THE DISCOVERY
OF NORTH AMERICA

The Discovery
of North America

W.P. Cumming
R.A. Skelton
D.B. Quinn

American Heritage Press, New York

© Paul Elek Productions Ltd, 1971
First American Edition 1972
All Rights Reserved. No part of this publication
may be reproduced, stored in a retrieval system,
or transmitted, in any form or by any means,
electronic, mechanical, photocopying, recording,
or otherwise, without the prior written permission
of the publisher.

Library of Congress Catalog Card Number: 73-165335
07-014905-4

Designed by Harold Bartram
Filmset in England by Photocomp Limited
Printed in Italy by Amilcare Pizzi SpA

Frontispiece: Indians round a fire. Drawing by John White, 1585.
London, British Museum.

CONTENTS

LIST OF ILLUSTRATIONS

PREFACE

The subject of this volume is the discovery of North America as seen, experienced, and recorded by Europeans from the earliest vaguely reported transatlantic voyages to the establishment of permanent settlements in the first third of the seventeenth century.

The selections and the accompanying illustrations are limited to those written or made in the period of discovery up to *c.* 1634. Wherever possible, the writings of the discoverers themselves have been used. A few exceptions to this policy, such as later illustrations of the arctic region, when no contemporary examples are known or preserved, are clearly indicated. The purpose and scope of the work excludes treatment, in the historical chapters, of numerous expeditions and attempted settlements which left no descriptive commentary or expanded knowledge. The discovery of the West Indies and Central America is omitted because it relates more closely to South America than to the northern continent, and will be dealt with in another volume.

Where original narratives have been selected, the exact wording has been reproduced, except for minor changes such as the substitution of *u* for *v* and *i* for *j* and vice versa, to accord with modern spelling practice, and the normalization of punctuation when needed for clarification. Brackets are inserted only for editorial emendation. The use of modern translations has been limited to cases where these are more accurate than those published earlier.

Professor D.B. Quinn has written the Introduction and the Epilogue; Dr R.A. Skelton, Chapters 1 and 5; and Professor W.P. Cumming, Chapters 2, 3, 4 and 6. The sudden death of Dr Skelton occurred within a week after his final examination of the proofs of this work, and it ended a career which established his pre-eminence throughout the world in the history of exploration and cartography.

The authors and publishers wish to thank Mrs Joyce Lorimer for her aid as research assistant; Mrs Alison Quinn and Mrs Mollie Skelton for preparing the valuable index; and Mrs Elizabeth Cumming for extensive research, proof-reading, critical aid, and versification in English of the selection from Villagrá's epic. Professor George Watts, Department of French, Davidson College, and Dr Mary Beaty, Department of Classics, University of Richmond, have generously made translations from the original French (anonymous letter from Florida, 1565) and Latin (from Sebastian Münster, *Cosmographia*, 1550). The authors wish also to express their appreciation to Miss Moira Johnston of Paul Elek Productions for her helpful cooperation and tireless effort in assembling the illustrations and editing the text.

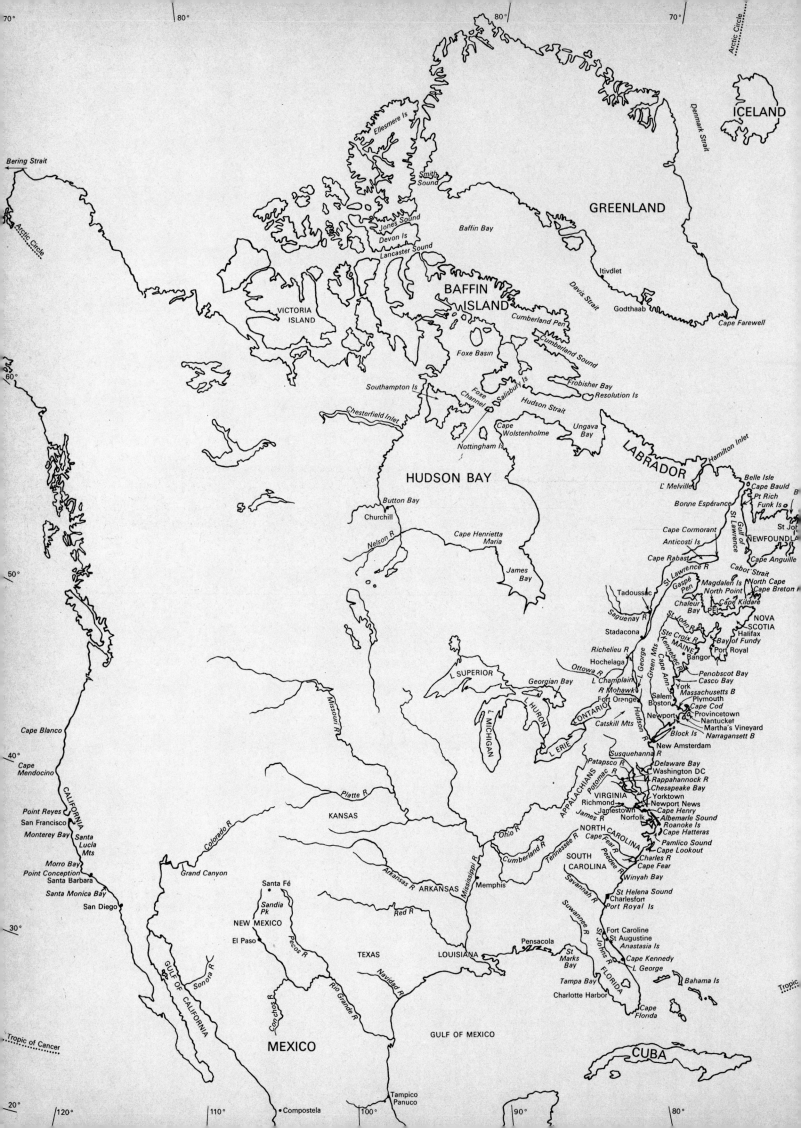

INTRODUCTION:
EUROPEAN TECHNOLOGY
AND PRECONCEPTIONS

The discovery of America was not an isolated event. It was made for purposes which were relevant to the European society from which the discoverers sprang. The exploration and exploitation which followed discovery were directly conditioned by the equipment and the mentality of the men who went across the ocean to involve themselves in one way or another with America: the trade in which they engaged and the settlements which they subsequently fostered were projections of Europe in a new environment. Most of the men—discoverers, explorers, fishermen, merchants, searchers for minerals or medicinal plants, and such like—were, in the earliest stages of contact with North America, wholly absorbed in what they were doing. They believed that when they were figuring out the lie of the land, getting an idea of the course of the rivers, trying to establish the main constituents of the vegetation, looking for cultivable lands, even observing those features of American Indian life which were novel and interesting, they were concerned with the thing-in-itself, with the objective situation in which they themselves were detached observers. Yet all had built into them the intention, conscious or unconscious, of involving North America with their European homeland. They were conditioned both by the outlook and needs of Renaissance Europe. In a book which is concerned mainly with the earliest stages of exploration and attempted settlement, it is entirely relevant that we should attempt to look briefly at what equipment, material and ideological, the first Europeans brought to the New World and to examine in what ways it influenced or governed their activities, the degree of success with which these were crowned, and their interaction both with their physical environment and with the aboriginal society with which they placed themselves in contact.

The white searchers of the ocean who found and explored North America in the sixteenth century were themselves at a point of transition in their technology, in their ideology and in the character of their social organization. They had, above all, developed the instruments of war so that they possessed not only the full accessories of the iron age—armor, swords and spears—but they had also passed into the phase of percussive weapons: they were able to use the longbow, and the mechanized crossbow, but these were giving place to the hand-gun (though still clumsy), and the cannon (now ship-portable) which placed them beyond the military resources of aboriginal Indian society, and the horse, providing both mobility and shock effect, in some ways their most effective military instrument. In static warfare they were immensely at an advantage, though this was counterbalanced to some extent by their vulnerability to surprise and ambush, and their insufficient mobility in the less open field.

It may seem a little surprising to put land weapons before ships in discussing the instruments with which Europeans began the exploration and conquest of America. But though

1
Shipbuilding in the Old World. Engraving by J. Sadeler. Slightly altered to indicate a similar activity in the New World, this engraving also appeared in Theodore de Bry's *America*, Part IV, Frankfurt, 1594 (see plate 362).

it was marine technology and navigational know-how that brought Europeans to America and enabled them to carry out a long, discontinuous sequence of exploration, if European arms had not been so overwhelmingly superior to those of the indigenous peoples, the European impact on North America—indeed on any part of the Americas—would have been marginal only, as was the case in the sixteenth century in European relations with China. That is not to say that without substantial developments in designing, propelling, and guiding ships the rediscovery of North America in lower latitudes than those used earlier by the Norsemen could have taken place when it did. But, unless weather conditions were quite exceptional (and since our knowledge of fifteenth and sixteenth century weather in the Atlantic is fragmentary one cannot be dogmatic about them), the transit of the Atlantic, with a probability of return eastwards, from the land limits of Europe between the latitudes of Gibraltar and north-west Ireland would scarcely have been possible much before 1500, when it took place. A rediscovery by way of the old northern route would have been more likely at an earlier stage, provided the old half-way houses in the Greenland settlements were still in existence.

If arms were what made European intervention effective, it was, of course, ships which not only took men there but enabled them to build up a remarkable chain of communications with the new continent. There is now a great deal known about the development of ships and rigging in the Mediterranean in the later Middle Ages and the gradual permeation of this knowledge into north-west Europe, with much more obtained empirically by the Portuguese and to some extent the Spaniards during the long probing voyages of the fifteenth century down the coast of Africa, out to the Atlantic islands, and finally across to the Columbus-found Caribbean. Less clearly we can see the development of the northern European ship. The Hanseatic League did something to develop the

foundland Banks in the late fifteenth and early sixteenth centuries. The French vessels which followed and soon outnumbered them had longer and more graceful lines. The Portuguese were able to deploy the rigging devices evolved on the African coast to develop their share of the North American fishery. The larger vessels used in exploration in the early stages of North American discovery are not known in any great detail, but, French and English alike, they owed something to the interplay between northern and Mediterranean techniques and to the Iberian trade which had developed with France and England in the later Middle Ages, and they continued to be influenced by the ship-building techniques of Portugal and Spain in the early sixteenth

2

older, rounder, northern ship into the longer, larger, more variably rigged carrack. The English ships which pioneered the Icelandic fishery in the late fourteenth and fifteenth centuries were the fishing doggers, and merchantmen following in their rather rugged lines, which formed the backbone of the fishing fleets that opened up the New-

2
'Searching the most opposite corners and quarters of the world'. This symbolic engraving illustrates both the aspirations of the European explorer and his technological equipment: the ocean-going ship, his instruments for navigation, his weapons and armament.
3
The figure of Columbus from a map of the Western Hemisphere in T. de Bry, *America*, Part IV, Frankfurt, 1594.

3

century. Hull-form, sail-plan and tonnage used for various purposes are technical matters on which detail would here be inappropriate, but navigational techniques were often as important as ships. The refinement of methods of dead-reckoning navigation (compass, lead and plain chart) ensured a basic competence in following a required route in normal weather conditions. The development of celestial navigation and the consequent capacity to determine latitude—though this remained imprecise at sea—made possible the correction of the major errors of dead reckoning. It might appear from the current state of knowledge that there was no single source of improvement: Italy, Portugal, France and England all had significant contributions to make to the building up of an effective capacity to master the ocean passage. The Spaniards possessed a great advantage in the exploration of North America in that they could use many small vessels built in the West Indies which might not easily have made the Atlantic passage, but there was little to choose between French, English and Portuguese in their capacity to sail across the Atlantic during the period under review in this book.

More specifically, the western European peoples varied in the degree to which they exploited the techniques of exploration in North America. Significantly, the Italians, who had taught so much to the Iberian nations, continued to appear prominently in the American field: Giovanni Caboto, Sebastiano Caboto, and Giovanni da Verrazzano—known better perhaps as John and Sebastian Cabot and Jean de Vérazane—are only the leading names in a fairly numerous brood. If many of the early sea-charts of Newfoundland, Labrador and the Maritimes were made by Portuguese, it was largely the Italians who worked them up into intelligible maps of the new continent, though they gradually gave place to the Dutch in the latter part of the sixteenth century and were almost submerged by them in the seventeenth century. Even in the later sixteenth century English explorers liked to have a Portuguese pilot with them—Drake rarely sailed without one—and a number of foreigners also appeared in the later French expeditions, even though the standard of French navigation was very high indeed by the later sixteenth century. To Spaniards and Portuguese the carrying of a painter on an expedition was usual, but his function was primarily to draw (or paint) maps from the crude charts made by the navigators and masters: he might perhaps sketch animals, plants or native peoples and decorate his finished maps with a few land curiosities as well as his sea with whales and monsters. The systematic use of a painter to record the natural products and peoples of North America begins with the French in 1564 when Jacques Le Moyne de Morgues was sent to make a survey of Florida; a selection of his drawings appeared in the form of engravings in 1591. The Spaniards had been less dependent on the brush before the great Mexican survey of Francisco Hernandez in the 1570s. The English were the first to exploit the technique of the Spanish 'geographical inquiry' (*relación geográfica*)—a questionnaire with answers—in combination with large numbers of naturalistic drawings of American Indians, fish, plants, birds and animals, so as to build up a systematic survey in words and pictures of the new land in which settlements were intended and which it was proposed to exploit systematically. The work of Thomas Harriot and John White in the years 1585–6, in what was then Virginia and is now North Carolina, was of great value to subsequent English expeditions and inquirers. Thomas Harriot's *A briefe and true report of the new found land of Virginia*, published in 1588, and reprinted with engravings of many of White's drawings by de Bry in 1590, did more to open up North America to the Europeans

(along with the parallel publication of Le Moyne) than any number of voyages themselves.

Publicity by narrative was also significant. Though Europeans could distribute information by means of print, it was not until the appearance of Ramusio's *Viaggi et navigationi* in the 1550s that a significant body of material on North America was circulated. The narratives of the Verrazzano and Cartier voyages were largely known, in the original Italian or in translations, from Ramusio. France did not publicize in print very systematically her North American exploits, but late in the sixteenth century, between 1582 and 1600, Richard Hakluyt put in print not only a great deal of material on English activities—almost every scrap he could find—but

4
No contemporary representation of Columbus' ship has survived. This woodcut (a copy of a picture published in 1486) illustrating his Letter on the first voyage printed in 1493, shows a ship similar in construction to his *Santa Maria. London, British Museum.*

much on French explorations as well. On the continent, his work was used and developed by Theodor de Bry in his famous series of illustrated volumes—those using drawings by Le Moyne and White have already been mentioned. In England Samuel Purchas continued the work of Richard Hakluyt between 1613 and 1625, while in France from 1603 onwards a stream of narrative emerged from the expeditions of Champlain and Lescarbot. This verbal recording derived in the main from participants in voyages at the time of their performance, rather than from vague reminiscences of their exploits after some time had elapsed. Many of them were based on the ship's log, with its column for 'occurrences'; and this information was built into detailed narrative journals of what took place. We lack journals for some major voyages and have inadequate ones for others, but in general we can follow the main explorations and early attempts at settlement firsthand in the words of the persons actually concerned. By the late sixteenth century a basic problem of communication had been solved: accounts of North American voyages were being written in simple vernacular language, accessible to all who could read and not confined to educated men who knew Latin, so that a popular bridge by means of printed words was erected across the Atlantic. Champlain's simple, honest prose was paralleled by the even more rugged and clear narrative style of Captain John Smith. The rise of a popular audience for information about North America was an essential stage in

This detail from the world map by Pierre Desceliers, dated 1550, shows a ship, probably intended to represent that of Jacques Cartier, in passage westward to America under greatly reduced sail. *London, British Museum, Add. Ms. 24065.*

6
A cross-staff in use, 1669. The cross-staff, an improvement over the astrolabe for accuracy in use, was introduced early in the sixteenth century. In bright sunshine it could cause damage to the eyes.

making its potential as an area of settlement as well as for trade known to the literate middle classes of western Europe, more especially in the early seventeenth century to the English but later to the French and Dutch as well.

Of the ideological equipment with which Europeans left their own societies, religion was the most important. It was religion, the sense of being involved in and sustained by the Church, which, more than color or national sentiment, made Europeans feel distinct from and superior to those peoples they met outside their own continent. To be non-Christian placed American Indians outside some sort of pale. Anti-Muslim feeling had bitten so deeply into Spaniards that they wore their religion like a sword not only against the Arabs and Turks but against all who were not, or who did not rapidly become, Christians. To some extent the Portuguese attitude was similar but not so dogmatic. This feeling existed amongst French and English too in more attenuated forms. The Reformation merely complicated these attitudes: Spaniards extended their desire to kill all non-Christians to those who had rebelled against the true Church. Protestants, French or English, could be almost as uncompromising as the Spaniards, though, emerging from societies themselves divided, they were more able to show a degree of inter-credal tolerance. The European urge to convert American Indians was partly expediency: the alternative of kill or convert was inter-mittently present in Spanish and English minds. Those who believed that Christianity offered a better life and that a better life ought to be offered to non-Christians were always few, but they grew more numerous in reaction against the intolerable inhumanity of the merely righteous. In the sixteenth century, however, the contacts of European Christians with North America, apart from Mexico, were slight and transient. Little sustained brutality against non-Christians took place (though the Spaniards several times showed their capacity for it); missionary activity, either for expediency's sake or for principle, was spasmodic and almost wholly ineffective. Christian ideology at this stage was more influential in determining attitudes than action.

There was a secular trend amongst the explorers which was often significant and sometimes dominant. Medieval theology had been more all-embracing in its theoretical ascendancy over men's minds than in practice. Latin and Greek literature, even if admitted to a quasi-Christian status, had kept open a less completely committed intellectual view of the world. The revived interest in and knowledge of the classical past, in literature at least, and its popularization by the circulation of printed works, left its mark on most educated men. If Europeans, when they went to America, sometimes employed archaic stereotypes drawn from the classics, they also used their secular mentors to point their curiosity and to stir them to objective comment or empirical relations with the indigenous peoples. It is hard to say, of course, how far classical

education was really the father of a lay, agnostic, and, to some extent, scientific attitude. Perhaps it was, in a society where the hold of the Church was slipping and where doctrinal certainties were being challenged, more of a vehicle for secularism than its creator. Spaniards were not all insulated from Renaissance secularism and some of their greatest observers, Oviedo for example, were products of the secular Italian Renaissance. There is no doubt that the Italians who played such a part in American exploration, Vespucci if not Columbus, Verrazzano if not John Cabot, were more secular-than Christian-oriented in their reactions to the new life of the American west. Throughout, Frenchmen too, like a few Englishmen, were essentially secular-minded and objective. And the Portuguese observer of de Soto's expedition, also, was less a victim of European blinkers than most Spaniards. Spaniards could be objective as well as repressive towards the Indians in so far as they studied them in order to exploit them or convert them, but, in North America at least, they did not seriously attempt to understand them, or collaborate with them, on either detached or on approximately equal terms (though this may be due not only to Christian aloofness but also to the fact that, by the time they met North American Indians in any numbers, they had many indigenous dependants in other parts of the Americas and had adopted a stereotyped attitude of familiar contempt towards them).

European society was hierarchical. The hierarchy of birth and of status (or order) informed every expedition from Europe to America. Men of gentle and noble birth took natural command over sailors, soldiers and settlers alike. In a settlement they expected and were accorded priority in war, in civil authority and in comfort: their views of American Indian life tended to prevail, at least in action. Spain had a superfluity of persons of noble birth and in the Americas more individuals than were qualified to receive the privileges of nobility claimed them: Spain was feudal but in America particularly there developed a feudalism open to talents so that almost everyone of any personality or education aspired to hold land and to rule men. The French had a certain, though qualified, respect for birth, and Frenchmen of quality expected to be singled out in American expeditions and settlements; the same was true of Englishmen, though they were perhaps stiffer in holding out for the privileges of gentility. All the Europeans consequently paid some attention to American Indian hierarchy: the existence of chiefs and elders, and of some degree of formality and ceremonial in their contacts, made it appear that these peoples were not wholly without signs of civilization in their social structure. Spaniards were most inclined to treat Indian chiefs as non-commissioned officers (*cacique* virtually equalled 'sergeant'), whose rank was to be respected by being kept subordinate to Spanish wishes and needs but whose status remained permanently at a level much lower than that of Spaniards. The French were most willing to take Indian status at its own valuation, to listen to interminable harangues in incomprehensible languages, to participate in formal festivals, to make alliances, to involve themselves in native wars. The rapport between Laudonnière and the Timucuan chief Satrioua—even if they often disagreed—is not paralleled in any other known relationship in sixteenth-century North America. The English again occupied an intermediate position: impressed by the claims of Indian 'kings', they were at times prepared to grant them feudal status (Manteo) or even recognition as subordinate kings (Powhatan). But in closer intercourse, Englishmen easily came to despise Indian social organization and, as they saw them, pretensions, and tended to become, as the French rarely did, equipped with a built-in attitude of superiority. But whenever they came ashore, and whenever they established a settlement, temporary or permanent, European hierarchies in some measure were established on American soil and contained in themselves elements of conflict with those of the indigenous population whose land they took, in most cases, without permission, and in which they began, in some degree, to recreate a European social order.

European society was acquisitive and mercantile. At every stage of European activity in North America, the profitable exchange of goods and the exploitation of natural resources were primary motives impelling men across the oceans and making their contact with the land and its inhabitants continuous and systematic. The exploitation of natural resources did not always and inevitably affect native society. Hundreds of European vessels could resort to the Grand Banks for fishing every season without affecting the American Indian peoples in any way—so long as they confined themselves to the Banks fishery and brought their fish green-salted to Europe. But so soon as they had developed an inshore fishery, and built stages and flakes and store and boat houses to dry fish, to render oil and shelter their boats, then an exploitation nexus was established with the native people of Newfoundland. It was not one-sided. Beothuk Indians could steal or seize European lines, nets, tools, weapons and even boats, as well as risk being killed if they were seen, and they could balance such loss of inshore fishing as they had suffered by the exchange of pelts for European commodities. But here, as elsewhere, when the less highly organized Indian groups had to deal with strongly individualistic fishermen, contact soon led to the retreat of the natives into the interior and to the less accessible bays: in the long run it meant their gradual extinction. Where the Indians were more numerous and more firmly organized, contacts over fishing and fur-trading might

7a

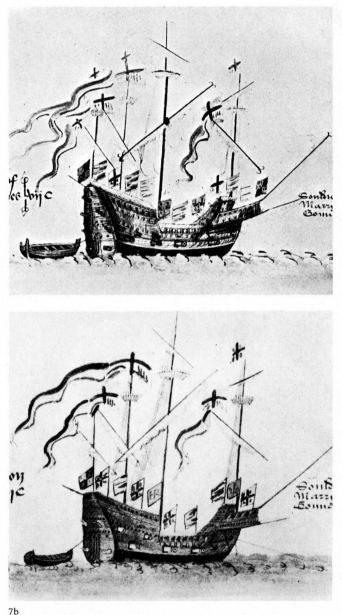

7b

involve occasional skirmishing, but no drastic changes in Indian life. It was possible, before European settlement began, to assimilate European and Indian demands into a reasonably equitable system of exchange. The French proved realistic and successful in developing a seasonal relationship of this nature along the shores of the Gulf and later the St Lawrence River and on the coast of the Maritimes down to Maine. But whenever Europeans established trading contacts of a regular character they tended to assume exclusive rights of access—Basques contested with Normans, Bretons with

12a

12
English merchantmen and ships of war and a French merchantman at the Battle of Smerwick, 1585:
a) The *Teager (Tiger)*; b) The *Revenge*; c) The *Swyfteswer (Swiftsure)*; d) The *Marlyon (Marlion)*; e) The *Ayd (Aid)*; f) The *Achates*; all these were warships; g) Captain Vaughan's ships, The *Victuler (Victualler)*, merchantmen; h) The *Jack*, a pinnace; i) The French merchantship, a Newfoundlander.
13
Portuguese ocean-going ships of the sixteenth century. From the *Livro das Armadas*, a set of drawings of the Portuguese fleets to India, made after 1566. Lisbon, Academia das Ciencias.

for settlement operated inside a framework of permissions derived from the nature and structure of the European nation state. Indeed, as North America was not regarded as being occupied by peoples with any stable political structure or with any inalienable rights of possession, exploration was normally taken in hand under the auspices of one or other of the western littorine states which gradually asserted its claims and ultimately its sovereignty to such American land as it could profess, effectively, to occupy and exploit. Spain demanded exclusive privileges over and sovereignty in the whole of eastern North America in virtue of a papal donation and a treaty with Portugal made before any Spaniard or Portuguese had set foot on any part of North America or even knew it existed, and was prepared to attempt to enforce that claim well into the seventeenth century. Portugal laid claim to a considerable extent of coastline on the basis of a false conclusion about longitude drawn from the 1494 treaty and from explorations made from 1500 onwards. France asserted, at one time or another, from the initial annexations made during Verrazzano's voyage in 1524 down to the time of Champlain, that New France extended from Florida to Hudson's Bay. English territorial claims were usually based on the Cabot voyages but sometimes on even earlier, alleged, discoveries.

The establishment of the simplest post required royal instructions or charters, which often set out in great detail the bureaucratic structure of the administration to be established there. The simplest trading post sported a governor, a cape merchant and a captain of soldiers at the least. Institutional buildings, a headquarters building for military, civil and commercial administration, for example, were amongst the earliest in all colonial settlements. A settlement of about a hundred men on Roanoke Island in 1585 had a governor (who doubled the role with that of colonel of the military arm of the colony), an admiral, a number of army captains, a council, a cape merchant, a surveyor, an artist, a metallurgist, so that between administrators and specialists there was only a small rank and file. Spanish administration in Florida was even more topheavy. The *adelantado* was, when absent, represented by a deputy governor; there was a treasurer, an accountant, a factor (sometimes assistants to each of these as well) in addition to a series of military officers in descending rank from the governor. Sometimes the superfluity of officers and of ranks could be an embarrassment to decisive action, but usually they had little effective power. Their significance was rather that their nation state which had despatched them, and which expected to continue to supervise them—directly in the case of Spain, indirectly, through companies, in the case of France and England—considered

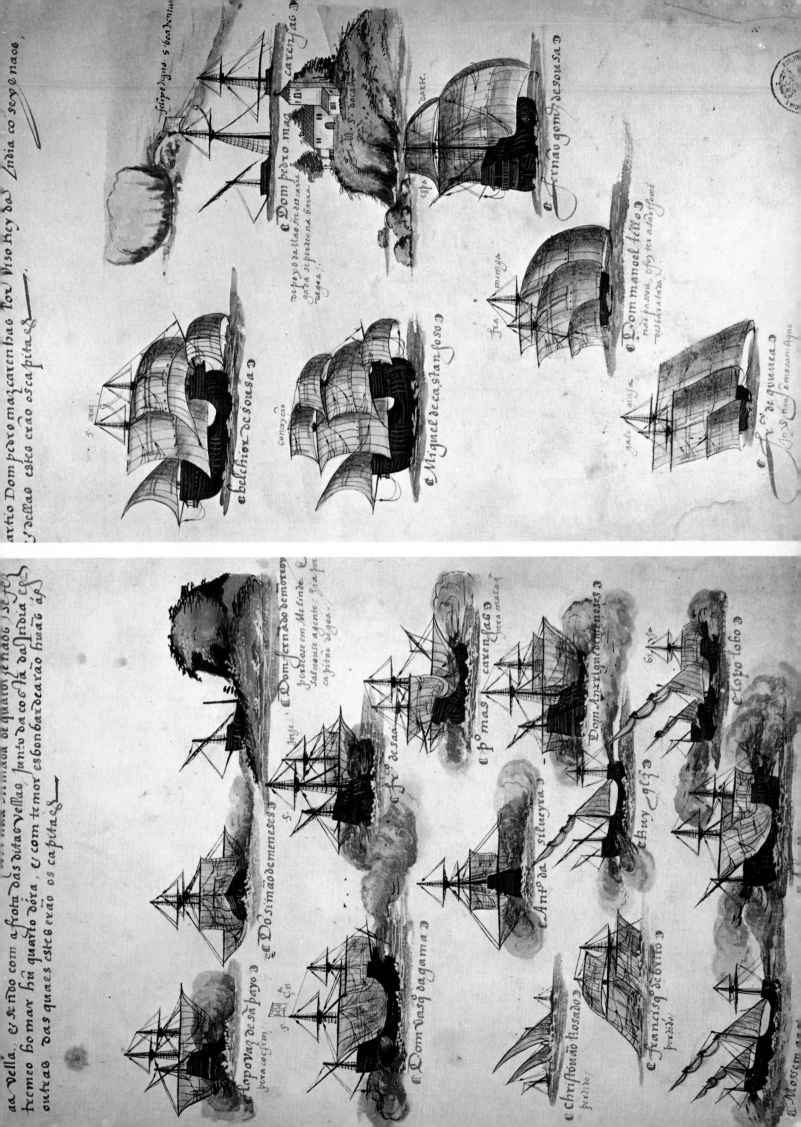

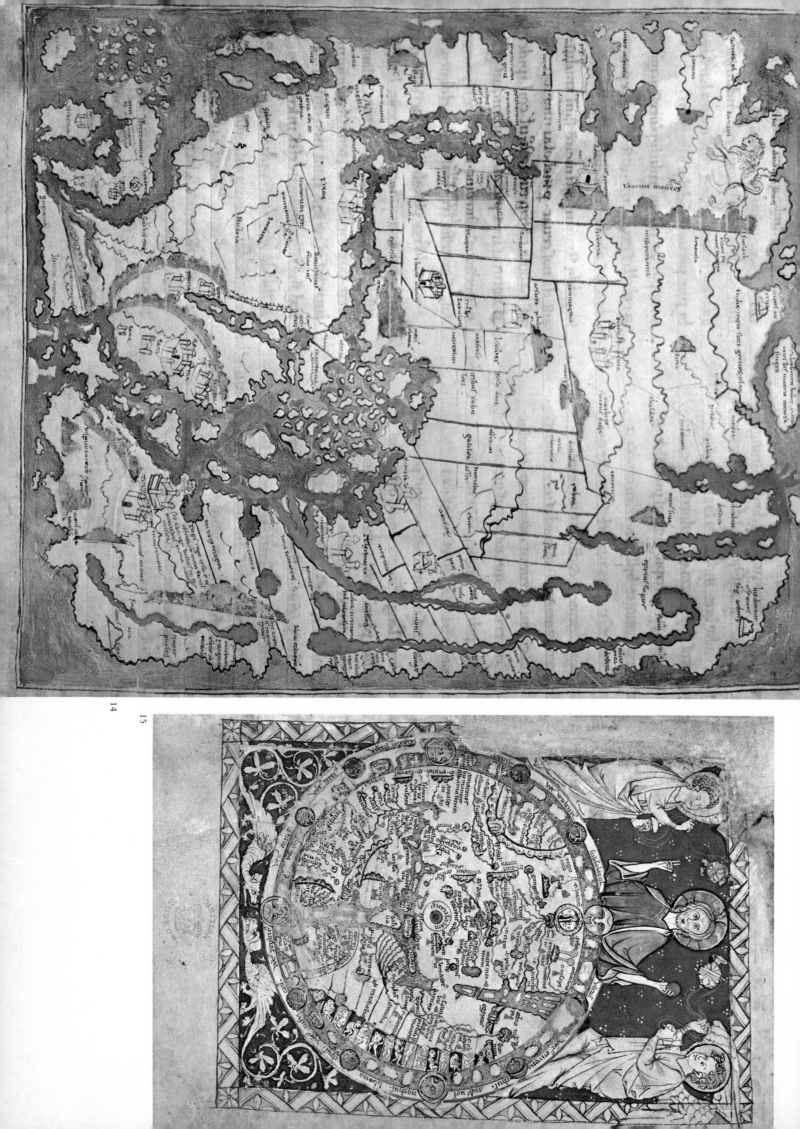

16
A fleet of ships of Dutch design from a chart showing Henry Hudson's discoveries of 1610–11, engraved by the Amsterdam engraver, Hessel Gerritsz, and published in *Descriptio ac delineatio geographica detenctionis freti,* Amsterdam, 1612.

17
A Portuguese fleet, probably Magellan's, from the world map of Diogo Ribero, 1529. *Biblioteca Apostolica Vaticana.*

17

16

14
The so-called 'Cottonian' or 'Anglo-Saxon' world map, eleventh century. *London, British Museum, Cotton Ms. Tiberius B.v, fo 56v.*

15
The so-called 'Psalter' world map, thirteenth century. *London, British Museum, Add. Ms. 28681, fo 9.*
These small 'mappaemundi', here reproduced in their original size, represent the world as seen by Christian cosmographers of the later Middle Ages. They agree in general design with the T-O maps (see plate 19), having east to the top and the Mediterranean as their central vertical axis. The monastic houses in which such maps were drawn preserved the writings and maps left by Latin geographers of the Roman Empire and the early Church, from the first to the fourth centuries. It was from these mainly literary sources that the *mappaemundi* took their schematic form, the pattern of land and water, and most of their names and descriptive legends. Over a thousand medieval world maps of this character have been preserved, ranging in size from great altarpieces six feet high to diagrammatic book-illustrations two or three inches in diameter.

The Psalter map, although drawn two centuries after the Cottonian, conforms more closely to the conventional type of the monastic *mappaemundi* and is more primitive in content. Circular in form and centered on Jerusalem, it depicts in detail the Biblical East and is enriched by pictorial illustrations of medieval lore, such as the monsters in Africa and the land of Gog and Magog walled in by Alexander the Great. Islands in the outer ocean, e.g. the British Isles, are compressed into the circular frame.

The Cottonian map owes most of its content to the description of the world, and perhaps a map, by the fifth-century Spanish priest Paulus Orosius. It illustrates the settlement of the Twelve Tribes of Israel and the boundaries of the Roman provinces. Jerusalem is however not in the center of the map, and the rectangular shape—which is exceptional among medieval world maps—allows room for a more generous delineation of the ocean and islands to the north-west of Europe (in the lower left-hand corner of the map). Here can be seen the British Isles, with a remarkably good outline, many 'islands in the ocean north of Britain' (as described by Dicuil in the ninth century), Iceland ('Tylen'), the Orkneys, and—in the position of the Scandinavian peninsula—a long island bearing the names 'Island' (the earliest appearance of this name in a map) and 'Skridefinnas' (i.e. Skrifinns). This information must be of northern origin, in a monastic community which was aware of Scandinavian and Irish voyaging in the Western Ocean. As this is the earliest known map to name a city in Ireland ('Arama', i.e. Armagh), it may well be the work of an Irish cleric.

these officials as in some sort representatives of its own sovereignty and the forerunners of a fully developed territorial administration. So, if a settlement could survive, whether with direct state aid or not, it automatically became a growing point for a projection of the national state, and was expected to carry forward with it the institutions of the state into its maturity, modified only in minor ways by local conditions in America. Europeans therefore went to America incapsulated in an administrative cocoon from which a network of organization would in the long run be spun.

It is unwise to linger too long on the more distant perspectives of European settlement at a point where we are mainly concerned with the more elementary aspects of discovery on the eastern side of the North Atlantic. Most of the explorers were absorbed in what they were doing, whether it was fishing, trading, looking for cultivable lands or prospecting for minerals—or even estimating the nature of the land, its topography, its vegetation, its human population in the most provisional way. But almost all of them had in their background, whether conscious of it or not, the intention to involve North America in the longer run with their European homeland. The type of society from which they sprung is thus entirely relevant to the story of exploration which must inevitably take up a major part of a book on the sixteenth century even if it is less easy to categorize Europeans than American Indians in ethnographic terms.

In the realm of social anthropology the Europeans had a number of advantages over their opposite numbers in American Indian society. They were more versatile artifact users. They had a religion with a firm institutional structure, which claimed to be ecumenical, and which gave them almost complete confidence in the rectitude of whatever they did. They had at their disposal (even those who were illiterate) a body of knowledge of human history and concepts which gave them a long historical perspective and which enabled them to envisage their historical role as, they believed, the representatives of the superior civilization of the world. They had enough scientific knowledge and curiosity to master the physical problems of transport and maintenance in a new environment (though they did not master them very rapidly). They had confidence that they could carry their institutional and bureaucratic structures into a completely different environment. They had a highly specialized acquisitiveness in the form of trading and exploitative objectives and techniques. They were, however, in some degree the prisoners of their European environment even when they were settling in North America. They found it hard to digest and harder to enjoy food of a kind different from that to which they were accustomed. They proved unskilful in the essential skills of hunting and sometimes (surprisingly) of fishing. Their science was often quite insufficient to guide them through divides of climate, diet and disease. They expected America to be too much like Europe too soon—they retained too long their cultural umbilical cord. Assimilation and settlement therefore was a slow, painful process of cultural adaptation, by no means satisfactorily achieved. By remaining subjectively Europeans for so long, they indicated some of the weaknesses which civilization can impose: by persisting in their occupation and in developing permanent settlements, in the end they enabled the strengths of their different cultural level to assert themselves. The white men studied the Indians as well as berated, attacked and missionized them. The wiser observers, like Harriot and Champlain, saw something of the rationale of their social practices, but most Europeans were slow to become, under the guidance, or in imitation of the American Indians, adjusted to American limits. Though in the end, they did acclimatize both themselves and their cultural imperatives in America, the way they did so helped to make inevitable the liquidation of the indigenous cultures.

18
Portuguese carracks off a rocky coast; an oil painting of about 1535 attributed to Cornelis Anthoniszoon. *Greenwich, National Maritime Museum.*

1 THE DISCOVERY OF THE ATLANTIC IN THE MIDDLE AGES

The prelude to the discovery of America was the discovery of the Atlantic Ocean and its navigation. It was made by seamen who had become acquainted with the winds and currents of the ocean and had learned how to use them. This is a constant factor which has controlled transatlantic navigation under sail in all periods. Those who ventured into the Western Ocean during the Middle Ages had limited objectives: land for settlement, opportunities for trade, new fishing grounds, or simply escape from society. Unlike the discoverers of the Renaissance, they did not consult world maps or the theories of armchair geographers about the distribution of land and water over the globe's surface. Before the fifteenth century, there was no empirical thought of a westward route to Asia, still less of the addition of a new 'continent' to the tripartite world of medieval cosmography.

The Mediterranean zone was the center of geographical culture in the Middle Ages. It was there that the schematic world map was adapted from Roman models to Christian tradition; and it was Mediterranean seamen who evolved the nautical chart and codified the sailing directions as practical guides to navigation of known waters. But the discoverers of North America, from the Vikings to the Bristol fishermen and John Cabot, made their voyages from north-west Europe. Until the very end of the medieval period, their landfalls did not enter the general stock of European ideas or create a common vision of the Atlantic Ocean bounded by land to east and west. To mapmakers of southern Europe, the Atlantic—the 'Sea of Darkness'—was simply that part of the outer ocean which marked the western boundary of the habitable world. But to the peoples of the northern and western seaboards of Europe, the ocean was a highway to be traversed with assurance by fishermen, merchants and settlers. For four centuries, almost unnoticed by Mediterranean geographers, the ocean passage between Norway and Greenland was regularly made by Scandinavian seamen; and a guidebook compiled for the use of merchants, probably in the late fourteenth century, recorded the distances from Bergen to Iceland and from Iceland to Greenland.[1] These were the stages by which the earliest ascertained voyages to North America were made.

In its glorious age of missionary expansion, after the collapse of Roman civilization in Europe, Celtic Christianity spread from Ireland to the western coasts and islands. The bearers were monks who established communities, priests who served churches, anchorites or wandering holy men who sought God in a desert or a solitude. They inherited a tradition of seafaring from their Celtic forebears, and it was by sea that the Irish carried their religion northward and westward. By the beginning of the seventh century they had colonized Scotland, the Orkneys and the Shetlands. Their further migration west to the Faeroes, by a sea-crossing of 200 miles, and to Iceland, barely 300 miles beyond, is well attested, and

19
Schematic world map, thirteenth century. *London, British Museum, Add. Ms. 22797, fo 99v.*
In the later Middle Ages, the habitable world was commonly visualized as a circular disc floating in the surrounding ocean. This concept was illustrated by the diagrams known as T-O maps, drawn with east to the top and showing the three parts of the known world—Asia, Europe, Africa— divided by water features: the Mediterranean formed the vertical stroke of the T, and the Rivers Don and Nile the horizontal stroke. From the eleventh century such maps were centred on Jerusalem. Even the largest *mappaemundi*, with detailed geographical representations and a wealth of names and legends, conformed to this simple structural pattern (see plates 14 and 15).

its chronology is approximately known. Dicuil, an Irish monk who wrote a geography about AD 825, talked with priests who had made these voyages under oar and sail in their well-found curraghs, the Celtic boats of cowhide stretched over greenwood frames. He learned that the Faeroes had been occupied for about a century by Irish hermits, but had by this time been 'vacated by the anchorites on account of the Norse brigands'. The priest who told him this had made the crossing from the Shetlands in two days and a night, and had found the islands full of sheep, doubtless introduced by the Irish and increased on the year-round grazing.[2]

Other priests interviewed by Dicuil had, 'some thirty years since', spent six months in Iceland, sailing in winter as the season in which fog and storm were less frequent. At that date, before AD 800, Irish monasticism must already have been established in Iceland. Fifty years after Dicuil wrote, the first Norse settlers found on the east coasts of Iceland 'Irish books, bells and croziers' left behind by monks who 'went away because they did not wish to live there with heathen men'.[3] Whither they went is a question to which historical records return no certain answer.

Around the seafaring of the Irish holy men, monastic story-

Marvellous adventures of St Brendan and his monks at sea.
(below) They encounter a siren. *(right)* They meet a holy man floating on
the sea. *(below left)* Their ship is attacked by a sea-monster. Woodcuts from
a German prose version of the *Navigatio,* printed at Ulm in 1499.

21 *Bottom right*
Walrus. Woodcut in Olaus Magnus, *Historia de gentibus septentrionalibus,*
Rome, 1555.

Uon fant Brandon ain
hübfch lefen.was er wunders auff dem mör
erfaren hat.

monks, then of other Irish wanderers. Among the landfalls
which can with more or less assurance be inferred from such
observations and from the details of navigation given are the
Faeroes, with their wealth of sheep and sea-birds; Iceland,
with a volcano in eruption; less confidently, the Azores and
the Sargasso Sea ('a thick curdled mass'), approximately where
later medieval mapmakers were to locate St Brendan's Island;
and a land forty days west of the Faeroes, where the voyagers
encountered whales, 'pygmies and dwarfs as black as coal'
(Eskimos?), and a 'sea-cat' with enormous eyes, whiskers and
tusks (a walrus?)—details suggesting the west coasts of Greenland on Davis Strait. These and other geographical identifications, in the context of the voyages described in the *Navigatio,*

tellers in Ireland wove travel-tales in which experience and
fantasy, Celtic legend and classical lore intermingled. In the
manner of older and fictitious sea-romances, or *immrama,*
they narrate the maritime adventures of the Irish missionary
saints who sailed western waters in the sixth century. The
most far-ranging of such voyages are those attributed to
St Brendan of Ardfert, a historical person who lived from
about 484 to about 577. They are chronicled in a remarkable
Latin narrative, the *Navigatio Sancti Brendani,* no doubt
transmitted orally until it was written down some three
centuries after the saint's death, and (with variants) in a
'Life' of him which exists in Irish and Latin versions.

These texts apparently refer to two voyages made by
Brendan in quest of a Land of Promise in the western ocean
and lasting in all seven years. They contain many records of
natural phenomena so precise and individual as to suggest an
origin in the experience, if not of Brendan and his crew of

are sufficiently numerous and consistent with the meteorology
and sailing conditions of the North Atlantic to admit the
historical possibility that Irish monks, fleeing from Iceland
before the Vikings, took refuge in Greenland.[4] There, in the
years 982–5, the first Norse settlers in fact found 'human
habitations, both in the east and west of the country, also the
remains of hide boats and implements of stone'.[5] The Icelandic
chronicler's association of these relics with 'Skrælings' or
Eskimos receives some support from modern archaeologists,
although the first wave of Eskimo migration from the Canadian
Arctic into Greenland, belonging to the so-called Dorset
culture, had spent itself, and there were apparently no
Eskimos in the country when the Norsemen came.[6]

The evidence for Irish voyaging and settlement still further
west is more insubstantial. There are visual clues in the
Brendan narrative pointing perhaps to the fogs of the Newfoundland Banks, to the southward drift of icebergs in the

spring, to a coral sea; and the Land of Promise which Brendan explored for forty days, and where one of his companions remained, seems to be mainland. The Icelandic chronicles and sagas tell of a 'White-Men's-Land' or 'Greater Ireland' to the west, where Norsemen, making chance landfalls in the late tenth and early eleventh centuries, found or heard of Christians speaking a language thought to be Irish; but the geographical context of these reports associates them with Greenland as plausibly as with America.[7]

On the methods of subsistence by which the Irish maintained themselves for a hundred years in the Faeroes (apart from the mention of sheep) and for nearly as long in Iceland, we have no evidence. The maritime economy of the Scandinavians who followed them is well known. They came, in the main, from the fjord country of Norway, and their farms on narrow coastal strips of arable and pasture were the bases from which they fished and went on raids for plunder across the sea. Men of violence and fiercely independent, they resented the dominant order imposed on Norway in the later ninth century and sought wider lands, free of political control, across the ocean. Attempts to establish themselves in the British Isles failed; and the first Viking settler in Iceland, in 870, was followed (in the chronicler's words) by 'a great movement of men out there from Norway'.[8] They quickly established a stable society, with voluntary political institutions, active commercial and cultural communication with Europe, and a lively interest both in the world about them and in their past. It is almost wholly in Icelandic literature—at first oral, and from the twelfth century written—that Norse exploration of the North Atlantic in the Middle Ages is recorded from a clear and retentive folk memory: in the sagas, in two great chronicles, the 'Book of the Settlements' (*Landnámabók*) and the 'Book of the Icelanders' (*Íslendingabók*), and in annals.

The sagas, in their original form, were essentially family histories, set in a genealogical framework and recounting the feats and adventures of notable forebears, seen with the eyes of the men who experienced them, though not without conscious embroidery or accretion and accidental confusion.[9] The two sagas which tell of the discovery of America—the 'Saga of the Greenlanders' and the later, more sophisticated 'Saga of Eirik the Red'—are historical in purpose and character. Their brisk and factual narratives reflect the observations and interests of the Norse voyagers—in conditions of navigation and pilotage, in the natural resources of lands encountered, in the possibilities of settlement.

It was land-hunger that impelled the Norsemen, in the period of Viking expansion, to reach out farther into the western ocean. This carried them across the two remaining stages of the sea-passage to America: from Iceland, after it was fully settled by the mid-tenth century, to Greenland, and from Greenland, with its limited scope for cultivators, to the Canadian Archipelago and the mainland south of it. In each case the first report of new land came from seamen storm-driven westward and southward in their square-sailed ships, in which course could not be maintained on a beam wind. In 981 or 982 Eirik the Red pioneered the sailing route due west from Iceland to the forbidding Greenland coast and south round Cape Farewell to the fjord region of the south-west. Here he spent three summers exploring the coasts of Davis Strait northward before returning to Iceland whence, in 985, he led a fleet of colonists and established on the fertile rims of the south-western fjords two settlements—the Western (at Julianehaab) and the Eastern (at Godthaab). No inhabitants were found, but the fjords offered good pasture, safe harbors, and access to the hunting and trapping grounds along the

coast to the north, the 'Nordrseta'. There, on their summer expeditions, they took fish and seals, walrus and narwhal, ice-bears, caribou, eider duck, and white falcons, returning to winter in their homesteads. To Norway they sent, by a regular traffic, the skins and furs, ivory and oil by which they purchased commodities that their land could not produce, notably iron, timber and grain. So long as communication with Europe remained open, the economic basis of the Greenland colonies was assured.[10]

By about 1070 the discovery of America made about three-quarters of a century earlier by Norsemen was known in northern Europe. The cleric Adam of Bremen heard of it from the King of Denmark: 'He told me too of yet another island,

22
A Norwegian Viking. Wood-carving on the wagon among the grave-goods in the ninth-century ship-burial at Oseberg in Vestfold, Norway, excavated in 1904. *Oslo, Universitetets Oldsaksamling.*

discovered by many in that ocean, which is called Wineland from the circumstance that vines grow there of their own accord, and produce most excellent wine. That there is abundance of unsown corn there we have learned . . . from the trustworthy report of the Danes'.[11] Because, of the two sagas which record the Vinland voyages, that of the Greenlanders is more concerned with the family of Eirik, and the 'Saga of Eirik the Red' with that of the Icelander Thorfinn Karlsefni, they disagree in the chronology and number of the voyages, in the selection of events and identification of localities, and in the credit given to different explorers. They concur however in their rendering of the central historical tradition: an accidental discovery made on a westward voyage

to Greenland, followed by exploratory reconnaissance and by expeditions for colonization of a land which seemed favorable in climate and vegetation, to be frustrated by the hostility of the inhabitants and by internal dissension. Since both sagas dip their bucket into the same well of experience, analysis of the sequence and geography of the voyages may be drawn from either; and in the following discussion the Greenlanders' Saga is indicated as *G*, the 'Saga of Eirik the Red' as *E*.

The initial discovery, and earliest known American landfall by Europeans, was made by Bjarni Herjolfsson in the year 985. His log-book (preserved only in *G*) tells how, in passage from Iceland to Greenland, he was blown off course to the south;

23

A sea-going sailing-ship of the Vikings: the Gokstad ship, excavated in a ninth-century burial at Gokstad in Vestfold, Norway, and reconstructed.

Above the keel, of a single oak beam nearly 58 feet long, she is clinker-built of oak strakes, with a beam of $17\frac{1}{2}$ feet and a draft of about 3 feet. The mast, deck and 16 pairs of oars were of pine, and she was steered by a side-rudder at the starboard quarter. A replica of this ship was, in 1893, sailed across the Atlantic, from Bergen to Newfoundland, in 28 days. *Oslo, Universitetets Oldsaksamling.*

navigational details of the voyage are recorded precisely and vividly, but Bjarni did not go ashore and noted only the general character of the three lands which he sighted in five days' sailing as he made his way north-east along the American coasts towards Greenland. Some fifteen years later (again according to *G*) Leif Eiriksson, in Bjarni's ship and probably with some of his crew, sailed from Eirik's Greenland home in the Eastern Settlement to reconnoitre these lands, following Bjarni's track in reverse. The first land, which he identified as that sighted last by Bjarni, he named Helluland ('Slab-land'), and his second landfall Markland ('Wood-land'). Two days to the south-west, in a sound between a headland and an island, Leif built houses ('Leifsbudir') and wintered; the length of the shortest day was noted, suggesting a latitude south of the St Lawrence.[12] Here they found wild grapes and bird's-eye maple, both pointing to the deciduous forests of New England;[13] and they took back to Greenland a cargo of vines (for cordage) and timber. Thorvald, Leif's brother, led the next expedition to Vinland, passing two winters at Leifsbudir and exploring the coast to the west. In the third summer, sailing east, north and then east past a headland which he named Kjalarnes ('Keel cape'), he selected a site for settlement on a wooded promontory. Here occurred the first recorded encounter between Europeans and natives of North America. Whether from fear or mere hunting instinct, the reaction of the Greenlanders was brutal: they killed the men whom they found sleeping under 'skin-boats'. In the attack by 'a great swarm of skin-boats' that followed, Thorvald was killed by an arrow. The 'skin-boats' (almost certainly birch-bark canoes) and the use of the bow and arrow, supplemented by archaeological evidence, identify the natives as Algonkian Indians, not Eskimos, and the locality of the fight as the neighborhood of Lake Melville in Labrador.[14]

Some years later the Icelander Thorfinn Karlsefni, married to the widow of Leif's brother Thorstein, led a larger expedition with two ships to establish a colony in America. The accounts of this differ in the two sagas. The longer version (in *E*) describes in more detail the topography and lands visited and the sailing-courses of the expedition, to which it attributes a length of three years, while the shorter version (in *G*) gives it a length of only two years and, though more summary, adds some circumstances to the report of trade and fighting between Norsemen and natives. Sailing north-west across Davis Strait, Karlsefni coasted southward along lands recognized as Leif's Helluland (Baffin Island) and Markland (probably Labrador); and passing Kjalarnes he spent the first winter, a 'severe' one, in a fjord which he called Straumfjord. In the summer, after a southward voyage lasting 'some time', he came to his second wintering-place (according to *E,* an enclosed fjord named Hóp, with climate and vegetation like

24
Sealing among ice-floes. Woodcut in Olaus Magnus, *Historia de gentibus septentrionalibus*, Rome, 1555.
25
The stern of the Gokstad ship, showing the steering-rudder to starboard. *Oslo, Universitetets Oldsaksamling.*
26
Polar bears on ice floes, one of which is eating a fish. Woodcut in Olaus Magnus, *Historia de gentibus septentrionalibus*, Rome, 1555.

25

24

26

The Vinland Map, c. 1440. *New Haven, Yale University Library.*
The Vinland Map is the only medieval world map to show both a realistic
Greenland and an island of almost continental proportions in the western
Atlantic, the latter being given the name of Vinland. It has thus been hailed
as embodying Norse traditions and cartographic knowledge of not only
the Greenland settlement but of the voyages from Greenland to North
America at the turn of the tenth and eleventh centuries, when Bjarni
Herjolfsson and Leif Eiriksson discovered North America. A Norse site which
can probably be associated with these voyages has been discovered at
L'Anse aux Meadows, Newfoundland.

The story of the discovery of the map and its eventual acquisition by
Yale University Library is told in *The Vinland Map and the Tartar Relation*
by R. A. Skelton, Thomas E. Marston and George D. Painter (New Haven and
London, 1965). Its publication caused a great stir, since it was regarded as
casting doubts on the priority of the discovery of America by Columbus,
with which, however, it was not concerned.

The Vinland Map was originally bound up with a document known as
'the Tartar Relation' and both formed part of a manuscript of the thirteenth-
century compendium, the *Speculum Historiale* of Vincent of Beauvais. This
manuscript was compiled about 1440, and the basis for the Vinland Map
contained in it was a version of the world map of Andrea Bianco, made
in 1436. This was a circular map, as were most world maps of the time, but
the Vinland Map has accommodated the world surface to a rectangular frame.
There remain doubts about the exact implications and even the authenticity
of the map, but it has been widely studied as an authentic document
recording unique information on the early cartography of America.

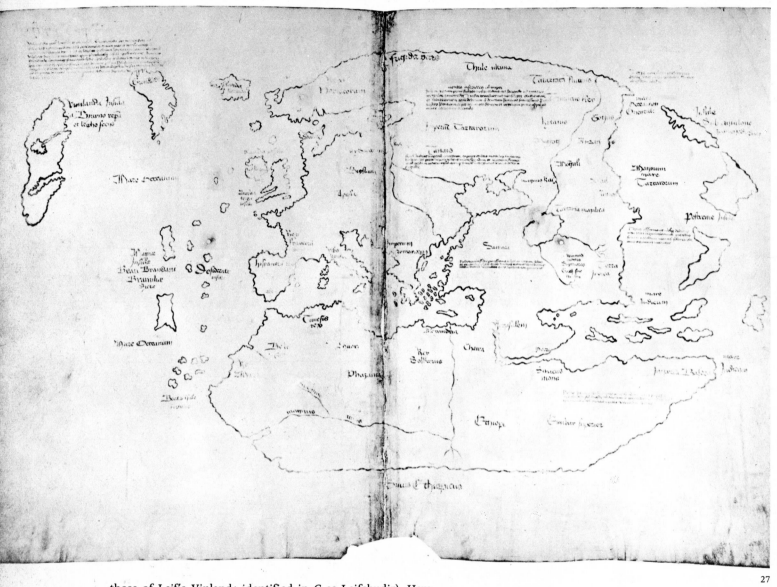

those of Leif's Vinland; identified in *G* as Leifsbudir). Here
natives came down to trade, offering 'furs and sables and pelts'
and asking in exchange for weapons, which 'Karlsefni
forbade his men to sell'. One of the natives (as narrated in *G*)
was killed by a Norseman 'for trying to steal some weapons',
and the rest fled into the woods.[15] Their physical characteristics, as observed by the voyagers, suggest that these were
Indians; and the weapons they used when, in the spring, they
attacked the colonists in their skin-boats have been identified
as characteristic of Algonkian Indians (catapults and a
'balista' or bombard), although it is curious that bows and
arrows—known to the Indians but not at this date to Eskimos
—are not mentioned.[16] Karlsefni now abandoned his plan for a
colony; he sailed off northward and wintered at Straumfjord.

28
Cathay and the Empire of the Great Khan, as depicted in the world map
executed by Fra Mauro at Murano, 1459. *Venice, Biblioteca Nazionale
Marciana.*
Fra Mauro's is the last of the great circular *mappaemundi* of the Middle Ages.
Though traditional in construction, it records the recent Portuguese
exploration of the West African coasts, and in the representation of the
Indian Ocean it draws on Arab information. The Far East is delineated from
Marco Polo's account of his travels a century and a half earlier. The artist
has conceived the imperial cities and palaces of Cathay in the
architectural styles of the Venetian Renaissance. This detail suggests the
brilliant vision of the wealth and splendor of the Far East which Columbus
and Cabot took from their reading of Marco Polo and carried in their mind's
eye as they sailed westward for its discovery.

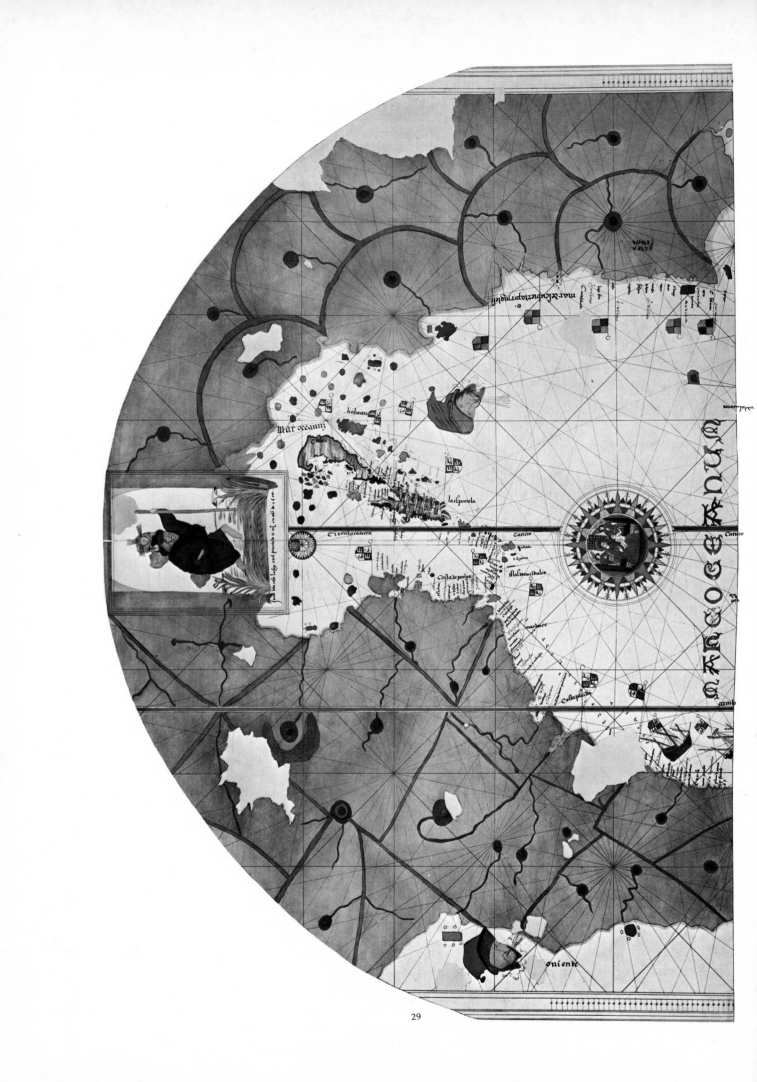

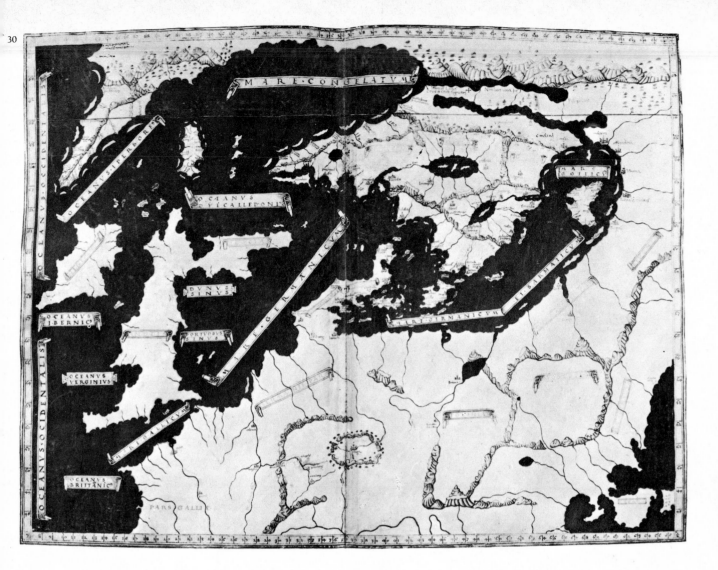

29

The New World from the world map, drawn by Juan de la Cosa, 1500. *Madrid, Museo Naval.*

Juan de la Cosa sailed with Columbus in 1493–4 and made three later voyages to America. On this map are legends showing the latest information concerning Spanish discoveries in the West Indies and South America. On the large landmass across the Atlantic in the latitude of England are five English standards with the legend 'sea discovered by the English'. These presumably refer to Cabot's voyages; the south-westward direction of the mainland coastline, in somewhat stylized cusps, is variously interpreted. It may intend to show the coastline of Asia, though no names or legends support this theory; it may record the knowledge derived from a voyage along the North American coast, though conclusive evidence of such explorations by surviving ships of John Cabot's 1498 expedition or by other vessels is lacking. La Cosa's map was constructed in two sections, the old world on a smaller scale than the new world. The tip of Brazil consequently is near the latitude of the Cape of Good Hope and Cuba is north of the Tropic of Cancer. The corruption of some place names on the map suggests that this is not the original but a copy of Cosa's map.

30

Map of the North, by Henricus Martellus Germanus, in a manuscript of Ptolemy's *Geographia,* c. 1485. *Florence, Biblioteca Nazionale Centrale, Cod. Magl. XIII.16, fos 104v-105r.*

This is derived from the lost second map of the North constructed by the Dane Claudius Clavus about 1430, which was to be the model for the representation of Greenland throughout the fifteenth and sixteenth centuries. Greenland is depicted as a peninsula connected to lands round the Pole and to northern Eurasia, and extending to the west of Iceland and south to a terminal cape in $62\frac{1}{2}°$N latitude. The maps of Clavus were the first in which the name Greenland appeared; although they were probably compiled only from written sources, such as medieval Norse sailing-directions, individual features of the coast are distinguished (but with fictitious names). A point on the west coast, in 70°N, is named by Henricus Martellus, following Clavus, as 'ultimus terre terminus', i.e. the furthest land known.

31

31

The extinction of the Norse settlements in Greenland, according to Eskimo folk memory. Woodcut in Henry Rink, *Tales and traditions of the Eskimos,* London, 1875.

Legends collected from the Greenland Eskimos in the nineteenth century by the Danish ethnologist Henry Rink tell of feuds between the 'Kablunaks' (Norsemen) and the Greenlanders. This wood-engraving, made by an Eskimo, illustrates the story in which, after the burning of the Eastern Settlement by Eskimos, a Kablunak chief Ungortok threw his young son into a lake on his flight south, 'so as to save his own life'.

On his voyage back to Greenland, in the spring, he touched at Markland where he took two native boys, of a people who 'lived in caves and holes in the ground'. If (as has been suggested) these were Beothuk Indians of Newfoundland,[17] the episode must have been introduced into the saga (*E*) out of its proper place.

The saga-story of the Norse voyages to America is told in episodic form. Each scene of the drama unfolds itself with a freshness and directness which without doubt mirror the visual experience, as well as the hopes and fears, of the venturers. Yet, from this first-hand testimony to the physical character, vegetation and inhabitants of the countries described, historians have been unable to reach agreement on the

32

identification of the principal localities of attempted settlement, Leifsbudir and Hóp. It is easy to see why no single theory is consistent with all the evidence in the sagas. In the course of their oral transmission, events were selected, rearranged or transposed, disturbing the chronological and geographical sequence of episodes; and, when brought into literary form, they were seen with the eyes of the writers two or more centuries after they occurred. At the time of the Vinland voyages there were Dorset Eskimos along the coasts of Labrador and Newfoundland, Beothuks in Newfoundland, and Indians of Algonkian stock to the west and south. In the Icelandic records of the voyages, the natives encountered by Thorvald and Karlsefni are uniformly called Skrælings, the name later applied by the Greenlanders to Eskimos of the Thule culture who advanced southward into Greenland in the thirteenth and fourteenth centuries.[18]

After Karlsefni, the Norsemen are not known to have made any later attempts to plant colonies in North America, though there are reports of a voyage to Vinland by a missionary bishop in the early twelfth century[19] and of a Greenland ship which in 1347 'made a voyage to Markland', perhaps for timber, and fetched Iceland, storm-driven, on her return.[20] This is the latest visit to American lands recorded in Icelandic literature. The geographical writings of southern Europe are

32

Map of the North drawn by Sigurdur Stefánsson (Sigurdus Stephanius) about 1590. *Copenhagen, Kongelige Bibliotek, Gl. kgl. Saml. 2881, 4°.*

This is the earliest of the maps drawn in Iceland and Denmark at the turn of the sixteenth and seventeenth centuries, when knowledge of the medieval Norse voyages to America was revived and a search for the lost Greenland colonies initiated. The original map by Sigurdur Stefánsson, schoolmaster of Skálholt in Iceland, is lost and now known in this copy made in 1668 by the Icelandic bishop Thordur Thorláksson. The date 1570 on the copy is erroneous.

As in other maps of this group, the cartographer has attempted to lay down the old Norse discoveries and settlements on the map of the North Atlantic as established in his own period by sixteenth-century exploration, attributing somewhat arbitrary latitudes to them. Following the tradition of Clavus as adopted by Mercator, Greenland is represented as a peninsula joined to lands in the north, with two marked innovations. In the top right-hand corner (at F on the map) a strait separating north-east Greenland from northern Russia ('Biarmaland') represents the passage by which the Dutch and English penetrated into the Kara Sea. The axis of Greenland, aligned SE-NW (instead of SW-NE as in Mercator's map), is turned through a right angle, probably because the cartographer supposed the Eastern and Western Settlements, here shown as two deep inlets on the south coast, to lie east and west of one another, though in fact they lie north and south. The only names on Greenland are 'Huidserk', the landmark picked up on the east coast by seamen sailing from Iceland, and 'Heriolfsnes', the home of Bjarni Herjolfsson, laid down in 62½°N. Southward from Greenland the American coast is shown as continuous, with the Norse landfalls of Helluland and Markland indicated as peninsulas separated by gulfs. Further south is a deep narrow bay with (on the east side) a conspicuous north-pointing cape named 'Promontorium Vinlandiae'; this outline seems to be a mental projection of the geographical features which the map maker noted in the description of Leif's Vinland in the Saga of the Greenlanders. West of this, as the accompanying text not shown here explains, is (A) 'land discovered by the English', presumably referring to Frobisher's expeditions of 1576–8, and (B) 'Vinland the Good'. The juxtaposition of these data, with the name 'Skrælinge Land', plainly arises from Frobisher's reports on the Eskimos of Baffin Island and from the cartographer's association of them with the natives of Vinland, whom the Icelandic historians supposed to be of the same race as the Eskimos or 'Skrælings' of Greenland.

33

A 'pygmy' or Eskimo of Greenland and the landmark of Hvitserk, as seen by a sixteenth-century historian. Woodcut in Olaus Magnus, *Historia de gentibus septentrionalibus*, Rome, 1555.

Hvitserk ('white shirt') was the name given in medieval Norse sailing directions to a navigation mark picked up on the east coast of Greenland by voyagers from Iceland; it suggests a glacier or the blink of the ice-cap inland. Olaus Magnus shows Hvitserk as a rocky island on which (as he narrates) Danish pirates were said to have set up a large compass-card, as a sea-mark, in the fifteenth century.

silent on the voyages westward from Greenland;[21] and the only medieval map to preserve their memory is the enigmatic Vinland Map (plate 27) which, if of the fifteenth century, remains the sole attempt, before about 1600, to illustrate in graphic form the knowledge of North America won by the Norse voyages and preserved in Iceland.

Not until the beginning of the fifteenth century did Italian mapmakers learn from a Scandinavian, Claudius Clavus, to

33

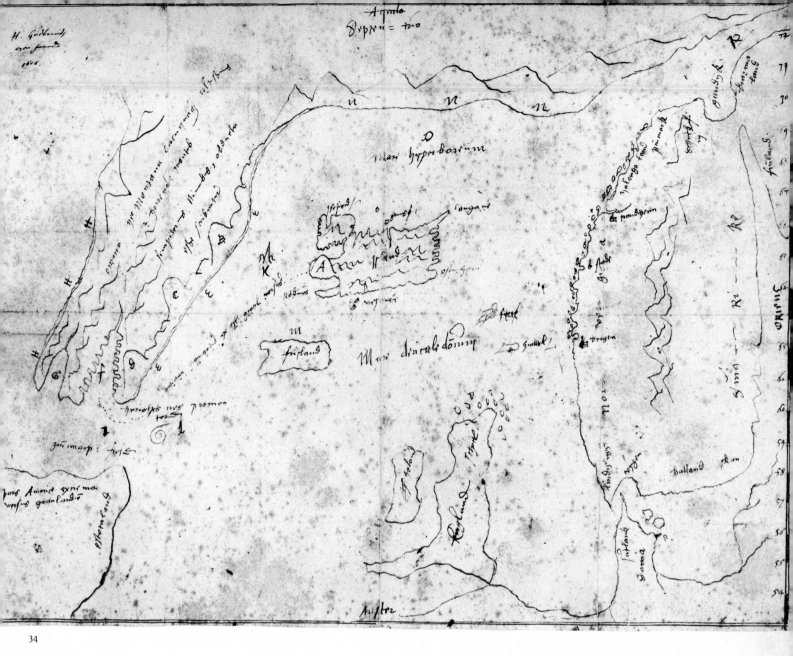

34

34

Map of the North drawn by Bishop Gudbrandur Thorláksson, 1606.
Copenhagen, Kongelige Bibliotek, Gl. kgl. 2876, 4°.
This map, drawn on a larger scale and with more detail than that of
Sigurdur Stefánsson (plate 32), is—like his—an attempt to reconcile the
geography of the medieval Norse voyages to America, as disclosed in the
Icelandic records, with the image of the North Atlantic created by more
recent explorers and cartographers. The representation of Greenland agrees
in general with Sigurdur Stefánsson's; but the peninsula is now oriented
SW-NE, with the Norse settlements still facing south, and its southernmost
point is brought down to 60°N. The ancient navigation route from Iceland
to Greenland ('antiqua navigatio ex Isl. Gronl. versus'), indicated by a
dotted line, begins at Snæfelsnes in Iceland (A), passes within sight of the
rock Hvitserk (K), and runs south-west, avoiding the East Greenland
ice-pack (E), to the Eastern Settlement (F). 'Ginnungagap', with a
whirlpool (L), in the strait south of Greenland is a relic of Norse mythology
which gave this name to a whirlpool fabled to lie at the end of the world.
From the Zeni map of 1558 (see plate 261) come the names 'Frisland', for an
imaginary island south of Iceland and duplicating it, and 'Estotiland', on
the North American coast.

   Gudbrandur Thorláksson, the Lutheran bishop of Hólar in Iceland,
prepared his map, which was received in Copenhagen in 1606, at the time
when King Christian IV of Denmark was sending expeditions in search of the
lost Greenland colonies.

lay down Greenland in its correct position to the west of
Iceland, though (following northern tradition) as a peninsula
connected to lands round the pole (see plate 30). By this time
the life-line connecting the Norse Greenland colonies with
Europe had been almost severed. The slow death of the
colonies is associated with the southward movement of the
Eskimos, with declining productivity of the settlers' farmland
and a diminishing European demand for their trade-goods,
with the colonists' failure to maintain their way of life in an
environment perhaps made harsher by a deteriorating climate,
with the irregularity and final cessation of sea communication
with Norway.[22] The Western Settlement was abandoned before
1350; its people were thought by later Icelanders either to
have fled west across Davis Strait or to have been absorbed,
perhaps by intermarriage, with 'the peoples of America'
(the Eskimos?).[23] The Eastern Settlement may have lingered
on for about three generations after the last supply ship is
known to have sailed, in 1410, from Norway to Greenland.
Only in the last years of the sixteenth century did European
geographers become aware that Norsemen had discovered
America six hundred years earlier. Icelanders and Danes,
searching the ancient records, then compiled maps in which
they attempted to locate the American landfalls of the Viking
period on the 'modern' map of the New World established by
explorers and cartographers of the sixteenth century[24];

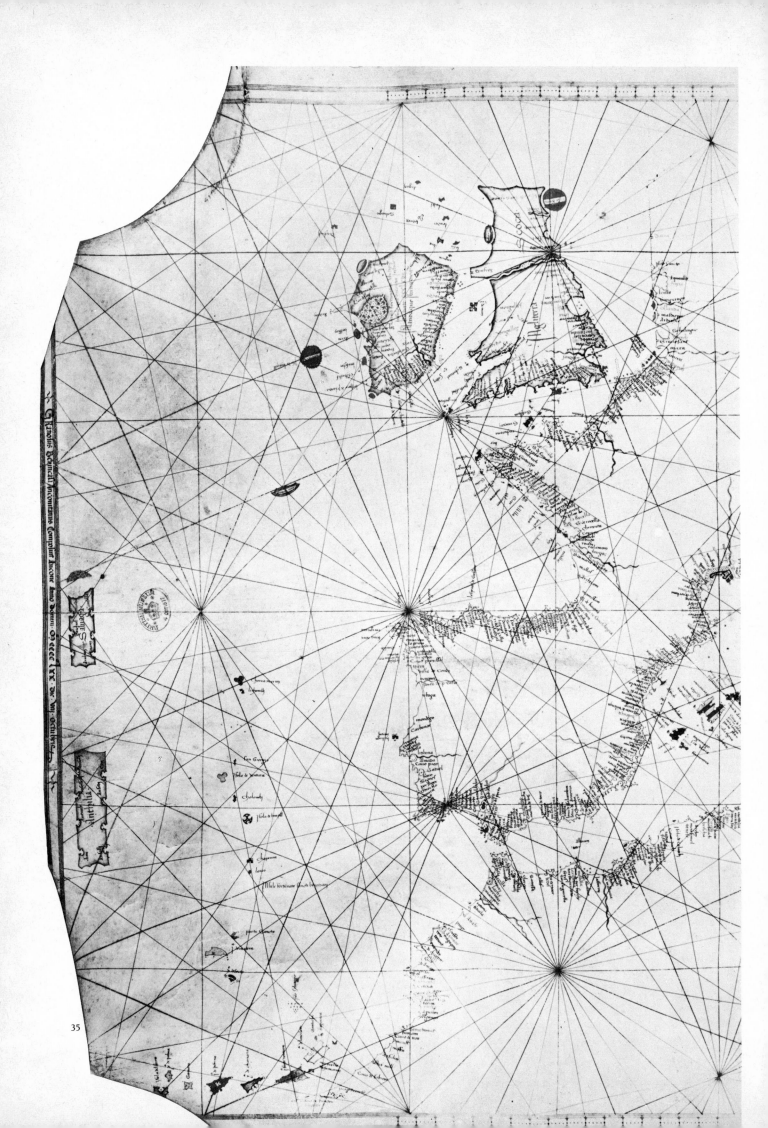

and
don
oper
of G
look
glas
ever
canc
as w

St
four
by c
as w
afte
the
On t
of th
the
'The
and
to o
havi
and
the
boat
the
to h
they

Islands of the Western Ocean, in a chart drawn by Andrea Benincasa at Ancona in 1470. *London, British Museum, Add. Ms. 31318.*
This chart illustrates the fusion of classical and medieval lore with data from discovery that characterizes fifteenth-century concepts of the Atlantic Ocean. The island groups of the Azores and the Canaries, discovered by the Portuguese since the mid-fourteenth century, are laid down as a long chain extending north-south. The name here applied to them, 'Insule fortunate sancti brandani' (i.e. The Fortunate Isles of St Brendan), contains echoes of Greek antiquity, in which the most westerly islands known were termed the Isles of the Blest or Fortunate Isles, and of the poetic legend of St Brendan, whose name had been associated with Atlantic islands on maps since the thirteenth century. The two large islands of 'Anthilia' and 'Saluaga', at the westernmost edge of the parchment, were introduced into cartography in the early fifteenth century; the first surviving chart to show them is dated 1424. This delineation certainly reflects contemporary rumor or surmise about land far out in the ocean, to which older Irish and Arab traditions of voyages to the west may well have contributed. In many Renaissance maps the larger island Antillia is named the 'Island of the Seven Cities', by association with an eighth-century legend. It has been forcefully argued, from the evidence of sailing conditions in the North Atlantic, from the etymology of the nomenclature, and from historical probability in the context of contemporary enterprise in navigation and exploration, that Antillia and Satanaxes in the maps record a Portuguese discovery of the West Indies of North America before 1424.

36
Manuscript chart of the North Atlantic by Alonso de Santa Cruz, cosmographer of the *Casa de Contractación*, Seville, in his 'Islario general del mundo', 1545. *Madrid, Biblioteca Nacional.*
The imaginary islands of Brasil, Las Maidas and 'ya verde' ('Green Island'), westward from Ireland, still form stepping-stones across the ocean.

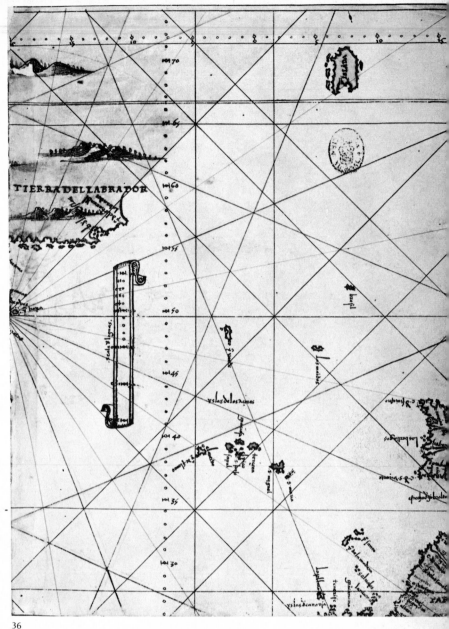

36

but the Danish expeditions which sought the lost Greenland colonies in 1605–7 found no trace of them.

It was however islands, and not mainland, that medieval mapmakers depicted in the fringe of ocean that lay along the western edge of their drawings. To islands of classical tradition or Irish lore (the Fortunate Isles, St Brendan's Isle, Brasil) they added, in the fourteenth and fifteenth centuries, islands revealed by discovery or settlement (Madeira, the Canaries, the Azores) and islands of conventional outline (Antillia or the Isle of the Seven Cities, Satanaxes) which may represent land reported but not surveyed (see plate 35). The principle of Christian cosmography, expressed by St Isidore in the seventh century, that 'beyond the Ocean there is not any land' had spent its force. Instead, men surmised that 'in the west [the ocean] is bounded in part by unknown land'.[25] Portuguese adventurers who, from about 1430, sailed from the Azores or Madeira in search of this land seem to have been beaten back by the westerly winds of the North Atlantic. Further south, other Portuguese seamen learnt how to navigate by the north-east trade winds in tropical latitudes; and further north, fishermen of western Europe—Basques, Bretons, English—were using the easterly winds which blow after the equinoxes to reach out to new banks and grounds in the ocean.

This practical experience of voyaging out and home in the Atlantic was to be harnessed to the belief that the East could be reached by sailing westward. Its intellectual basis was the concept that the earth was a sphere, a belief never entirely extinguished in the Middle Ages and revived with the recovery of Greek geographical thought in the fifteenth century. The imaginative motive was provided by Marco Polo's description of the splendours of Cathay (China) and Cipangu (Japan), in far eastern Asia. Columbus, who had sailed in Portuguese ships to West Africa, chose the trade-wind route, 'south till the butter melts' and then west. It was in tropical latitudes that his maps laid down Antillia and Cipangu, that he could count on fair winds outward, and that he made his Caribbean landfall. But it was by the northern route that Bristol fishermen, between 1482 and 1494, and John Cabot in 1497 rediscovered North America. The Atlantic Ocean could now be visualized as a 'middle sea', like the Mediterranean, carrying traffic between its littoral lands. A Portuguese cosmographer expressed this idea in 1505: 'The sea does not surround the earth, as Homer and other authors affirmed, but rather the earth in its greatness surrounds and contains all the waters in its concavity and centre'.[26]

37

38

40

Woodcut of sea monsters inhabiting the north Atlantic and of animals found in northern lands appeared in Sebastian Münster's *Cosmographia*, Basle, 1550 and in many subsequent editions of his work.

Most of the monsters shown here are found in Olaus Magnus' map of northern Europe and adjacent waters, published in 1539; Münster's popular cosmography, however, was probably the immediate source of the sea monsters that decorate and enliven the charts of many European mapmakers in the latter half of the sixteenth century. Münster's accompanying description of the figures in the woodcut did little to lessen the apprehension of seafarers into unknown waters. Its translation from the Latin below is by Dr M. Beaty.

The following is a description of the sea and land monsters which are pictured in the illustration. The letters A, B, C, etc. which appear in this description correspond to those on the drawing.

A Huge fish the size of mountains are sometimes seen close to Iceland. They overturn ships unless frightened away by the sound of trumpets, or they may play with empty barrels thrown in the water, a game which amuses them greatly. Occasionally sailors are endangered when they drop anchor on the backs of these whales, mistaking them for islands. The Icelanders call them Fish of the Devil. Many people of Iceland even today build their houses from the ribs and bones of these whales.

B There is a fearful species of whale called physeters, mentioned by Pliny and Solinus. When it stands erect this monster of the sea can sink even a large ship by sucking in water and then blowing it out again in clouds through holes in its forehead.

C These hydrae or serpents, 200 or 300 feet in length, are found in northern waters. They throw themselves on ships with the purpose of turning them over. They are extremely troublesome to sailors, especially in strong northern winds.

D One of these enormous sea monsters has terrible tusks, the other is horrifying with horns, flames, and huge eyes sixteen or twenty feet across. On its square head is a long beard. The rest of its body is quite small.

E This creature is an insatiable glutton. By squeezing itself between trees it empties its belly and then rushes back to continue eating. Hunters, creeping up, kill this animal for its beautiful skin, which noblemen enjoy wearing; but those who wear the skin sometimes become like the animal.

F Reindeer, raised in herds, can pull carriages faster than any horses, especially in the snow, covering almost 30 German miles a day. They also provide milk for household use and move about in herds like cattle. They are larger than stags, with splendid antlers which are more slender than those of stags and with fewer prongs.

G In the wilds of the North, in Biarmia far beyond Sweden, is a huge forest said to extend for 80 miles. Here live many animals whose fur is valued by noblemen, animals such as martens, sables, ermines, lynxes, otters, various genets, and beavers everywhere you look.

H This is a horrible sea monster, called a Ziphius, which devours seals.

I The fruit of certain trees produces ducks.

K A sea monster somewhat resembling a pig was sighted in 1537.

L The Norwegians call this a Spring whale because of its agility. It has a broad, high hump on its back.

M There are crabs so large and strong that they can kill a swimmer who is caught in their claws.

N A creature resembling a rhinoceros is able to devour a crab twelve feet long. It has a sharp-pointed nose and a sharp-edged back which goes up in a peak.

O The lynx, found in the most remote parts of Sweden, is somewhat like a wolf in nature and is often caught in wolf traps. Lynxes eat cats which live in the forests.

P In the interior of Sweden elk are used to pull carriages through the snow at great speed. This isn't allowed in Gothia, though, where it is feared that their speed may be used by those wishing to spy on the country. In winter the elks stay together in herds and fight the wolves which try to devour them. We have drawn as good a likeness of this animal as a pen can provide.

Q Hunters search for pheasants which may lie hidden under the snow for two or three months without food.

R The pelican, a bird at least as large as a goose, can fill its throat with water and let out a noise as loud as the braying of a donkey. Under its beak

it has a sack-like swelling.
S   These fish are noted for their kindness, for they save swimmers from being eaten by sea monsters.
T   The sea cow has a body shaped like that of a cow on land.
V   A thick book could be written about the many other types and amazing appearance of the animals, fish, and birds found in northern areas, if anyone were willing to study the species with which it has pleased God to adorn that ice region. For just as the torrid zone of Africa has its own peculiar and wonderful creatures which can barely exist without the heat of that climate, so the Creator has given to the cold northern region its own creatures which cannot bear the heat of the sun. This was done in order that the glory of God might be known throughout the world and so that mankind in all parts of the world might find creatures whose appearance would grip him with a sense of wonder at the wisdom and power of God.

41

he was driven westwards off course and discovered the Gunnbjarnar Skerries; he added that he would come back to visit his friends if he found this country.

He put out to sea past Snæfells Glacier. He found the country he was seeking and made land near the glacier he named Mid Glacier; it is now known as Blaserk. From there he sailed south down the coast to find out if the country were habitable there. He spent the first winter on Eiriks Island, which lies near the middle of the Eastern Settlement. In the spring he went to Eiriksfjord, where he decided to make his home. That summer he explored the wilderness to the west and gave names to many landmarks there. He spent the second winter on Eiriks Holms, off Hvarfs Peak. The third summer he sailed

41
Eiriksfjord, in south-west Greenland, where Eirik the Red settled in 986. This was the base from which the Norse voyages for the discovery and colonization of North America were made early in the eleventh century.

3.
The Norse discovery and colonization of Greenland, *c*. 981–5

From *Grænlandinga Saga*: 'Saga of the Greenlanders'.

About 900, some thirty years after the settlement of Iceland by Norwegian Vikings had begun, an Icelander named Gunnbjorn Ulfsson was blown to the west by a gale and made the first chance sighting of islands off the Greenland coast near Angmagssalik. Gunnbjorn's discovery was remembered in Iceland and prompted an abortive attempt at colonization in 978. Soon after, about 981, Eirik Thorvaldsson, called the Red, who had emigrated from Norway 'because of some killings', got into further trouble in Iceland and decided to try his luck in the land to the west. Rounding Cape Farewell he spent three summers exploring Davis Strait and established his settlement, with colonists brought from Iceland, on the west coast.

Eirik was sentenced to outlawry at the Thorsness Assembly. He prepared his ship in Eiriksbay for a sea voyage, and when he was ready, Styr and the others accompanied him out beyond the islands. Eirik told them he was going to search for the land that Gunnbjorn, the son of Ulf Crow, had sighted when

all the way north to Snæfell and into Hrafnsfjord, where he reckoned he was farther inland than the head of Eiriksfjord. Then he turned back and spent the third winter on Eiriks Island, off the mouth of Eiriksfjord.

He sailed back to Iceland the following summer and put in at Breidafjord. He named the country he had discovered GREENLAND, for he said that people would be much more tempted to go there if it had an attractive name. Eirik spent the winter in Iceland. Next summer he sailed off to colonize Greenland, and he made his home at Brattahlid, in Eiriksfjord.

It is said by learned men that in the summer in which Eirik the Red set off to colonize Greenland, twenty-five ships sailed from Breidafjord and Borgarfjord, but only fourteen reached there; some were driven back, and some were lost at sea.

Text used: Translation by Magnus Magnusson and Hermann Pálsson, The Vinland Sagas, Harmondsworth, 1965, pp. 49-51.

4.
The discovery of North America by Greenlanders, 985–6 and 1001–2

From *Grœnlandinga Saga:* 'Saga of the Greenlanders'.

Bjarni Herjolfsson sailed from Norway in 985 to join his father in Iceland, but found that Herjolf had just emigrated with Eirik the Red to Greenland. Deciding to join him, Bjarni was blown off-course south and west to make the first recorded landfalls on the American continent.

Bjarni arrived in Iceland at Eyrar in the summer of the year that his father had left for Greenland. The news came as a shock to Bjarni, and he refused to have his ship unloaded. His crew asked him what he had in mind; he replied that he intended to keep his custom of enjoying his father's hospitality over the winter—'so I want to sail my ship to Greenland, if you are willing to come with me'.

They all replied that they would do what he thought best. Then Bjarni said, 'This voyage of ours will be considered foolhardy, for not one of us has ever sailed the Greenland Sea'.

However, they put to sea as soon as they were ready and sailed for three days until land was lost to sight below the horizon. Then the fair wind failed and northerly winds and fog set in, and for many days they had no idea what their course was. After that they saw the sun again and were able to get their bearings; they hoisted sail and after a day's sailing they sighted land.

They discussed amongst themselves what country this might be. Bjarni said he thought it could not be Greenland. The crew asked him if he wanted to land there or not; Bjarni replied, 'I think we should sail in close'.

They did so, and soon they could see that the country was not mountainous, but was well wooded and with low hills. So they put to sea again, leaving the land on the port quarter; and after sailing for two days they sighted land once more.

Bjarni's men asked him if he thought this was Greenland yet; he said he did not think this was Greenland, any more than the previous one—'for there are said to be huge glaciers in Greenland'.

They closed the land quickly and saw that it was flat and wooded. Then the wind failed and the crew all said they thought it advisable to land there, but Bjarni refused. They claimed they needed both firewood and water; but Bjarni said, 'You have no shortage of either'. He was criticized for this by his men.

He ordered them to hoist sail, and they did so. They turned the prow out to sea and sailed before a south-west wind for three days before they sighted a third land. This one was high and mountainous, and topped by a glacier. Again they asked Bjarni if he wished to land there, but he replied, 'No, for this country seems to me to be worthless'.

They did not lower sail this time, but followed the coastline and saw that it was an island. Once again they put the land astern and sailed out to sea before the same fair wind. But now it began to blow a gale, and Bjarni ordered his men to shorten sail and not to go harder than ship and rigging could stand. They sailed now for four days, until they sighted a fourth land.

The men asked Bjarni if he thought this would be Greenland or not.

'This tallies most closely with what I have been told about Greenland,' replied Bjarni. 'And here we shall go into land.'

They did so, and made land as dusk was falling at a promontory which had a boat hauled up on it. This was where Bjarni's father, Herjolf, lived, and it has been called Herjolfsness for that reason ever since.

About fifteen years later, Leif Eiriksson went in search of the western lands seen by Bjarni, traversing them in the reverse order, namely north to south, from Baffin Island along the Labrador coast to the Gulf of St Lawrence, or perhaps further south.

Some time later, Bjarni Herjolfsson sailed from Greenland to Norway and visited Earl Eirik, who received him well. Bjarni told the earl about his voyage and the lands he had sighted. People thought he had shown great lack of curiosity, since he could tell them nothing about these countries, and he was criticized for this. Bjarni was made a retainer at the earl's court, and went back to Greenland the following summer.

There was now great talk of discovering new countries. Leif, the son of Eirik the Red of Brattahlid, went to see Bjarni Herjolfsson and bought his ship from him, and engaged a crew of thirty-five . . .

They made their ship ready and put out to sea. The first landfall they made was the country that Bjarni had sighted last. They sailed right up to the shore and cast anchor, then lowered a boat and landed. There was no grass to be seen, and the hinterland was covered with great glaciers, and between glaciers and shore the land was like one great slab of rock. It seemed to them a worthless country.

42
An animal head carved in wood, as a charm against evil spirits, on a sledge found in the Oseberg ship-burial, ninth century. *Oslo, Universitetets Oldsaksamling.*

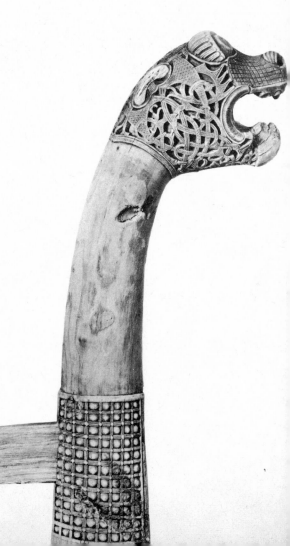

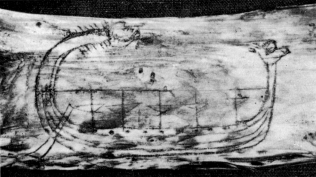

43

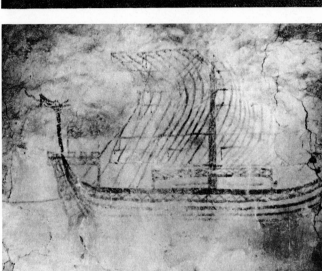

44

43
A Norse dragon-ship. Carving on a stick found at the German Quay in Bergen. *Bergen, Historisk Museum.*
44
A Viking ship under sail. Wall-painting in the church of Siljan in Telemark, Norway, showing the single square sail of woollen cloth, hoisted on a big yard and loose-footed. *Oslo, Riksantikvaren.*
45
Cape Bauld, Newfoundland (Strait of Belle Isle): perhaps the 'Promontorium Vinlandiae' of Sigurdur **Stefánsson**'s map of the North, *c.* 1590 (plate 32).
46
Cape Farewell (named by John Davis in 1585), seen from the south-west. Drawing by William Richey, midshipman, July 1810. *(Hydrographic Department, British Ministry of Defence, 'Coastal Views: Arctic', vol. II.)*

45

46

Then Leif said, 'Now we have done better than Bjarni where this country is concerned—we at least have set foot on it. I shall give this country a name and call it HELLULAND.'

They returned to their ship and put to sea, and sighted a second land. Once again they sailed right up to it and cast anchor, lowered a boat and went ashore. This country was flat and wooded, with white sandy beaches wherever they went; and the land sloped gently down to the sea.

Leif said, 'This country shall be named after its natural resources: it shall be called MARKLAND.'

They hurried back to their ship as quickly as possible and sailed away to sea in a north-east wind for two days until they sighted land again. They sailed towards it and came to an island which lay to the north of it.

They went ashore and looked about them. The weather was fine. There was dew on the grass, and the first thing they did was to get some of it on their hands and put it to their lips, and to them it seemed the sweetest thing they had ever tasted. Then they went back to their ship and sailed into the sound that lay between the island and the headland jutting out to the north.

They steered a westerly course round the headland. There were extensive shallows there and at low tide their ship was left high and dry, with the sea almost out of sight. But they were so impatient to land that they could not bear to wait for the rising tide to float the ship; they ran ashore to a place where a river flowed out of a lake. As soon as the tide had refloated the ship they took a boat and rowed to it and brought it up the river into the lake, where they anchored it. They carried their hammocks ashore and put up booths. Then they decided to winter there, and built some large houses.

There was no lack of salmon in the river or the lake, bigger salmon than they had ever seen. The country seemed to them so kind that no winter fodder would be needed for livestock: there was never any frost all winter and the grass hardly withered at all.

In this country, night and day were of more even length than in either Greenland or Iceland: on the shortest day of the year, the sun was already up by 9 a.m., and did not set until after 3 p.m.

When they had finished building their houses, Leif said to his companions, 'Now I want to divide our company into two parties and have the country explored; half of the company are to remain here at the houses while the other half go exploring—but they must not go so far that they cannot return the same evening, and they are not to become separated . . .'

Tyrkir, a 'Southerner' (German) in Leif's crew, wandered off on his own and found vines, from which Leif named the country.

At first Tyrkir spoke for a long time in German, rolling his eyes in all directions and pulling faces, and no one could understand what he was saying. After a while he spoke in Icelandic.

'I did not go much farther than you,' he said. 'I have some news. I found vines and grapes.'

'Is that true, foster-father?' asked Leif.

'Of course it is true,' he replied. 'Where I was born there were plenty of vines and grapes.'

They slept for the rest of the night, and next morning Leif said to his men, 'Now we have two tasks on our hands. On alternate days we must gather grapes and cut vines, and then fell trees to make a cargo for my ship.'

This was done. It is said that the tow-boat was filled with grapes. They took on a full cargo of timber; and in the spring they made ready to leave and sailed away. Leif named the country after its natural qualities and called it VINLAND.

Thorvald, Leif's brother, thought that 'the country had not been explored extensively enough' and led a second expedition to Vinland, where he wintered and was killed in an affray with Indians.

Thorvald prepared his expedition with his brother Leif's guidance and engaged a crew of thirty. When the ship was ready they put out to sea and there are no reports of their voyage until they reached Leif's Houses in Vinland. There they laid up the ship and settled down for the winter, catching fish for their food.

In the spring Thorvald said they should get the ship ready, and that meanwhile a small party of men should take the ship's boat and sail west along the coast and explore that

47
Cape Porcupine and the adjoining strand, south of Hamilton Inlet, Labrador:
perhaps the 'Kjalarnes' and 'Furdustrands' of the Vinland voyages.

region during the summer.

They found the country there very attractive, with woods stretching almost down to the shore and white sandy beaches. There were numerous islands there, and extensive shallows. They found no traces of human habitation or animals except on one westerly island, where they found a wooden stack-cover. That was the only man-made thing they found; and in the autumn they returned to Leif's Houses.

Next summer Thorvald sailed east with his ship and then north along the coast. They ran into a fierce gale off a headland and were driven ashore; the keel was shattered and they had to stay there for a long time while they repaired the ship.

Thorvald said to his companions, 'I want to erect the old keel here on the headland, and call the place KJALARNES.'

They did this and then sailed away eastward along the coast. Soon they found themselves at the mouth of two fjords, and sailed up to the promontory that jutted out between them; it was heavily wooded. They moored the ship alongside and put out the gangway, and Thorvald went ashore with all his men.

'It is beautiful here,' he said. 'Here I should like to make my home.'

On their way back to the ship they noticed three humps on the sandy beach just in front of the headland. When they went closer they found that these were three skin-boats, with three men under each of them. Thorvald and his men divided forces and captured all of them except one, who escaped in his boat. They killed the other eight and returned to the headland, from which they scanned the surrounding country. They could make out a number of humps farther up the fjord and concluded that these were settlements.

Then they were overwhelmed by such a heavy drowsiness that they could not stay awake, and they all fell asleep—until they were awakened by a voice that shouted, 'Wake up, Thorvald, and all your men, if you want to stay alive! Get to your ship with all your company and get away as fast as you can!'

A great swarm of skin-boats was then heading towards them down the fjord.

Thorvald said, 'We shall set up breastworks on the gunwales and defend ourselves as best we can, but fight back as little as possible.'

They did this. The Skrælings shot at them for a while, and then turned and fled as fast as they could.

Thorvald asked his men if any of them were wounded; they all replied that they were unhurt.

'I have a wound in the armpit,' said Thorvald. 'An arrow flew up between the gunwale and my shield, under my arm—here it is. This will lead to my death.

'I advise you now to go back as soon as you can. But first I want you to take me to the headland I thought so suitable for a home. I seem to have hit on the truth when I said that I would settle there for a while. Bury me there, and put crosses at my head and feet, and let the place be called KROSSANES for ever afterwards.'

With that Thorvald died, and his men did exactly as he had asked of them. Afterwards they sailed back and joined the rest of the expedition and exchanged all the news they had to tell.

They spent the winter there and gathered grapes and vines as cargo for the ship. In the spring they set off on the voyage to Greenland; they made land at Eiriksfjord, and had plenty of news to tell Leif.

Text used: Translation by Magnus Magnusson and Hermann Pálsson, The Vinland Sagas, *Harmondsworth, 1965, pp. 52–61.*

5.
Attempted Norse colonization in North America, *c.* 1010

From *Eiríks Saga Randa:* 'Eirik the Red's Saga'.

Some years later Thorfinn Karlsefni, an Icelandic merchant, came to Brattahlid, where he married Gudrid, widow of another brother of Leif, and planned a larger expedition to make a permanent settlement in Vinland, with three ships and 160 men and women including his wife, Leif's sister Freydis and Bjarni Grimolfsson. The ships sailed north up Davis Strait and then southward along the Labrador coast. The first winter was spent at 'Straumfjord', the second at 'Hóp', and the third at 'Straumfjord'; these places have been variously located between the St Lawrence and the Hudson river. In spite of extensive exploration, they failed to find Leif's Vinland. The hostility of the Indians and discord between the men of the expedition discouraged settlement, and in the fourth summer Karlsefni returned to Greenland.

There were great discussions at Brattahlid that winter about going in search of Vinland where, it was said, there was excellent land to be had. The outcome was that Karlsefni and Snorri Thorbrandsson prepared their ship and made ready to search for Vinland that summer . . .

They sailed first up to the Western Settlement, and then to the Bjarn Isles. From there they sailed before a northerly wind and after two days at sea they sighted land and rowed ashore in boats to explore it. They found there many slabs of stone so huge that two men could stretch out on them sole to sole. There were numerous foxes there. They gave this country a name and called it HELLULAND.

From there they sailed for two days before a northerly wind and sighted land ahead; this was a heavily-wooded country abounding with animals. There was an island to the south-east, where they found bears, and so they named it BJARN ISLE; they named the wooded mainland itself MARKLAND.

After two days they sighted land again and held in towards it; it was a promontory they were approaching. They tacked along the coast, with the land to starboard.

It was open and harbourless, with long beaches and extensive sands. They went ashore in boats and found a ship's keel on the headland, and so they called the place KJALARNES. They called this stretch of coast FURDUSTRANDS because it took so long to sail past it. Then the coastline became indented with bays and they steered into one of them . . .

The expedition sailed on until they reached a fjord. They steered their ships into it. At its mouth lay an island around which there flowed very strong currents, and so they named it STRAUM ISLAND. There were so many birds on it that one could scarcely set foot between their eggs.

They steered into the fjord, which they named STRAUM-FJORD; here they unloaded their ships and settled down. They had brought with them livestock of all kinds and they looked around for natural produce. There were mountains there and the country was beautiful to look at, and they paid no attention to anything except exploring it. There was tall grass everywhere.

They stayed there that winter, which turned out to be a very severe one; they had made no provision for it during the summer, and now they ran short of food and the hunting failed. They moved out to the island in the hope of finding game, or stranded whales, but there was little food to be found there, although their livestock throve . . .

In the spring they went back to Straumfjord and gathered supplies, game on the mainland, eggs on the island, and fish from the sea . . .

Karlsefni sailed south along the coast, accompanied by Snorri and Bjarni and the rest of the expedition. They sailed for a long time and eventually came to a river that flowed down into a lake and from the lake into the sea. There were extensive sandbars outside the river mouth, and ships could only enter it at high tide.

They did so. The newcomers rowed towards them and stared at them in amazement as they came ashore. They were small and evil-looking, and their hair was coarse; they had large eyes and broad cheekbones. They stayed there for a while, marvelling, and then rowed away south round the headland.

Karlsefni and his men had built their settlement on a slope by the lakeside; some of the houses were close to the lake, and others were farther away. They stayed there that winter. There was no snow at all, and all the livestock were able to fend for themselves.

Then early one morning in spring, they saw a horde of skin-boats approaching from the south round the headland, so

Karlsefni and his men sailed into the estuary and named the place HÓP [Tidal Lake]. Here they found wild wheat growing in fields on all the low ground and grapevines on all the higher ground. Every stream was teeming with fish. They dug trenches at the high-tide mark, and when the tide went out there were halibut trapped in the trenches. In the woods there was a great number of animals of all kinds.

They stayed there for a fortnight, enjoying themselves and noticing nothing untoward. They had their livestock with them. But early one morning as they looked around they caught sight of nine skin-boats; the men in them were waving sticks which made a noise like flails, and the motion was sunwise.

Karlsefni said, 'What can this signify?'

'It could well be a token of peace,' said Snorri. 'Let us take a white shield and go to meet them with it.'

48
Hvalsey Church at East Settlement, the best preserved Norse ruin.

dense that it looked as if the estuary were strewn with charcoal; and sticks were being waved from every boat. Karlsefni's men raised their shields and the two parties began to trade.

What the natives wanted most to buy was red cloth; they also wanted to buy swords and spears, but Karlsefni and Snorri forbade that. In exchange for the cloth they traded grey pelts. The natives took a span of red cloth for each pelt, and tied the cloth around their heads. The trading went on like this for a while until the cloth began to run short; then Karlsefni and his men cut it up into pieces which were no more than a finger's breadth wide; but the Skrælings paid just as much or even more for it.

Then it so happened that a bull belonging to Karlsefni and

his men came running out of the woods, bellowing furiously. The Skrælings were terrified and ran to their skin-boats and rowed away south round the headland.

After that there was no sign of the natives for three whole weeks. But then Karlsefni's men saw a huge number of boats coming from the south, pouring in like a torrent. This time all the sticks were being waved anti-clockwise and all the Skrælings were howling loudly. Karlsefni and his men now hoisted red shields and advanced towards them.

When they clashed there was a fierce battle and a hail of missiles came flying over, for the Skrælings were using catapults. Karlsefni and Snorri saw them hoist a large sphere on a pole; it was dark blue in colour. It came flying in over the heads of Karlsefni's men and made an ugly din when it struck the ground. This terrified Karlsefni and his men so much that their only thought was to flee, and they retreated farther up the river. They did not halt until they reached some cliffs, where they prepared to make a resolute stand.

Freydis came out and saw the retreat. She shouted, 'Why do you flee from such pitiful wretches, brave men like you? You should be able to slaughter them like cattle. If I had weapons, I am sure I could fight better than any of you.'

The men paid no attention to what she was saying. Freydis tried to join them but she could not keep up with them because she was pregnant. She was following them into the woods when the Skrælings closed in on her. In front of her lay a dead man, Thorbrand Snorrason, with a flintstone buried in his head, and his sword beside him. She snatched up the sword and prepared to defend herself. When the Skrælings came rushing towards her she pulled one of her breasts out of her bodice and slapped it with the sword. The Skrælings were terrified at the sight of this and fled back to their boats and hastened away.

Karlsefni and his men came over to her and praised her courage. Two of their men had been killed and four of the Skrælings, even though Karlsefni and his men had been fighting against heavy odds.

They returned to their houses and pondered what force it was that had attacked them from inland; they then realized that the only attackers had been those who had come in the boats, and that the other force had just been a delusion.

The Skrælings found the other dead Norseman, with his axe lying beside him. One of them hacked at a rock with the axe, and the axe broke; and thinking it worthless now because it could not withstand stone, they threw it away.

Karlsefni and his men had realized by now that although the land was excellent they could never live there in safety or freedom from fear, because of the native inhabitants. So they made ready to leave the place and return home. They sailed off north along the coast. They came upon five Skrælings clad in skins, asleep; beside them were containers full of deer-marrow mixed with blood. Karlsefni's men reckoned that these five must be outlaws, and killed them.

Then they came to a headland on which there were numerous deer; the headland looked like a huge cake of dung, for the animals used to spend the winters there.

Soon afterwards Karlsefni and his men arrived at Straumfjord, where they found plenty of everything.

Karlsefni set out with one ship in search of Thorhall the Hunter, while the rest of the company stayed behind. He sailed north past Kjalarnes and then bore west, with the land on the port beam. It was a region of wild and desolate woodland; and when they had travelled a long way they came to a river which flowed from east to west into the sea. They steered into the river mouth and lay to by its southern bank.

They returned to Straumfjord and spent the third winter

49
The remains of the farmhouse at Sandnes, in the Western Settlement, the home of Thorstein Eiriksson, and then of Thorfinn Karlsefni who married Thorstein's widow. Here, in 1930, an arrowhead of Labrador quartzite was found, similar to Indian arrows found in 1956 near Lake Melville in Labrador, where Thorvald Eiriksson was killed by 'Skrælings'.

there. But now quarrels broke out frequently; those who were unmarried kept pestering the married men.

It was in the first autumn that Karlsefni's son, Snorri, was born; he was three years old when they left.

They set sail before a southerly wind and reached Markland, where they came upon five Skrælings—a bearded man, two women, and two children. Karlsefni and his men captured the two boys, but the others got away and sank down into the ground.

They took the boys with them and taught them the language and baptized them. The boys said that their mother was called Vætild and their father Ovægir. They said that the land of the Skrælings was ruled by two kings, one of whom was called Avaldamon and the other Valdidida. They said that there were no houses there and that people lived in caves or holes in the ground. They said that there was a country across from their own land where the people went about in white clothing and uttered loud cries and carried poles with patches of cloth attached. This is thought to have been HVITRAMANNA-LAND.

Finally they reached Greenland, and spent the winter with Eirik the Red.

Text used: Translation by Magnus Magnusson and Hermann Pálsson, The Vinland Sagas, Harmondsworth, 1965, pp. 93-103.

2 CABOT TO CARTIER: THE DISCOVERY AND EXPLORATION OF THE EAST COAST OF NORTH AMERICA

Gold and pearls were the lures of the south; fish and fur were the lodestones of the north. The tropics turned explorers into conquistadors; the Newfoundland Banks and the mainland forests turned fishermen and, later, traders into explorers. Yet both in the south and in the north the mirage of a sea-route to the Spice Islands and the fabulous wealth of the Orient drew the earliest explorers across the Atlantic.

The eyes of the Portuguese and Spanish explorers turned southward or westward, not to the north. The landfall of Columbus on San Salvador on 12 October 1492, was the most northerly of his four voyages. In 1493 he first arrived at Dominica in the Lesser Antilles; in 1498 he turned north eventually from his projected route to discover Trinidad and sailed on to his first sight of the South American mainland. On his last voyage of 1502 he explored the coast of Honduras, still expecting to find the gold-paved mansions of Cipangu there or beyond. Amerigo Vespucci and the Portuguese Cabral went even farther south along the Atlantic coast of South America in their discoveries. If Columbus visited Iceland sometime before 1492, as certain historians have claimed, he must have been convinced that gold and glory did not lie to the north; there is little probability and no proof that he had ever heard of the Skrælings or Vinland. The early voyages from the Iberian peninsula across the Atlantic do not concern us in this book; any Spanish or Portuguese explorations that reached the Atlantic coast of North America in the years immediately after Columbus' discovery were clandestine or officially unrecorded. From more northern ports, however, there were recorded explorations in this period and possibly earlier.

Although tantalizing and indefinite contemporary references to discoveries of land beyond the Atlantic in the decade preceding Columbus exist (see, for example, the Day letter, page 80), the first clearly documented voyage of exploration along the North American coast is that of John Cabot. Giovanni Caboto, a naturalized Venetian, received a patent for discovery from Henry VII of England in 1496. In the same year he sailed from Bristol harbor but soon turned back because of storms, inadequate provisions, and disagreements with the crew.

His next venture, a three months' voyage starting in May 1497 from Bristol in a small vessel, the *Matthew*, was more successful. The letter of the English merchant, John Day, provides the best account of this expedition, but other contemporary reports furnish added detail. Raimondo de Soncino wrote from London to his master the Duke of Milan on 18 December 1497 that, 'Messer Zoane Caboto . . . started from Bristol, a port on the west of this kingdom, passed Ireland, which is still further west . . . After having wandered for some time he at length arrived at the mainland, where he hoisted the royal standard and took possession for the king here; and after taking certain tokens he returned . . . This Messer Zoane has a description of the world in a map, and also

in a solid sphere, which he had made, and shows where he has been. In going toward the east [the Orient] he passed far beyond the country of the Tanais. They say the land is excellent and temperate, and they believe that Brazil wood and silk are native there. They assert that the sea there is swarming with fish, which can be taken not only with the net, but in baskets let down with a stone, so that it sinks in the water. I have heard this Messer Zoane state so much.

'These same English, his companions, say that they could bring back so many fish that this kingdom would have no need of Iceland, from which place comes a very great quantity of the fish called stock fish. But Messer Zoane has his mind set upon even greater things, because he proposes to keep along the coast from the place at which he touched, more and more toward the east, until he reaches an island called Cipango [Japan], situated in the equinoctial region, where he believes that all the spices of the world have their origin, as well as the jewels.'[1]

Cabot thought he had reached Asia, 'the country of the great Khan' or the 'Island of the Seven Cities'.[2] After making landfall on 24 June on a wooded shore near his first sight of land, he sailed along the coast for a month or more without going ashore before returning to England. Where he landed is uncertain; it may have been as far north as Labrador or near Cape Bauld, Newfoundland. Probably, but not certainly, he sighted land somewhere along the Maine coast; his last view of the shore was a cape, possibly Cape Breton or Cape Race, Newfoundland.[3]

In May 1498 Cabot set out again from Bristol in a small fleet of four ships equipped by the merchants of that seaport and a fifth fitted out by the king.[4] Cabot never returned; he found, said a contemporary, 'new lands nowhere but on the very bottom of ocean'.[5] No record of the voyage survives nor of how many of the ships returned eventually to Bristol. Unsupported English claims that Cabot or surviving ships in his fleet explored the coast to Florida or beyond date from the latter half of the next century.

Cabot's maps, mentioned by Soncino, and his report to Henry VII upon his return from his first voyage, are lost; but copies of his maps reached Spain by 1498 and are reflected in a map made by Juan de la Cosa in the summer of 1500 (plate 29).[6] La Cosa (not the man of the same name who was the owner and master of the *Santa Maria* on Columbus' first voyage) served as a seaman in the *Niña* on Columbus' second voyage of 1493.

Reports of Cabot's voyages reached Portugal as well as Spain; several expeditions by Portuguese soon sailed for northern waters with the encouragement of the King, Dom Manoel. The King was concerned because the land might be within the sphere of influence, east of the longitudinal line agreed upon and assigned to him by the Treaty of Tordesillas in 1494[7], and because in that region he might find a shorter

way to the East than the route by the Cape of Good Hope[8] taken by Vasco da Gama, who had returned from his two-year voyage in 1499. In that year King Manoel gave letters-patent to John (João) Fernandes,[9] a labrador, or small landowner, of Terceira in the Portuguese Azores, for discoveries 'at his own expense'. Fernandes reached Greenland, which subsequently was named Labrador because he, a 'labrador', had 'discovered' it. The transference of the name from Greenland to the coast north of Newfoundland on maps and in contemporary reports did not occur until the latter half of the sixteenth century. Fernandes soon went to Bristol, where he took part in an English-Portuguese expedition of 1501.[10]

Perhaps Fernandes turned to England because in 1500 King Manoel gave a grant for the discovery of islands and a mainland, with full perquisites of trade and governorship, to Gaspar Corte-Real, son of a governor of Terceira.[11] In the same year Gaspar made a voyage in which he discovered 'a land that is very cool and with big trees [which] he named *Terra Verde* [Newfoundland]'.[12] On 15 May 1501, Gaspar left Lisbon with a fleet of three ships on his second voyage. According to a letter written on 9 October 1501 to the Duke of Ferrara from his emissary in Lisbon, Alberto Cantino, 'they found the sea to be frozen. [Turning west after three months' sailing] they caught sight of a very large country . . . numerous large rivers flowed into the sea . . . They made their way about a league inland [where] on landing they found abundance of most luscious and varied fruits, and trees and pines of such measureless height and girth, that they would be too big as a mast for the largest ship that sails the sea.'[13]

Only two ships returned; the third, with Gaspar aboard, was never heard of again. Cantino, who had meanwhile made further personal contact with those who had returned, wrote again to the Duke of Ferrara, giving the first ethnological account of the native inhabitants: 'No corn grows there, but the people of that country say they live altogether by fishing and hunting animals, in which the land abounds, such as very large deer, covered with extremely long hair, the skins of which they use for garments and also make houses and boats thereof and again wolves, foxes, tigers, and sables. They affirm that there are, what appears to me wonderful, as many falcons there as there are sparrows in our country, and I have seen some of them and they are very pretty. They forcibly kidnapped about fifty men and women of this country [actually fifty-seven[14]] and have brought them to the king. I have seen, touched, and examined these people, and beginning with their stature, declare they are somewhat taller than our average, with members corresponding and well formed. The hair of the men is long . . . and [they] have their face marked with great signs . . . Their speech is unintelligible but nevertheless is not harsh but rather human. Their manners and gestures are most gentle.'[15]

50

Chart of the North Atlantic, from an Italian portolan atlas, c. 1508–10, showing part of the coast of America. *London, British Museum, Egerton Ms. 2803, fo 8b.*
This chart is attributed to the cartographer Vesconte Maggiolo of Genoa. East is at the top. See also plate 59.

51 *Overleaf*
The Contarini world map, 1506. *London, British Museum, c.2.cc.4.*
The great promontory of Asia extending eastward to the North Atlantic is part of the province of Tangut, mentioned by Marco Polo; its discovery is attributed to the Portuguese, a reference to the voyages of the Corte-Reals. Only 'Zimpangu' (Japan) lies between the West Indies and Cathay, 60° farther west. The legend between Zimpangu and Cathay refers to the fourth voyage of Columbus to 'Ciamba'. This world map was the first printed map to show any part of the New World, and was designed by the Venetian G. M. Contarini and engraved at Florence by Francesco Roselli; the only remaining impression is in the British Museum.

On 10 May 1502, Gaspar's brother Miguel sailed from Lisbon with three ships to find his brother. Miguel's ship never returned. The following year the King of Portugal sent a third brother to continue the search; he came back without finding his lost brothers or their ships. The voyages of Fernandes and the Corte-Reals succeeded in reaching the shores of Greenland, modern Labrador, and Newfoundland but they did not open a way to the Spice Islands, and the land appeared inhospitable. Portuguese exploration in this region ceased. The exploitation of the Newfoundland Banks by Portuguese fishing fleets, however, increased so rapidly that by 1506 a tax was levied on the Newfoundland cod brought to Portugal.[16]

The discoveries by the Corte-Reals, who by the very nature

50

and purpose of their search must have explored the coast rather carefully, soon appeared on maps. Some showed the isle of Verde or the land of the Corte-Reals as islands in the mid-Atlantic; others connected these new regions with Greenland or with Asia.

The first map to show the Portuguese explorations to the North is the Cantino planisphere (plate 53), one of the primary cartographical documents of the New World.[17] Alberto Cantino, already mentioned, had it made in Lisbon for his master, Ercole d'Este, Duke of Ferrara, in 1502 for the sum

A lande Crab.

55

56

57

Garopa.

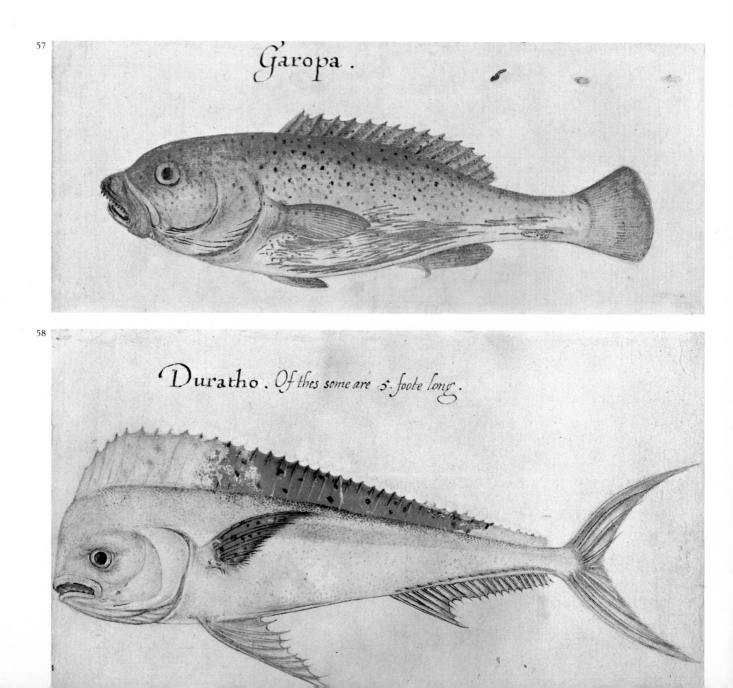

58

Duratho. Of thes some are 5. foote long.

Florida. On 10 February 1521, he wrote to Charles V, King of Spain: 'Among my services I discovered, at my own expense, the Island of Florida and others in its district . . . I intend to explore the coast of the said island further, and see whether it is an island, or whether it connects with [Cuba], or any other; and I shall endeavor to learn all I can. I shall set out to pursue my voyage hence in five or six days.' With two ships and 250 men he attempted settlement, probably at Charlotte Harbor or the Bay of Tampa; but again the Indians made a ferocious attack and killed or wounded many men. De León was severely wounded and died a few days after reaching Cuba. Thus ended the career of a conquistador, resourceful and indomitable, who made the first known exploration of the Florida peninsula and unwittingly discovered the Gulf Stream.

It was not Ponce de León, however, but Alonzo Alvarez de

59

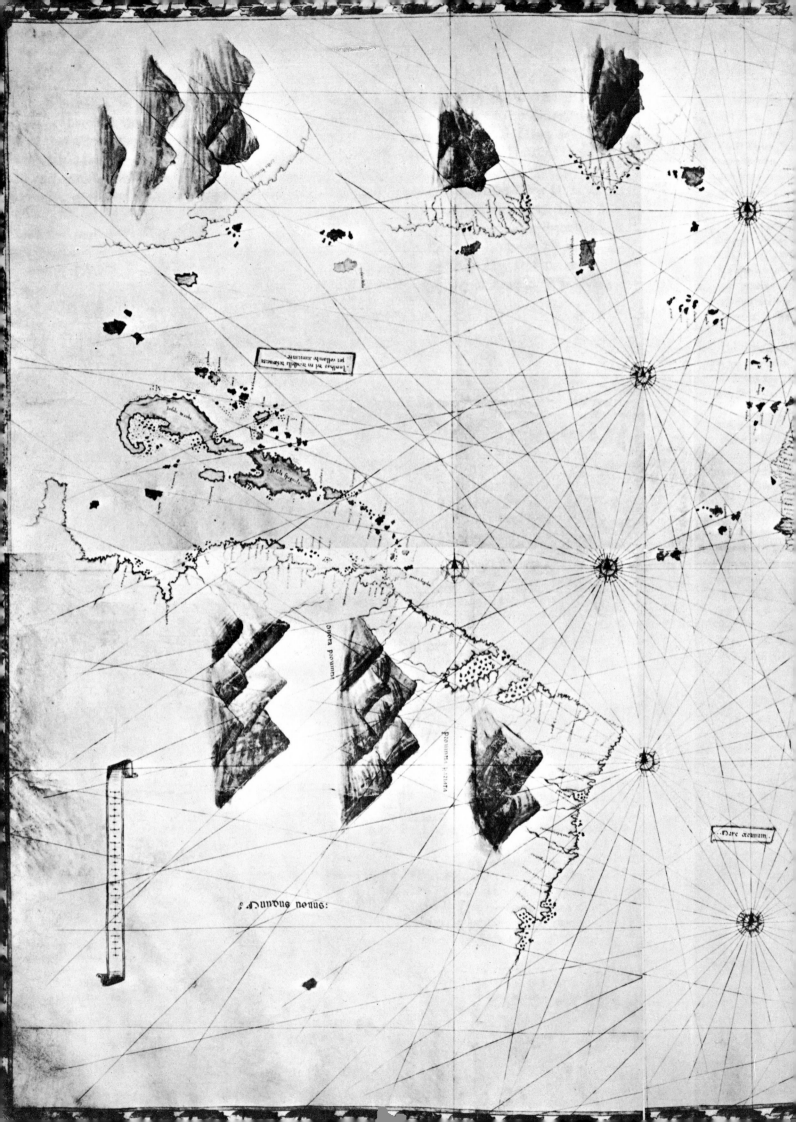

60
The Oliveriani or Anonymous World Map, c. 1508–10. *Pesaro, Italy,
Biblioteca e Musei Oliveriani.*

The chief interest in the 'Oliveriani' map is its representation of the northern
sections of the New World in an attempt to interpret information gathered
from various sources. The three large land masses in the North Atlantic
show a conception of a land running east to west, somewhat like the Cosa
map, to which the West Indies and the western hooked end of Cuba also
bear a resemblance. To the north of Cuba is a coast which may be an eastern
promontory of Asia or the land shown on the Cantino map and its
successors. To the east of this is the land discovered by Cabot (Labrador-
Newfoundland); on it is 'Terra de Corte', probably a reference to the
Corte-Reals, and 'rivo de los bacalaos', the river of cod. Below Greenland is a
large island, 'Insula de labardor', the land discovered by the labrador,
João Fernandes; this is probably a reduplication of Greenland. The
differences between the Oliveriani map and its contemporaries show the
variation in interpretation possible to mapmakers with the same sources of
information. It may be a copy of an early map by Amerigo Vespucci, whose
discoveries in South America are shown on it.

61
Ponce de León, from A. Herrera y Tordesillas, *Historia General,* Madrid,
1728–30.

62
Indian dwellings in Florida; detail from the Lázaro Luís atlas, 1563.
Lisbon, Academia das Ciencias, fo 7v. West is at the top.

61

62

Pineda who in 1519 determined conclusively in an eight-
or nine-months' voyage that Florida was part of a mainland
extending without break to Mexico, and who charted the
northern shores of the Gulf of Mexico.[24] Pineda was in command
of four caravels fitted out by Francisco de Garay, the wealthy
Governor of Jamaica. Garay planned to establish a province
or to find some strait to the Pacific. No report by Pineda or
Garay is known; but the royal grant of 1521 to Garay describes
Pineda's voyage from Panuco River in Mexico to the Cape of
Florida or 'Bimjnj' and refers to an accompanying chart.
A map attached to the grant is usually referred to as the
Pineda map of 1519 (plate 68). Garay did not live to exploit his
'Province of Amichel', described in the charter as abounding
in gold, with a mighty river having eighty towns on its banks
within six leagues of the mouth (not the Mississippi delta),[25]
giants ten palms in height and pigmies only five palms high.
He sailed to occupy his yet unconquered land in 1523 but fell
into the hands of Cortés, who was not one to suffer gladly
rivals near the throne. Garay died shortly after in Mexico City.
Amichel never became a reality; but for years Spanish maps
showed the Land of Garay [Tierra de Garay] across present-
day Texas, Louisiana, and Mississippi.

Meanwhile, Lucas Vásquez de Ayllón, a wealthy auditor
and judge of Hispaniola, and a man of education and nobility
of character, obtained a license to search out new lands to the
north.[26] Late in 1520 he sent out a caravel under the command
of Francisco Gordillo; on 20 June 1521, Gordillo joined forces
with Pedro de Quexos, the master of a slave-hunting caravel
whom he had met while cruising in the Bahamas, and made
land at the mouth of a large river at north latitude 30° 30'.
They gave it the name Rio de San Juan Bautista; it may have
been the Peedee River at Winyah Bay.[27] Going ashore, they
took formal possession of the country and made brief explorations of the surrounding region. Contrary to the express orders
of Ayllón to encourage friendly relations with the natives, they
enticed some one hundred and fifty Indians aboard their ships
for the slave trade and returned to Hispaniola. There, a
commission under Diego Columbus ordered, at Ayllón's
request, that the natives be returned to their country and
freed.[28] One of them learned Spanish and was baptized with the
name Francisco of Chicora; Ayllón took Francisco to Spain
as a personal servant when he returned in 1523 to plead for a

63 *Overleaf*
The Grynaeus world map, attributed to Holbein the Younger, from
Novus Orbis, Basel, 1555.

This oval-projection woodcut map, surrounded with finely executed designs
of cannibals, hunting scenes, and monsters, is commonly attributed to
Hans Holbein the Younger. The New World is based on out-of-date
conceptions found in the Waldseemüller map (1507) and globes by
Johann Schöner (1515–20); artistically it is one of the most interesting maps
of the sixteenth century. The land mass above the West Indies is called
the Land of Cuba; Japan (Zipangri) is close to the west coast; an isthmus in
Central America opens a sea passage to the South Sea. It first appeared in a
book of travels, by Simon Grynaeus and John Huttich, *Novus Orbis,* 1532.
This reproduction is taken from the 1555 edition of the same work, in
which there are minor changes in the type-printed insertions of the map.

Latitudo 80 Septentrionalis

Cizaig

Islandia

Iberna

Moſco
uia

OCEANVS
MAGNVS

Anglia

Dacia
Germania Sarmatia

PA

Terra
de
Cuba

Terra Cor
teſia

Liſbona

EVRO
Galia

Ita
lia

Grecia

Hiſpa
nia

Mare
mediterra
neum

Chozus

Inſulæ
Antigliæ

Iſabella

Portus Sanctus

Barbaria

Atlas mons

Aegyp
tus

Spagnolla

Medera
inſulæ Canariæ

Ziu
pan
gri

TROPICVS CANCRI

Terra alba
Caput album

Getulia
NIGRITAE

Dargin
Alba
Gazara

Inſula bon inſus
Sinus magnus
Sagres
Sinus tru begs

Hodeni
Caput uiride

Aethiopia
sanga flu.
APHRICA

Gambra regnū

270 280 290 300 310 320 330 340 350 360

Beſigna
Ginega

AETHIOPIA
interior

10   20   30   40   50   60 70

Fauonig

Parias

Canibali

AEQVINOCTIALIS

Regnum
Melli &
Nebeorum

Reg

AMERICA

Origo
Nili

TERRA NOVA

Priſilia

TROPICVS CAPRICORNI

Terra pſi
tacorum

Lips

Caput bo
ne ſpei

OCEANVS MERIDIONALIS

CANIBALI

Aphzich

Latitudo 80 Meridionalis

63

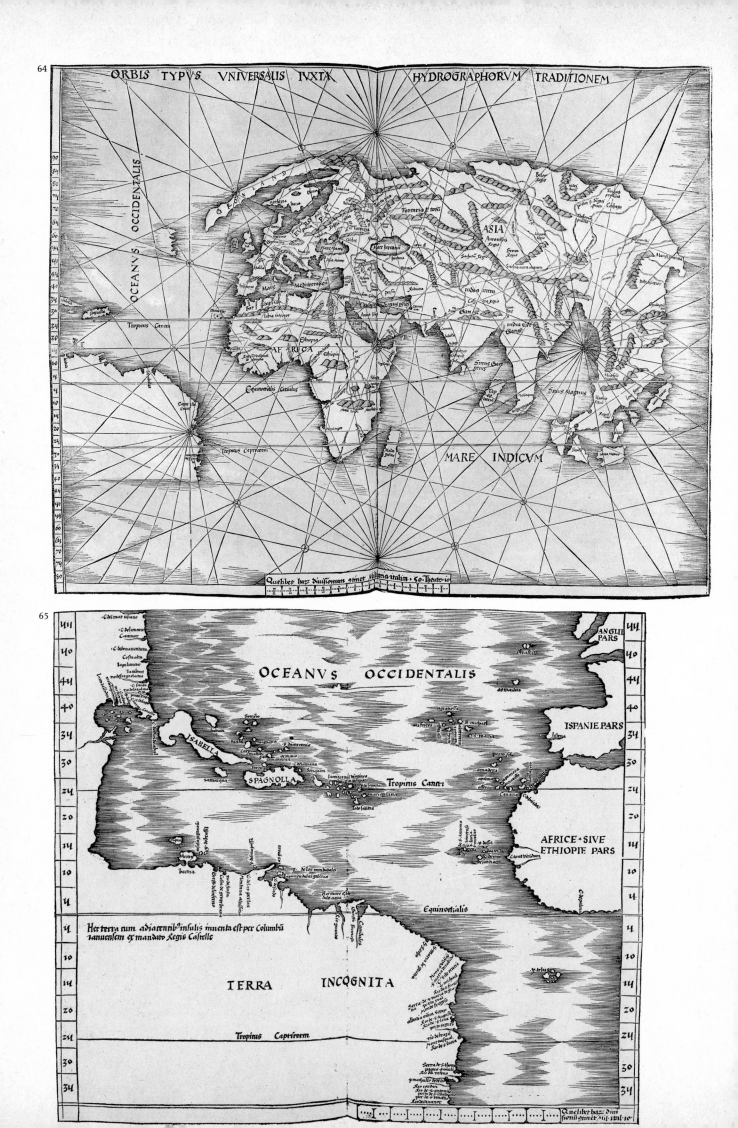

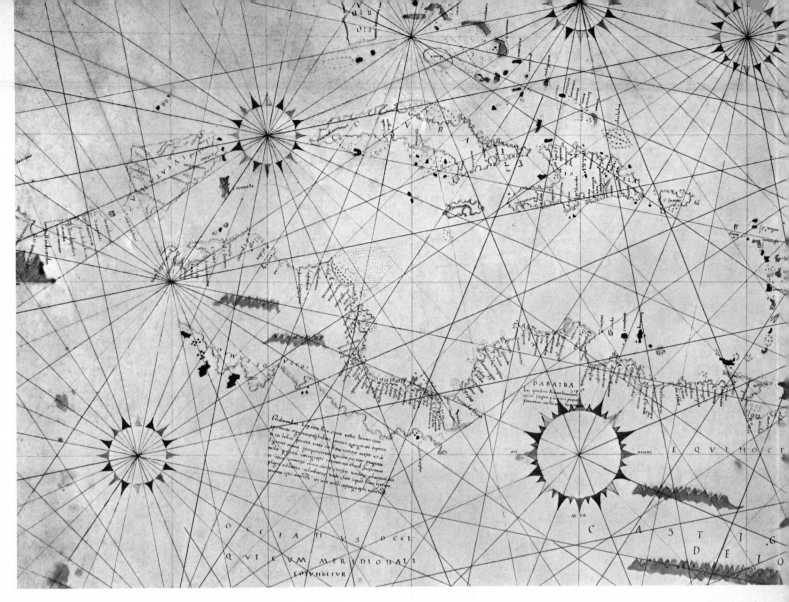

64

'Orbis Typus Universalis', from the Claudius Ptolemy (Waldseemüller) *Geographia*, Strassburg, 1513.

A source of the information on this map, according to an editorial comment, was 'the Admiral', possibly a reference to Columbus. Both this map and the following one, 'Tabula Terre Nove', have been called the 'Admiral's map'; there is some question as to which the editorial comment refers to.

Both charts first appear in the Supplement to the edition of Claudius Ptolemy's *Geographia*. In this sea map or 'hydrograph', the Portuguese Labrador-Newfoundland discoveries are shown south-west of Greenland, which is a peninsula extending westward from Asia. Unlike 'Tabula Terre Nove', this map has no uninterrupted continent continuing north from South America to the west and north of the West Indies.

65

'Tabula Terre Nove', from the Claudius Ptolemy (Waldseemüller) *Geographia*, Strassburg, 1513.

The Supplement to the Strassburg 1513 edition of Ptolemy's *Geographia*, composed of twenty maps containing new information gathered from many travels and voyages of discovery, made it 'the first modern atlas of the world'. Martin Waldseemüller of St Dié began work on this new edition of Ptolemy about 1505 and compiled the maps; two Strassburg citizens, Eszler and Übelin, edited and published Waldseemüller's text.

66

The hydrographic world chart known as the 'Wolfenbüttel', c. 1523–5.
Wolfenbüttel, Herzog August Bibliothek, Aug. fo 103.

This detail from the hydrographic chart, with a broken coastline extending from Florida to southern Brazil, shows Ponce de León's conception of Florida as an island before Pineda's voyage of 1519 demonstrated that it was part of a continent extending to Mexico. Marcel Destombes attributes the map to the cartographer and navigator Girolamo Verrazzano, the brother of the explorer, on the basis of similarity in calligraphy to the signed work of Girolamo and to Italicisms in phraseology. Below the Yucatan peninsula, here an island, the open coastline implies a possible westward passage to the Pacific. Destombes suggests that the map was made before the ill-fated second expedition of discovery by

Verrazzano in 1528, on which Girolamo saw his brother eaten by cannibals on a West Indian island. The map could not have been made long after 1525, for the discoveries of Ayllón and Gomes extending from Florida northward were well known before the end of that year.

It is apparently derived from a Spanish chart like the Turin, c. 1523, map in the Turin Royal Library, to which it is similar in the insular representation of Florida, the indeterminate coastline at the base of Yucatan, and nomenclature.

patent of possession for his discoveries.[29] Peter Martyr, who said that he had the two at his table a number of times, related in his *Decades* several extraordinary tales with which Francisco embellished his descriptions of his native land of Chicora and the surrounding provinces. The king and ruling family of the neighboring kingdom of Duhare were of gigantic size, Francisco said, the result of special bone-softening herbs given in infancy, followed by a process of stretching the limbs. He apparently mingled folklore with factual description, as in the tale of a small race of men who in time past had landed on their shores; they had stiff tails for which it was necessary to dig holes in the earth when they sat.

In 1525 Ayllón, who had obtained, with the support of Peter Martyr at court, a royal cédula for settling the new land, sent Pedro de Quexos on a further voyage of exploration which covered 250 leagues of the coast and which sailed as far north as the Outer Banks of North Carolina and perhaps Chesapeake Bay. It was not until June 1526 that Ayllón, with a company of some six hundred, set sail in three large vessels and landed

Map of the Gulf of Mexico, published with a letter of Ferdinand Cortés, 1524. *Seville, Archivo General de Indias.*
This map of the Gulf of Mexico, found on the same page with a larger map of Mexico City, was published in Nuremberg in 1524 with the second letter of Cortés in *Praeclara Ferdinandi Cortesii de Nova maris Oceani Hispanica Narratio*, which he wrote in 1520. In the letter Cortés said that he was given a drawing of the coast by Montezuma. The northern shoreline, with its Spanish names, may have come from reports by members of Pineda's 1519 voyage of exploration whom Cortés captured at Panuco. On this map at Panuco is Provincia Amichel, the name given by Garay to his proposed colony for which Pineda made his expedition. The conception of Yucatan as an island may have influenced later geographers. This is the earliest printed map to use the name Florida. West is at the top.

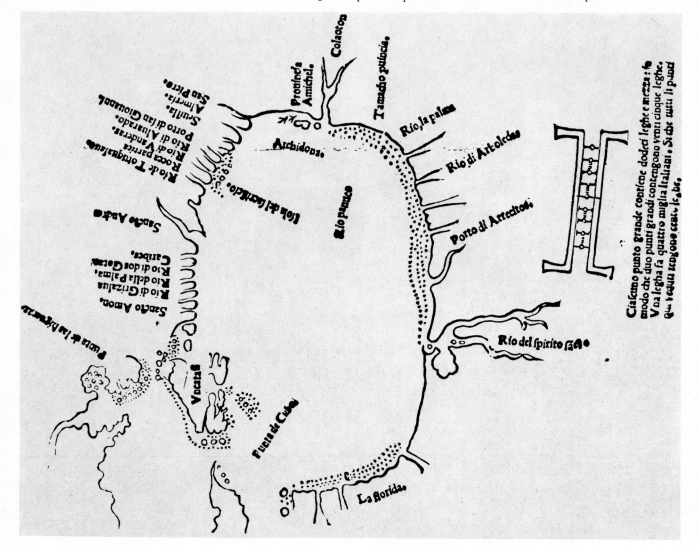

at the mouth of a big river. Quexos had found and named it the River Jordan in 1525;[30] if his reading of 33° 40′ was correct, it was the Cape Fear River. Here, near the land of Chicora, Francisco escaped, probably to tell his listeners tales about Spain as incredible as those he had related to Peter Martyr.

The exploring party gave an unfavorable report of the country, and Ayllón soon moved his settlement down the coast.[31] Oviedo, the appointed historiographer of the Indies and a resident official in the New World for thirty-four years, who names Quexos as one of his informants, says, 'they went to a large river (forty or fifty leagues from their landing) which is called Gualdape: and there they pitched their camp and began to build houses . . . The land was level and very marshy but the river very powerful . . . at the entrance of it was a bay which ships could enter only at high tide. The region was sparsely inhabited, the Indians living in great communal houses, far from each other, constructed of very tall and beautiful pines, leaving a crown of leaves at the top . . . with a space between the two sides of from fifteen to twenty feet, the length of the walls being three hundred or more feet . . . They cover it all with matting interwoven between the logs where there may be hollows or open places. Furthermore, they cross these beams with other pines placed lengthwise on the inside, increasing the thickness of their walls . . . Their temples have walls of stone or mortar (which mortar they made of oyster shells).'[32]

The settlers pitched their camp near the coast and prepared for permanent settlement, for Ayllón had brought women and children as well as Negro slaves. This was the first introduction of African slavery into the territory of the United States; yet, as Dr Gilmary Shea notes,[33] also in the company was the famous Dominican, Father Antonio Montesinos, the storm center of opposition to slavery in the West Indies. San Miguel de Gualdape, as Ayllón called the settlement, was probably on the north shore of Winyah Bay, a large but shallow bay into which the Peedee and four other rivers flow. San Miguel did not prosper. Ayllón himself died of a fever in October, the slaves revolted, and the Indians killed some of the settlers. The colonists abandoned the undertaking in the winter of 1527 but their hardships were not over; of the 150 survivors who sailed for Hispaniola seven men froze to death aboard the *Catalina*.

Before Ayllón had sent Quexos on his second trip of 1525 along the Carolina coast, Charles V of Spain had despatched one

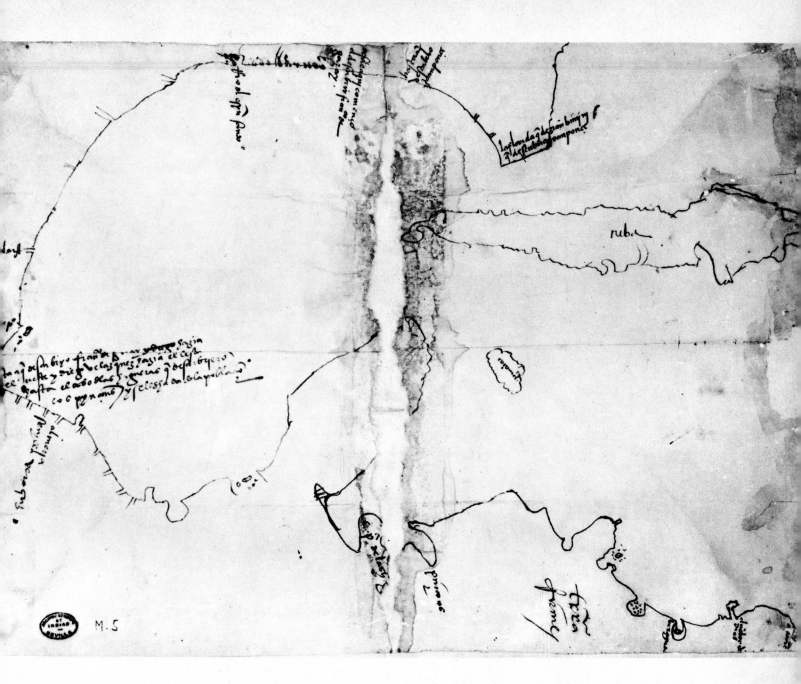

M.5

68

The 'Pineda' chart, c. 1520. *Seville, Archivo General de Indias.*
The earliest map to show correctly the main outlines of the Gulf of Mexico
is attached to a royal authorization of 1521 granting Francesco de Garay the
right to colonize the country between 'Florida, formerly Bimjnj' and
Mexico. It is presumably the drawing sent to the King by Garay and made
by Pineda and his pilots, who explored the northern coast for Garay.
Pineda's voyage showed that there was no passage to the Pacific from the
Gulf; from Mexico southward the coast was already known. The Yucatan
peninsula is here correctly shown as part of the mainland, not an island as
on many later maps of the period.

of his ablest navigators, Estevão Gomes,[34] on a voyage along the
entire east coast of the continent to discover a shorter route
to the Spice Islands than by the Straits of Magellan. Gomes,
a Portuguese who had entered the service of the Spanish Casa
de Contratación (Board of Trade) in 1518, had been to India,
had deserted Magellan after reaching the Pacific, and had
argued convincingly for a more direct passage to the east at the
Badajoz Commission inquiry of 1524. On 24 September 1524
he sailed from Coruña in a seventy-five ton caravel as captain
and pilot. First crossing to Santiago de Cuba, where he probably
learned details of Ayllón's 1520–1 explorations along the

south-east coast,[35] he sailed north and explored the coast
carefully from southern New England to Nova Scotia in a
seven-month's voyage, returning to Coruña on 21 August 1525.
Frustrated by failure in finding a westward passage, he
captured fifty-eight Indians whom he expected to sell as
slaves; but Charles V ordered their release. At first the report
spread like wildfire that Gomes had reached the Spice Islands,
Peter Martyr writes,[36] because a horseman galloped off to
the royal court with the news that the caravel was laden with
precious stones and *clavos* (cloves), having missed the first
syllable of *esclavos* (slaves). This error, when corrected, filled
the opponents of Gomes with glee. The information gathered
by Gomes and Ayllón's captains became the basis for the
Spanish cartography of the east coast from Florida to Newfoundland during the rest of the sixteenth century.

France was the last of the four great European powers
bordering on the Atlantic to take an active part in trans-
oceanic exploration; her political and military involvements in
Europe occupied her attention. Eventually, however, the
thoughts of Francis I, deeply in need of money, turned to
possibilities of wealth that he might be missing. The return of
Magellan's *Victoria* to Spain in 1522 laden with cloves from the

69

'The land discovered by the Pilot Estevan Gómez', from the Islario General of Alonso de Santa Cruz, c. 1545. *Madrid, Biblioteca Nacional.* This chart of the Spanish royal cosmographer shows the New England coast and extends from present-day North Carolina to Newfoundland. 'R. de los gamos' (Deer River) in the center, with its many islands, is Penobscot River and Bay. Cabot Strait is shown as the bay leading to 'Tierra de Bacallaos', although the French had been using it as the passageway to the Gulf of St Lawrence for ten years. Breton fishing fleets had been frequenting the area since the early years of the century.

70

Giovanni da Verrazzano, drawn by G. Zocchi and engraved by F. Allegrini, 1767. *New York, Pierpont Morgan Library.*

69

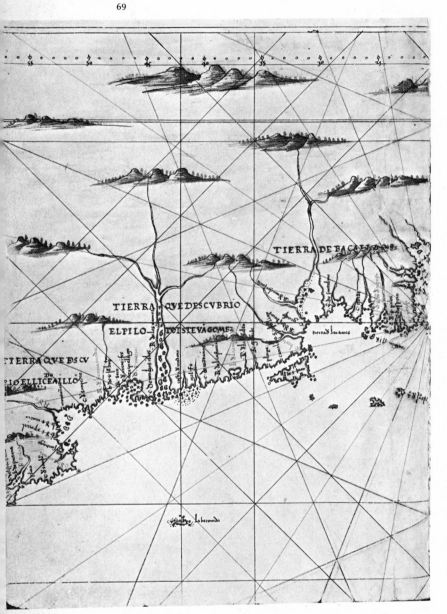

70

Spice Islands;[37] the capture by a French corsair of three galleons sent by Cortés with Montezuma's treasures; and the reports of the fishing grounds off Newfoundland to which Bretons had been making their way since 1504, all stimulated his imagination.

The harbinger of later French activities in the New World was the voyage of Giovanni da Verrazzano in 1524, made at the behest of Francis I. His exploration of the North American coast, the first under official French auspices, had as its chief purpose the discovery of a way to Cathay, although the possibilities of trade in the New World may also have had a share. Verrazzano, a Florentine of a prominent family with wide trade and banking connections, was in close contact with Italian merchants in Lyons and elsewhere in France. He was also an expert navigator, a product of the same extraordinary flowering of genius in the Italian Renaissance that gave Christopher Columbus to Spain, Amerigo Vespucci to Portugal, and John Cabot to England.

In 1523 Francis I sent Verrazzano with four ships 'to discover new lands';[38] the fleet ran into a storm and only two vessels reached port in Brittany. These two, refitted, made a successful foray along the coast of Spain, with whom France was at war. Upon return, Verrazzano received orders to search for a route to Cathay. Having refitted his ship, the *Dauphine*, with naval armaments, with the latest navigational instruments, and with provisions for an eight-months' voyage, he sailed due west with a crew of fifty from an island of the Portuguese Madeiras on 17 January 1524. Landfall was at north latitude 34°, near Cape Fear, North Carolina. After coasting south-west for fifty leagues without finding a good harbor, he returned to this first landfall for a brief exploration. Then he sailed along the long stretch of narrow Outer Bank Islands that separate the

70

Atlantic Ocean from the Carolina Sounds. This stretch he described as 'an isthmus a mile in width and 200 long'; Pamlico Sound he thought was the Pacific Ocean. As he continued northward along the coast, he missed the eleven-mile entrance to Chesapeake Bay but became the first European to enter and describe New York Bay and the Hudson River. After landing and observing the country and the natives at various places, he reached Newfoundland; his provisions were failing and he returned to France, reaching Dieppe early in July 1524.

Verrazzano's account of his voyage found in a draft of his report to Francis I, sent to friends, is the earliest known geographical and topological description of a continuous

71
Map of the mainland and West Indies (the 'Ramusio' map), 1534. *Providence, John Carter Brown Library.*
This woodcut 'general map of the mainland and West Indies . . ., taken from two nautical charts made in Seville by the pilots of His Imperial Majesty', is found in the *Summario de la generale historia de l'Indie occidentali,* Venice, 1534, attributed to Ramusio. To the south the 'Stretto de magallanes' appears for the first time on a printed map; Tumbez (in Peru) and Temistitan (Mexico) refer to recent Spanish conquests; Yucatan is an island. Off Florida and Ailon (Province of Ayllón) the dotted area indicates dangerous shoals along the shallow coast. The name of 'Gomez' appears by the Penobscot River, and farther north Bacalaos includes Newfoundland and Labrador; laborator (Labrador) still refers to Greenland.

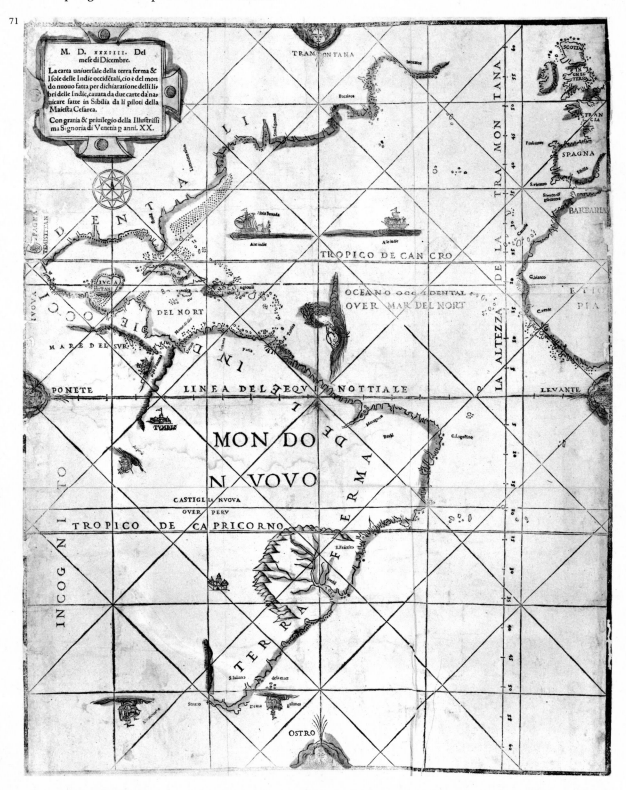

71

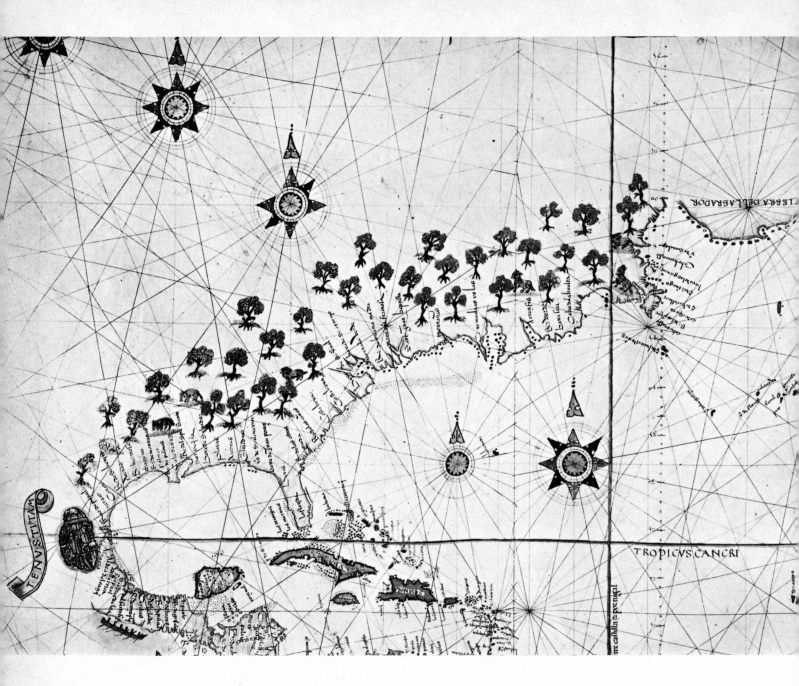

72

The east coast of North America and the Gulf of Mexico, from the
'Salviati' world map, c. 1525. *Florence, Biblioteca Mediceo-Laurenziana.*
Although this beautifully executed world map could not have been made
earlier than September, 1525, it presents a conception of the east coast of
North America shown on this detail different from and earlier than the
Castiglioni (1525, plate 74), Vespucci (1526, plate 87), and Ribero (1529,
plate 115) maps. The names given to the New England coastal features by
Gomes, who returned to Coruña in August 1525, begin with the bays of
'S. [Christ]oual' and 'S. antonjo' north of the conspicuous promontory of
Cape Cod on the later Spanish maps. Here, however, they are written by the
island-studded bay which represents the North Carolina Sounds/Chesapeake
Bay region, which for fifty years the Spanish called 'baya de Santa Maria'.
It was discovered by the expedition sent out by Ayllón in 1521. The seven
animals roaming among the trees along the coast are not easily identifiable.
The map was made for or presented to some member of the powerful
Florentine family of Salviati, whose arms are emblazoned on the chart.

voyage along the eastern coast of North America. He found no
passage to the Orient; but his misconception of a narrow
isthmus which alone barred the way to the Pacific continued
to stimulate the imagination of Europeans. Even after explorations disproved the existence of the isthmus, the theory that
'Verrazzano's Sea' formed an arm of the Pacific, corresponding
to the Gulf of Mexico from the Atlantic, continued to raise
hopes and to result in expeditions for a century and a half.[39]

The return of Verrazzano to France coincided with a series
of disastrous defeats which Francis I suffered in his Italian
wars against Charles V; he was captured at the battle of Pavia
in 1525, taken prisoner to Madrid, and forced to sign the
Peace of Madrid before his release. He repudiated the treaty,
was defeated again, and forced to pay two million crowns.
More desperately than ever he needed gold. In 1533, he
succeeded in obtaining from Pope Clement VII[40] a statement
that Spain and Portugal had no inherent rights over lands which
they had not discovered before Christmas 1492—an interpretation of the bull of Alexander VI in 1493 which both
Iberian powers actively repudiated. Supported now by papal
law, Francis renewed his plans for overseas discovery.

Verrazzano was no longer alive; on an island off the coast of South America in 1528 he had been killed and eaten by Caribs in sight of his horrified but helpless crew. The King knew another experienced sailor, however, who had been across the Atlantic and who inspired him with hope of profitable adventure. This was Jacques Cartier, a Breton of St Malo, who was an expert navigator and cartographer. Francis entrusted to him the responsibility of a voyage to unknown lands and seaways beyond Newfoundland.

The King's purpose in his order to Cartier was clear: 'To discover certain islands and lands where it is said a great quantity of gold and other precious things are to be found'.[41] On 20 April 1534 Cartier left St Malo with two sixty-tonners and a crew of sixty-one men. He made a remarkably fast run of twenty days to Cape Bonavista on the east Newfoundland coast. From there, impeded by ice floes and fog, he made his way to the northern entrance of the Gulf of St Lawrence, the

Strait of Belle Isle. This strait, known to Cartier as the Bay of Castles (Baie des Chasteaulx) because within it lay two tower-like basaltic rock islands, was an objective to be reached in the plans made before Cartier left France.[42] He may have been there before himself; it was known to the Breton cod fishermen who frequented the Newfoundland Banks at the time. They knew something of the vast bay beyond; after entering the Gulf and stopping at a water and wood depot named the Port of Brest, Cartier met a ship from Rochelle that had lost its way en route there. Brest was on the north or Labrador coast, beyond which stetched a barren and rocky shore that Cartier called 'the land God gave to Cain'. He turned his ships to the south-east and crossed to the west coast of Newfoundland. From there he made a roughly clockwise circle of the entire Gulf of St Lawrence, bestowing names on capes, rivers, bays and islands as he examined or passed by them. He missed Cabot Strait between Nova Scotia and Newfoundland; although previous explorers or unknown fishermen may have entered, Cartier's discovery of it on his second voyage is the first clear record of the southern entrance to the gulf. He also crossed the mouth of the St Lawrence River from Gaspé Peninsula to Anticosti Island, but dismissed it as a great circular bay; he was deceived by the fog or mist. His record of what he did observe is acute and interesting. He noted areas 'encircled by sand as far as the eye can see, overlaid by marshes and standing pools'; he commented with enthusiasm when he found islands 'with goodly trees, meadows, fields of wild corn and peas in bloom as thick and fair as any you can see in Brittany'. With a Frenchman's interest in food he described the taste of the meat, the fowl, and the fish they ate,

73

The east coast of North America, from the world map by Girolamo da Verrazzano, 1529. *Biblioteca Apostolica Vaticana.*

Giovanni da Verrazzano, a Florentine, was sent by Francis I mainly to search for a westward passage to Asia. Sailing along the Carolina coast in April, 1524, Verrazzano thought that the narrow strip of the Outer Banks Islands was an isthmus separating the Atlantic and Pacific Oceans. Consequent belief in a deep indentation of the Pacific coast at this latitude influenced maps and explorers for a hundred and fifty years. A large world map, of which a part is here reproduced, was drawn by Girolamo da Verrazzano, the brother of the navigator. The coastal nomenclature given by Verrazzano differs from the names found on Spanish maps (see Castiglioni, Salviati, and Ribero, plates 72, 74 and 115), and was not widely followed by later geographers and mapmakers.

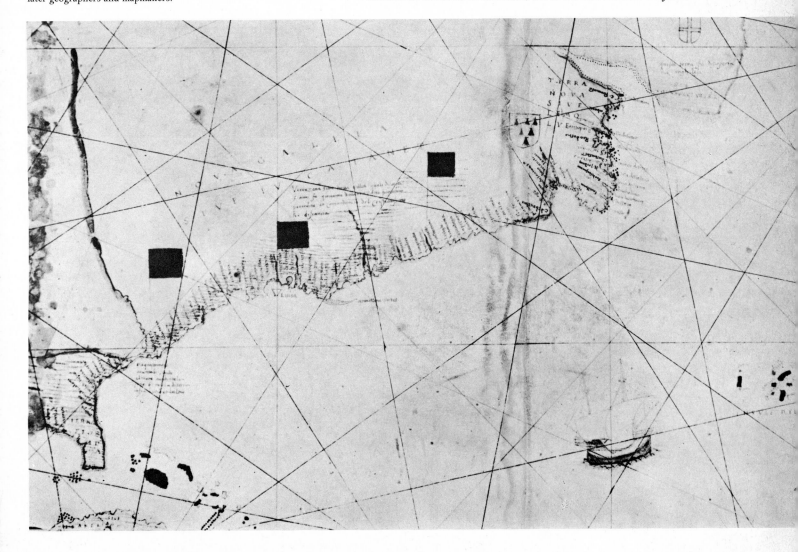

The Western Hemisphere, from the 'Castiglioni' world map, 1525.
Mantua, Archivo Marchesi Castiglioni.
The Castiglioni world map records the new discoveries between Florida and
Newfoundland made on the voyages of Ayllón's pilots and of Gomes in
1524–5. It is the earliest map to follow the delineation of the east coast
which is found after this date on maps derived from the official charts of
the Pilot Major in Seville, as may be seen by comparing this detail with the
Ribero planisphere of 1529 (plate 115). Above the New England coast is the
legend that it is the 'Land which Estevan Gómez discovered this year of
1525 by order of his Majesty'. Examination of the coast south of New
England by Gomes was very cursory; he may have relied entirely on
reports from the voyage sent out by Ayllón in 1520–1. Gomes missed
New York Harbor, which Verrazzano had discovered a few months earlier.
The bay half way up the coast may be Long Island Sound; on some maps
the cape has two prongs similar to the east end of Long Island. The
projection is commonly identified as Cape Cod. Unlike other coastlines on
the map, the coastal contours between Florida and Newfoundland are
lightly drawn with few place names; Professor Ganong has suggested that
the map, based on the official *padrón real*, was prepared earlier but awaited
the return of Gomes, with hoped-for news of a westward passage, for its
completion.

According to a family tradition in Mantua, the map was given by
Charles V to Count Baldassare Castiglioni, papal nuncio of Clement VII,
who had won the Emperor's friendship and admiration. Charles V may have
intended the great chart for presentation to the Pope; if so, a rapid
sequence of events would have prevented it. A few months later, early
in 1526, Clement VII made a league with Francis I, the Emperor's bitter foe.
The next year the Pope, pursued from the Vatican by the victorious troops
of Charles V, barely escaped with his life. Although in 1529 the two were
reconciled, the noble Baldassare, torn with grief by his divided loyalties
and by the accusation of treachery, had died. The map, for whomever it
may have been intended, went to Mantua.

naming the varieties and where they were found.

Although he did not return to France with gold or news of a
route to Cathay, Francis and the court received him with honor
for his undoubted skill and achievements. He traded and made
valuable friendships with the Indians he met. He sailed in
unknown waters with rocks and shoals, through a labyrinth
of islands, and with the additional hazards of field ice, fogs,
and heavy storms. He had a motley crew, with convicts from
the jails, whom he kept under control. He found a vast new sea
bordered by lands yet unexplored. And he returned to France
with both ships and without having lost a man.

With this voyage of Cartier a period in the discovery of

76

The east coast of North America from the world map by Sebastian Cabot,
1544. *Paris, Bibliothèque Nationale.*
This is a section of a large elliptical copper-engraved chart ($47\frac{1}{3} \times 84\frac{2}{3}$ ins),
which has printed legends pasted on either side of the map. One of these
inscriptions states that the map was made by Sebastian Cabot in 1544;
another describes the country discovered by 'Juan Cabot, a Venetian, and
by Sebastian, his son', and places the 'land first seen' at Cape Breton, on
Cabot Strait. Sebastian was about fifteen at that time. The St Lawrence
shows the discoveries of Jacques Cartier, and it has been suggested that the
map was here attempting to establish the priority of English over French
claims to the country. The accuracy of several statements in the inscriptions,
which were not written by Sebastian, has been questioned, including his
authorship of the map. Sebastian left England for the service of Spain in
1512 as a captain in the navy, and held the important official position of
Pilot Major in the Casa de Contratación from 1518 to 1547. In the latter
year he returned again to England, where he died about 1557. There are
numerous contemporary references to other maps made by Sebastian Cabot;
this is the only extant map, however, attributed to him.

74

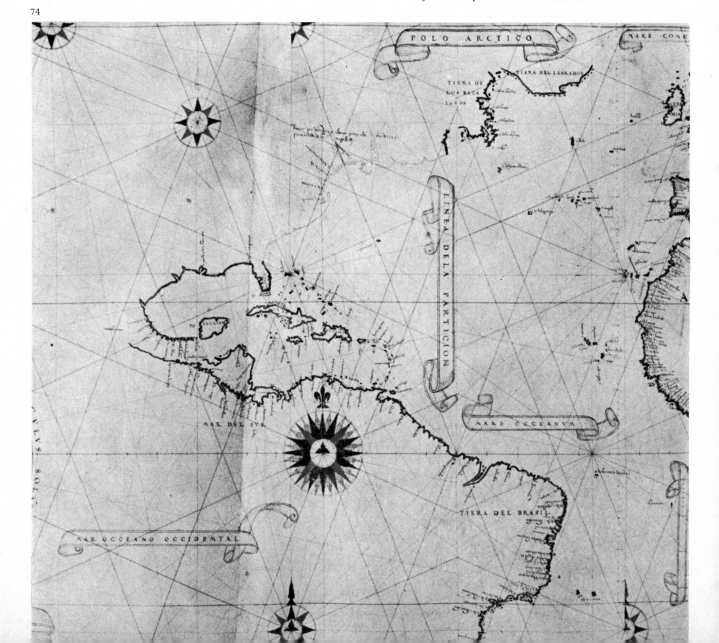

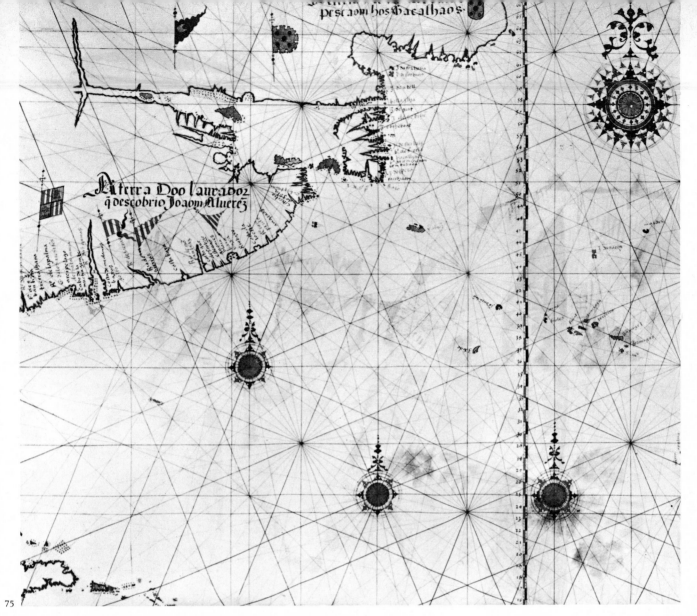

75

75

Map of North America and the Atlantic, from the Lázaro Luís atlas, 1563.
Lisbon, Academia das Ciencias, fo 3.
This Portuguese map has an interesting legend in the Nova Scotia/Cape
Breton Island region that the land of 'Lavrador' was discovered by 'Joaom
Aluerez'. From other documents we know that by 1520 a Portuguese
nobleman, João Alvares Fagundes, had explored the east and south coast
of Newfoundland under a charter of governorship granted by King
Emmanuel and that he gave names to landmarks which are found on many
later maps. Afterwards he explored the maritime region south of
Newfoundland, and he or other Portuguese made attempts to establish
colonies on Cape Breton Island which did not succeed. The Lázaro Luís map
has 'Fagundes' names along the coast and also is one of many Portuguese
maps that show Cartier's discoveries.

77 *Overleaf*
'Nova totius terrarum orbis iuxta neotericorum traditiones descriptio',
world map of Ortelius, 1564. *London, British Museum.*
Ortelius' world map of 1564, of which the upper left part is here
reproduced, is an engraved map on the popular cordiform projection.
On it he attempted to reconcile, not very successfully, information from
various earlier sources. The Gulf of St Lawrence leads to an open sea,
although several names derived from Cartier's discoveries are on the
northern shore of the continent. The Golfo de las Gamas, a name given
by Gomes to the Penobscot Bay and River, is influenced by the shape of the
Bay of Fundy on the maps of Lopo and Diogo Homem (plate 140); it is a
seaway to the North-west passage. The southern part of the continent
follows Spanish maps, as does the west coast with the region of Quivira
and the Strait of Anian.

NOVA TOTIVS TERRARV

TERICORVM TRADIT

ABRAH. ORTELIO
ANVERPIANO AVCT.

SEPT
Tramon
Moor

ZONA

OCEANVS HYPERBOREVS SIVE
SEPTENTRIONALIS

CIRCVLVS ARCTICVS

SIVE BOREALIS.

GRON LAN

TERRA DE LABRADOR

Littora Septentrionalia Americæ
nondum sunt perlustrata, eoq́
prorsus incognita, an mare
hic sit an terra nondum constat.

C. de Paramantia
Los Jardinos

LA NVOVA FRANZA

TERRA DE
NORVMBEGA

CANADA

TERRA
NVOVA

CALICVAZ

TAGIL

AVACAL

MOCOZA

APALCHEN

FLORI DA

DI MEXICO

La Vermeia

La Trinita

La Bermuda

OCEANVS OCCIDENTALIS
uulgo
MAR DEL NORT

INSVLAE DE
LAS AÇORAS

Tortugas

S. Michel

Faial   Pico

Quern o   Gracifsa S. Georgio

Bahama

Lucaio grande

La Catholica

INSVLAE
CANARIAE

Palma
Gomera

Madera

Tana
rifa

y. del ferro

SPAGNVOLA

OCEANVS ATLANTICVS

VENEZVELA

S. MARTA

Bocca di Dragone

S. Vincente

77

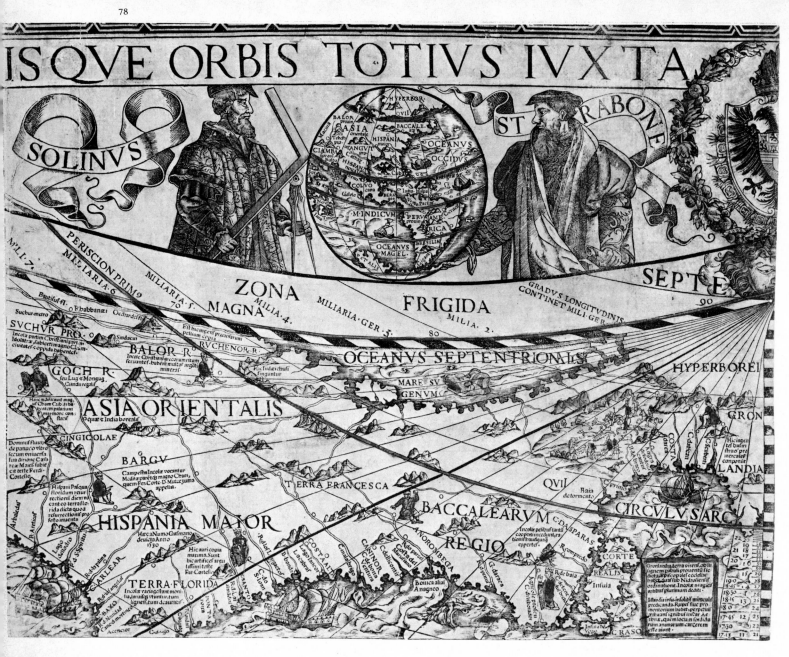

ISQVE ORBIS TOTIVS IVXTA

SOLINVS · ST · RABONE

SEPTE

ZONA MAGNA · FRIGIDA

78

North American section of the Vopell world map, 1558. *Harvard, Houghton Library.*

North America is here shown as an eastern extension of Asia on a large cordiform wall map of the world, approximately four by six feet, designed by Caspar Vopell, professor of mathematics at the University of Cologne and a famous map- and globe-maker. It was printed from twelve woodcut blocks cut by the Venetian cartographer Giovanni Andrea Vavassore, and is a re-engraving of a 1545 map by Vopell of which no copy is now extant.

It is a beautifully decorated map, with many important geographical notes by Vopell. One of these is an account of an audience he had with Charles V on an imperial visit to Cologne. Vopell had delayed publishing his map until he could learn from Charles V, who received reports of all important discoveries, whether a land mass connected the northern continent with Asia, or the two were separated, as rumored, by a strait. Charles V stated categorically that new Spanish discoveries west and north of Mexico showed that 'the aforementioned countries were in no way separated by a sea in between but connected with the eastern countries'. Therefore, Charles V pointed out, the western country extends to and includes China and its people in the sphere of Spain.

79

Jacques Cartier; engraving in Charlevoix, *Histoire de la Nouvelle France*, Paris, 1744, after the portrait in St Malo.

79

The New World by Jean Bellere, from Gómara's *México*, Antwerp, 1554.
Bellere's 'New, brief and exact description of the new world and its islands'
appeared in Gómara's *México,* and in several works by other authors.
The North American coastal names are those of the Ayllón, Gomes and
Fagundes expeditions; this map influenced the mid-sixteenth century
conception of South America, although not many maps showed the Amazon
flowing from the south.

North America comes to an end. From Mexico to Greenland
Europeans have explored, described, and mapped the coastline. Geographical misconceptions are still numerous; the
outlines are frequently vague or faulty; a few major gaps in
discovery, such as the Chesapeake Bay and Cabot Strait, still
remain to be filled in later voyages; the names given to capes,
rivers, bays, and islands are often transitory, changing, and
unidentifiable. Different names are given to the same landmark and the same name is applied to different locations.

These explorers, however, have not made settlements as
did the Spanish in the West Indies and Mexico. The exceptions
are negligible: temporary summer encampments by fishermen
in Newfoundland, the short-lived colony of Ayllón in South
Carolina, and a few Portuguese left stranded on Cape Breton
Island by João Alvares Fagundes shortly after 1520. The
coastal explorers of this period have not come to stay, but to
search out the land, which they have found rough and
difficult, its natives hostile and primitive, and the gold and
spices of their dreams unattained.

1.

A letter from John Day to the Lord Grand Admiral

This is an extract from a report by John Day, an English merchant in Andalusia, to the 'Lord Grand Admiral' of Spain, presumably Columbus, written in the winter of 1497–8. He describes the 1497 voyage of John Cabot, an earlier abortive Cabot voyage of the previous year, and mentions other earlier Bristol Atlantic expeditions of discovery, vague in destination and time. He forwarded with his missive 'a copy of the land which has been found' which is no longer with the manuscript.

From the said copy your Lordship will learn what you wish to know, for in it are named the capes of the mainland and the islands, and thus you will see where land was first sighted, since most of the land was discovered after turning back. Thus your Lordship will know that the cape nearest to Ireland is 1800 miles west of Dursey Head which is in Ireland, and the southernmost part of the Island of the Seven Cities is west of Bordeaux River, and your Lordship will know that he [Cabot] landed at only one spot of the mainland, near the place where land was first sighted, and they disembarked there with a crucifix and raised banners with the arms of the Holy Father and those of the King of England, my master; and they found tall trees of the kind masts are made, and other smaller trees, and the country is very rich in grass. In that particular spot, as I told your Lordship, they found a trail that went inland, they saw a site where a fire had been made, they saw manure of animals which they thought to be farm animals, and they saw a stick half a yard long pierced at both ends, carved and painted with brazil, and by such signs they believe the land to be inhabited. Since he was with just a few people, he did not dare advance inland beyond the shooting distance of a cross-bow, and after taking in fresh water he returned to his ship. All along the coast they found many fish like those which in Iceland are dried in the open and sold in England and other countries, and these fish are called in English 'stockfish'; and thus following the shore they saw two forms running on land one after the other, but they could not tell if they were human beings or animals; and it seemed to them that there were fields where they thought might also be villages, and they saw a forest whose foliage looked beautiful. They left England toward the end of May, and must have been on the way 35 days before sighting land; the wind was east-north-east and the sea calm going and coming back, except for one day when he ran into a storm two or three days before finding land; and going so far out, his compass needle failed to point north and marked two rhumbs below. They spent about one month discovering the coast and from the above mentioned cape of the mainland which is nearest to Ireland, they returned to the coast of Europe in fifteen days. They had the wind behind them, and he reached Brittany because the sailors confused him, saying that he was heading too far north. From there he came to Bristol, and he went to see the King to report to him all the above mentioned; and the King granted him an annual pension of twenty pounds sterling to sustain himself until the time comes when more will be known of this business, since with God's help it is hoped to push through plans for exploring the said land more thoroughly next year with ten or twelve vessels—because in his voyage he had only one ship of fifty 'toneles' and twenty men and food for seven or eight months—

and they want to carry out this new project. It is considered certain that the cape of the said land was found and discovered in the past by the men from Bristol who found 'Brasil' as your Lordship well knows. It was called the Island of Brasil, and it is assumed and believed to be the mainland that the men from Bristol found.

Since your Lordship wants information relating to the first voyage, here is what happened: he went with one ship, his crew confused him, he was short of supplies and ran into bad weather, and he decided to turn back.

The original manuscript is in the Archivo General de Simancas, Estado de Castilla, Leg. 2, fo 6. Translation: L. A. Vigneras, 'The Cape Breton Landfall: 1494 or 1497'. Canadian Historical Review, XXXVIII (1957), pp. 220-8. Text used: J. A. Williamson, The Cabot Voyages and Bristol Discoveries under Henry VII. Cambridge: Hakluyt Society, Ser. II, No. CXX, 1962, Doc. 25, pp. 211-14.

2.

The voyage of Giovanni da Verrazzano, 1524

A letter, the *Cellère Codex*, in the Pierpont Morgan Library, New York, written in Italian by Verrazzano, from his ship the *Dauphine*, in Dieppe Harbor, on 8 July 1524.

Verrazzano, a Florentine, was sent by Francis I of France in the *Dauphine* to explore and to find a western passage to Asia. He was equipped, he said, with a variety of navigational instruments; the accuracy of some of his observations bears good testimony to his skill in using them. His point of departure was from a 'deserted rock' in the neighborhood of the Madeiras on 17 January 1524. After enduring 'a tempest as severe as ever a man who has navigated suffered', he made landfall in the neighborhood of Cape Fear, North Carolina. His impressions of the region and its inhabitants follow.

In XXV more days we sailed more than 400 leagues where there appeared to us a new land never before seen by anyone, ancient or modern.

THE LAND FIRST SEEN IN 34°N. LATITUDE

At first it appeared rather low; having approached to within a quarter of a league, we perceived it, by the great fires built on the shore of the sea, to be inhabited. We saw that it ran toward the south; following it, to find some port where we could anchor with the ship and investigate its nature, in the space of fifty leagues we did not find a port or any place where it was possible to stay with the ship. And having seen that it trended continually to the south (in order not to meet with the Spaniards) we decided to turn about to coast it toward the north, where we found the same place. We anchored by the coast, sending the small boat to land. We had seen many people who came to the shore of the sea and seeing us approach fled, sometimes halting, turning back, looking with great admiration. Reassuring them by various signs, some of them approached, showing great delight at seeing us, marvelling at our clothes, figures and whiteness, making to us various signs where we could land more conveniently with the small boat, offering to us of their foods.

We were on land, and that which we were able to learn of their life and customs I will tell Your Majesty briefly:

They go nude of everything except that at the private parts they wear some skins of little animals like martens, a girdle of fine grass woven with various tails of other animals which hang around the body as far as the knees; the rest nude; the head likewise. Some wear certain garlands of feathers of birds. They are of dark color not much unlike the Ethiopians, and hair black and thick, and not very long, which they tie together back on the head in the shape of a little tail. As for the symmetry of the man, they are well proportioned, of medium stature, and rather exceed us. In the breast they are broad, their arms well built, the legs and other parts of the body well put together. There is nothing else, except that they incline somewhat to broadness in the face; but not all, for in more we saw the face clear-cut. The eyes black and large, the glance intent and quick. They are not of much strength, in craftiness acute, agile and the greatest runners. From what we were able to learn by experience, they resemble in the last two respects the Orientals, and mostly those of the farthest Sinarian regions. We were not able to learn with particularity of the life and customs of these people because of the shortness of the stay we made on land, on account of there being few people and the ship anchored in the high sea.

'FOREST OF LAURELS' AND 'FIELD OF CEDARS'

We found on the shore, not far from these, other people whose lives we think are similar. I will tell Your Majesty about it, describing at present the site and nature of said land. The maritime shore is all covered with fine sand XV feet high, extending in the form of little hills about fifty paces wide. After going ahead, some rivers and arms of the sea were found which enter through some mouths, coursing the shore on both sides as it follows its windings. Near by appears the spacious land, so high that it exceeds the sandy shore, with many beautiful fields and plains, full of the largest forests, some thin and some dense, clothed with as many colors of trees, with as much beauty and delectable appearance as it would be possible to express. And do not believe, Your Majesty, that these are like the Hyrcanian Forest or the wild solitudes of Scythia and northern countries, full of rugged trees, but adorned and clothed with palms, laurels, and cypresses, and other varieties of trees unknown in our Europe (We baptized this land 'Forest of Laurels' and a little farther down on account of the beautiful cedars it was given the name 'Field of Cedars' [between Cape

81

Woodcut of a deer, from the title page of A. Thevet, *Les singularités de la France Antarctique*, Paris, 1558.

Fear and Bogue Banks]); which, for a long distance, exhale the sweetest odors (We smelled the odor a hundred leagues, and farther when they burned the cedars and the winds blew from the land); the property of which we were not able to learn, for the cause above narrated, not that it was difficult for us to travel through the forests, because their density is not so great but that they are entirely penetrable. We think that partaking of the Orient on account of the surroundings, they are not without some medical property or aromatic liquor. And other riches: gold, to which land of such a color has every tendency. It is abundant of many animals, stags, deer, hares; likewise of lakes and pools of living water, with various numbers of birds, adapted and convenient for every delectable pleasure of the hunt.

The region enjoyed a moderate climate, placid seas, and a coast free from rocks with good anchorage close in land. As the vessel coasted eastward, Verrazzano noticed many fires lit by the inhabitants. Observing the Outer Banks Islands between Cape Lookout and Cape Henry, Verrazzano mistook them for a long isthmus and thought Pamlico and Albemarle Sounds behind them were the Pacific Ocean. Arcadia, mentioned at the end of the following extract, is identified as the Eastern Shore of Virginia or Maryland.

Sending ashore by swimming one of our young sailors carrying to them some trinkets, such as little bells, mirrors, and other favors, and being approached within 4 fathoms of them, throwing the goods to them and wishing to turn back he was so tossed by the waves that almost half dead he was carried to the edge of the shore. Which having been seen, the people of the land ran immediately to him: taking him by the head, legs and arms, they carried him some distance away. Where, the youth, seeing himself carried in such way, stricken with terror, uttered very loud cries, which they did similarly in their language, showing him that he should not fear. After that, having placed him on the ground in the sun at the foot of a little hill, they performed great acts of admiration, regarding the whiteness of his flesh, examining him from head to foot. Taking off his shirt and hose, leaving him nude, they made a very large fire near him, placing him near the heat. Which having been seen, the sailors who had remained in the small boat, full of fear, as is their custom in every new case, thought that they wanted to roast him for food. His strength recovered, having remained with them awhile, he showed by signs that he desired to return to the ship; who, with the greatest kindness, holding him always close with various embraces, accompanied him as far as the sea, and in order to assure him more, extending themselves on a high hill, stood to watch him until he was in the boat. Which young man learned of this people that they are thus: of dark color like the others, the flesh more lustrous, of medium stature, the face more clear-cut, much more delicate of body and other members, of much less strength and even of intelligence. He saw nothing else.

(We called it Annunciata from the day of arrival, where was found an isthmus a mile in width and about 200 long, in which, from the ship, was seen the oriental sea between the west [corrected from 'east' in the text] and north. Which is the one, without doubt, which goes about the extremity of India, China and Cathay. We navigated along the said isthmus with the continual hope of finding some strait or true promontory at which the land would end toward the north in order to be able to penetrate to those blessed shores of Cathay. To which isthmus was given by the discoverer [the name Isthmus] Verrazanio: as all the land found was named Francesco for our Francis.)

Having departed thence, following always the shore which turned somewhat toward the north, we came in the space of fifty leagues to another land which appeared much more beautiful and full of the largest forests.

Verrazzano had missed the eleven-mile entrance to Chesapeake Bay entirely. The vessel anchored north of the mouth of the Bay, however, and twenty men explored about two leagues inland, the natives fleeing before them. The party discovered an old woman and a young girl with a group of children. One boy was taken from them to carry back to France. The young woman strenuously resisted efforts to remove her also. Verrazzano wrote the following account of the Indians and the terrain explored.

These we found lighter colored than those past, dressed in certain grasses which grow, pendant from the branches of the trees, which they weave with various ends of wild hemp. The head bare in the same form as the others. Their food in general is of pulse with which they abound, differing in color and size from ours, of excellent and delectable flavor; also, from hunting, fishes and birds, which they take with bows and with snares. They make (the bows) of tough wood, the arrows of reeds, placing at the extremities bones of fishes and of other animals. The beasts in this part are much wilder than in our Europe because they are continually molested by the hunters. We saw many of their barges constructed from a single tree twenty feet long, four wide, which are not fabricated with stones, iron or other kind of metals, because in all this land, in the space of two hundred leagues which we traveled, only one stone of any species was seen by us. They aid themselves with the fourth element, burning such part of the wood as suffices for the hollow of the barge, also of the stern and prow, so that, navigating, it is possible to plough the waves of the sea.

The land in situation, goodness and beauty, is like the other; the forests open; full of various kinds of trees, but not of such fragrance, on account of being more north and cold. We saw in that (land) many vines of natural growth which, rising, entwine themselves around the trees, as they are accustomed in Cisalpine Gaul; which, if they had the perfect system of culture by the agriculturists, without doubt would produce excellent wines, because [of] finding many times the dry fruit of those [vines] sweet and agreeable, not different from ours. They are held in esteem by them, because wherever they [the vines] grow, they lift up the surrounding bushes in order that the fruit may be able to mature. We found wild roses, violets and lilies, and many sorts of herbs, and fragrant flowers different from ours.

Having remained in this place three days, anchored off the coast, we decided on account of the scarcity of ports to depart, always skirting the shore (which we baptized Arcadia on account of the beauty of the trees). In Arcadia we found a man who came to the shore to see what people we were: who stood hesitating and ready for flight. Watching us, he did not permit himself to be approached. He was handsome, nude, with hair fastened back in a knot, of olive color. We were about XX [in number] ashore and coaxing him he approached to within two fathoms, showing a burning stick as if to offer us fire. And we made fire with powder and flint-and-steel and he trembled all over with terror and we fired a shot. He stopped, as if astonished and prayed, worshipping like a monk, lifting his fingers to the sky, and pointing to the ship and the sea he appeared to bless us.

At the end of a hundred leagues we found a very agreeable situation located within two small prominent hills [entrance to New York Harbor], in the midst of which flowed to the sea a very great river [Hudson River], which was deep within the mouth; and from the sea to the hills of that [place] with the rising of the tides, which we found eight feet, any laden ship might have passed. On account of being anchored off the coast in good shelter, we did not wish to adventure in without knowledge of the entrances. We were with the small boat, entering the said river to the land, which we found much populated. The people, almost like the others, clothed with the feathers of birds of various colors, came toward us joyfully, uttering very great exclamations of admiration, showing us where we could land with the boat more safely. We entered said river, within the land [within the Narrows], about half a league, where we saw it made a very beautiful lake with a circuit of about three leagues [the Upper Bay]; through which they [the Indians] went, going from one and another part to the number of XXX of their little barges, with innumerable people, who passed from one shore and the other in order to see us. In an instant, as is wont to happen in navigation, a gale of unfavorable wind blowing in from the sea, we were forced

Hyoscyamus luteus.
Seelen Bilsen.

82

Seelen Bilsen: yellow henbane or *Nicotiana rustica*, from Rembert Dodoens' *Cruÿdeboeck*, Antwerp, 1554.

This is the first drawing of *Nicotiana rustica* to appear in a published work, but the chewing or inhaling of tobacco by the American Indians was reported by the earliest explorers. Among the gifts the natives offered to Columbus upon his first landing were some dried leaves of tobacco. Waldseemüller, recording the manners of the Venezuelan natives encountered by Vespucci, Ojeda, and Cosa, notes that 'the customs and manners of this tribe are of this sort: in looks and behavior they were very repulsive, and each had his cheeks bulging with a certain green herb which they chewed like cattle, so that they could scarcely speak. And hanging from his neck each carried two dried gourds, one of which was full of the very herb he kept in his mouth.'

to return to the ship, leaving the said land with much regret because of its commodiousness and beauty, thinking it was not without some properties of value, all of its hills showing indications of minerals.

The anchor raised, sailing towards the east, as thus the land turned, having traveled LXXX leagues always in sight of it, we discovered an island triangular in form, distant ten leagues from the continent [Block Island], in size like the island of Rhodes, full of hills, covered with trees, much populated [judging] by the continuous fires along all the surrounding shore which we saw they made. We baptized it in the name of your most illustrious mother [Luisa]; not anchoring there on account of the unfavorableness of the weather.

The next landfall was made at Narragansett Bay, titled 'Refugio' by the explorers. The vessel anchored at present day Newport. The party once more encountered friendly Indians, seemingly more civilized than those contacted in the south.

There were among them two Kings, of as good stature and form as it would be possible to tell; the first of about XXXX years, the other a young man of XXIIII years, the clothing of whom was thus: the older had on his nude body a skin of a stag, artifically adorned like a damask with various embroideries; the head bare, the hair turned back with various bands, at the neck a broad chain ornamented with many stones of diverse colors. The young man was almost in the same style. This is the most beautiful people and the most civilized in customs that we have found in this navigation. They excel us in size; they are of bronze color, some inclining more to whiteness, others to tawny color; the face sharply cut, the hair long and black, upon which they bestow the greatest study in adorning it; the eyes black and alert, the bearing kind and gentle, imitating much the ancient [manner]. Of the other parts of the body I will not speak to Your Majesty, having all the proportions which belong to every well built man. Their women are of the same beauty and charm; very graceful; of comely mien and agreeable aspect; of habits and behavior as much according to womanly custom as pertains to human nature; they go nude with only one skin of the stag embroidered like the men, and some wear on the arms very rich skins of the lynx; the head bare, with various arrangements of braids, composed of their own hair, which hang on one side and the other of the breast. Some use other hair-arrangements like the women of Egypt and of Syria use, and these are they who are advanced in age and are joined in wedlock. They have in the ears various pendant trinkets as the orientals are accustomed to have, the men like the women, among which we saw many plates wrought from copper, by whom it is prized more than the gold; which, on account of its color, they do not esteem; wherefore among all it is held by them more worthless; on the other hand rating blue and red above any other. That which they were given by us which they most valued were little bells, blue crystals and other trinkets to place in the ears and on the neck. They did not prize cloth of silk and of gold nor even of other kind, nor did they care to have them; likewise with metals like steel and iron . . .

The expedition remained in Newport for fifteen days establishing a firm friendship with the Indians. Although the menfolk frequently boarded the ship, the women were never allowed to come amongst the Europeans. The latter made several exploratory trips inland.

Many times we were from five to six leagues inland which we found as pleasing as it can be to narrate, adapted to every kind of cultivation,—grain, wine, oil. Because in that place the

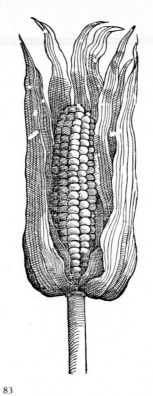

83

Ear of corn, from G. B. Ramusio, *Navigationi et Viaggi,* Venice, 1556.

fields are from XXV to XXX leagues wide, open and devoid of every impediment of trees, of such fertility that any seed in them would produce the best crops. Entering then into the woods, all of which are penetrable by any numerous army in any way whatsoever, and whose trees, oaks, cypresses, and others, are unknown in our Europe. We found Lucallian apples (or cherries), plums and filberts, and many kinds of fruits different from ours. Animals there are in very great number, stags, deer, lynx, and other species, which, in the way of the others, they capture with snares and bows which are their principal arms. The arrows of whom are worked with great beauty, placing at the end, instead of iron, emery, jasper, hard marble, and other sharp stones, by which they served themselves instead of iron in cutting trees, making their barges from a single trunk of a tree, hollowed with wonderful skill, in which from fourteen to XV men will go comfortably; the short oar, broad at the end, working it solely with the strength of the arms at sea without any peril with as much speed as pleases them.

'THE COUNTRY OF REFUGIO'

Going further, we saw their habitations, circular in form, of XIIII to XV paces compass, made from semi-circles of wood separated one from the other, without system of architecture, covered with mats of straw ingeniously worked, which protect them from rain and wind. There is no doubt that if they had the perfection of the arts we have, they would build magnificent edifices, for all the maritime coast is full of blue rocks, crystals and alabaster; and for such cause is full of ports and shelters for ships. They change said houses from one place to another according to the opulence of the site and the season in which they live. Carrying away only the mats, immediately they have other habitations made. There live in each a father and family to a very large number, so that in some we saw XXV and XXX souls. Their food is like the others; of pulse (which they produce with more system of culture than the others, observing the full moon, the rising of the Pleiades, and many customs derived from the ancients), also of the chase and fish.

Verrazzano went on to describe the physical features of Narragansett Bay, and particularly its western entrance, dominated by Whale Rock. The latter he christened 'Petra Viva'.

On 6 May the *Dauphine* weighed anchor and left Narragansett. They traced the shore northwards and navigated the hazardous shoals off Nantucket and Cape Cod with great difficulty. The land appeared more mountainous. Fifty leagues farther on the company reached a wilder coast and had their first experience of hostile Indians. The land of the Bad People is identified as being near Casco Bay.

THE LAND OF BAD PEOPLE

In the space of fifty leagues, holding more to the north, we found a high land and full of very thick forests, the trees of which were pines, cypresses [red cedar] and such as grow in cold regions. The people all different from the others, and as much as those passed were of cultivated manners, these were full of uncouthness and vices, so barbarous that we were never able, with howsoever many signs we made them, to have any intercourse with them. They dress with the skins of bear, lynxes, sea-wolves, and other animals. The food, according to that which we were able to learn through going many times to their habitations, we think is of the chase, fish and some products which are of a species of roots which the ground yields by its own self. They do not have pulse, nor did we see any signs of cultivation, nor would the ground, on account of its sterility, be adapted to produce fruit or any grain. If, trading at any time with them, we desired their things, they came to the shore of the sea upon some rock where it was very steep, and—we remaining in the small boat,—with a cord let down to us what they wished to give, continually crying on land that we should not approach, giving quickly the barter, not taking in exchange for it except knives, hooks for fishing, and sharp metal. They had no regard for courtesy, and when they had nothing more to exchange, at their departing the men made at us all the signs of contempt and shame which any brute creature could make. Contrary to their wish, XXV armed men of us were inland two and three leagues, and when we descended to the shore they shot at us with their bows, sending forth the greatest cries, then fled into the woods. We do not know any value of any moment in this land except the very great forests, with some hills which possibly have some metal, because on many [natives] we saw 'pater-nosters' of copper in the ears.

Verrazzano pursued his course east-south-east and north-north-east, completely bypassing the Bay of Fundy, until he reached Cape Breton. Shortage of victuals and naval stores put an end to further exploration. The company restocked with wood and water and sailed for France, reaching Dieppe on 8 July 1524. Verrazzano concluded in his report that his purpose in finding a sea passage to Cathay failed because there was no strait to the Eastern sea and that the whole New World formed a vast continent larger than Asia, with an unbroken coastline.

Text used: Translation by E. H. Hall in Fifteenth Annual Report of the American Scenic and Historic Preservation Society, *Appendix A. Albany, 1910, pp. 179-202. Marginal notes in the* Cellère Codex, *probably in Verrazzano's own hand, appear in parentheses; editorial identifications of places and names are in brackets.*

3.
The first voyage of Jacques Cartier, 1534

From an anonymous manuscript copy, now in the Bibliothèque Nationale, Paris, Moreau Collection, No. 841, of an original, probably not by Cartier but by Jehan Poullet, who accompanied Cartier on the voyage.

Jacques Cartier sighted Cape Bonavista, Newfoundland, on 10 May after a fair voyage from France. Faced with dangerous ice floes off the coast, his expedition repaired to Catalina Harbour. From this haven on 21 May they proceeded northwards to Funk Island, called by Cartier the 'Isle of Birds'.

The island was completely surrounded and encompassed by a cordon of loose ice, split up into cakes. In spite of this belt (of ice) our two long-boats were sent off to the island to procure some of the birds, whose numbers are so great as to be incredible, unless one has seen them; for although the island is about a league in circumference, it is so exceeding full of birds that one would think they had been stowed there. In the air and round about are an hundred times as many more as on the island itself. Some of these birds are as large as geese, being black and white with a beak like a crow's. They are always in the water, not being able to fly in the air, inasmuch as they have only small wings about the size of half one's hand,

84
Flying-fish. Drawing by John White, 1585. *London, British Museum.*
85
Portuguese Man-o'-War. Drawing by John White, 1585. *London, British Museum.*
86
The head of a Brown Pelican. Drawing by John White, 1585. *London, British Museum.*
87 *Overleaf*
The Planisphere made by Juan Vespucci, 1526. *New York, Hispanic Society of America.*
The first known map to record the explorations of Ayllón and to establish a new type of nomenclature for the south-east coast is a holograph *mappamundi* by Juan Vespucci, nephew of Amerigo Vespucci, which was made in 1526. Juan was appointed pilot of the Casa de Contratación in May 1512; in 1515 he was a member of the junta that was brought together to improve existing charts; and he was a member of the Badajoz Commission of 1524. In the year that he made the map, he was appointed, with Miguel García, to examine pilots in the place of the Pilot Major, Sebastian Cabot, who was then leading an expedition in Brazil. The map shows care in giving only what Juan Vespucci felt was sufficiently certain to justify inclusion; he shows nothing below Newfoundland and the Nova Scotia coast until he reaches the 'trá nueva de ayllón', which he marks with a Spanish flag. Ten names are entered along the south-east coast; since they do not include the 'R.S. Juan' (Rio de San Juan Bautista) where Gordillo and Quexos landed in 1521 or 'aguarda', which are usually found on maps having 'R.S. Juan', this map apparently does not report Ayllón's first expedition under Gordillo in 1521. Vespucci could hardly have included information derived from Ayllón's own attempt at settlement in 1526, since the colonists endured part of the winter of 1526–7 before returning to Hispaniola. Vespucci's map may therefore be taken to show the information gained by Pedro de Quexos on his journey of exploration along the coast in 1525 and reported to the office of the Pilot Major in Seville.
Along the Ayllón coast 'baya de sa maria' shows that Quexos went as far north as the Carolina Sounds or Chesapeake Bay; 'c[abo] da sāta elena' is the first appearance of St Helena Sound which remains one of the earliest names still used on the North Atlantic coast. 'Rio de sa terazanas' shows that a report of Verrazzano's landing near Cape Fear River in 1524 was known in Spain; strangely the map gives no record of the Spanish voyage of Gomes in 1525.

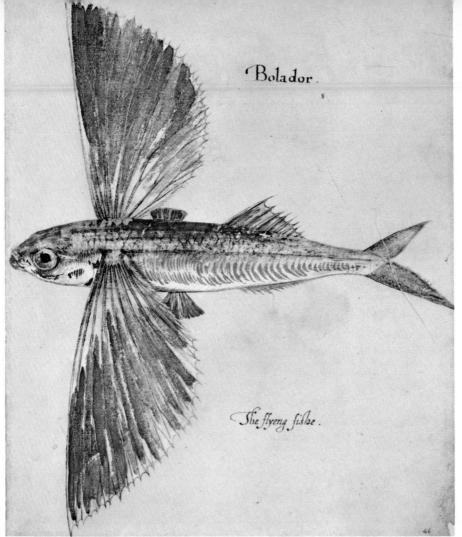

Bolador.

The flyeng fishe.

84

This is a lyuing fish, and flote vpon the Sea. Some call them Caruels

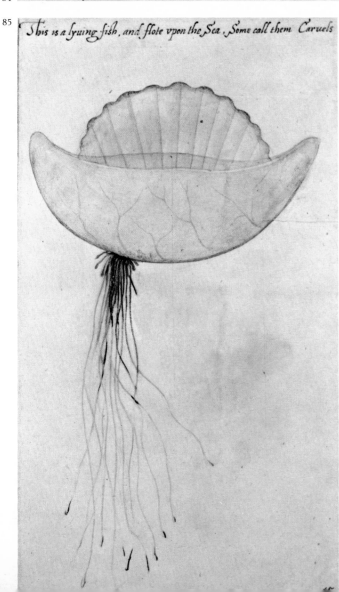

Alcatralsa. This fowle is of the greatnes of a Swanne. and of the same forme sauing the heade, w.ᶜʰ is in length 16. ynches.

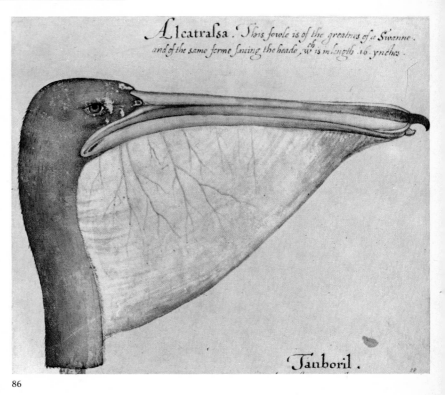

Tanboril.

86

Note, *These Fowls never fly, for their Wings are very short, most like the Fins of a Fish, having nothing upon them but a sort of Down and short Feathers.*

90

88
Loggerhead Turtle. Drawing by John White, 1585. *London, British Museum.* The only sea turtle which breeds on the Carolina Banks.
89
Terrapin. Drawing by John White, 1585. *London, British Museum.*
90
The great auk, unable to fly and easily caught, was often described by early trans-Atlantic explorers as a source of food after they reached the coastal islands off the shore of Newfoundland. It was extinct by 1844 through indiscriminate killing by boat crews. This crude drawing appeared in various editions of *The English Pilot, Fourth Book,* first published in 1689, for nearly a hundred years.
91
Bears, taken from the Pierre Desceliers world map of 1550. *London, British Museum, Add. Ms. 24065.*

with which however they move as quickly along the water as the other birds fly through the air. And these birds are so fat that it is marvellous. We call them apponats [the great auk, extinct since 1844]; and our two long-boats were laden with them as with stones, in less than half an hour. Of these, each of our ships salted four or five casks, not counting those we were able to eat fresh.

OF TWO KINDS OF BIRDS, THE ONE CALLED TINKERS AND THE OTHER GANNETS; AND HOW THEY ARRIVED AT KARPONT

Furthermore there is another smaller kind of bird that flies in the air and swims in the sea, which is called a tinker [the razor-billed auk or common penguin]. These stow and place themselves on this land underneath the larger ones. There were other white ones larger still that keep apart from the rest in a portion of the island, and are very ugly to attack; for they bite like dogs. These are called gannets. Notwithstanding that the island lies fourteen leagues from shore, bears swim out to it from the mainland in order to feed on these birds; and our men found one as big as a calf and as white as a swan that sprang into the sea in front of them. And the next day, which was Whitsuntide, on continuing our voyage in the direction of the mainland, we caught sight of this bear about half way, swimming towards land as fast as we were sailing; and on coming up with him we gave chase with our long-boats and captured him by main force. His flesh was as good to eat as that of a two-year-old heifer.

On 27 May the two vessels reached the mouth of Belle Isle Strait. Icebergs and bad weather induced them to retire to neighboring Karpont (now Grand-Kirpon) Harbour until 9 June. Cartier described the north-east Newfoundland coast between Cape Rouge and Cape Degrat thus:

The coast from cape Rouge to cape Degrat, which is the point at the entrance to the bay, runs from cape to cape north-north-east and south-south-west, and all this part of the coast has islands off it and near to one another, so that there are nothing but narrow channels where ships' boats may go and pass among them. And on this account there are several good harbours of which the said Karpont harbour and the harbour of Degrat are in one of these islands, that which is the highest of all [Kirpon Island], from the top of which one can see clearly the two Belle Isles [the Groais Islands] that are near cape Rouge, whence to the harbour of Karpont the distance is twenty-five leagues.

Cartier went on to describe the shoals and bars near Grand-Kirpon and the soundings he had taken there. Three islands were observed at the mouth of Belle Isle Strait, and the positions of various harbors established during progress along the northern coast of the latter passage. Greenly Island off Blanc Sablon was titled Bird Island

91

because of the myriad tinkers and puffins seen there. The coast between Islets Harbour, now Bradore Bay, and the Port of Brest (Bonne Espérance Harbour, within the Gulf of St Lawrence, on the Labrador coast) appeared to him thus:

From the Islets to this place there are islands; and Brest lies among islands. And furthermore ranging the coast at a distance of three leagues out there are islands all along for more than twelve leagues from Brest, which islands are low and one can see the high shore over the tops of them.

The expedition entered Brest on 10 June. The next day a party set out in long-boats to explore the coast westwards. Passing through innumerable islands, they discovered Rocky, Lobster and Shecatica Bays, and encountered a Rochelle fishing vessel which had lost its bearings. The party then proceeded to Cumberland Harbour in company with the ship from Rochelle. Cartier commented further:

This harbour is in my opinion one of the best in the world. It was named port Jacques Cartier. If the soil were as good as the harbours, it would be a blessing; but the land should not be called the New Land, being composed of stones and horrible rugged rocks; for along the whole of the north Shore (of the Gulf), I did not see one cart-load of earth and yet I landed in many places. Except at Blanc Sablon there is nothing but moss and short, stunted shrub. In fine I am rather inclined to believe that this is the land God gave to Cain. There are people on this coast whose bodies are fairly well formed but they are wild and savage folk. They wear their hair tied up on the top of their heads like a handful of twisted hay, with a nail or something of the sort passed through the middle, and into it they weave a few bird's feathers. They clothe themselves with the furs of animals, both men as well as women; but the women are wrapped up more closely and snuggly in their furs; and have a belt about their waists. They (all) paint themselves with certain tan colours. They have canoes made of birch bark in which they go about, and from which they catch many seals. Since seeing them [Beothuk Indians], I have been informed that their home is not at this place but that they come from warmer countries to catch these seals and to get other food for their sustenance.

The long-boats returned to Brest, and on 15 June Cartier's two ships left harbor sailing southwards. They touched the north-west coast of Newfoundland at Point Rich, naming it Cape Double because it appeared to be 'a large cape doubled one part above the other'.

The next day [Tuesday], the sixteenth of the month [of June], we ran along this coast to the south-west, one quarter south, for some thirty-five leagues from cape Double, when we came to a region of very high and rugged mountains, among which was one in appearance like a barn and on this account we named this region the Barn mountains [the Highlands of St John]. These highlands and mountains are cut up and hewn out; and between them and the sea are low shores.

back towards cape Royal [Bear Head] to try and find a harbour. We set out with our long-boats to examine the coast between cape Royal [Bear Head] and Lath cape [Cape Cormorant], and found that on either side on the low shores, there is a large bay [Port-au-Port Bay] running back a long way, with islands in it. It is land-locked to the south of the low shores, which form one side of the entrance, while cape Royal [Bear Head] forms the other. These low shores stretch out into the sea for more than half a league [Long Point], with shoal water and bad ground; and in the middle of the entrance there is an island [Fox Island].

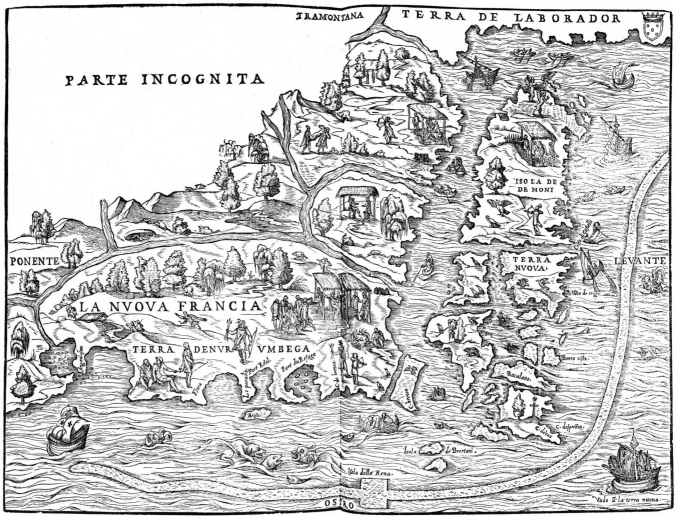

92

On 17 June they ran south-west before a storm, sighting Bay of Islands, and two headlands which they called Cape Royal and Lath Cape, present-day Bear Head and Cape Cormorant. Cartier observed:

Between these two capes [Bear Head and Cape Cormorant] are low shores, beyond which are very high lands with apparently rivers among them. Two leagues from cape Royal there is a depth of twenty fathoms and the best fishing possible for big cod. Of these cod we caught, while waiting for our consort, more than a hundred in less than an hour.

OF SOME ISLANDS BETWEEN CAPE ROYAL AND LATH CAPE

On the next day [Thursday], the eighteenth of the said month [of June], the wind came ahead and blew hard; and we put

92
'La Nuova Francia', from Giovanni Baptista Ramusio's *Navigationi et viaggi*, Venice, 1556.
This woodcut map, designed by Gastaldi for Ramusio's collection of travels, influenced numerous later maps with its many-islanded Newfoundland and narrow off-shore banks. Although it was published in 1556 in Ramusio's third volume of voyages, which includes an account of Cartier's exploration of the Gulf of St Lawrence in 1534, it shows no knowledge of Cartier's discoveries, but is based chiefly on Verrazzano's voyage of 1524.
95
The land of Labrador, from an anonymous atlas, c. 1550–60. *Greenwich, National Maritime Museum, Portolan Atlas No. 14, fo 14v.*
This Portuguese map of the Gulf and River of St Lawrence, with east at the top, in an undated atlas, shows the discoveries of Jacques Cartier. Its nomenclature and the configuration of the St Lawrence River show that it is based on some recent French map, such as that of Vallard in 1547; but the peacock and castellated fort are inappropriate, ornamental additions.

93
Drawings of three kinds of dog-tooth violets and five kinds of *hepatica* from Johannes T. de Bry, *Florilegium renovatum et auctum*, Frankfurt, 1641.

94
A walrus cow with her calf, from Johan de Laet, *Nieuwe Wereldt ofte beschrijvinghe van West-Indien*, Leyden, 1630.

Provins roses, as well as parsley and other useful, strong-smelling herbs. Round about this island are many great beasts, like large oxen, which have two tusks in their jaw like elephant's tusks and swim about in the water [walruses]. There was one asleep on shore near the water's edge, and we set out in our long-boats to try and catch him; but as soon as we drew near, he threw himself into the sea. We also saw there bears and foxes. This island was named Brion island. In the neighbourhood of these islands the tides are strong and run to all appearance south-east and north-west. I am rather inclined to think from what I have seen that there is a passage between Newfoundland and the Breton's land [Cabot Strait]. If this were so, it would prove a great saving both in time and

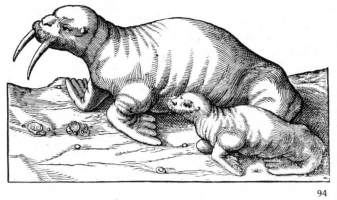

94

95

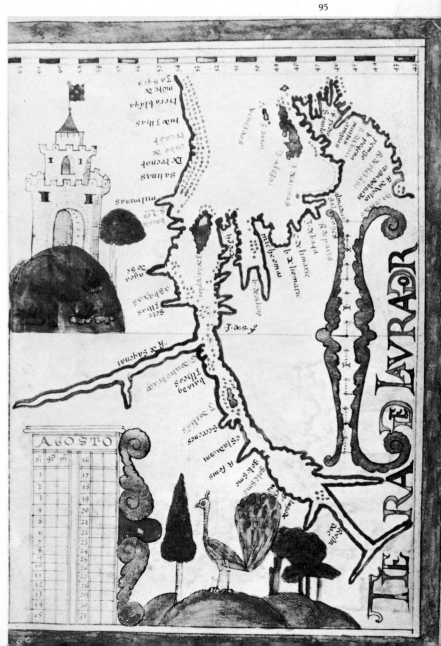

On 19 June stormy weather drove them south-west. They discovered a cape on St John's Day (24 June) and named it St John (probably Cape Anguille). On 26 June, leaving the Newfoundland coast, they reached three islands. Two of these, the Bird Rocks, were named the Gannet Islands owing to the huge numbers of gannets, murres and puffins found nesting there. The third, Brion Island, made a great impression on Cartier.

This island is fringed with sand-banks, and there is excellent bottom and anchorage all around it in six and seven fathoms. This island is the best land we have seen; for two acres of it are worth more than the whole of Newfoundland. We found it to be covered with fine trees and meadows, fields of wild oats, and of pease in flower, as thick and as fine as ever I saw in Brittany, which might have been sown by husbandmen. There are numerous gooseberry bushes, strawberry vines, distance, should any success be met with in this voyage. Four leagues from the said (Brion) island to the west-south-west lies the mainland [actually the Magdalen Islands], which has the appearance of an island surrounded by islets of sand. On it stands a fine cape which we named cape Dauphin [North Cape on Grosse Island], as it is the beginning of the good land.

On (Saturday) the twenty-seventh of the said month of June, we ranged this coast, which runs east-north-east and west-south-west. From a distance it looks as if there were dunes, as the shores are low and sandy. We could not approach nor land there as the wind came off the shore. We ranged it that day about fifteen leagues.

After following this coast westward, the party passed almost a day without sight of land, until it descried what appeared to be two islands. On 30 June they arrived off Prince Edward Island. Cartier again thought that this was the mainland.

And pursuing our course we came in sight of what had looked to us like two islands, which was mainland [actually, Prince Edward Island], that ran south-south-east and north-north-west as far as a very fine headland, named by us cape Orleans [Cape Kildare].

All this coast is low and flat but the finest land one can see, and full of beautiful trees and meadows. Yet we could find along it no harbour; for the shore is low and skirted all along with sand banks, and the water is shallow. We went ashore in our long-boats at several places, and among others at a fine river of little depth, where we caught sight of some Indians in their canoes who were crossing the river. On that account we named this river Canoe river. But we had no further acquaintance with the savages as the wind came up off the sea, and drove upon the shores, so that we deemed it advisable to go back with our long-boats to the ships. We headed north-east until the next morning [Wednesday], the first day of July, at sunrise, at which hour came up fog with overcast sky, and we lowered the sails until about ten o'clock, when it brightened up and we had sight of cape Orleans and of another cape that lay about seven leagues north, one quarter north-east of it, which we named Indian cape [North Point]. To the north-east of this cape, for about half a league, there is a very dangerous shoal and rocky bar. At this cape a man came in sight who ran after our long-boats along the coast, making frequent signs to us to return towards the said [Indian] point. And seeing these signs we began to row towards him, but when he saw that we were returning, he started to run away and to flee before us. We landed opposite to him and placed a knife and a woollen girdle on a branch; and then returned to our ships. That day we coasted this shore some nine or ten leagues to try and find a harbour, but could not do so; for, as I have already mentioned, the shore is low and the water shallow. We landed that day in four places to see the trees which are wonderfully beautiful and very fragrant. We discovered that there were cedars, yew-trees, pines, white elms, ash trees, willows and others, many of them unknown to us and all trees without fruit. The soil where there are no trees is also very rich and is covered with pease, white and red gooseberry bushes, strawberries, raspberries and wild oats like rye, which one would say had been sown there and tilled. It is the best-tempered region one can possibly see and the heat is considerable. There are many turtle-doves, wood-pigeons and other birds. Nothing is wanting but harbours.

96

96
Barley, from N. Monardes, *Joyfull newes out of the newe founde world,* Englished by J. Frampton, London, 1577.

97

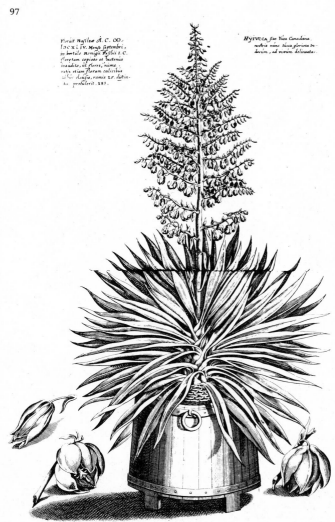

97
Hyiucca sive Yuca Canadana, from J. T. de Bry, *Florilegium renovatum et auctum,* Frankfurt, 1641.

98

The Mercator world map, 1569. *Rotterdam, Prins Hendrik Maritiem Museum.*
Mercator's map is one of the most important and influential in the history
of mapmaking; this importance is not based on the topographical accuracy
of his maps, however, but on the value of the projection which he evolved
for portraying the spherical earth on a two-dimensional surface. Mercator
produced a chart on which a straight line joining any two points on the
chart determines the compass direction a navigator must steer in sailing the
most direct route from one place to another. The value of Mercator's
projection is shown in its continued use to this day.

   The most obvious distortion in this projection is the increased size of an
area the farther it is from the equator; the most famous illustration is that
Greenland on a Mercator map is larger than South America, whereas it is
actually only one ninth the size. Any projection of the earth on a flat
surface must be a compromise; Mercator's great achievement was to make

his maps conformal in shape and to aid the navigator in plotting his course.
It was not until the end of the sixteenth century, however, that sailors
began to accept and use maps with this projection; they were skeptical of
the distortions and of parallels and meridians drawn at right angles to each
other. In 1599 an Englishman, Edward Wright, made another chart and
explained the projection in terms and tables of calculations that navigators
could understand and use.

   Mercator's world map of 1569 is the first map to show the Appalachians
as a continuous mountain range stretching parallel to the east coast in a
south-west/north-easterly direction. The New England/Nova Scotia coast
extends too pronouncedly east-west, as in most sixteenth-century maps; this
is the result of the declination of the magnetic compass at this latitude,
which caused the navigators to err in recording their direction along the
coast.

COSTE DE LA FLOVRIDE

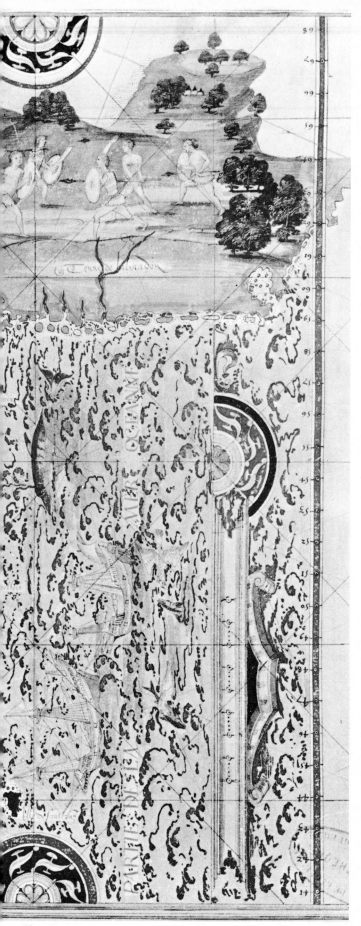

99

Florida, Canada and Labrador, from the *Cosmographie Universelle* of Guillaume le Testu, 1555. (See also plates 141, 147 and 163.) *Paris, Ministère des Armées, D.I.Z.14, fo 57v.*

On 4 July Cartier coasted the north shore of Chaleur Bay, discovering a small cove which he named after St Martin (Port Daniel). His ships remained there until 12 July. Meanwhile, on the 6th, he set out with a long-boat to examine a cape farther into the bay.

And when we were half a league from this point, we caught sight of two fleets of Indian canoes that were crossing from one side [of Chaleur Bay] to the other, which numbered in all some forty or fifty canoes. Upon one of the fleets reaching this point, there sprang out and landed a large number of Indians, who set up a great clamour and made frequent signs to us to come on shore, holding up to us some furs on sticks. But as we were only one boat we did not care to go, so we rowed towards the other fleet which was on the water. And they (on shore), seeing we were rowing away, made ready two of their largest canoes in order to follow us. These were joined by five more of those that were coming in from the sea, and all came after our long-boat, dancing and showing many signs of joy, and of their desire to be friends, saying to us in their language: 'Napou tou daman asurtat', and other words, we did not understand. But for the reason already stated, that we had only one of our long-boats, we did not care to trust to their signs and waved to them to go back, which they would not do but paddled so hard that they soon surrounded our long-boat with their seven canoes. And seeing that no matter how much we signed to them, they would not go back, we shot off over their heads two small cannon. On this they began to return toward the point, and set up a marvellously loud shout, after which they proceeded to come on again as before. And when they had come alongside our long-boat, we shot off two fire-lances which scattered among them and frightened them so much that they began to paddle off in very great haste, and did not follow us any more.

HOW THESE INDIANS COMING TOWARDS THE SHIPS AND OUR PEOPLE GOING TOWARDS THEM, SOME FROM EACH PART WENT ON SHORE AND HOW THE INDIANS IN GREAT GLEE BEGAN TO BARTER WITH OUR MEN

The next day (Tuesday, July 7) some of these Indians came in nine canoes to the point at the mouth of the cove [West Point at the mouth of Port Daniel], where we lay anchored with our ships. And being informed of their arrival we went with our two long-boats to the point where they were, at the mouth of the cove. As soon as they saw us they began to run away, making signs to us that they had come to barter with us; and held up some furs of small value, with which they clothe themselves. We likewise made signs to them that we wished them no harm, and sent two men on shore, to offer them some knives and other iron goods, and a red cap to give to their chief. Seeing this, they sent on shore part of their people with some of their furs; and the two parties traded together. The savages showed a marvellously great pleasure in possessing and obtaining these iron wares and other commodities, dancing and going through many ceremonies, and throwing salt water over their heads with their hands. They bartered all they had to such an extent that all went back naked without anything on them; and they made signs to us that they would return on the morrow with more furs.

HOW, WHEN OUR PEOPLE HAD SENT TWO PEOPLE ON SHORE WITH GOODS, ABOUT THREE HUNDRED INDIANS MET THEM IN GREAT GLEE; OF THE NATURE OF THIS COUNTRY AND OF ITS PRODUCTS; AND OF A BAY NAMED CHALEUR BAY

On Thursday the ninth of the said month [of July] as the wind was favourable for getting underway with our ships, we fitted up our long-boats to go and explore this [Chaleur] bay; and we ran up it that day some twenty-five leagues. The next day [Friday, July 10], at daybreak, we had fine weather and sailed on until about ten o'clock in the morning, at which hour we caught sight of the head of the bay, whereat we were grieved and displeased. At the head of this bay, beyond the low shore, were several very high mountains. And seeing there was no passage, we proceeded to turn back.

100

A sixteenth-century seaman taking the altitude by observing a star with a cross-staff, from an anonymous atlas, c. 1550–60. *Greenwich, National Maritime Museum, Portolan Atlas No. 14, fo 15v.*

On their return journey the French encountered more friendly Indians. Cartier noted that the countryside on the north shore of the bay resembled that of the Isle Brion and the west coast of Prince Edward Island. On 12 July the ships weighed anchor and followed the coast up as far as Gaspé Bay. Fog and high wind detained them there from the 14 to the 25 July. While they were at anchor in Gaspé harbor, over three hundred Indians arrived to fish for mackerel. These natives were again delighted to see the Europeans. Cartier described them as follows:

The wind increased to such an extent that one of our ships lost an anchor, and we deemed it prudent to go farther up some seven or eight leagues, into a good and safe harbour, which we had already explored with our long-boats. On account of the continuous bad weather with over-cast sky and mist, we remained in that harbour and river, without being able to leave, until the twenty-fifth of the said month [of July]. During that time there arrived a large number of savages, who had come to the river [Gaspé basin] to fish for mackerel, of which there is great abundance. They [the savages] numbered, as well men, women as children, more than 300 persons, with some forty canoes. When they had mixed with us a little on shore, they came freely in their canoes to the sides of our vessels. We gave them knives, glass beads, combs and other trinkets of small value, at which they showed many signs of joy, lifting up their hands to heaven and singing

and dancing in their canoes. This people may well be called savage; for they are the sorriest folk there can be in the world, and the whole lot of them had not anything above the value of five sous, their canoes and fishing-nets excepted. They go quite naked, except for a small skin, with which they cover their privy parts, and for a few old furs which they throw over their shoulders. They are not at all of the same race or language as the first we met. They have their heads shaved all round in circles, except for a tuft on the top of the head, which they leave long like a horse's tail. This they do up upon their heads and tie in a knot with leather thongs. They have no other dwelling but their canoes, which they turn upside down and sleep on the ground underneath. They eat their meat almost raw, only warming it a little on the coals; and the same with their fish. On St Magdalen's day [22 July], we rowed over in our long-boats to the spot on shore where they were, and went on land freely among them. At this they showed great joy, and the men all began to sing and to dance in two or three groups, exhibiting signs of great pleasure at our coming. But they had made all the young women retire into the woods, except two or three who remained, to whom we gave each a comb and a little tin bell, at which they showed great pleasure, thanking the captain by rubbing his arms and his breast with their hands. And the men, seeing we had given something to the women that had remained, made those come back who had fled to the woods, in order to receive the same as the others. These, who numbered some twenty, crowded about the captain and rubbed him with their hands, which is their way of showing welcome. He gave them each a little tin ring of small value; and at once they assembled together in a group to dance; and sang several songs. We saw a large quantity of mackerel which they had caught near the shore with the nets they use for fishing, which are made of hemp thread, that grows in the country where they ordinarily reside; for they only come down to the sea in the fishing-season, as I have been given to understand. Here likewise grows Indian corn like pease, the same as in Brazil, which they eat in place of bread, and of this they had a large quantity with them. They call it in their language, *Kagaige.* Furthermore, they have plums which they dry for the winter as we do, and these they call *honnesta*; also figs, nuts, pears, apples and other fruits, and beans which they call *sahe.* They call nuts, *caheya,* figs, *honnesta,* apples . . . If one shows them something they have not got and they know not what it is, they shake their heads and say, *nouda,* which means, they have none of it and know not what it is. Of the things they have, they showed us by signs the way they grow and how they prepare them. They never eat anything that has a taste of salt in it. They are wonderful thieves and steal everything they can carry off.

HOW OUR PEOPLE SET UP A LARGE CROSS ON THE POINT AT THE MOUTH OF THIS HARBOUR, AND HOW THE CHIEF OF THAT TRIBE CAME AND AFTER A LONG HARANGUE WAS QUIETED BY OUR CAPTAIN AND ALLOWED TWO OF HIS SONS TO DEPART WITH THE LATTER

On the twenty-fourth of the said month [of July], we had a cross made thirty feet high, which was put together in the presence of a number of the Indians on the point at the entrance to the harbour [Gaspé], under the cross-bar of which we fixed a shield with three *fleurs-de-lys* in relief, and above it a wooden board, engraved in large Gothic characters, where was written, LONG LIVE THE KING OF FRANCE. We erected this cross on the point in their presence and they watched it being put together and set up. And when it had been raised in the air, we all knelt down with our hands joined, worshipping it before them; and made signs to them, looking up and pointing

Details of animals from a map of North America, 'America Septentrionalis', 1638, from Jan Jansson, *Nouveau theatre du monde*, Amsterdam, 1640.

towards heaven, that by means of this we had our redemption, at which they showed many marks of admiration, at the same time turning and looking at the cross.

When we had returned to our ships, the chief, dressed in an old black bear-skin, arrived in a canoe with three of his sons and his brother; but they did not come so close to the ships as they had usually done. And pointing to the cross he [the chief] made us a long harangue, making the sign of the cross with two of his fingers; and then he pointed to the land all around about, as if he wished to say that all this region belonged to him, and that we ought not to have set up this cross without his permission. And when he had finished his harangue, we held up an axe to him, pretending we would barter it for his fur-skin. To this he nodded assent and little by little drew near the side of our vessel, thinking he would have the axe. But one of our men, who was in our dinghy, caught hold of his canoe, and at once two or three more stepped down into it and made the Indians come on board our vessel, at which they were greatly astonished. When they had come on board, they were assured by the captain that no harm would befall them, while at the same time every sign of affection was shown to them; and they were made to eat and to drink and to be of good cheer. And then we explained to them by signs that the cross had been set up to serve as a land-mark and guide-post on coming into the harbour, and that we would soon come back and would bring them iron wares and other goods; and that we wished to take two of his [the chief's] sons away with us and afterwards would bring them back again to that harbour [Taignoagny and Domagaia, who returned to Canada with Cartier in 1535]. And we dressed up his two sons in shirts and ribbons and in red caps, and put a little brass chain round the neck of each, at which they were greatly pleased; and they proceeded to hand over their old rags to those who were going back on shore. To each of these three, whom we sent back, we also gave a hatchet and two knives at which they showed great pleasure. When they had returned on shore, they told the others what had happened. About noon on that day [24 July] six canoes came off to the ships, in each of which were five or six Indians, who had come to say good-bye to the two we had detained, and to bring them some fish. These made signs to us that they would not pull down the cross, delivering at the same time several harangues which we did not understand.

Having mistaken the passage into the St Lawrence for a bay, the expedition had stood over from Gaspé to the south shore of the Isle of Anticosti. They then coasted eastwards, rounding Heath Point and Table Head to sight the Quebec coast opposite.

At sunrise on Saturday the first of August, we descried and came in sight of another coast that lay to the north and north-east of us [the Quebec coast opposite Anticosti Island]. It was a marvellously high coast cut up into peaks; and between them and us the shore was low with rivers and timber thereon. Heading north-west we ranged these coasts, first on one side and then on the other, to see if this was a bay or a strait, until Wednesday the fifth of the said month (of August)—the distance from shore to shore is about fifteen leagues and the centre is in latitude 50° 20′—without ever being able to advance up it more than about twenty-five leagues, on account of the heavy head-winds and of the tides, that set against us. And we made our way as far as the narrowest part of it, where one can easily see the shore on both sides. There it begins to broaden out again. And as we kept continually falling off before the wind, we set out for the shore in our long-boats, to try and make our way as far as a cape on the south shore, which stretched out the longest and the farthest of any we saw from the water [North Point or Cape Rabast], the distance to which was about five leagues. On reaching the shore we found cliffs and a rocky bottom, which we had not met with in all the places visited towards the south since leaving cape St John.

After consultation on the unfavorableness of the winds and the tides and the lateness of the season, the decision was taken to return to France. Friendly Indians were encountered at Natashkwan Point, on the Quebec coast. Cartier's last descriptive passage concerns this region.

From this cape onward the coast runs east-south-east and west-north-west, and is a very fine low shore but bordered with sand-banks. There are also a great number of shoals and reefs for the space of some twenty leagues, when the coast begins to run east and east-north-east, and is all skirted with islands to a distance of two or three leagues off shore. In the neighbourhood of these are dangerous reefs to a distance of more than four or five leagues from shore.

The ships continued eastwards to touch the Newfoundland coast just south of Cape Double. Coasting northwards they crossed Belle Isle Straits to the harbor of Blanc Sablon. From the latter haven Cartier set course for France on 15 August. His expedition survived severe tempests off Newfoundland and Cape Breton and reached St Malo safely on 5 September 1534.

Text used: H. P. Biggar, ed. and transl., The Voyages of Jacques Cartier. *Ottawa: Publications of the Public Archives of Canada, No. 11, 1924, pp. 3-79, passim, pp. 40-3, 59-63, 64-7.*

3 THE PENETRATION OF THE INTERIOR AND THE EXPLORATION OF THE WEST COAST

102
John Hawkins, from H. Holland, *Herwologia*, London, 1620.

The exploration of coastal North America was an enterprise shared by several nations. It was the Spanish, however, who opened the interior of the continent in the sixteenth century, and to whose eyes the land, in the sense of inland North America, first appeared. To the Spanish also belonged the first sight of its unknown western coast.

In spite of the dangers of storm and wreck and uncertain navigation along uncharted shores, the hazards of plunging, by foot and horseback, into unknown forests and deserts, inhabited by incalculable 'savages' and furnished by no guaranteeable food supply, were far greater. The motivations for undertaking inland exploration, therefore, had to be very strong. For centuries the Spanish nobles and their foot soldiers had been engaged in conquest—the recovery of their land from the Moor. Warfare had become a profession with them, and a nationally held militant faith a far more potent justification for the subduing of pagans than the desire of small groups for freedom of worship. Furthermore, they were lured inland by the craving of the royal court, and of themselves, for the portable riches of gold and silver and precious stones. They had also been greatly encouraged by the extraordinary success they had had in finding such wealth in Central and South America. Another Mexico City and another Peru

glimmered on before them, nor could they accept for many years the evidence that there was no other comparable treasure horde.

Another lure was provided by the legends, fragile but indestructible: the Seven Cities, which moved from island to desert when they reappeared in Indian tales; the fabled city of Quivira, where men had golden eagles on the prows of canoes; the pearl-ringed island of California, kingdom of Amazons; and the Strait of Anian, much sought seaway to Cathay, through which persons were not lacking to declare they had already sailed.[1] Many of these features were attractively emblazoned on maps, and as Henry Wagner wrote, 'There is nothing that has such an air of verisimilitude as a map'.[2] Lastly, the Spanish were spurred on by prying corsairs from other nations, and by persistent rumors that the English, French, or Portuguese had discovered the key to the inner fastnesses, were about to take possession, and must be forestalled.

There was an exception to the Spanish monopoly of sixteenth-century penetration of the interior. Cartier, on his later voyages, followed the St Lawrence waterway some way into the continent, but made only short sallies away from its tidal shores, as did other French and English explorers from the east coast. But an English sailor named David Ingram, set ashore on the Mexican coast near present Tampico in 1568 by Sir John Hawkins, apparently crossed some part of North America on foot.[3] The two other English sailors who he said were his companions died before he was closely questioned. Ingram said he was picked up eventually by the captain of a French vessel, on or near Cape Breton Island. This appears to be impossible because of the factors of distance and time. Professor Quinn points out that the French were trading and refitting their ships along the South Carolina coast in 1568 after de Gourges's victory over the Spanish forts on the St Johns; Ingram could have been taken aboard there, or by a privateer somewhere on the Gulf of Mexico, and the vessel could have touched at Cape Breton. No copy is now known of the version of his adventures published in 1583, but the record of his examination before Sir Francis Walsingham the year before is full of patent falsehoods, such as elephants encountered and fabulous wealth of Indian chiefs seen.[4] The basic fact of his journey and survival, however, is little open to question; this English sailor penetrated some part of the interior on a remarkable walking trip.

Curiously, it was another epic walk, this time by three Spaniards and a Negro slave, which began the exploration of inland America and greatly stimulated its continuance. Cabeza de Vaca had planned not to walk but to ride horseback, and to move into the interior with a large band of armed men. A native of Jéréz de la Frontera, he had set sail from Spain in June 1527, as treasurer of the expedition commanded by Pánfilo de Narváez, who had received a royal grant to conquer and colonize the country between Rio de las Palmas in eastern Mexico and the Cape of Florida. To the Spaniards seated in the West Indies, Florida seemed the natural entrance to the unknown land to the north. Ponce de León and Ayllón had both made brief, impermanent forays on the coast, and other ships had touched and even been wrecked there. In April 1528, Narváez landed near Tampa Bay on the west coast of the Florida peninsula with three hundred men[5]. Hearing of much gold in a province called Apalachen, Narváez wanted to march there, leaving the ships to follow along the coast to a good port somewhere ahead to the west. Despite de Vaca's pleas that the ships be left only in a known, safe port, Narváez prevailed and 'ordered to each man going with him two

103
Stalks of maize or American corn, from Rembert Dodoens' *Frumentorum, leguminum . . .*, Antwerp, 1566.
104
'The apples of love' (the tomato plant) from John Gerard, *The Herball or generall historie of plantes,* London, 1633.

pounds of biscuit and a half a pound of bacon; and thus victualled we took up our march into the country'.[6] They never saw the ships again.

Marching northward, Narváez and his company encountered bitter hardships of starvation, sickness, Indian hostility, and difficult terrain. Crossing the Suwannee, they found in the Apalachen region of the north Florida lake country only little maize and less wealth. They struggled on to Aute, near the head of St Mark's Bay; no ships were there and, except for a few oysters, no prospect of food. Narváez, as foolishly optimistic about sea travel as he had been about the wilderness, persuaded them to build a fleet in which to escape to Mexico. Although constructed with an extraordinary display of ingenuity, the overcrowded boats were unseaworthy; after passing the mouth of the Mississippi, where the fresh water drove them out to sea, they were wrecked one by one along the unknown coast. Finally that captained by Cabeza de Vaca was cast up on Malhado, or Misfortune Island, somewhere on the Texas coast. As de Vaca says, 'The Indians, at sight of what had befallen us, and from the sorrow and pity they felt,

they all began to lament so earnestly that they might have been heard at a distance . . . It was strange to see these men, wild and untaught, howling like brutes over our misfortunes.'[7] Many of the Spaniards drowned or died from the harsh treatment of the Indians, who made them slaves. For years de Vaca endured incredible hardships, grubbing up edible roots from under the water for his Indian masters. Finally, he made connection with three of his shipmates, Castillo, Dorantes, and Estevan, Dorantes's Negro slave, and they managed to escape from their masters. De Vaca's principle was to move parallel to the coast and then westward; he refused to go north, even though the Indians told him of treasure there. After a rough beginning his relations with the natives changed completely. He became a much sought-after trader and a deeply reverenced healer, whose prayers over the sick and simple remedies were almost miraculously efficacious. Later explorers picked up his traces on the edge of the great plains, along the Rio Grande below El Paso, and in Sonora, northern Mexico.[8] The little group was passed from tribe to tribe until the day in 1536 when, after eight years of wandering, they suddenly appeared to a party of slave hunters near the Pacific coast sent out by Guzmán, the cruel Governor of New Galicia, the most northerly province of New Spain. 'They stood staring at me a length of time, so confounded that they neither hailed me nor drew near to make an inquiry'.[9] De Vaca found a sympathetic ear when he was taken to the Viceroy of New Spain. Mendoza, like him, while eager to explore the possibility of conquest to the north, wanted to serve the Indians with far more humane treatment than that so far accorded them by the Spaniards.

De Vaca had seen great rivers, plains, and mountains but no treasure except a few turquoises and a copper bell; nor did he say he had. He never disguised the privations he had undergone nor the poverty of the land or Indians. He did, however, state that he had heard of strong, well-built cities to the north of where he had been, and after his return to Spain was given to suggesting sagely that he knew of matters which he could disclose only to the king.[10] This small spark, coupled with another from an Indian who had told Guzmán that he had been taken as a child to treasure cities in the north, was enough to ignite the already smoldering ambitions of the Spaniards, and to help launch four more expeditions of discovery into North America: those of de Soto, Fray Marcos de Nizza, Coronado, and Alarcón.

The second Spanish expedition into inland North America, like that of Narváez, landed near Tampa Bay to attempt the conquest of Florida; its discoveries, however, were wider than those of Narváez, including parts of present Florida, Georgia, North and South Carolina, Tennessee, Alabama, Mississippi, Arkansas, Texas, and Oklahoma.[11] Its leader, Hernando de Soto, son of an esquire of Estremadura, had accompanied Pizarro in the conquest of Peru, where he may well have sharpened both his brilliance and his cruelty.[12] At the Spanish court, he put on a great show of elegance, and won from the Emperor his title: Governor of the Island of Cuba and Adelantado of Florida. The Gentleman of Elvas, one of the Portuguese who joined the expedition and later became its best chronicler, reported that, at the first muster, the Castilians turned out 'very showily, in silk over silk, pinked and slashed'[13]; de Soto sent them back to find their suits of mail, many of which turned out to be 'very sorry and rusty'. In April 1538, the five ships set sail. In Cuba, de Soto left his wife Doña Ysabel, a governor's daughter, to rule the island. In May 1539, now with nine vessels, he landed at or near Tampa Bay.[14] This Mendoza, the Viceroy, viewed with alarm, since Florida had no bounds, and might, for aught he knew, furnish an approach to those mysterious cities and treasure lands somewhere to the north, on which he also had designs. Quietly he despatched his own expeditions; but de Soto, buried in the wilderness, knew nothing of them, at least for many months.

There are four early accounts of the de Soto expedition: the diary of the Gentleman of Elvas, the factual accounts of Biedma the factor and Ranjel the secretary, and the flowery one of Garcilaso the Inca, written later from tales.[15] In all is revealed the character of the leader: intrepid, resourceful, ruthless, cruel to the Indians, and relentlessly determined to find treasure or perish in the attempt, as he did. From every source also comes the impression of the extraordinary nature of the

106
Hernando de Soto, from A. Herrera y Tordesillas, *Historia General*, Madrid, 1728–30.

troupe for wilderness travel. Compared with the lightfooted Indian and later forest scout in his moccasins and portable canoe, the sheer weight of the Spaniards appals: hundreds of men in plumes, banners, and heavy coats of mail; horses plunging through the dense underbrush; bearer Indians weighted not only with the baggage and their sorrows, but with chains; and, above all, the squealing recalcitrant food supply. Determined that his men should not starve, de Soto had brought along thirteen hogs, and bred them till the drove increased to several hundred. All these, so laden, marched, rode, rooted, or swam on this amazing journey.

Early Spanish writers are not much given to detailed description of the land. Nevertheless, it is in all their accounts, wild, difficult, baffling. Any report of treasure turned de Soto in a new direction, whatever the terrain. It was said that in Cale, 'toward the sunset', the people wore golden hats, and so the march veered west. However, de Soto planned far more shrewdly than had Narváez. On the way to Apalachen, and by a route along which he knew he could obtain food, he had the luck to pick up Ortiz, a Narváez survivor, now an excellent interpreter to the Indians. From Aute, where lay the skulls of Narváez' horses, de Soto sent his fleet back to Cuba for supplies, and instructed it to meet him at Ochus, or Pensacola Bay. He then pressed north and east to Cutifachiqui (near Silver Bluff on the Savannah River), of whose lady *cacique* or chief and prosperity he had heard.[16] He found some pearls, and traces of Ayllón, whose Atlantic settlement had been near.[17] All wished to establish a colony here, except the Governor, who had heard of mountains and possible gold to the north. Northward they went, across the 'very rough and lofty ridges' of the lower Appalachians, through forests and across rivers. The mountains appeared to them to run east and west, and were so drawn on later maps. De Soto alternatively captured, cajoled and kidnapped the Indians; he took along the *cacica*, but she gave him the slip in a forest. Turning west, they found fertility and food again in Chiaha and Coça, northern Alabama.[18] They fought a terrible battle at Mavilla in present Clarke County, Alabama, with heavy loss. Then de Soto learned that his ships were at Ochus, six days' journey south. Yet that granite spirit refused even to send word to them. He had no gold; he had lost his pearls at Mavilla; they would go on!

West again and north, toward the country hinted at by de Vaca, moved the cavalcade. Fighting again at Chicaça, they came at last to the banks of a huge river. The Mississippi appeared in its majesty. De Soto crossed in piraguas (dug-out canoes), played tribe against tribe, set up huge crosses in the cowed Indian villages, told them he was the Child of the Sun. He worked west, through swamps and 'a huge, pathless

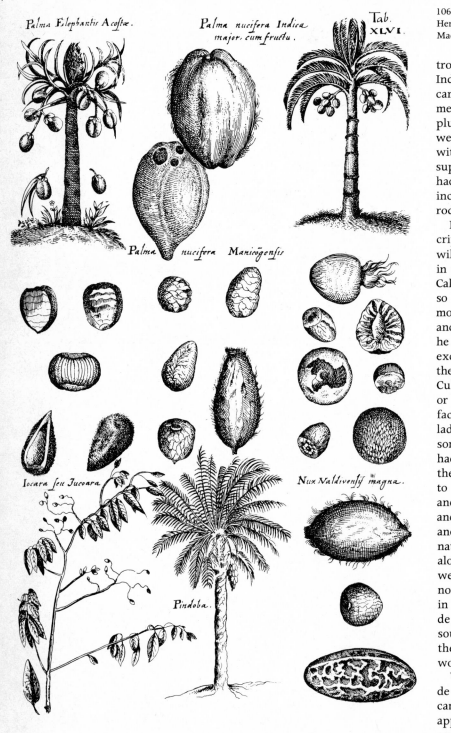

Palma Elephantis Acostæ.
Palma nucifera Indica major, cum fructu.
Tab. XLVI.
Palma nucifera Maniöogensis
Iocara seu Jucoara
Nux Naldivensis magna.
Pindoba.

105
Types of American palm trees and their nuts, from J. T. de Bry, *Florilegium renovatum et auctum*, Frankfurt, 1641, plate XLVI.

thicket' to Arkansas, where he heard of, though did not see, the buffalo plains which Coronado was discovering from the west. Forced to turn south, he wintered at Autiamque, near the Mississippi again. As the Gentleman of Elvas said simply: 'Three years had elapsed since he [de Soto] had been heard of by Doña Ysabel, or any person in a civilized community. Two hundred and fifty of his men were dead, likewise one hundred and fifty horses.'[19] De Soto was tired. In Guachoya, close to the river, he gave way to depression, made a great repentant speech, and died. Since it could not be admitted to the Indians that this had befallen the Child of the Sun, they weighted his body and cast it into the Mississippi in the dead of night.

Moscoso, his successor, was faced with a terrible dilemma. Should they push west, and attempt to reach New Spain by the painful route of de Vaca, or build a fleet and try the unknown river? This seemed the more terrifying. Says the Gentleman of Elvas, 'Nor was there captain nor pilot, needle nor chart, nor was it known how distant might be the sea . . . or if the river did not take some great turn through the land, or might have some fall over rocks where they might be lost. Some, who had seen the sea-card, found that by the shore,

from the place where they were to New Spain, there should be about 500 leagues.'[20] What 'sea-card' this was is unknown. So they went west, finding wilderness, 'great heats', no news of Spaniards ahead, a few turquoises and cotton blankets, and not much food save de Vaca's prickly pears (see page 118). Back to the Mississippi, they adopted the second desperate alternative. They must have built better boats than Narváez, because on 10 September 1543, 311 weary Spaniards, clothed largely in deerskins, landed at Panuco in northern Mexico, to the amazement of the Viceroy Mendoza, who had long supposed them all dead.

In the meantime, Mendoza, spurred on by rumors of the Seven Cities, had not been idle. In 1539, within a few months

108

107
Various types of cacti, from J. T. de Bry, *Florilegium renovatum et auctum*, Frankfurt, 1641, plate LXXX.
108
De Soto's cruelties in Florida, from T. de Bry, *America*, Part V, 1595, plate XVII.

107

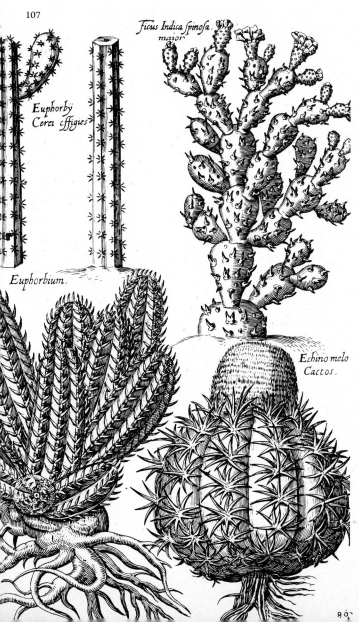

Ficus Indica spinosa.
major

Euphorbÿ
Cerei effigies

Euphorbium.

Echino melo
Cactos.

of de Soto's landing in Florida, he had sent a small expedition north in preparation for a large-scale attempt at discovery and colonization under Coronado. He thought it prudent to check the hints of de Vaca concerning great cities, and chose for this an enterprising friar and explorer named Fray Marcos de Nizza, who had been born in France, campaigned in Peru, and walked barefoot from lower Central America to Mexico.[21] He had been trained in theology, cosmography, and the arts of the sea. With him on this reconnaissance Mendoza sent the sole member of de Vaca's company who could be persuaded, or forced, to go: Estevån, the Negro slave whom he had purchased from Dorantes. He also sent along a supporting company of Indians. The story is dramatic. Estevån, greatly enjoying his new status, was supremely confident in his ability to deal with the Indians. From Sonora, northern Mexico, Fray Marcos sent him on ahead with a few Indians, perhaps not liking the way he collected Indian women. His instructions were to send back a cross if he made a discovery, and a larger cross if it was an important discovery. Larger and larger crosses appeared each day, with Indians who assured the friar that the Seven Cities were just beyond the wilderness, with houses four stories high, turquoise decorations, finely clothed people, and greater cities beyond. Fray Marcos, pushing through the mountains of Arizona, sent Estevån word to wait at the edge of the 'wilderness'; but Estevan was in his glory. Bedecked with turquoises and feathers, lording it over his troupe and his traveling harem, he approached the Seven Cities, the Zuñi pueblos, which were indeed many stories high and under one lord.[22] To the first of these, Hawikuh, he sent his medicine man's rattle which, in the south, had always brought reverence. It was a fatal gesture, for these tribes were mortal enemies of the tribe from which the gourd came. Furthermore, it seemed illogical to the pueblo chief that a black man should claim to represent white conquerors. Estevan was confined to a hut outside the city, and when he tried to escape, the Indians pursued and killed him. Frightened fugitive Indians met Fray Marcos with the news. All he could

109
Map of the Californian area by Castillo, from Hernando Cortés, *Historia de Nueva Espagna*, Mexico, 1770.
Castillo, maker of this map, was a pilot on the expedition of Alarcón, which explored the coasts and the head of the Gulf of California in 1540–2, while Coronado penetrated the interior. They sailed twice up the Colorado River, hearing from Indians of Coronado's arrival at Cibola, shown here as the City of Cibora. Their explorations made it clear that California was a peninsula, not an island. The original of this map is now lost; it is known only by this copy, on which the name 'California' may have been added.

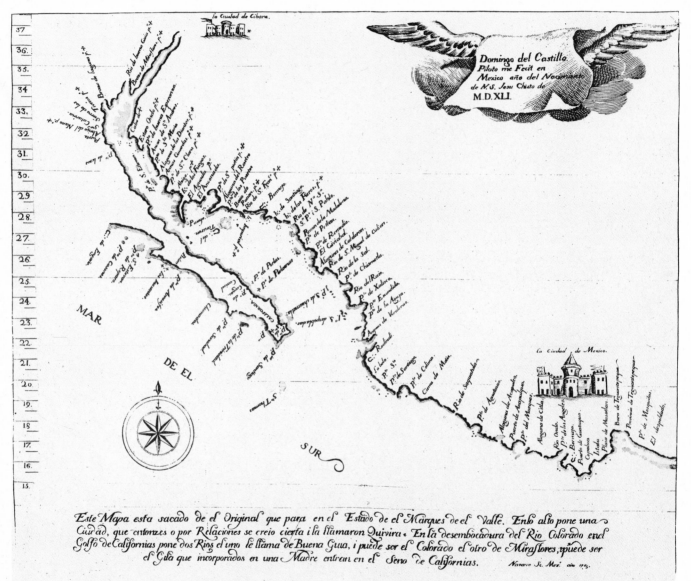

persuade his companions to do was to go with him to a hill, from the top of which he could descry from afar the many-tiered pueblo. Then he turned in his tracks and raced for Mexico.

A great controversy has ensued as to whether or not Fray Marcos told the truth on his return.[23] 'Seven Cities,' he said; there were indeed seven Zuñi pueblos. 'Built of stone'; or at least mortar. 'Many storied'; indisputable to anyone, then or now, who has tried to climb the ladders from terrace to terrace. 'Turquoises' and 'blankets made of cotton'; these were there. And if he did say that Cibola looked to him bigger than Mexico City, he did not say it was. It seems hard that the good friar was blamed because the imaginations of the eager inhabitants of New Spain seized on these facts and blew them up into a dream of a rich civilization. It is possible that the rumors reached de Soto by way of his ships awaiting him at Ochus and accounted for his continuing westward push.[24]

In Mexico Mendoza continued his elaborate preparations. He gave strict instructions that every effort was to be made to win the Indians by peaceful methods. Melchior Díaz was sent ahead to scout but failed to reach Cibola. He returned disillusioned; his report was suppressed. Alarcón went by sea to sail up the Gulf of California or Mar Verméjo; he made no contact with the main expedition but entered the Colorado River twice and was probably the first European to set foot in modern California.[25] Mendoza mustered an immense force at Compostela which he put under the command of Francisco Vásquez de Coronado, the vigorous young Governor of New Galicia. There were 250 Spaniards on horseback with banners; 300 Indians; possibly as many as a thousand servants, many with crossbows; every sort of artisan; and many friars.[26] Coronado moved northward ahead of his great force, eager for the first sight of the Seven Cities of Cibola. Past the red adobe of Chichilticale, across the Arizona 'wilderness'; at last they were there! Their reaction can best be expressed in their own words. 'It is a little, cramped village, looking as if it had been all crumpled up together . . . when they saw it, such were the curses that some hurled at Friar Marcos that I pray God may protect him from them.'[27]

The shock of disappointment in the failure to find rich mines and treasure, the many hardships encountered, and the dissensions and mutinies which made the planting of a lasting settlement impossible continued to haunt the Coronado expedition long after the last soldier straggled back to New Spain. Some of its members, however, were not altogether blind to the fascination and tremendous possibilities of the vast new land which they had entered for the first time. Castañeda, who wrote his absorbing chronicle of it twenty years later, mourned over how much more men value explorations afterwards than when making them. He felt that they should not have abandoned their discovery; it was 'the marrow of the land in these western parts'.[28] They had moved east from Cibola to find the pueblos of Tiguex along the Rio Grande, which they thought quite probably rose in Asia.[29] They had seen Acoma,[30] the amazing pueblo on a huge rock. They had penetrated a great range of mountains and encountered snow and bitter cold. A band under Cardeñas had gazed into the Grand Canyon, which seemed to them only a horrendous barrier to their progress.[31] They had fought fierce wars with the Indians but also had some peaceful dealings with them; they had learned much about the customs, food, crafts, and beliefs of the pueblo dwellers.

Another will-of-the-wisp had led them to discover an absolutely different part of this astonishing country. This was the tales of the Turk, an Indian slave who, it later transpired, had been bribed to lead them away from people longing to be rid of their conquerors, by stories of the kingdom of Quivira. There, he said, 'was a river . . . two leagues wide, in which there were fishes as big as horses, and large numbers of very big canoes, with more than twenty rowers on a side, and that they carried sails, and that their lords sat on the poop under awnings, and on the prow they had a great golden eagle.'[32] Coronado with a small force accompanied the Turk to Cicuye (modern Pecos) and thence out onto the boundless plains, where they encountered tremendous herds of bison and also nomad Indians, the Apaches and Tejas. After terrible wanderings first east and then north, they reached Quivira, a pleasant, fertile region in the present state of Kansas; but it was furnished

110

North America by Bolognino Zaltieri, Venice, 1566.

An Italian map, by Zaltieri of Bologna. This map is, according to the title, 'a draught of the discovery of New France, made lately from the most recent voyages of the French to that place'. Its chief importance, however, is that it is the first printed map to name the narrow body of water between Asia and North America the Strait of Anian.

CIRCVLVS ARCTICVS:

POLVS MVNDI ARCTICVS:

TIERA DE LLABRAD

TIERA NOVA:
DE CORTEREAL

TIERA DE ESTEVA GOMEZ

TIERA DE AYLLON:

TIERA DE GARAY

TROPICVS CANCRI

CANCER

TAVRVS

MAIVS

IVLIVS

VIRGO

SEPTEMBER

NVEVA ESPAÑA

LINEA EQVINOCTIALIS

GVATIMALA

MAR DEL SVR:

CASTILLA DELORO

OCCEANVS OCCIDENTALIS:

PERV

PISCES

IANVARIVS

NOVEMBER

SCORPIVS

CAPRICORN

MVNDVS
NOWS

TERA BRASILIS:

TROPICVS CAPRICORNI:

TIERA DE SOLIS

TIERA DE PATA
GONES:

CIRCVLVS ATARCTICVS:

POLVS MVNDI ATARCTICVS:

115

to have reached 44° latitude, which would put them north of the southern border of present Oregon. Both ships managed to return to Navidad in Mexico in April 1543, after a year of navigating the entire coast of California.[39]

Justice cannot be done to the role of the friars in a brief treatment of the Spanish invasion of new territory. Seeking souls, they often led the way with amazing courage and endurance, often possessed skill in navigation and cosmography, and, more often than not, lost their lives by remaining alone among their unpredictable and half-hostile Indian converts. Such missionaries were Fray Rodríguez, Fray López, and Fray Santa María, who set out in 1581 to find again the pueblo Indians,[40] unforgotten since the return of Coronado. Mendoza had long since ceased to be the Viceroy, who was now the Count of Coruña; he gave them permission to go, with nine soldiers under Chamuscado, and sixteen Indian servants. They started from Santa Barbara, the new northernmost mining town, and followed a new route, down the Conchos River and up the Rio Grande. Several of the soldiers made declarations upon return. They said they found Indians in cotton garments along the lower river, living in 'rancherías'; that they passed through an uninhabited section, and then came to a region of large, terraced peublos. Fray Santa María, attempting to return, was killed by Maguas. The others reached Puaray, the central pueblo of Coronado's Tiguex, where his harshness was remembered. They visited the salt mines, the buffalo plains, Acoma and Zuñi. Fray Rodríguez and Fray López remained at Puaray with a few servants; the soldiers returned. Later, one of them, Barrado, told the Viceroy that he had met in Mexico one of the Indians left with the friars. The Indian said that the people of Puaray had killed Fray López; frightened, he had run away, and hearing a commotion behind him, had concluded that they had murdered Fray Rodríguez also.

Before this news arrived, however, another expedition had set out to support or rescue the missionaries.[41] Fray Beltrán, a Franciscan, was anxious to go to the help of his companions; to his aid came Antonio de Espéjo, a wealthy citizen who volunteered to go and pay expenses. They took some fifteen soldiers, a number of servants, and at least one soldier's family, named Valenciano, consisting of a wife and children aged three and a half and twenty months. Espéjo wrote a lively account upon his return. The Jumanos, on the lower Rio Grande, remembered de Vaca. At Puaray they learned of the murder of the friars, but both Fray Beltrán and Espéjo were

determined on further exploration. They visited the Maguas, the pueblo of Sia, 'very large . . . had eight plazas, and better houses . . . whitewashed, and painted with colors and pictures';[42] Acoma, where they were impressed with the dancing and the irrigation; and Cibola, or Zuñi. Here Fray Beltrán and some of the party turned back, among whom were understandably the Valencianos. Espéjo had heard, however, both from the Jumanos and in Cibola, of a very large lake to the west, where people wore rich ornaments of gold. Either the Indians were following their frequently used ruse to get rid of the Spaniards, or they were speaking of the Gulf of California;[43] but this non-existent Lake of Gold appeared on maps for years, and influenced the final colonizing expedition under Oñate. Espéjo did not find his lake, but did visit the turquoise mines in the Arizona mountains. He made friends with the New Mexican Indians who had been so frightened by Spaniards; in Moqui he was given 4,000 cotton blankets. He went to the buffalo plains, and, guided by the Jumanos, took a new route south from there back to the Conchos River and Santa Barbara.[44] Espéjo wrote the Viceroy, 'I shall not be satisfied till I reach the coasts of the North and South Seas'.[45] Viceroy and king were immensely interested; but it was fourteen years later that the great colonizing expedition was launched.

In the meantime, the Pacific coast was being reached from another direction. A Spanish fleet under Villalobos, sent by Mendoza, had landed in the Philippines in 1542 and taken possession, while Cabrillo was exploring the California coast. In 1565, Legazpi subdued the islands. Trade was established with an annual Manila galleon; but the return voyage to Mexico proved extremely difficult because of prevailing winds and currents. Urdaneta finally worked out the best plan, and Arellano first carried it out: to sail north and east, strike the California coast somewhere about Cape Mendocino, and come down it to the home ports.[46] To the desire to find the Strait of Anian and forestall the English was now added the need for a harbor refuge for the returning Manila galleon. Several made landings. Francisco Gali was sure that he had been in the mouth of the Strait of Anian.[47] Pedro de Unamuno described vividly his landing at Morro Bay in 1587.[48] On his way home, he was warned of 'the English Corsair', who was Cavendish, loose along the South and Central American coasts. In 1595, Sebastian Cermeño landed and traded in the present Drake's Bay, which he called San Francisco Bay, ran his ship, the *San Agustín,* aground there, losing his food, and managed to reach Mexico, starving, in the ship's launch.[49]

Cermeño may not have been first to have used Drake's Bay as an anchorage, nor was Cavendish the only English corsair to have visited Pacific coasts. In 1578–9 Sir Francis Drake, in the *Golden Hind,* had made an epic voyage which was part of the stirring of serious English interest in the New World. To quote Henry Wagner: 'About the middle of the sixteenth century it began to dawn on them [the English] that they were being left out in the cold. They were in the position of a hungry man on a sidewalk looking through a window at two gentlemen seated at a banquet table within. A Spaniard seemed to have on his side all that part of the world where the precious metals were to be found and a Portuguese opposite, the other part where spices were produced.'[50] One result of this realization was the efforts of Frobisher and Hudson to find the North-west Passage. Another was Ralegh's colonizing attempts on Roanoke Island. A third was what was called in one account of it, 'The World Encompass'd, by Sir Francis Drake'.

The primary object of Drake's voyage was the opening of trade routes; exploration and plunder were secondary.[51] With

116
Map of North America and the West Indies from the atlas of Jean Rotz, 1542. *London, British Museum, Royal 20.E.IX, fos 23v and 24r.*
The first picture of an Indian wigwam appears on this map, which is found in a handsome atlas made for Henry VIII by Jean Rotz (John Roze), a Frenchman of Scots descent. The atlas was completed in 1542 but the information on this map was compiled earlier; it shows the discoveries of Cartier in the Gulf of St Lawrence in 1534, but not those of his 1535 voyage up the river. Newfoundland itself is made up of numerous islands, not a Cartier concept; the entire coastline and the names along it are based on some Spanish map. Off the coast at the bottom is the interesting note, 'The new fonde londe quhar men goeth a fisching'; for over thirty years vessels from European ports had been visiting the Great Banks regularly.

117 *Overleaf*
Pacific section of Christian Sgrooten's world map, from his manuscript atlas, 1592. *Madrid, Biblioteca Nacional, fo 2.B.1.*
On this part of Sgrooten's world map the north-west coast of America is clearly separated from Asia by an arctic waterway, and also the North-west Passage across the continent is shown. Anian is not a strait but a kingdom on the mainland north of Quivira. Tiguex is also on the coast; 'Cevola' is inland on the Colorado River. For Japan, Sgrooten may have used details from a Jesuit map.

his small fleet, and several captured additions, he rounded South America through Magellan's Strait and moved up the west coast. At Guatulco he decided to go north instead of west to the Philippines. He sailed to approximately 42°, and coasted south, looking for a sheltered harbor where he might repair his vessel. This he found at about 38°, made landfall, and careened his ship. According to the account in 'The Famous Voyage of Sir Francis Drake', included by Hakluyt in his *Principall navigations* of 1589, Drake's relations with the Indians were happy and they asked him to be their king. He took possession in the name of Queen Elizabeth, named the country New Albion, and left there an inscribed brass plate, which is lately believed to have been found.[52] Much recent

archaeological, ethnological, and cartographical research has been expended on the question of the exact place of Drake's landing. Because of Indian words quoted by him, and other evidence, it is agreed that he was among the Miwoks, and not, as Wagner contended, at Trinidad Bay, which is in Yurok territory. But whether his cove was on the shore of Drake's Estero, which opens into what is now called Drake's Bay, ringed by the white cliffs which looked like home and inspired his name of New Albion, or whether he actually sailed the *Golden Hind* through the Golden Gate, and anchored by the Tiburon Peninsula on the shore of northern San Francisco Bay, is a matter of fierce dispute.[53] Both sites claim a likeness to Drake's *Portus* in the inset on the Hondius (1590) map (plate

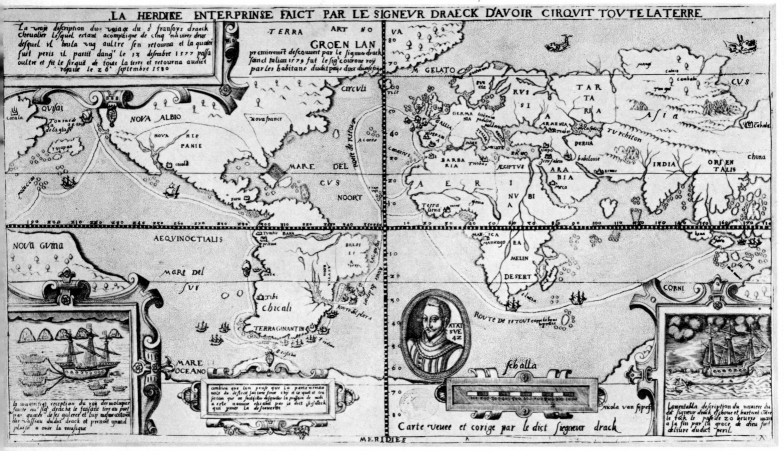

118

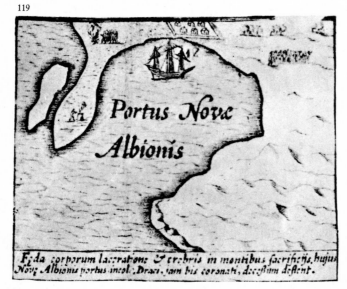

119

118
Map of Drake's circumnavigation of the globe by Nicola van Sijpe, *c.* 1589. *London, British Museum.*
Sir Francis Drake's circumnavigation is portrayed on this contemporary world map, with legends in French. A note at the bottom states that the chart has been seen and corrected by the said 'Siegneur drack'.
119
Drake's anchorage, from the Hondius world map, *c.* 1590. *London, British Museum.*
This inset on the map by Jodocus Hondius, 'Vera totius expeditionis nautica' ('The Broadside Map'), purports to be a map of the bay on the California coast where in 1578 Drake careened his ship, *The Golden Hind,* established his New Albion, and left the plate of brass announcing his claim. It has caused more controversy than its dubious accuracy warrants. Chief among modern contenders to be the place are a cove near the mouth of Drake's Estero, off Drake's Bay, just north of the Golden Gate, and another within San Francisco Bay.
120
Thomas Cavendish from H. Holland, *Herwologia*, London, 1620.
121
Sir Francis Drake; engraving (first state) attributed to Jodocus Hondius.

112

120

121

122

122

Map of North America by Henry Briggs, published in *Hakluytus Posthumus or Purchas his Pilgrimes*, London, 1625.

This detail from the Briggs map of 1625 shows the erroneous conception of California as an island which he did much to popularize. Chiefly responsible for this error was Father Antonio Ascensión, who accompanied Vizcaino on his exploration of the Pacific coast in 1602. He proclaimed in 1620 that California was an island on the basis of a north-east turn of the coast above Cape Mendocino which they thought they saw, Oñate's doubts about the head of the Gulf of California, and the reports of Juan de la Fuca and Martin d'Aguilar. Although Father Kino refuted this on the basis of exploration in 1698, the misconception remained on maps well into the eighteenth century. Finally, in 1747, Ferdinand VII stated in a royal decree, 'California is not an Island'.

119); Indian mounds marking the sites of villages and hills answering Drake's description surround both; and unfortunately there are two claimants and two locations for the first finding of the brass plate. Wherever they were, Drake and his men were much refreshed by their brief stay; they sailed off to the Philippines and the rest of their remarkable circumnavigation.

Spurred on by Drake, the Spanish now made a concerted effort to explore and colonize both the western coast and the interior of New Mexico. Vizcaino, who captained the coast voyage, was a Basque, and a trader between Mexico and the East, who had once explored the Gulf of California. In 1602, he was sent with three ships, by royal order, up the outer coast. His instructions[54] were to seek a port for the galleons; not to go inland; not to change Cabrillo's names, which he nonetheless did; to sail to Cape Mendocino, and, if the wind allowed, to Cape Blanco at 44°. If the land turned westward toward Asia between these points he was to follow it for one hundred leagues. His captain was Gómez, his cosmographer Palacios, who was to make maps, and who did chart the coast in detail. Three Carmelite friars went also, one of whom, Fray Ascensión, was himself a cosmographer. In his account of the voyage, he asserted that another object was to look for a river, perhaps entering the northern strait, which would lead to the city of Quivira.

It was already November when they reached San Diego Bay, but they pressed north into the winter. The north-west wind, which Fray Ascensión called 'the king and absolute master of this sea and coast',[55] often drove the ships apart. Their sufferings from scurvy were terrible. Nevertheless, they discovered a beautiful, protected, hitherto unknown bay which they named Monterey for the current Viceroy. Here they sent back one ship, laden with sick, to announce the finding of the port for the Manila galleon and request supplies; the other two sailed bravely on northwards. Again they were separated by hostile snow and storm. The larger ship, the *San Diego*, anchored in Drake's Bay, was driven north to 43° where they saw 'a cape of white earth close to some high sierras covered with snow',[56] and made her way down the coast with scarcely a man strong enough to man the sails. The fruit of the agave caused a cure as miraculously quick as that of Cartier's men in Canada.

The little fragata, the *Tres Reyes*, was driven even farther north. Somewhere about Cabo Blanco, the pilot died; the boatswain said in his later declaration that in that region the coast ran north-east, and near Cape Mendocino they found a bay and a great river coming in from the east. This was thought to connect with the Strait of Anian. Fray Ascensión, writing in 1620, made a great deal of the word *north-east* concerning the coast, and of Palacios's chart of this.[57] Using the suggestion of Oñate, who went down the Colorado to the head of the Gulf of California, that beyond the river entrance the gulf turned west and north, he vigorously proclaimed that the gulf, or Mediterranean Sea of California, joined the Strait to the north, and that California was an island. The Briggs map (plate 122) and others perpetuated this notion for some time. Therefore this brave voyage of exploration ended in the creation of a great geographical error. Vizcaino, however, concentrated on urging the colonization of Monterey. This project was abandoned by a new Viceroy, who thought it unwise to draw the attention of other nations to that coast.[58]

Meanwhile, along the mighty Rio del Norte, the Rio Grande, with the northern mystery still luring them on, a settlement was finally made by the Spanish in the interior of western North America, second only to St Augustine in point of time. The New Mexico of Coronado had been almost forgotten; but after the discoveries of Espéjo in 1582 came a resurgence of interest. Many candidates applied for royal permission to conquer and colonize; two groups started off without it.[59] Sosa, with a company of 170, got to Taos before he was arrested and brought back. Humaña, also unauthorized, in 1593 actually reached the Arkansas River in Kansas and advanced as far north as the River Platte in Nebraska. However, Humaña murdered his partner Leyba, and the greater part of the group was in turn slaughtered by the Indians. The Council of the Indies was seeking a leader who would undertake colonization without cost to them and who would abide as far as possible by the new policy toward the Indians. The friars had pleaded for them, the outside world had criticized Spanish cruelty, and the new laws forbade enslavement and oppressive military conquest of new territories.

In 1595 the contract was awarded to Don Juan de Oñate, wealthy citizen of Zacatecas. His wife was a granddaughter of Cortés and a great-granddaughter of Montezuma! In the contract, Oñate proposed to provide '1000 cattle, 3000 sheep, 1000 rams, 1000 goats, 100 black cattle, 150 colts, 150 mares',[60] and much more. Because the Viceroy was now Monterey, who viewed with alarm Oñate's new governorship, obstacles were raised and the expedition did not start till 1598. They were now able to take a more direct route than that of the Conchos River to the Rio Grande. Here, near El Paso, the ford, a tremendous scene took place.[61] There was a sermon and a great religious and secular celebration. A comedy by Farfán was presented, and the royal standard was blessed. All the young noble officers like Oñate's nephews the Zaldivars had their banners too. One member of the expedition was Gaspar de Villagrá, already beginning to compose the epic poem which he published in Spain in 1610, and which is not only a glowing

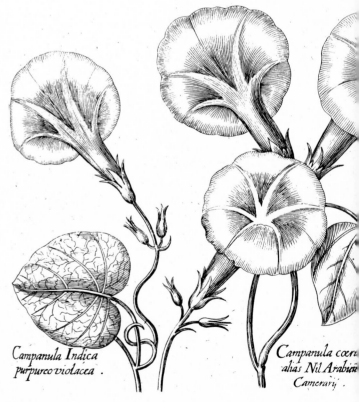

Campanula Indica purpureo violacea .

Campanula cœru alias Nil Arabicū Camerarij .

123

Morning glory or *Convolvulus*, from J. T. de Bry, *Florilegium renovatum et auctum,* Frankfurt, 1641.

but a reliable account of events. After this, 400 men, 130
families, 83 carts, and 7000 cattle began the ascent of the
Rio Grande, often through dense forest.

Oñate established his first capital, called San Juan de los
Caballeros, on the east bank, north of present Bernalillo.
He later moved it to San Gabriel on the west bank. With
exceptions, the Indians accepted them peacefully. Churches
were built, and the pueblos divided among the friars. A great
deal was learned about the culture of the pueblo Indians,
though not enough to prevent instances of over demand and
harassment. Such a misunderstanding caused the killing of one
Zaldivar at Acoma, and the terrible laying waste of that
mountain-top pueblo in revenge. Oñate sent his young captains
out to follow Coronado's exploration routes and find new ones.
Another Zaldivar went to the buffalo plains. Farfán pushed
north-west to the mines. Oñate himself visited the salt mines,
reached the Quivira region by way of the Canadian and
Arkansas Rivers, and traveled down the Colorado River to the
Gulf. Discontent among colonists and Indians, however, piled
up while he was away. Finally, in 1608, Oñate resigned as
governor, returning to face trial in Mexico on charges
including his fierce punishment of Acoma. How could the
Spanish maintain such a distant colony? Yet how could they
desert their baptized Indian converts? In 1609, it was decided
to maintain a royal colony and a mission field, but not to
extend it by conquest. The next year, Peralta moved the capital
to Santa Fé,[62] which since then has been continuously occupied.
In 1620, when the Pilgrims landed in Massachusetts, Santa Fé
was 'a villa of fifty residents'; sixteen friars were in the
province. Today, many people of the region are of Spanish
blood, an ethnically distinct group.

The Spanish never developed a viable colonial policy in
North America. It was, however, their courage, their curiosity,
their zeal for the faith, as well as their greed for wealth and
their fear of outsiders, to which we owe the discovery and
penetration of the mountains, the vast plains, and the
intractable western coast of the country.

124
A scene from the Spanish conquest of the New World from T. de Bry,
America, Part VI, 1596.

1.

The Narváez expedition and Cabeza de Vaca's journey from Florida to Mexico, 1528–36

From *Relacion* by Nuñez Cabeça de Vaca, Zamora, 1542.

The ill-organized expedition of Pánfilo de Narváez, which had landed at Tampa Bay on the west coast of Florida in April 1528, was reduced to starvation and despair when they reached Aute (St Mark's Bay) and could not find their ships. Cabeza de Vaca, the treasurer, describes their attempt to escape from 'a country so remote and malign, so destitute of all resource, whereby either to live in it or go out of it'.

We coincided in one great project extremely difficult to put in operation, and that was to build vessels in which we might go away. This appeared impossible to every one; we knew not how to construct, nor were there tools, nor iron, nor forge, nor tow, nor resin, nor rigging; finally, no one thing of so many that are necessary, nor any man who had a knowledge of their manufacture; and, above all, there was nothing to eat, while building, for those who should labor.

The next day it was His will that one of the company should come saying that he could make some pipes out of wood, which with deer-skins might be made into bellows; and, as we lived in a time when anything that had the semblance of relief appeared well, we told him to set himself to work. We assented to the making of nails, saws, axes, and other tools of which there was such need, from the stirrups, spurs, crossbows, and the other things of iron there were. We caused many palmitos [small palms with fan-like leaves] to be collected for the woof or covering, twisting and preparing it for use in the place of tow for the boats.

We commenced to build on the fourth, with the only carpenter in the company, and we proceeded with so great diligence that on the twentieth day of September five boats were finished, twenty-two cubits in length, each caulked with the fibre of the palmito. We pitched them with a certain resin, made from pine trees by a Greek, named Don Theodoro; from the same husk of the palmito, and from the tails and manes of the horses we made ropes and rigging, from our shirts, sails, and from the savins growing there we made the oars that appeared to us requisite. Such was the country into which our sins had cast us, that only by very great search could we find stone for ballast and anchors, since in it all we had not seen one. We flayed the horses, taking the skin from their legs entire, and tanning them to make bottles wherein to carry water.

During this time some went gathering shell-fish in the coves and creeks of the sea, at which employment the Indians twice attacked them and killed ten men in sight of the camp, without our being able to afford succor. We found their corpses traversed from side to side with arrows; and for all some had on good armor, it did not give adequate protection or security against the nice and powerful archery of which I have spoken.

Before we embarked there died more than forty men of disease and hunger, without enumerating those destroyed by the Indians. By the twenty-second of the month of September, the horses had been consumed, one only remaining. After the provisions and clothes had been taken in, not over a span of the gunwales remained above water; and more than this, the boats were so crowded that we could not move: so much can necessity do, which drove us to hazard our lives in this manner, running into a turbulent sea, not a single one who went having a knowledge of navigation.

125

Five Indians in a dugout; detail from T. de Bry's map 'Hispaniae Novae sive magnae . . .' in *America*, Part V, 1595.

De Vaca and three other survivors of the wrecked fleet, Castillo, Dorantes, and his Negro slave Estev010n, became slaves of several tribes of south Texas Indians, among whom were the Yguazes. De Vaca describes the miserable life which they shared with these people.

This is likewise the practice of their neighbors the Yguazes, but of no other people of that country. When the men would marry, they buy the women of their enemies: the price paid for a wife is a bow, the best that can be got, with two arrows: if it happens that the suitor should have no bow, then a net a fathom in length and another in breadth. They kill their male children, and buy those of strangers. The marriage state continues no longer than while the parties are satisfied, and they separate for the slightest cause. Dorantes was among this people, and after a few days escaped.

Castillo and Estevanico went inland to the Yguazes. This people are universally good archers and of a fine symmetry, although not so large as those we left. They have a nipple and a lip bored. Their support is principally roots, of two or three kinds, and they look for them over the face of all the country. The food is poor and gripes the persons who eat it. The roots require roasting two days: many are very bitter, and withal difficult to be dug. They are sought the distance of two or three leagues, and so great is the want these people experience, that they cannot get through the year without them. Oc-

126

Map of Florida and Apalche, from Cornelius Wytfliet, *Descriptionis Ptolemaicae augmentum*, Louvain, 1597.

This atlas is known as the first distinctively American one, since all its maps are of the New World. The map of Florida and Apalche, with its Indian settlements reported by the de Soto expedition, enlarges the area of and adds details to the Ortelius map of Florida, 1584.

The early geographers had no knowledge of the size of the Mississippi River; from the narratives of the de Soto expedition they believed that a range of mountains extended east-west above the Gulf, which would preclude a great river. Wytfliet's rectangular Florida peninsula, with a bottle-neck at the top, is unlike the V-shaped form of most earlier maps. The pronged Secco-Sola (Savannah) River on the Georgia coast was probably based on reports of the network of islands and rivers there.

127

A battle between Spaniards and Indians, from T. de Bry, *America*, Part V, 1595, plate XVI.

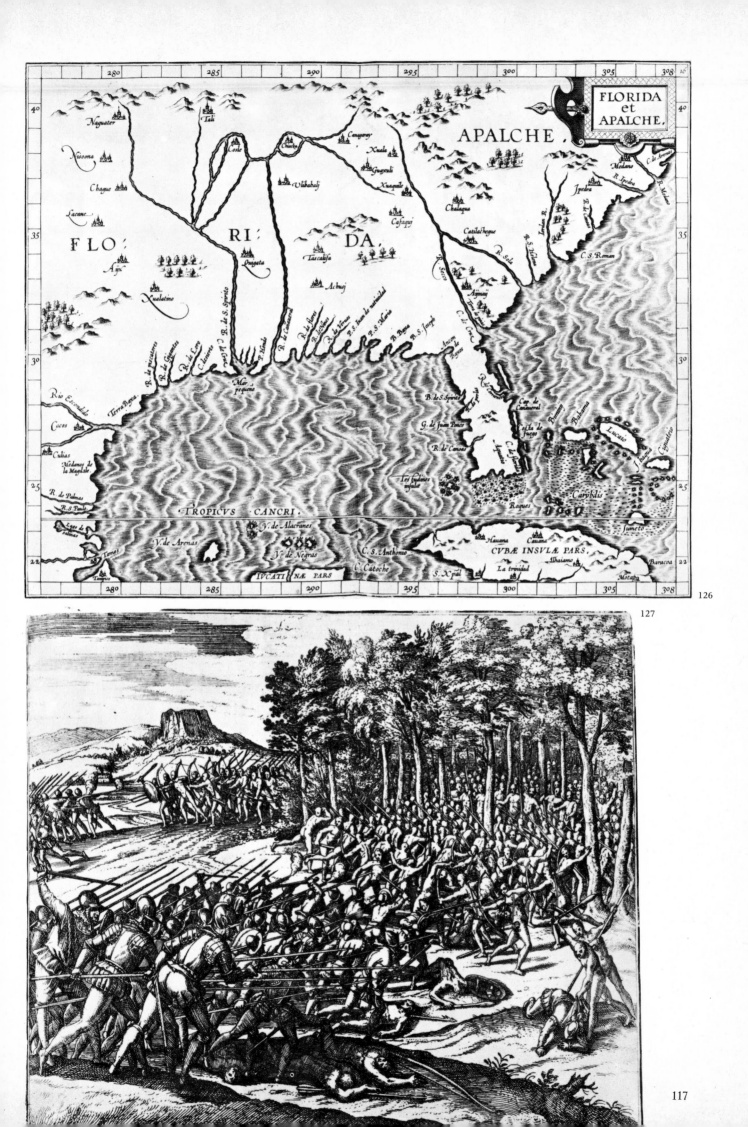

casionally they kill deer, and at times take fish; but the quantity is so small and the famine so great, that they eat spiders and the eggs of ants, worms, lizards, salamanders, snakes, and vipers that kill whom they strike; and they eat earth and wood, and all that there is, the dung of deer, and other things that I omit to mention; and I honestly believe that were there stones in that land they would eat them. They save the bones of fishes they consume, of snakes and other animals, that they may afterwards beat them together and eat the powder. The men bear no burthens, nor carry anything of weight; such are borne by women and old men who are of the least esteem. The majority of the people are great thieves; for though they are free to divide with each other, on turning

128
An iguana, from Johan de Laet, *Nieuwe Wereldt ofte beschrijvinghe van West-Indien*, Leyden, 1630.
129
Cactus, from G. B. Ramusio, *Navigationi et Viaggi*, Venice, 1565.
130
Another cactus, from Ramusio, *Navigationi et Viaggi*, Venice, 1565.
The happiest time of year for the Indians was the 'season of the prickly pear', when they drank the sweet juicy fruit of several species of cactus.
131
Bison with a bird on its back; a detail from a map by T. de Bry, 'Hispaniae Novae sive magnae . . .' in *America*, Part V, 1595.

128

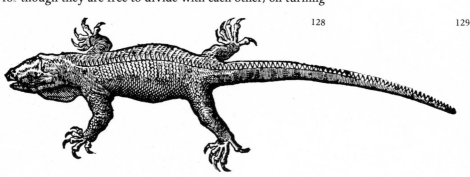

129

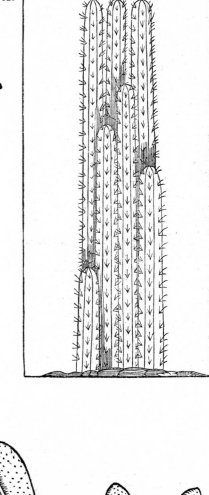

the head, even a son or a father will take what he can. They are great liars, and also great drunkards, which they became from the use of a certain liquor.

These Indians are so accustomed to running, that without rest or fatigue they follow a deer from morning to night. In this way they kill many. They pursue them until tired down, and sometimes overtake them in the race. Their houses are of matting, placed upon four hoops. They carry them on the back, and remove every two or three days in search of food. Nothing is planted for support. They are a merry people, considering the hunger they suffer; for they never cease, notwithstanding, to observe their festivities and *areytos* [superstitions]. To them the happiest part of the year is the season of eating prickly pears; they have hunger then no longer, pass all the time in dancing, and eat day and night. While these last, they squeeze out the juice, open and set them to dry, and when dry they are put in hampers like figs. These they keep to eat on their way back. The peel is beaten to powder.

We found mosquitos of three sorts, and all of them abundant in every part of the country. They poison and inflame, and during the greater part of the summer gave us great annoyance. As a protection we made fires, encircling the people with them, burning rotten and wet wood to produce smoke without flame. The remedy brought another trouble, and the night long we did little else than shed tears from the smoke that came into our eyes, besides feeling intense heat from the many fires, and if at any time we went out for repose to the seaside and fell asleep, we were reminded with blows to make up the fires. The Indians of the interior have a different method, as intolerable, and worse even than the one I have spoken of, which is to go with brands in the hand firing the plains and forests within their reach, that the mosquitos may fly away, and at the same time to drive out lizards and other like things from the earth for them to eat. They are accustomed also to kill deer by encircling them with fires.

130

Escaping from slavery and moving westward with his three companions, de Vaca, who was always interested in the life of the Indians, relates the vigilance in war and hunting of the Aguenes or Koguenes, another Texas coastal tribe.

While I was among the Aguenes, their enemies coming suddenly at midnight, fell upon them, killed three and wounded many, so that they ran from their houses to the fields before them. As soon as these ascertained that their assailants had withdrawn, they returned to pick up all the arrows the others had shot, and following after them in the most stealthy manner possible, came that night to their dwellings without their presence being suspected. At four o'clock in the morning the Aguenes attacked them, killed five, and wounded numerous others, and made them flee from their houses, leaving their bows with all they possessed. All these nations, when they have personal enmities, and are not of one family, assassinate at night, waylay, and inflict gross barbarities on each other.

They are the most watchful in danger of any people I ever knew. If they fear an enemy they are awake the night long, each with a bow at his side and a dozen arrows. He that would sleep tries his bow, and if it is not strung, he gives the turn necessary to the cord. They often come out from their houses, bending to the ground in such manner that they cannot be seen, looking and watching on all sides to catch every object. If they perceive anything about, they are at once in the bushes with their bows and arrows, and there remain until day, running from place to place where it is needful to be, or where they think their enemies are. When the light has come, they unbend their bows until they go out to hunt. The strings are the sinews of deer.

The method they have of fighting, is bending low to the earth, and whilst shot at they move about, speaking and leaping from one point to another, thus avoiding the shafts of their enemies. When they use arrows in battle and exhaust their store, each returns his own way, without the one party following the other, although the one be many and the other few, such being their custom. Oftentimes the body of an Indian is traversed by the arrow; yet unless the entrails or the heart be struck, he does not die but recovers from the wound.

I believe these people see and hear better, and have keener senses than any other in the world. They are great in hunger, thirst, and cold, as if they were made for the endurance of these more than other men, by habit and nature.

Thanks to their skill in trading and healing, the Spaniards' lot improved steadily. They reached the Jumanos, the relatively prosperous and well-fed pueblo Indians of the Rio Grande north of its junction with the Conchos. De Vaca makes one of the earliest references to herds of bison.

Here Castillo and Estevanico arrived, and, after talking with the Indians, Castillo returned at the end of three days to the spot where he had left us, and brought five or six of the people. He told us he had found fixed dwellings of civilization, that the inhabitants lived on beans and pumpkins, and that he had seen maize. This news the most of anything delighted us, and for it we gave infinite thanks to our Lord. Castillo told us the negro was coming with all the population to wait for us in the road not far off. Accordingly we left, and, having travelled a league and a half, we met the negro and the people coming to receive us. They gave us beans, many pumpkins, calabashes, blankets of cowhide and other things. As this people and those who came with us were enemies, and spoke not each other's language, we discharged the latter, giving them what we

received, and we departed with the others. Six leagues from there, as the night set in we arrived at the houses, where great festivities were made over us. We remained one day, and the next set out with these Indians. They took us to the settled habitations of others, who lived upon the same food.

From that place onward was another usage. Those who knew of our approach did not come out to receive us on the road as the others had done, but we found them in their houses, and they had made others for our reception. They were all seated with their faces turned to the wall, their heads down, the hair brought before their eyes, and their property placed in a heap in the middle of the house. From this place they began to give us many blankets of skin; and they had nothing

131

they did not bestow. They have the finest persons of any people we saw, of the greatest activity and strength, who best understood us and intelligently answered our inquiries. We called them the Cow nation, because most of the cattle [bison] killed are slaughtered in their neighborhood, and along up that river [?Pecos] for over fifty leagues they destroy great numbers.

When he finally reached Mexico near the Pacific coast, de Vaca found the Indians in terror from the slave-hunting and oppression of the Spanish settlers. He tried to mediate between them unsuccessfully.

Our countrymen became jealous at this, and caused their interpreter to tell the Indians that we were of them, and for a long time we had been lost; that they were the lords of the land who must be obeyed and served, while we were persons of mean condition and small force. The Indians cared little or nothing for what was told them; and conversing among themselves said the Christians lied: that we had come whence the sun rises, and they whence it goes down; we healed the sick, they killed the sound; that we had come naked and barefooted, while they had arrived in clothing and on horses with lances; that we were not covetous of anything, but all that was given to us we directly turned to give, remaining with nothing; that the others had the only purpose to rob whomsoever they found, bestowing nothing on any one.

The Indians, at taking their leave, told us they would do what we commanded, and would build their towns, if the Christians would suffer them; and this I say and affirm most positively, that, if they have not done so, it is the fault of the Christians.

Translation used: Buckingham Smith in The Narrative of Alvar Nuñez Cabeça de Vaca, *ed. John Gilmary Shea. New York, 1871. Reprint used:* F. W. Hodge and T. H. Lewis, eds, Spanish Explorers in the Southern United States, 1528–1543. *New York: Scribner, 1907, pp. 34-7, 65-7, 84-6, 102-3, 114-15.*

2.
The expedition of Hernando de Soto, 1539–43

From *Relacam verdaderia dos trabalhos . . . pur hun fidalgo D elvas* (by the Gentleman of Elvas), Evora, Portugal, 1557.

De Soto, appointed Royal Governor of Cuba and of Florida, a land of unknown extent and boundaries, landed at or near Tampa Bay 25 May 1539 with 620 men and 223 horses. After extensive marching, he reached the province of Cutifachiqui almost a year later. Here he found a woman chieftain.

After a little time the Cacica came out of the town, seated in a chair, which some principal men having borne to the bank, she entered a canoe. Over the stern was spread an awning, and in the bottom lay extended a mat where were two cushions, one above the other, upon which she sate; and she was accompanied by her chief men, in other canoes, with Indians.

The Cacica presented much clothing of the country, from the shawls and skins that came in the other boats; and drawing from over her head a large string of pearls, she threw them about his [de Soto's] neck, exchanging with him many gracious words of friendship and courtesy. She directed that canoes should come to the spot, whence the Governor and his people passed to the opposite side of the river. So soon as he was lodged in the town, a great many turkeys were sent to him. The country was delightful and fertile, having good interval lands upon the streams; the forest was open, with abundance of walnut and mulberry trees. The sea was stated to be distant two days' travel. About the place, from half a league to a league off, were large vacant towns, grown up in grass, that appeared as if no people had lived in them for a long time. The Indians said that, two years before, there had been a pest in the land, and the inhabitants had moved away to other towns. In the barbacoas [containers] were large quantities of clothing, shawls of thread, made from the bark of trees, and others of feathers, white, gray, vermilion, and yellow, rich and proper for winter. There were also many well-dressed deer-skins, of colors drawn over with designs, of which had been made shoes, stockings, and hose. The Cacica, observing that the Christians valued the pearls, told the Governor that, if he should order some sepulchres that were in the town to be searched, he would find many; and if he chose to send to those that were in the uninhabited towns, he might load all his horses with them. They examined those in the town, and found three hundred and fifty pounds' weight of pearls, and figures of babies and birds made of them.

The inhabitants are brown of skin, well formed and proportioned. They are more civilized than any people seen in all the territories of Florida, wearing clothes and shoes.

To all it appeared well to make a settlement there, the point being a favorable one, to which could come all the ships from New Spain, Peru, Sancta Marta, and Tierra-Firme, going to Spain; because it is in the way thither, is a good country, and one fit in which to raise supplies; but Soto, as it was his object to find another treasure like that of Atabalipa, lord of Peru, would not be content.

132

Passion flower, from J. T. de Bry, *Florilegium renovatum et auctum*, Frankfurt, 1641.

Probably the most important of de Soto's discoveries was that of the Mississippi River. Their crossing of it, here described, was near the Indian Quizquiz, below Memphis at Council Bend or Walnut Bend, Mississippi.

There was little maize in the place, and the Governor moved to another town, half a league from the great river [Mississippi], where it was found in sufficiency. He went to look at the river, and saw that near it there was much timber of which piraguas might be made, and a good situation in which the camp might be placed. He directly moved, built houses, and settled on a plain a crossbow-shot from the water, bringing together there all the maize of the towns behind, that at once they might go to work and cut down trees for sawing out planks to build barges. The Indians soon came from up the stream, jumped on shore, and told the Governor that they were the vassals of a great lord, named Aquixo, who was the suzerain of many towns and people on the other shore; and they made known from him, that he would come the day after, with all his people, to hear what his lordship would command him.

The next day the cacique arrived, with two hundred canoes filled with men, having weapons. They were painted with ochre, wearing great bunches of white and other plumes of many colors, having feathered shields in their hands, with which they sheltered the oarsmen on either side, the warriors

Sketch of the de Soto expedition, *c.* 1544. *Seville, Archivo General de Indias.*

This pen-and-ink sketch is the only contemporary map to illustrate the de Soto expedition of 1539–43. It shows the southern part of North America and includes the coast from St Elena (Port Royal, South Carolina) to the Panuco River in Mexico, where the survivors arrived under Moscoso, after the death of their leader and after their epic wanderings of four years. Many of the 127 legends, rivers, and names of Indian towns on the map are to be found in narratives of the expedition by Ranjel, Biedma, and the Gentleman of Elvas. The map was found among the papers of the royal cartographer, Alonso de Santa Cruz, and was probably made by him from written and oral reports of members of the expedition.

standing erect from bow to stern, holding bows and arrows. The barge in which the cacique came had an awning at the poop, under which he sate; and the like had the barges of the other chiefs; and there, from under the canopy, where the chief man was, the course was directed and orders issued to the rest. All came down together, and arrived within a stone's cast of the ravine, whence the cacique said to the Governor,

who was walking along the river-bank, with others who bore him company, that he had come to visit, serve, and obey him; for he had heard that he was the greatest of lords, the most powerful on all the earth, and that he must see what he would have him do. The Governor expressed his pleasure, and besought him to land, that they might the better confer; but the chief gave no reply, ordering three barges to draw near, wherein was great quantity of fish, and loaves like bricks, made of the pulp of plums [persimmons], which Soto receiving, gave him thanks and again entreated him to land.

Making the gift had been a pretext, to discover if any harm might be done; but, finding the Governor and his people on their guard, the cacique began to draw off from the shore, when the crossbowmen who were in readiness, with loud cries shot at the Indians, and struck down five or six of them. They retired with great order, not one leaving the oar, even though the one next to him might have fallen, and covering themselves, they withdrew. Afterwards they came many times and landed; when approached, they would go back to their barges. These were fine-looking men, very large and

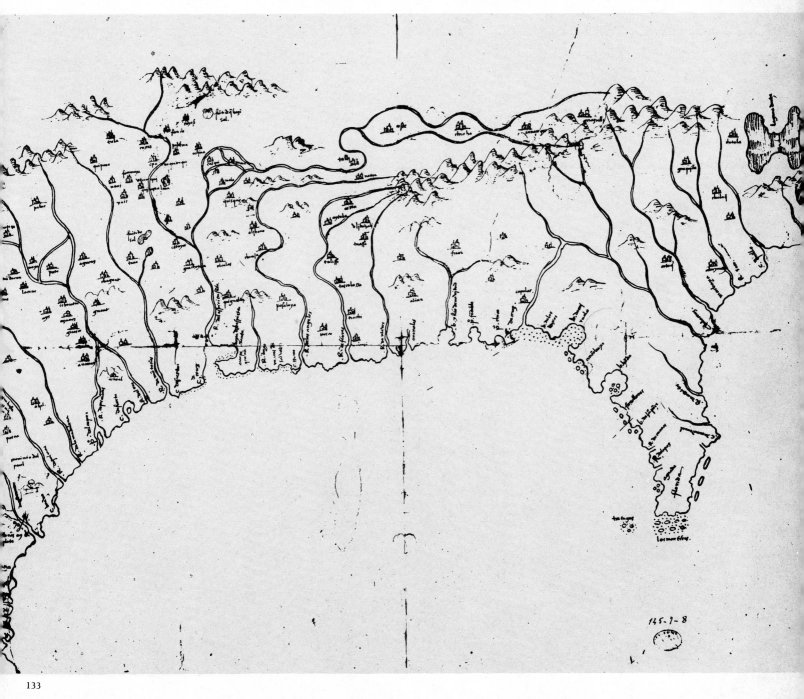

well formed; and what with the awnings, the plumes, and the shields, the pennons, and the number of people in the fleet, it appeared like a famous armada of galleys.

During the thirty days that were passed there, four piraguas were built, into three of which, one morning, three hours before daybreak, the Governor ordered twelve cavalry to enter, four in each, men in whom he had confidence that they would gain the land notwithstanding the Indians, and secure the passage, or die.

So soon as they had come to shore the piraguas returned; and when the sun was up two hours high, the people had all got over. The distance was near half a league: a man standing on the shore could not be told, whether he were a man or something else, from the other side. The stream was swift, and very deep; the water, always flowing turbidly, brought along from above many trees and much timber, driven onward by its force.

At the end of his account the Gentleman of Elvas summarizes the regions through which they passed. Though his measurements of distance are not accurate, he conveys vividly the diversities of the vast terrain they had covered.

From the port of Espiritu Santo, where the Christians went on shore, to the province of Ocute, which may be a distance of four hundred leagues, a little more or less, the country is very level, having many ponds, dense thickets, and, in places, tall pine-trees: the soil is light, and there is not in it a mountain nor a hill.

The land of Ocute is more strong and fertile than the rest, the forest more open; and it has very good fields along the margins of the rivers. From there to Cutifachiqui are about one hundred and thirty leagues, of which eighty leagues are of desert and pine forests, through which run great rivers. From Cutifachiqui to Xuala there may be two hundred and fifty leagues, and all a country of mountains: the places themselves are on high level ground, and have good fields upon the streams.

Thence onward, through Chiaha, Coça, and Talise, the country of which is flat, dry, and strong, yielding abundance of maize, to Tascaluça, may be two hundred and fifty leagues; and thence to Rio Grande [Mississippi], a distance of about three hundred leagues, the land is low, abounding in lakes. The country afterward is higher, more open, and more populous than any other in Florida; and along the River Grande, from Aquixo to Pacaha and Coligoa, a distance of one hundred and fifty leagues, the land is level, the forest open, and in places the fields very fertile and inviting.

From Coligoa to Autiamque may be two hundred and fifty leagues of mountainous country; thence to Guacay may be two hundred and thirty leagues of level ground; and the region to Daycao, a distance of one hundred and twenty leagues, is continuously of mountainous lands.

There are many lions and bears in Florida, wolves, deer, jackals, cats, and rabbits; numerous wild fowl, as large as peafowl; small partridges, like those of Africa, and cranes, ducks, pigeons, thrushes, and sparrows. There are blackbirds larger than sparrows and smaller than stares; hawks, goshawks, falcons, and all the birds of rapine to be found in Spain.

Translation used: Buckingham Smith in The Career of Hernando de Soto in the Conquest of Florida as told by a Knight of Elvas. *New York: Bradford Club, No. 5, 1866. Reprint used: F. W. Hodge and T. H. Lewis, eds,* Spanish Explorers in the Southern United States, 1528–1543. *New York: Scribner, 1907, pp. 173-5, 203-4, 270-2, 308-9, 362-3.*

134
Photograph of the mesa and pueblo of Acoma, by A. C. Vroman, 1897. *Los Angeles County Museum of Natural History.*
135
Bald Eagle. Dr Hans Sloane manuscript. *London, British Museum.* 'Nahyapuw. The Grype, almost as bigg as an Eagle.' A seventeenth-century copy of a lost original drawing by John White.
136
Brown Thrasher and Baltimore Oriole. Dr Hans Sloane manuscript. *London, British Museum.* A seventeenth-century copy of an original by John White.
137
Red-breasted Merganser. Dr Hans Sloane manuscript. *London, British Museum.* A winter coastal visitor to North Carolina. This is a seventeenth-century copy of a lost John White drawing.

135

Qvúnziuck . Of the bignes of a Duck.

3.
The death of Estaván,
May 1539

Ever since the expedition of Fray Marcos de Nizza into New Mexico in 1539, there has been a legend current among the Zuñi Indians concerning the death of Estaván the Negro. A version recorded by Hammond follows.

It is to be believed that a long time ago, when roofs lay over the walls of KYA-KI-ME [Hawikuh], when smoke hung over the house-tops, and the ladder-rounds were still unbroken in KYA-KI-ME, then the Black Mexicans came from their abodes in Everlasting Summerland . . . Then and thus was killed by our ancients, right where the stone stands down by the arroyo of KYA-KI-ME, one of the Black Mexicans, a large man, with chilli lips . . . Then the rest ran away, chased by our grandfathers, and went back toward their country in the land of Everlasting Summer.

Text used: George P. Hammond, Coronado's seven cities. *Albuquerque, United States Coronado Exposition Commission, 1940, p. 8. The author says he is setting down a legend still current in pueblos.*

4.
Discoveries of the Coronado
expedition, 1540–2

From a manuscript copy made in Seville in 1599 of Castañeda's narrative of the Coronado expedition.

The first great expedition from Mexico to attempt the colonization of North America was under the command of Francisco Vásquez de Coronado. It followed the route of Fray Marcos to Cibola (Zuñi) and then moved eastward to the Rio Grande. The most remarkable pueblo encountered by one of the exploring parties was that of Acoma, probably the oldest continuously occupied settlement in the United States.

Captain Alvarado started on this journey and in five days reached a village which was on a rock called Acuco [Acoma], having a population of about two hundred men. These people were robbers, feared by the whole country round about. The village was very strong, because it was up on a rock out of reach, having steep sides in every direction, and so high that it was a very good musket that could throw a ball as high. There was only one entrance by a stairway built by hand, which began at the top of a slope which is around the foot of the rock. There was a broad stairway for about two hundred steps, then a stretch of about one hundred narrower steps, and at the top they had to go up about three times as high as a man by means of holes in the rock, in which they put the points of their feet, holding on at the same time by their hands. There was a wall of large and small stones at the top, which they could roll down without showing themselves, so that no army could possibly be strong enough to capture the

138

138
Indians selling in an open market, from T. de Bry, *America*, Part V, 1595, plate X.
139
The east coast of North America from the world map by Pierre Desceliers, 1550. *London, British Museum, Add. Ms. 24065.*
This beautiful, elaborately illustrated planisphere, made at Arques, near Dieppe, is one of the fine examples of the work of the cartographer-artists who flourished in Dieppe around the middle of the sixteenth century.
The map is signed and dated 1550 by Desceliers; the St Lawrence region was influenced by the work of an anonymous Portuguese cartographer who had access to charts of Jacques Cartier's expeditions. In a long legend Desceliers describes the discovery of Canada by Cartier and the privations of the colony under Roberval in 1542. In its improved conception of Newfoundland and in details added from Cartier's second and third voyages up the St Lawrence, this map shows the advance in knowledge made since Rotz's map of 1542 (plate 116).

140 *Overleaf*
A map of North America and the North Atlantic by Diogo Homem, 1558.
London, British Museum, Add. Ms. 5451.A, fos 19b and 20a.
Two features of this map by the capable Portuguese cartographer Diogo Homem are especially noticeable: the interpretation of Jacques Cartier's discovery of the St Lawrence, and the representation, surprisingly belated, of the Bay of Fundy. These features first appear in a map of 1554 by Lopo Homem, Diogo's supposed father, and are repeated in their later maps. The St Lawrence River is open to a great ocean on the north, the Paramantium Sea, separated from it by a series of islands with non-Cartier names gratuitously added on the seaward coast. Apparently Homem drew openings wherever Cartier reported that he had tried to find a westward passage to the Pacific on the north shore of the Gulf and River.

The second and more important feature of the map is the great bay on the New England coast which represents the Bay of Fundy. Why so important and large a coastal indentation as the Bay of Fundy was not shown on earlier maps is difficult to understand. Professor Ganong suggests that Verrazzano sailed across the mouth of the bay without noticing it, and that Gomes did not sail far enough north to discover it. The east coast of Newfoundland on this map, he adds, shows the explorations of João Alvares Fagundes before 1521. Shortly after 1521, Fagundes, or other Portuguese associates, attempted to settle Cape Breton Island, and at that time must have discovered the Bay of Fundy. Apparently the Homems knew and used Fagundes's documents which other cartographers did not use. These documents were in all probability lost, with many other important primary sources, in the fire following the great Lisbon earthquake of 1755. South of New England to Florida the Homems, although dependent on Spanish maps, differ from them in so many details that they must have used independent sources or reports.

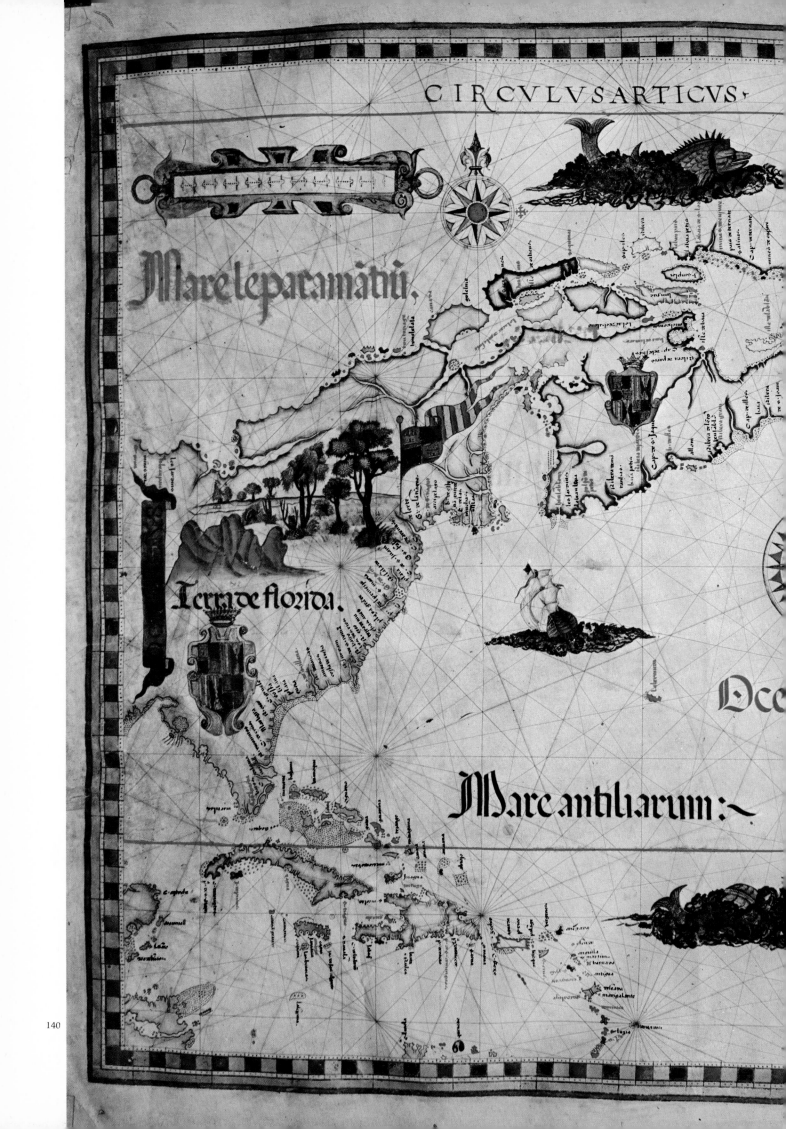

CIRCVLVSARTICVS·

Mare leparamatu.

Terra de florida.

Mare antiliarum:

140

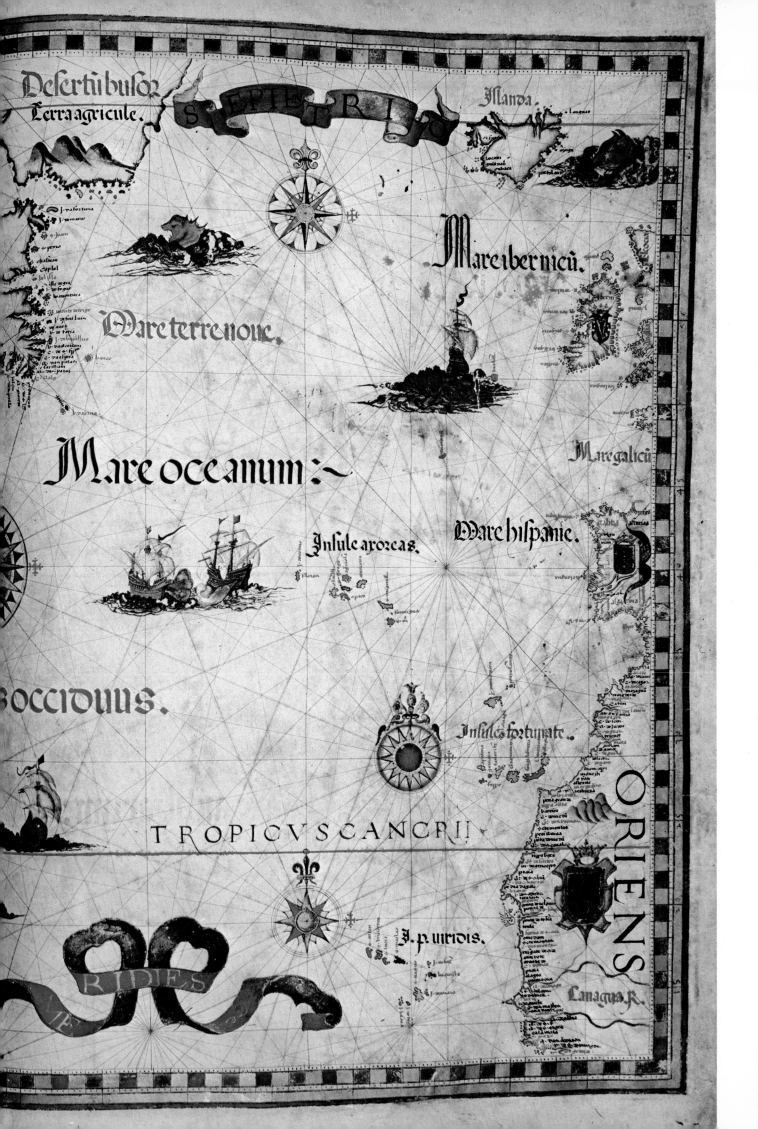

village. On the top they had room to sow and store a large amount of corn, and cisterns to collect snow and water. These people came down to the plain ready to fight, and would not listen to any arguments. They drew lines on the ground and determined to prevent our men from crossing these, but when they saw that they would have to fight they offered to make peace before any harm had been done. They went through their forms of making peace, which is to touch the horses and take their sweat and rub themselves with it, and to make crosses with the fingers of the hands. But to make the most secure peace they put their hands across each other, and they keep this peace inviolably. They made a present of a large number of [turkey] cocks with very big wattles, much bread, tanned deerskins, pine [piñon] nuts, flour [cornmeal], and corn.

Coronado established his headquarters in the Tiguex pueblo region of the upper Rio Grande in northern New Mexico. Here Castañeda describes as highly developed an Indian culture as any in North America.

Tiguex is a province with twelve villages on the banks of a large, mighty river; some villages on one side and some on the other. It is a spacious valley two leagues wide, and a very high, rough, snow-covered mountain chain [the Sandia Mountains] lies east of it.

In general, these villages all have the same habits and customs, although some have some things in particular which the others have not. They are governed by the opinions of the elders. They all work together to build the villages, the women being engaged in making the mixture and the walls, while the men bring the wood and put it in place. They have no lime, but they make a mixture of ashes, coals, and dirt which is almost as good as mortar, for when the house is to have four stories, they do not make the walls more than half a yard thick. They gather a great pile of twigs of thyme [sagebrush] and sedge grass and set it afire, and when it is half coals and ashes they throw a quantity of dirt and water on it and mix it all together. They make round balls of this, which they use instead of stones after they are dry, fixing them with the same mixture, which comes to be like stiff clay. Before they are married the young men serve the whole village in general, and fetch the wood that is needed for use, putting it in a pile in the courtyard of the villages, from which the women take it to carry to their houses.

The young men live in the estufas, which are in the yards of the village. They are underground, square or round, with pine pillars. Some were seen with twelve pillars and with four in the centre as large as two men could stretch around. They usually had three or four pillars. The floor was made of large, smooth stones, like the baths which they have in Europe. They have a hearth made like the binnacle or compass box

of a ship, in which they burn a handful of thyme at a time to keep up the heat, and they can stay in there just as in a bath. The top was on a level with the ground. Some that were seen were large enough for a game of ball. When any man wishes to marry, it has to be arranged by those who govern. The man has to spin and weave a blanket and place it before the woman, who covers herself with it and becomes his wife. The houses belong to the women, the estufas to the men. If a man repudiates his woman, he has to go to the estufa. It is forbidden for women to sleep in the estufas, or to enter these for any purpose except to give their husbands or sons something to eat. The men spin and weave. The women bring up the children and prepare the food. The country is so fertile that they do not have to break up the ground the year round, but only have to sow the seed, which is presently covered by the fall of snow, and the ears come up under the snow. In one year they gather enough for seven. A very large number of cranes and wild geese and crows and starlings live on what is sown, and for all this, when they come to sow for another year, the fields are covered with corn which they have not been able to finish gathering.

There are a great many native fowl in these provinces, and cocks with great hanging chins. When dead, these keep for sixty days, and longer in winter, without losing their feathers or opening, and without any bad smell, and the same is true of dead men.

The villages are free from nuisances, because they go outside to excrete, and they pass their water into clay vessels, which they empty at a distance from the village. They keep the separate houses where they prepare the food for eating and where they grind the meal, very clean. This is a separate room or closet, where they have a trough with three stones fixed in stiff clay. Three women go in here, each one having a stone, with which one of them breaks the corn, the next grinds it, and the third grinds it again. They take off their shoes, do up their hair, shake their clothes, and cover their heads before they enter the door. A man sits at the door playing on a fife while they grind, moving the stones to the music and singing together. There are no fruits good to eat in the country, except the pine nuts. They have their preachers. Sodomy is not found among them. They do not eat human flesh nor make sacrifices of it. The people are not cruel. In all these provinces they have earthenware glazed with antimony and jars of extraordinary labor and workmanship, which were worth seeing.

The scouting expedition under Cardeñas was the first group of white men to visit the Grand Canyon of the Colorado. To them it was an obstacle rather than a sight of awe-inspiring beauty.

As Don Pedro de Tovar was not commissioned to go farther, he returned from there and gave this information to the general, who dispatched Don Garcia Lopez de Cardeñas with about twelve companions to go to see this river. He was well received when he reached Tusayan and was entertained by the natives, who gave him guides for his journey. They started from here loaded with provisions, for they had to go through a desert country before reaching the inhabited region, which the Indians said was more than twenty days' journey. After they had gone twenty days they came to the banks of the river, which seemed to be more than three or four leagues in an air line across to the other bank of the stream which flowed between them. This country was elevated and full of low twisted pines, very cold, and lying open toward the north, so that, this being the warm season, no one could live there on account of the cold. They spent three days on this bank

141
Map of Florida, Canada and Labrador from the *Cosmographie Universelle* of Guillaume Le Testu, 1555. *Paris, Ministère des Armées, D.I.Z.14, fo 56v.*
This map of New France, showing the discoveries of Cartier and Roberval in the Gulf of St Lawrence and up the 'River of Canada', is in the *Cosmographie Universelle*, one of the great decorative atlases of the sixteenth century. Superbly illustrated, it was made for Admiral Coligny by Le Testu, a pilot of Havre de Grace. The names on this map show that Le Testu used an intermediary Portuguese source instead of basing his work directly upon Cartier's own charts, which were still in existence in France.
  Le Testu, a Huguenot, had already crossed the Atlantic by 1550 as a pilot; he went on expeditions to Brazil, Africa and the East Indies, perhaps to Australia. In 1572 Drake encountered him on the Isthmus of Panama, where they briefly joined forces in the capture of Spanish booty. (See also plates 99, 147 and 163).

142

looking for a passage down to the river, which looked from above as if the water was six feet across, although the Indians said it was half a league wide. It was impossible to descend, for after these three days Captain Melgosa and one Juan Galeras and another companion, who were the three lightest and most agile men, made an attempt to go down at the least difficult place, and went down until those who were above were unable to keep sight of them. They returned about four o'clock in the afternoon, not having succeeded in reaching the bottom on account of the great difficulties which they found, because what seemed to be easy from above was not so, but instead very hard and difficult. They said that they had been down about a third of the way and that the river seemed very large from the place which they reached, and that from what they saw they thought the Indians had given the width correctly. Those who stayed above had estimated that some huge rocks on the sides of the cliffs seemed to be about as tall as a man, but those who went down swore that when they reached these rocks they were bigger than the great tower of Seville.

Coronado, in search of the rumored wealth of Quivira, led another party across the great plains to southern Kansas, meeting bison and nomad Indians on the way.

The country is like a bowl, so that when a man sits down, the horizon surrounds him all around at the distance of a musket shot. There are no groves of trees except at the rivers, which flow at the bottom of some ravines where the trees grow so thick that they were not noticed until one was right on the edge of them. They are of dead earth. There are paths down into these, made by the cows [bison] when they go to the water, which is essential throughout these plains. As I have related in the first part, people follow the cows, hunting them and tanning the skins to take to the settlements in the winter to sell, since they go there to pass the winter, each company going to those which are nearest, some to the settlements at Cicuye, others toward Quivira, and others to the settlements which are situated in the direction of Florida. These people are called Querechos and Teyas. They travel like the Arabs, with their tents and troops of dogs loaded with poles and having Moorish pack-saddles with girths. When the load gets disarranged, the dogs howl, calling some one to fix them right. These people eat raw flesh and drink blood. They do not eat human flesh. They are a kind people and not cruel. They are faithful friends. They are able to make themselves very well understood by means of signs. They dry the flesh in the sun, cutting it thin like a leaf, and when dry they grind it like meal to keep it and make a sort of sea soup of it to eat. A handful thrown into a pot swells up so as to increase very much. They season it with fat, which they always try to secure when they kill a cow. They empty a large gut and fill it with blood, and carry this around the neck to drink when they are thirsty.

They cut the hide open at the back and pull it off at the joints, using a flint as large as a finger, tied in a little stick, with as much ease as if working with a good iron tool. They give it an edge with their own teeth. The quickness with which they do this is something worth seeing and noting.

There are very great numbers of wolves on these plains, which go around with the cows. They have white skins. The deer are pied with white. Their skin is loose, so that when they are killed it can be pulled off with the hand while warm, coming off like pigskin. The rabbits, which are very numerous, are so foolish that those on horseback killed them with their lances. This is when they are mounted among the cows. They fly from a person on foot.

Translation used: George P. Winship in 'Account of the Expedition to Cibola which took place in 1540 . . . Written by Pedro de Castañeda'. Fourteenth Annual Report of the Bureau of Ethnology. Washington: U.S. Gov't Printing Office, 1896. Reprint used: F. W. Hodge and T. H. Lewis, eds, Spanish explorers in the Southern United States, 1528–1543. *New York: Scribner, 1907, pp. 311-2, 352-5, 362-3.*

5.
Cabrillo's discovery of the coast of California, 1542–3

From an untitled account of the voyage, attributed to Juan Paez.

Cabrillo is important as the first explorer of the California coast, although the names he gave were later replaced. The landings here described were made north of Los Angeles, along the coast of Santa Barbara County.

On Wednesday, the 1st day of November, at midnight, standing off, they encountered a heavy wind from the north-northwest, which prevented them from carrying a palm of sail, and by dawn it had freshened so that they were forced to seek shelter, and they therefore went to take refuge under Cape Galera [Point Concepcion: 34° 27′N]. There they cast anchor and went ashore; and although there was a large pueblo which they call Xexo, because wood did not appear to be close at hand they decided to go to the pueblo of Las Sardinas [the Sardines, where they caught many sardines 17 October], because there the water and wood were close and handy. This shelter under Galera they called the port of Todos Santos [El Coxo anchorage; 34° 28′N]. On the following Thursday they went to the pueblo of Las Sardinas, where they remained three days, taking on water and wood. The natives of the country aided them and brought the wood and water to the ships. The ruler of these pueblos is an old Indian woman, who came to the ships and slept two nights on the captain's ship, as did many Indians. The pueblo of Ciucut appeared to be the capital of the rest, for they came there from other pueblos at the call of this ruler. The pueblo which is at the cape they call Xexo. From this port to the pueblo of Las Canoas is another province which they call Xucu. Their houses are round and very well covered clear to the ground. They wear skins of many kinds of animals. They eat oak acorns, and a seed the size of maize. It is white, and from it they make tamales; it is a good food. They say that in the interior there is much maize, and that men like us are going about there.

On Monday, the 6th of said month of November, they left

142
Indians shooting bison; detail from T. de Bry's map, 'Hispaniae Novae sive magnae . . .', *America,* Part V, 1595.

143
Map of the southern part of North America in a portolan atlas, probably by Battista Agnese, c. 1557. *Chicago, Newberry Library, Ayer Collection xii (3), fos 3b and 4b.*

This interesting map differs in style from the usual work of Agnese. It is one of the earliest maps to show the place names given by Cabrillo to features of the California coast, and to illustrate the 'Sierra nevados', the snowy mountains seen by him from the sea. Coronado's discoveries appear in such names as Tigues (Tiguex) and Axa (Acoma) on the Rio Grande (R. de Tiguex), but his Quivira has been moved from Kansas to the California coast, where it remained on many maps, and above it appears the legend, 'Fin qui scoperse Franc Vasquez de Coronado'. This transfer is accounted for by the fact that Gómara, in his *Historia de las Indias* (1552), fails to say in which direction Coronado went to Quivira, and states that he saw 'on the coast' ships decked with gold and silver which he thought were from Cathay. Mendoza also told Cabrillo to search for a river with such ships on it, which might flow into the Pacific. On this map, in 40°N, is another legend, 'Ship of Cataio, or China'. The Appalachians here run from east to west and are also snow-covered.

the said port of Sardinas; that day they made almost no progress, and until the following Friday they sailed with very light wind. That day we arrived at Cape Galera. During all this course they could make no use of the Indians who came aboard with water and fish, and appeared very friendly. They have in their pueblos large plazas, and have an enclosure like a fence; and around the enclosure they have many blocks of stone set in the ground, and projecting three palms above it. Within the enclosures they have many timbers set up like thick masts. On these poles they have many paintings, and we thought that they worshipped them, because when they dance they go dancing around the enclosure.

On the following Saturday, the day of San Martin, the 11th of this said month of November, they held on their course. All this coast which they ran this day is bold and entirely without shelter. All along it runs a chain of very high mountains. It is as high at the sea coast as in the interior, and the sea beats upon it. They saw no settlement nor any smokes, and all the coast, which has no shelter from the north, is uninhabited. They named these mountains the Sierras de San Martin [the Santa Lucía Mountains].

Translation used: Buckingham Smith of a manuscript in the Archives of the Indies, 1-1-1/20.R.23. Reprint used: H. R. Wagner, Spanish voyages to the Northwest coast of America in the sixteenth century. *San Francisco: California Historical Society, 1929, pp. 29-30.*

143

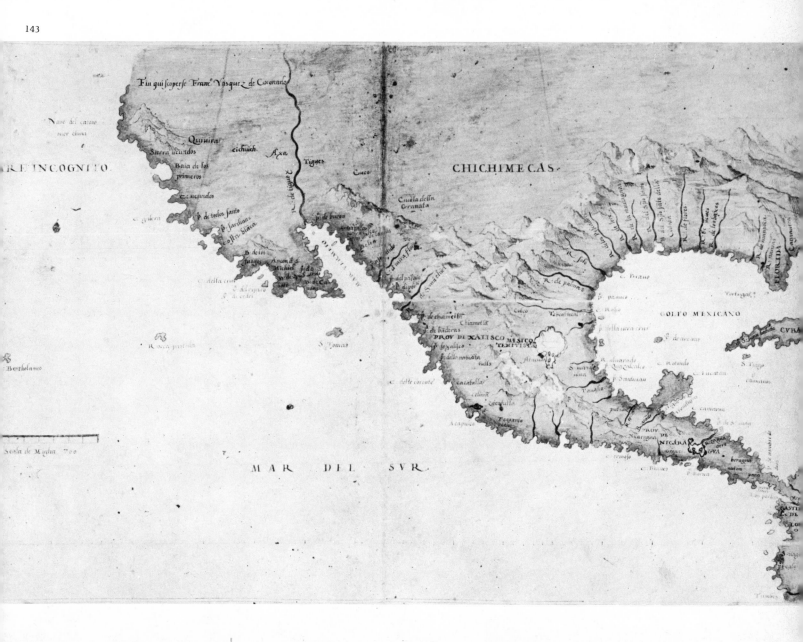

6.
Sir Francis Drake in Nova Albion, 1578

From Richard Hakluyt, 'The famous voyage of Sir Francis Drake . . .', *The principall navigations*. London, 1589.

On his westward voyage of circumnavigation, Drake made a landing on the California coast at Drake's or San Francisco Bay. Here he took possession in the name of Queen Elizabeth.

The newes of our being there, being spread through the Countrey, the people that inhabited round about came downe, and amongst them the King himselfe, a man of goodly stature, & comely personage, with many other tall, and warlike men.

In the fore front was a man of goodly personage, who bare the scepter, or mace before the King, whereupon hanged two crownes, a lesse and a bigger, with three chaines of a marvelous length: the crownes were made of knit worke wrought artifically with fethers of divers colours: the chaines were made of a bonie substance, and few be the persons among them that are admitted to weare them.

In comming towards our bulwarks and tents, the scepter bearer began a song, observing his measures in a daunce, and that with a stately countenance, whom the King with his Garde, and every degree of persons following, did in like manner sing and daunce, saving onely the women which daunced, & kept silence. The Generall permitted them to enter within our bulwarke, where they continued their song and daunce a reasonable time. When they had satisfied themselves, they made signes to our General to sit downe, to whom the King, and divers others made several orations, or rather supplications, that he would take their province & kingdome into his hand, and become their King, making signes that they would resigne unto him their right and title of the whole land, and become his subjects.

The common sorte of people leaving the King, and his Garde with our Generall, scattered themselves together with their sacrifices among our people, taking a diligent viewe of every person: and such as pleased their fancie, (which were the yongest) they inclosing them about offred their sacrifices unto them with lamentable weeping, scratching, and tearing the flesh from their faces with their nailes, whereof issued abundance of bloode. But wee used signes to them of disliking this, and staied their hands from force, and directed them upwards to the living God, whome onely they ought to worshippe. They shewed unto us their wounds, and craved helpe of them at our hands, whereupon wee gave them lotions, plaisters, and ointments agreeing to the state of their griefes, beseeching God to cure their diseases. Every thirde day they brought their sacrifices unto us, until they understoode our meaning, that we had no pleasure in them: yet they could not be long absent from us, but daily frequented our companie to the houre of our departure, which departure seemed so greevous unto them, that their joy was turned into sorrow. They intreated us, that being absent we would remember them, and by stelth provided a sacrifice, which we misliked.

Our necessarie busines being ended, our Generall with his companie travailed up into the Countrey to their villages, where wee found heardes of Deere by 1000. in a companie, being most large, and fat of bodie.

We found the whole Countrey to be a warren of a strange

144
The *Golden Hind,* inset from the 'Hondius Broadside' (?1595), '*Vera totius expeditiones nauticae*'.
This engraving is accepted as an authentic picture of Drake's famous *Golden Hind,* since Hondius, living in London at the time, must have seen it at Deptford. Beside the inset Hondius notes that it seems miraculous that a ship of this size, laden with gold and silver, could survive a journey of at least 8500 German miles, after being tossed on the rocks for twenty hours; it is now, Hondius adds, preserved at Deptford on the Thames.

kind of Connies, their bodies in bignes as be the Barbarie Connies, their heads as the heads of ours, the feete of a Want [mole], and the taile of a Rat being of great length: under her chinne on either side a bagge, into the which she gathereth her meate, when she hath filled her bellie abroad. The people eate their bodies, and make great accompt of their skinnes, for their Kings coate was made of them [ie gophers].

Our Generall called this Countrey, NOVA ALBION, and that for two causes: the one in respect of the white bankes and cliffes, which lie towards the sea: and the other, because it might have some affinitie with our Countrey in name, which sometime was so called.

There is no part of earth here to be taken up, wherein there is not a reasonable quantitie of gold or silver.

The above extract appears, inserted between pages 643 and 644 in The principall navigations.

From
hizo
el en

Vizc
port

On
fou
on
Sier
Phil
whi
sno
all
stra
othe
Two
rive
acro
port
this
fron
seer
'Mo
who

Two
stor

Whe
Jant
and
like
each
with
latit
well
(it w
to th
wind
port
had
find
ever
W
Men
told
cabi

147
Map
Unive
West

7.

Landing of Unamuno on the California coast, 1587

From Unamuno's report of his voyage, probably sent by the Viceroy from Mexico in 1587.

Unamuno, one of the Spanish captains returning from the Philippines by the recently discovered northern route, hoped to find a California port for the Manila galleons. He describes a landing at Morro Bay, where he takes formal possession of the country.

When we had landed in the harbor, a consultation was held as to what direction should be taken, whether toward the place where the Indians had been seen shortly before, or toward the pine woods where some fires had been seen that morning, as there were many trails leading in different directions. We decided to go towards the place where the two Indians had been seen, because the trail that way seemed to be the most trodden, and so we began our march in that direction. Having reached the top of the hill toward the east-northeast, we saw a good-sized river [Chorro Creek] in a plain below, and many beaten trails leading in every direction, but saw no sign of the Indians we had previously seen on the slope. Considering the diversity of the trails leading in every direction, it was agreed to follow one of them, which led southeast toward a high hill from whence what lay about could be seen. With Father Martin leading, his cross in his hand, we set off towards it, two of our Indians ahead as scouts. When we had marched a quarter of a league the Indians discovered people, and having reported that they had seen five persons, went after them. At the same time we hastened our pace in order to speak with them, and meanwhile decided to send Diego Vasquez Mexia, the sergeant, and another soldier with the two Indians to entertain them with pleasant words and show them peace and good will, if they could overtake them. The sergeant went ahead with the scouts after the five persons and although he made every effort they could not be overtaken, for they were high up on the hill. They were naked and fleet, and although the rest of the party advanced at a good gait, they had time to get into a pine wood by way of another high hill. We found two bundles like baskets wrapped up in two deerskins on a steepe slope along the trail to the hill. We found nothing in them but two deerskins, little pelts, like rabbit skins, cut and fashioned like a chain, and a few flowers like wild marjoram, which must serve them for food or drink, as no other seed was found. There were two women among the five persons they had seen, according to

the report of the Indian scouts, for they carried two children on their backs. We took one of the two deerskins, leaving in its place two handkerchiefs with their other plunder. Our men were not allowed to take anything of theirs. This done, we went up to the top of the hill, where we halted and looked about to see what could be seen. As it was already late, we returned toward the ship and when we came near, we found on and about a little hill a great quantity of very large pearl-oyster [abalone] shells and others of numerous shell-fish. When we reached this hill, as it seemed to be a suitable place to take possession in His Majesty's name of the port and the country, seeing that I and the rest of the party had landed and traversed the country round about and the port quietly and

146

145 and 146
Map of California, from the *Atlas* of Vaz Dourado, 1580. *Munich, Bayerische Staatsbibliothek, fo 17.*
Vaz Dourado is considered the chief Portuguese artist-cartographer of his time. The map from which these details are taken is lavishly decorated with pictures of Indians, Spanish horsemen, and a geographically misplaced bison.

pacifically, as in territory belonging to his domain, I did so in the name of King Philip, our master, in due legal form, through Diego Vasquez Mexia (one of the alcaldes elected for this purpose) in his capacity of Justicia, setting up a cross as a sign of the Christian faith and of the possession taken in His Majesty's name of the port and the country, cutting branches from the trees which grew thereabouts, and performing the other customary ceremonies. We then went aboard the vessel.

Text used: H. R. Wagner, transl. and ed., Spanish voyages to the Northwest coast of America in the sixteenth century. *San Francisco: California Historical Society, 1929, pp. 143-5. Original manuscript in the Archives of the Indies, 1-1-3/25.*

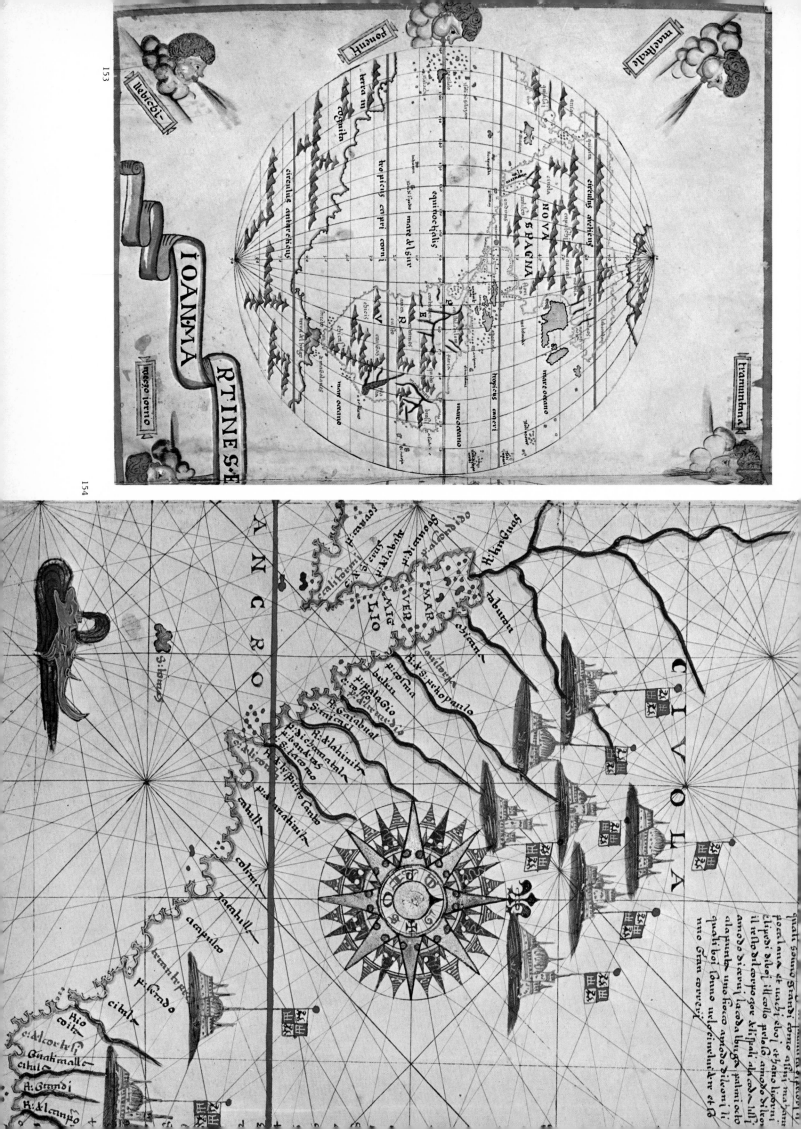

10.
Oñate's colonizing expedition to New Mexico, 1598

155

From *Relaciones que envio Don Juan de Oñate de algunas journadas.*

Oñate sent his nephew Zaldivar with a troup to hunt bison on the great plains to the east in 1598.

He spent the night by that river, and the next day, on his way back to camp, came upon a ranchería of fifty tents made of tanned skins which were very bright red and white in color. They were round like pavilions, with flaps and openings, and made as neatly as those from Italy. They are so large that in the most common ones there is ample room for four individual mattresses and beds. The tanning is so good that even the heaviest rain will not go through the skin, nor does it become hard.

To carry these tents, the poles with which they set them up, and a bag of meat and their pinole, or maize, the Indians use medium-sized, shaggy dogs, which they harness like mules. They have large droves of them, each girt around the breast and haunches, carrying a load of at least one hundred pounds. They travel at the same pace as their masters. It is both interesting and amusing to see them traveling along, one after the other, dragging the ends of their poles, almost all of them with sores under the harness. When the Indian women load these dogs they hold their heads between their legs, and in this manner they load them or straighten their loads. This is seldom necessary, for they travel at a pace as if they had been trained with fetters.

On returning to camp, they rested that day and the next, as it was Saint Francis' day. On October 5 they set out to find the main herd of the buffalo, and in three days traveled fourteen leagues, at the end of which they came upon and killed large numbers of them. A day later they went on three leagues farther in search of a good location for a corral and the material with which to build it. Having located a site, they proceeded to build the corral of large cottonwood logs, which took them three days. It was so large and had such long wings that they thought they could enclose ten thousand head, because during those days they had seen so many cattle and they roamed so close to the tents and the horses. In view of this fact and that when they run they look as if they were hobbled, taking small leaps, the men took their capture for granted. They assert that at that place alone there were more cattle than in three of the best-stocked ranches in New Spain. This was maintained by those who had seen both.

The corral being completed, they set out on the following day toward a plain where, on the preceding afternoon, they had seen about 100,000 head of cattle. As they rushed them, the buffalo began to move toward the corral, but in a little while they stampeded with great fury in the direction of the men and broke through them, even though they held close together; and they were unable to stop the cattle; because they are stubborn animals, brave beyond praise, and so cunning that if one runs after them, they run, and if one stops or moves slowly, they stop and roll, just like mules, and after this rest they renew their flight. For a few days the men tried in a thousand ways to drive them inside the corral or round

them up, but all methods proved equally fruitless. This is no small wonder, because they are unusually wild and fierce; in fact, they killed three of our horses and wounded forty others badly. They have very sharp horns, about one span and a half long, bent upward toward each other. They attack from the side, lowering the head way down, so that whatever they attack they gash easily. Nevertheless, many of them were killed and more than eighty arrobas of fat were obtained. Without any question, it is far superior to lard. The meat of the bulls is better than our beef, and that of the cows equals our most tender veal or mutton.

153
A map of the Western Hemisphere by Joan Martinez, 1578. *London, British Museum, Harley Ms.3489, fo 1.*
Joan Martinez was a Spanish or Catalan mapmaker of Messina, Sicily. His work was artistic and popular; eighteen of his atlases are still preserved. This map of the western hemisphere has an unusual conception of New England and Nova Scotia as an island. Quivira is placed in the extreme north-west, separated by a strait from the Asiatic province of Anian. A North-west Passage is above the Arctic Circle; a great Antarctic continent, found also on the maps of Mercator, Le Testu, and many other cartographers of the period, was believed in as a 'balance' to the great land masses north of the equator.

154
Map of the south-west coast of North America from the atlas of Joan Martinez, 1578. *London, British Museum, Harley Ms. 3450, fo 10.*
The maps of Martinez are useless for navigation but extremely beautiful. He based his conception of the south-west coast of America largely upon the maps of Ortelius and Zaltieri (see plate 110). This map is chiefly notable for its graphic illustration of the hold which the legend of the Seven Cities of 'Civola' had on the imagination of the explorers, and their expected magnificence.

155
The bison, from Johan de Laet, *Nieuwe Wereldt ofte beschrijvinghe van West-Indien*, Leyden, 1630.
No animal of North America made a more profound impression on the Spanish explorers than the bison. Totally unknown to Europeans, they were found in huge herds on the great plains between the Mississippi and the Rio Grande, and with them nomadic tribes of Indians whose whole life and culture depended on their hunting of 'the cows'. Descriptions of them are vivid, especially by the chroniclers of the Coronado and Oñate expeditions. European attempts to make pictures of them are often amusing.

156 *Overleaf*
Northern part of the New World map by Diego Gutiérrez, 1562. *London, British Museum.*
This is the largest and most detailed map of the New World to be engraved and published up to the time of its appearance. Made by a royal cosmographer and acting Pilot Major who had access to the latest Spanish charts and reports, it shows clearly current conceptions and knowledge then available in Spain. It does not, however, show the explorations of de Soto or other recent voyages of discovery by French and Spanish. The original work, of which this reproduction shows the northern half, must have been designed before 1554, when Diego Gutiérrez, senior, died.

Although Mercator used this map for part of the New World in making his great wall map of 1569, he did not depend on it for his topography of the east coast of North America, which differs from and is better than that of Gutiérrez.

UNIVERSALE DESCRITTIONE DI T

144

Rapids, which they later ascended with difficulty in two boats, only to hear of three other rapids beyond which extended a continuous waterway for three months' journey westward. Cartier, appointed by Francis as captain and pilot of the King 'to go west as far as possible,'[2] must have begun to grasp with amazement the enormous size of the continent which he had penetrated.

Some eight months after his return from his first voyage, Cartier had set out again in three ships with a hundred and ten men. Entering the Gulf of St Lawrence in the only way he knew, by the strait between Labrador and northern Newfoundland, he explored in vain for a passageway to the South Sea. From Taignoagny and Domagaia, the Indian lads whom he had taken back to France and trained as interpreters, he learned of the great 'river of Hochelaga [the St Lawrence], which went so far upwards, that they had never heard of any man who had gone to the head of it, and that there is no other passage but with small boats.'[3] He passed Anticosti Island and moved into the river, briefly exploring the tributary Saguenay, and after 300 miles reaching Stadacona, 'as goodly a plot of ground as possibly may be seen,' the present site of Quebec. There he was joyfully greeted by 'the Lord of Canada,' Chief Donnacona, father of his young interpreters.

When he informed his hosts of his intention to visit Hochelaga, the Indians, wanting the protection and trade of the French, offered bribes to dissuade him. Failing, they 'went and dressed three men like Devils, being wrapped in dogges skins white and blacke, their faces besmeared as blacke as any coales, with hornes on their heads more than a yard long,'[4] who prophecied they would die of ice and snow if they went. The French did not improve their friendship with the Indians by ridiculing the antics of the medicine men.

On the way to Hochelaga, Cartier saw the St Lawrence country in all its October glory. 'We saw as goodly and pleasant a countrey as possibly can be wished for, full of all sorts of goodly trees, that is to say, Okes, Elmes, Walnut-trees, Cedars, Firres, Ashes, Boxe, Willows, and great store of Vines, all as full of grapes as could be, so that if any of our fellowes went on shore, they came home laden with them: there are likewise Cranes, Swannes, Geese, Duckes, Feasants, Partriges, Thrushes, Blackbirds, Turtles, Finches, Redbreasts, Nightingales [?Thrushes], Sparrowes of diverse kinds, with many other sorts of birds . . . There is also great store of Stags, Deere, Beares, and other such like sort of beasts, as Connies, Hares, Materns, Foxes, Otters, Bevers, Weasels, Badgers, and Rats [Muskrats] exceeding great and divers other sortes of wilde beasts. They cloth themselves with the skinnes of those beasts.'[5]

Cartier returned to winter at Stadacona, where, as fresh meat and vegetables disappeared, the French succumbed to scurvy, thinking it caught from the Indians. Legs swelled,

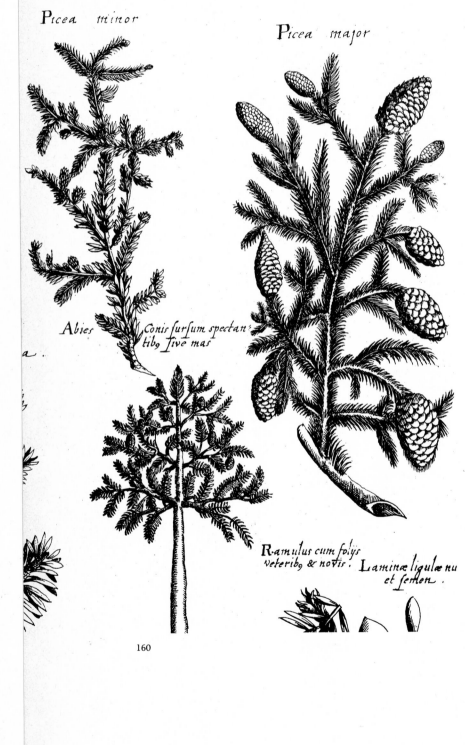

Picea minor

Picea major

Abies

Conis sursum spectantibₛ sive mas

Ramulus cum folijs veteribₛ & notis. Laminæ ligulæ nu et semen.

160

160
Spruce (*Picea minor* and *Picea major*) from J. T. de Bry, *Florilegium renovatum et auctum*, Frankfurt, 1641.
161
'Typus Orbis Terrarum' by Ortelius in his *Theatrum*, 1570, *Greenwich, National Maritime Museum*.
Abraham Ortelius (1527–98), next to Mercator the greatest geographer of the sixteenth century, was born and died in Antwerp. In 1570 he published *Theatrum Orbis Terrarum*, 'the first modern atlas'; to its 53 maps he added many others in a series of later supplements. He had access to a large collection of Italian, French, English, Portuguese, and Spanish maps; to these he added knowledge gained from wide reading and extensive correspondence. In 1575 Philip II of Spain appointed him geographer, and he published several important regional maps of Spanish territories in the New World.
162 *Overleaf*
Map of the east coast of North America from the 'Harleian Map', c. 1544. *London, British Museum, Add. Ms. 5413.*
This is part of a large undated, unsigned manuscript map, approximately four by eight feet, which derives its name from a former owner, Edward Harley, Earl of Oxford. Its style is that of the Dieppe school of mapmakers; it was probably made about 1544 by Pierre Desceliers or Jean Rotz. The St Lawrence River shows the discoveries of Jacques Cartier on his second voyage in 1535; it may be based on Cartier's own map, now lost, of that voyage. The river and Chaleur Bay are too large; the Gulf of St Lawrence too small; the maps from which they were drawn may have been of different scales. The older assumption that the central figure in the group below the river is an actual portrait of Cartier is now disputed. The coastline from Cape Breton to the south of Cape Cod is probably based upon a copy of the lost *padrón general* of Alonso de Chaves, 1536. Above Florida is a strait connecting the Atlantic with the Pacific at Verrazzano's imagined bay; John White, on his general map of the south-east, plate 199, shows this same strait.

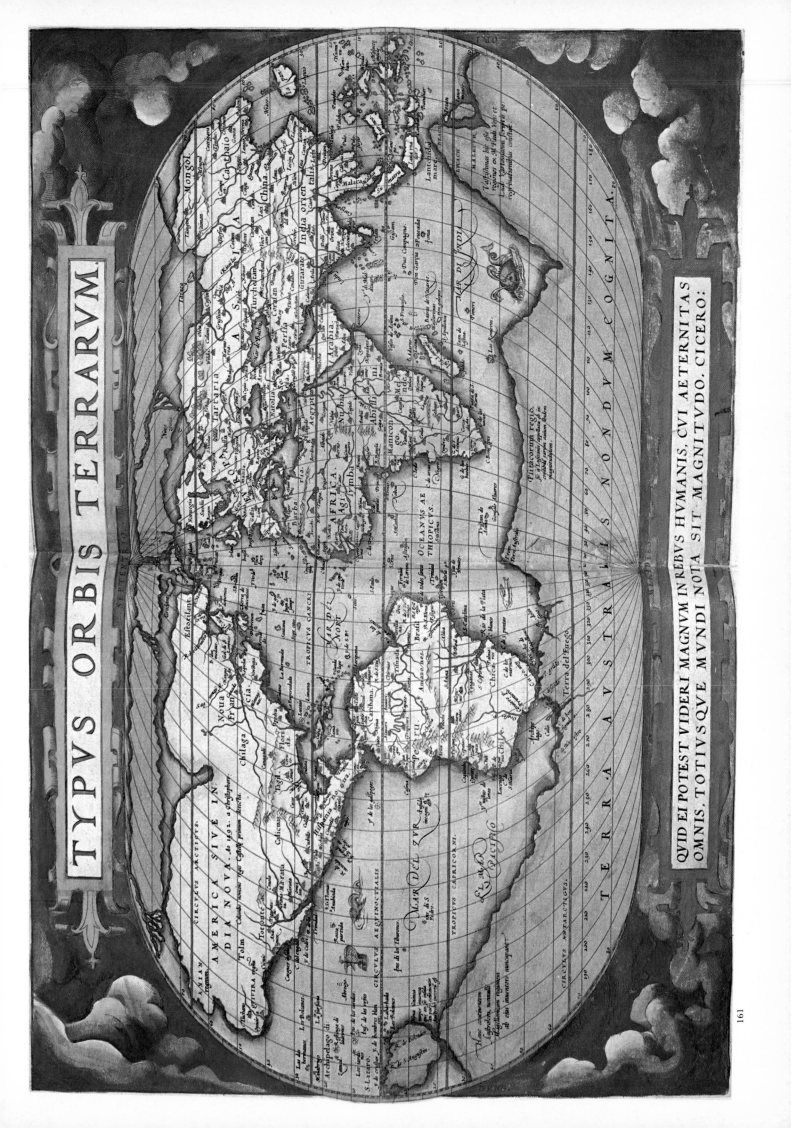

TYPVS ORBIS TERRARVM

SEPTENTRIO

QVID EI POTEST VIDERI MAGNVM IN REBVS HVMANIS, CVI AETERNITAS
OMNIS, TOTIVSQVE MVNDI NOTA SIT MAGNITVDO. CICERO:

CANADA

CANADA

TERRE DV LABOVREVE

162

TERRE DE LA FLORIDE

PARTIE DE LA MER OCEANNE

LA COVBE

ESPAIGNOL

PARTIE DE LA MER DE LENTILLE

skin blackened, gums rotted away. Twenty-five died; only four, among them Cartier, escaped the sickness. Ice froze to a depth of twelve feet; snow mounted higher than the sides of the ship; drink froze in the vessels. Then in March Domagaia, previously a disfigured scurvy victim, suddenly appeared well and sound. The seemingly miraculous remedy was a drink made from boiling the bark and needles of spruce or white pine. 'If all the physicians of Montpelier and Louvaine had beene there with all the drugs of Alexandria, they would not have done so much in one yere, as that tree did in six days.'[6]

Spring of 1536 brought recuperation and the return to France. Sailing down the St Lawrence, Cartier increased his knowledge, especially in discovering Cabot Strait between Newfoundland and Cape Breton. He encountered French fishing vessels off Newfoundland. From Cape Race to St Malo took only seventeen days; he arrived on 6 July 1536.

When Cartier sailed from Newfoundland, he missed by only a few days crossing the track of two English vessels on a voyage both ludicrous and gruesome. It is the first recorded conducted tour to America; of the sixty aboard the ships, thirty were young bloods of the Inns of Court and gentlemen about town, filled with zest for a sight of the wonders of the New World.[7] The conductor of the excursion was Master Richard Hore, a London leather-seller 'much given to the study of cosmographie'. After a boring two-months' trip from Gravesend, they reached Cape Breton and sailed up the east coast of Newfoundland early in July. They went ashore at Penguin Island, stretched their sails from their boats to the shore, and had great sport driving great auks aboard without even the trouble of catching them. 'They dressed and eate them and found them to be very good and nourishing meat.'[8]

One day Mr Oliver Dawbeny, a London merchant, saw some of 'the natural people of the country' approaching in a boat. All his companions were below the hatches, possibly gaming; upon his call, they hastily manned a ship's boat and set out in hot pursuit to capture some of the wild men as souvenirs for their return. The Indians escaped; the men returned to the ship, the only tokens of their 'victory' a leather boot and 'a certain warm mitten'. As they sailed farther north, they encountered great fields of drift ice; also, as in many another expedition, their food gave out. Their hunger became intense; they went ashore to find food. Some returned well fed; others never came back. 'By this meane the company decreased, and the officers knew not what was become of them,' until one man, led by the 'savour of broyled flesh', was told 'if thou

wouldst needes know, the broyled meat that I had was a piece of such a man's buttocke'.[9] The captain made a 'notable Oration' against such iniquity; the only effect was that they agreed to pursue their course more fairly by casting lots as to who should provide the next meal. At this juncture a well-provisioned French fishing ship appeared and was captured; its crew was transferred to the English ship and to an unrecorded fate. The 'tourists' sailed back in the better equipped French ship to St Ives in Cornwall, which they reached in October after a six-months' excursion. Fifty years later Richard Hakluyt published the details of the voyage as told him by Thomas Butts, the only survivor still living. Documents in a lawsuit against Hore for failure to carry out certain contractual terms in the voyage, recently discovered, do not mention any gentlemen passengers or, quite understandably, cannibalism.[10] The bizarre tale of Butts, it has been suggested, reflects the cultural shock of pampered townsmen unprepared for life aboard a fishing vessel. As Hakluyt drily comments, the gentlemen were actually reduced to drinking water from mugs accustomed to more potent beverage.

Four years passed before Cartier was able to return to Canada. The king listened eagerly to the fabulous tales told him by the chief Donnacona, whom with nine other Indians Cartier had captured and brought back to France. Francis, though anxious to establish a colony and explore the possibilities raised by those tales and a few pellets of gold, some beaver skins and Saguenay copper, lacked money.[11] He rewarded Cartier with the gift of the *Grande Hermione*, the ship in which he had sailed, and commissioned him 'Captain-General and master pilot' for discoveries in the 'countries of Canada and Ochelaga right into the domain of the Saguenay . . . comprising an end of Asia', but he could not finance him. At this point, Jean-François de la Roque, Seigneur de Roberval, offered to raise funds and lead a colonizing enterprise; an able and adventurous soldier, knowing mining, he fancied himself a French conquistador. On 15 January 1541 Francis commissioned him lieutenant general of the country.[12] This brought a sharp protest from Charles V of Spain, to the Pope and to Francis, for violation of the bull of Alexander VI.[13] Pope Paul III ignored the matter; Francis asked the Spanish ambassador why he had been left out when the world was divided between Spain and Portugal. Had Father Adam, he asked with Gallic wit, left a last will or testament designating these two as his sole heirs? These verbal skirmishes stiffened Spanish determination to maintain by force their exclusive right to America. Francis, on the other hand, maintained 'the freedom to navigate upon the common sea'[14] and the principle that effective occupation of a territory is the only criterion for possession, and continued to support French colonization of the St Lawrence.

Roberval, assembling his expedition, allowed Cartier to precede him with three ships. Cartier reached the St Lawrence in August 1541, and settled at Charlesbourg Royal, a high bluff overlooking the Cape Royal River. There, after some short exploratory trips, he wintered. All but one of the Indians that Cartier had taken to France had died there, including Donnacona; the new chief, Agona, seemed unconcerned. At Charlesbourg Royal, where the French were planting a crop, they made a discovery which galvanized them into action. Near the fort they found 'a quantity of stones that were believed to be diamonds', and by the river's edge 'certain leaves of gold as thick as the nail of a man'.[15] They gathered ten barrels of the yellow metal and over a thousand pounds of the glittering stones, and in June 1542 set sail for France. At St John's, Newfoundland, they met Roberval, with a motley assortment of settlers, from noblemen to assassins from

163
Map of Florida from the *Cosmographie Universelle* of Guillaume Le Testu, 1555. *Paris, Ministère des Armées, D.I.Z.14, fo 52v.*
The *Cosmographie Universelle*, an atlas of 56 maps by Le Testu, is the most detailed and beautifully decorative work produced by the Dieppe school of cartographers, which flourished in the middle of the sixteenth century. It was made for Gaspard de Coligny, who had been made admiral of the French navy in 1552 and who was to become the leader of the French Huguenots and supporter of the colonizing expeditions to Brazil in 1555 and to Florida in 1562 and 1564. This atlas, based upon a collection of recent charts from French, Spanish and Portuguese sources, furnished Admiral de Coligny with one of the most complete cartographical records available at the time. The maps in the atlas are widely varied in accuracy. Le Testu was especially interested in the supposed Antarctic continent, Terre Australle; six maps portray this region, with entirely imaginary tropical flora, strange beasts, and inhabitants.

The map of Florida, soon to be the object of French Huguenot exploration, is derived from a Portuguese map closely following a Spanish source. Opposite the map is a folio page of description: 'In this region gold is abundant, with emeralds and pearls; also it nourishes beasts of marvellous strength'.

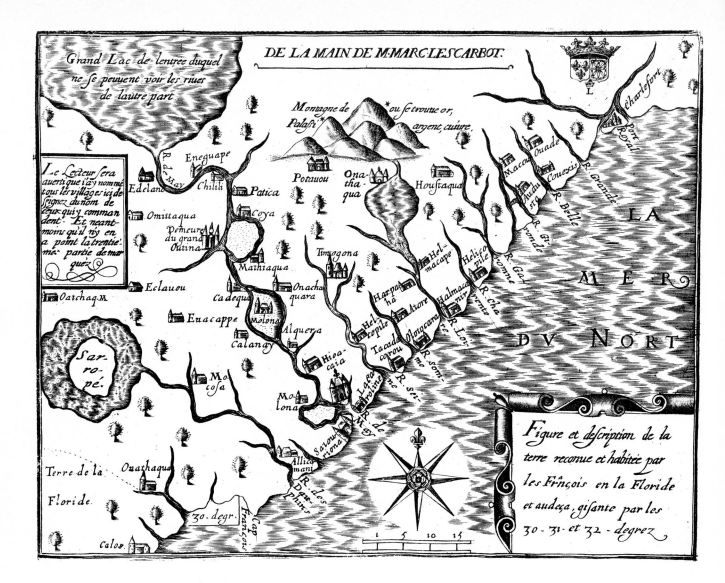

On the map:

DE LA MAIN DE M. MARC LESCARBOT.

Grand Lac de l'entree duquel ne se peuuent voir les riues de l'autre part

Le Lecteur sera auerti que i'ay nommé tous les villages icy designez du nom de ceux qui y commandent. Et neantmoins qu'il n'y en a point la trentié'mᵃ partie de marquez

Montagne de Palaffi   *où se trouue or, argent, cuiure.*

Terre de la Floride.

Figure et description de la terre reconue et habitée par les Frnçois en la Floride et audeça, gisante par les 30. 31. et 32. degrez

LA MER DU NORT

164

Map of French Florida by Lescarbot, from his *Histoire de la Nouvelle France*, Paris, 1612.

Marc Lescarbot's charming but inaccurate map of French Florida shows the River May (St Johns) flowing from a great lake beyond the Appalachian Mountains, and places Fort Caroline on the north instead of the south bank of the May.

jail.[16] Roberval wanted Cartier to turn back; but after a furnace test 'proved' the metal to be gold of 'good quality', Cartier continued his voyage to report to the king his joyful news.

Disaster, however, lay ahead. Roberval reached Charlesbourg Royal, which he renamed France-Roy, and built lodgings for the settlers;[17] but he attempted unsuccessfully to ascend the Lachine Rapids, and failed to reach the fabulous country of Saguenay. By the summer of 1543 news came that Francis was withdrawing his support; the entire colony returned to France. In Paris the high hopes of Cartier had collapsed. The gold turned out to be iron pyrites; the diamonds quartz crystals! Roberval returned to lawsuits and financial ruin; Cartier retired to his home of Limoilou, still held in esteem by Francis and revered as noble captain by his fellow townsmen. None of Cartier's maps, to which there were contemporary references, has survived; but they were known to and used by French mapmakers of the period, such as Nicolas Desliens, Pierre Desceliers, Jean Rotz, and Portuguese cartographers (see plates 116, 139 and 162).

Until the closing decades of the sixteenth century, the colonizing enterprises of France in Canada languished.[18] Fishing for cod on the Newfoundland Banks continued and fur trading with the Indians steadily increased along the Labrador coast and even up the St Lawrence to Tadoussac at the mouth of the Saguenay. In France itself, darkening clouds

of fanaticism and hate gathered strength as fratricidal religious divisions appeared. The bitter fight of the Huguenots for survival and against persecution prompted other attempts at settlement in America. Under the two sons of Francis, Henry II (1547–59) and Charles IX (1560–74), a new colonial policy emerged which encouraged outposts on transatlantic coasts much closer to Spanish and Portuguese activities than Newfoundland.

The next colonizing venture of the French in North America was to Florida, a name at that time given to the entire southeastern region. It was planned by Admiral Gaspard de Coligny, Huguenot leader, French patriot, and vowed opponent of Spain; it was supported financially by the highest members of the French court. Jean Ribaut of Dieppe was placed in command; a Huguenot and one of France's ablest seamen, he proved a wise and resourceful leader. With one hundred and fifty men in two three-masted Dutch vessels and a sloop, he left Le Havre in February 1562. Taking a mid-Atlantic course to avoid Spanish observation, he reached the coast of present-day Florida at the cape of St Anastasia Island near present-day St Augustine, to which he gave the name Cap François.[19] The day after their arrival, the first of May, the French entered the mouth of St Johns River, which Ribaut called the River of May. There he set up a stone column to signify French possession; when Laudonnière returned two years later, he found that the local Indians had made it an object of worship. (See plate 210 and the account by the anonymous letter writer on page 182.) Ribaut made friendly contacts with the local Timucuan Indians and went up the river for several leagues. He then sailed northeastward along the coast, exploring carefully the inlets, rivers, and harbors.[20] The names which he gave to the rivers and coastal islands are found on the maps of European geographers until the eighteenth century, but their identity remained in dispute until the recent discovery in the Museo Naval, Madrid, of the

165

'The French sail to the River of May'. Drawing by Jacques Le Moyne, engraving from T. de Bry, *America,* Part II, 1591, plate II.

'Re-embarking, they sailed to another place; and, before landing again, were received with salutations by another crowd of Indians, some of whom waded into the water up to their shoulders, offering the visitors little baskets full of maize and of white and red mulberries, while others offered to help them in going on shore. Having landed, they saw the chief, who was accompanied by two sons, and a company of Indians armed with bows and quivers full of arrows. After an exchange of salutations, our men went on into the woods, in hopes to discover many wonderful things. They found nothing, however, except trees bearing white and red mulberries, on the boughs of which were numerous silk-worms. They named this river the River of May [St Johns], because they sighted it on the first day of that month.'—Le Moyne.

The descriptive comments given here as well as with other engravings of Le Moyne's paintings are the artist's own explanation which de Bry printed under the engravings. These illustrations are in an appendix to Le Moyne's narrative of the French expeditions to Florida under Ribaut in 1562 and under Laudonnière in 1564. They were published by Theodor de Bry as the second volume of *America,* his series of voyages to the New World, under the title *Brevis narratio eorum quae in Florida Americae provincia Gallis acciderunt . . . auctore Jacobo le Moyne,* Frankfurt, 1591. The translation from the Latin is by Fred B. Perkins.

copy of a map made in 1562 by Nicolas Barré, a pilot who accompanied Ribaut.[21] After examining and naming a score of landmarks, he reached a bay (Baye de Santa Elena), 'one of the greatest and fayrest havens of the world', which he called Port Royal, a name which it still retains. 'In this porte are many armes of the sea depe and lardg,' wrote Ribaut, 'where without danger all the shippes in the world might be harbored.'[22] Here on a high bank of Port Royal Island on 'Chenonceau River' (Battery Creek), reasonably safe from prying Spanish eyes, he raised a small wooden structure, Charlesfort, for thirty men who volunteered to stay behind while he returned to France for supplies and reinforcements. 'He had discovered more in six weekes,' wrote a gentleman on the voyage, René de Laudonnière, 'then the Spaniards had done in two yeares in the conquest of their New Spaine.'[23] When the ships reached Dieppe on 22 July 1562, open religious and civil war had broken out; Ribaut fought with the Huguenots at Dieppe until its surrender and then fled to England early in 1563.[24]

Meanwhile, the little settlement at Charlesfort fared badly. Captain Albert della Pirie, whom Ribaut left in charge, became homicidally tyrannical in his efforts to preserve discipline; he hanged one man and exiled another, La Chère, to imminent starvation on an island. Albert was killed, probably by a man who acted in self-defense. After rescuing La Chère, the colonists elected Nicolas Barré as their leader. Barré, who had discovered and helped to put down a mutiny at Fort Coligny in Brazil, quickly restored order. The French visited and made friends with the surrounding Indians, who gave them food when their own supply was exhausted. The old story of improvidence repeated itself; the colonists planted nothing, counting on what they had brought with them and on Indian stores to provide food. When Ribaut did not return in the promised six months, they built a small pinnace and set sail for France. For weeks they were becalmed. Famished and starving, they cast lots; the choice fell on La Chère, whom they had rescued.[25] They ate him. Shortly after, probably in July 1563, an English ship picked them up, put the ill ashore,

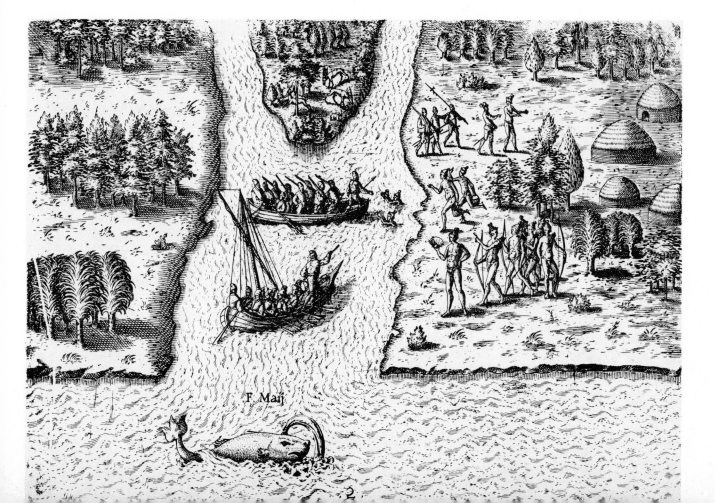

F. Maij

166

167

'Leaving the River of May, the French discover two other rivers'.
Drawing by Le Moyne, engraving from T. de Bry, *America*, Part II, 1591, plate III.

'A little afterwards they went on board again, hoisted anchors, and sailed farther on along the coast, until they entered a beautiful river [St Mary's], which the commander himself chose to explore in company with the chief of that vicinity and some of the natives, and which he named the Seine because it was very like the River Seine in France. It is about fourteen leagues from the River of May. Returning to the ships, they sailed still farther north; but, before going far, they discovered another fine river, and sent two boats to explore it. In it they discovered an island, whose chief was no less friendly than the others. This river they named the Aine [Satilla]. It is six miles from the Seine.'—Le Moyne.

167
'The French left in Fort Charles suffer from scarcity of provisions'.
Drawing by Le Moyne, engraving from T. de Bry, *America*, Part II, 1591, plate VII.

'Not long after the departure of Ribaud from Florida, the men whom he left in Charles fort (the work erected by him on an island on a stream entering the greater channel of Port Royal from the north) began to find their provisions fail them. They concluded that the wisest plan was to apply to the chief Ouadé and to his brother Couëxis. Those who were sent on this business went in Indian canoes by the inland waters, and at a distance of some ten miles discovered a large and beautiful river of fresh water, in which they saw numerous crocodiles, much larger than those of the Nile. The banks of this stream were wooded with lofty cypresses. They went on to the chief Ouadé; and, being received by him in the most friendly manner, they laid before him the object of their journey, and prayed him not to desert them in such a strait. The chief sent messengers to his brother Couëxis after maize and beans. The latter responded promptly; for next morning very early the messengers came back with the provisions, which the chief ordered on board the canoe. Next morning he showed them his fields of millet, or maize, and intimated that they should not want for food as long as that millet existed. Being now dismissed by the king, they returned by the way they had come.'—Le Moyne.

168
Chart of the coast of 'French Florida', by Nicolas Barré of Tours, a pilot in Ribaut's expedition of 1562: a near-contemporary tracing by a Spanish hand.
Madrid, Museo Naval, Col. Nararrete, vol XIV, fo 459.

The original chart, which is now lost, was evidently drawn by Barré as Ribaut's ships ran along the coast northward from their landfall near St Augustine to Port Royal in South Carolina, giving the coastal features names which remained on maps for three centuries. As the only surviving first-hand cartographic record of the first French expedition to Florida, Barré's sketch-chart has (since its recent discovery) thrown valuable light on Ribaut's exploration of this coast, and especially on the location of the settlement established by him at 'Charlesfort' (Port Royal) on Battery Creek, South Carolina. This map also shows knowledge of the coast north of Port Royal which was obtained by the French after Ribaut sailed back to France. This tracing of Barré's map by a Spanish spy in London was sent to the King of Spain, who despatched an expedition to destroy the French colony on Port Royal Island. The Spanish did not know that the French had abandoned their fortified settlement, here shown beside a ship at the extreme right of the map.

and took the others with them to London. Among the latter was Nicolas Barré, who was held in England for a year and a half in spite of efforts of the French ambassador to have him released for return to France.[26] Like Ribaut, Barré was a pawn in international schemes for colonization. Both England and France had plans for settling Florida and wanted these two men. Barré, a pilot with considerable transatlantic experience, had a detailed map of the Florida coast; an English translation of Ribaut's report of his voyage to the French admiral was published in London in July 1963.

The uneasy peace of Amboise between the Huguenots and Roman Catholics in 1563 gave Coligny freedom to renew his attempts to weaken Spain and to establish a strong foothold

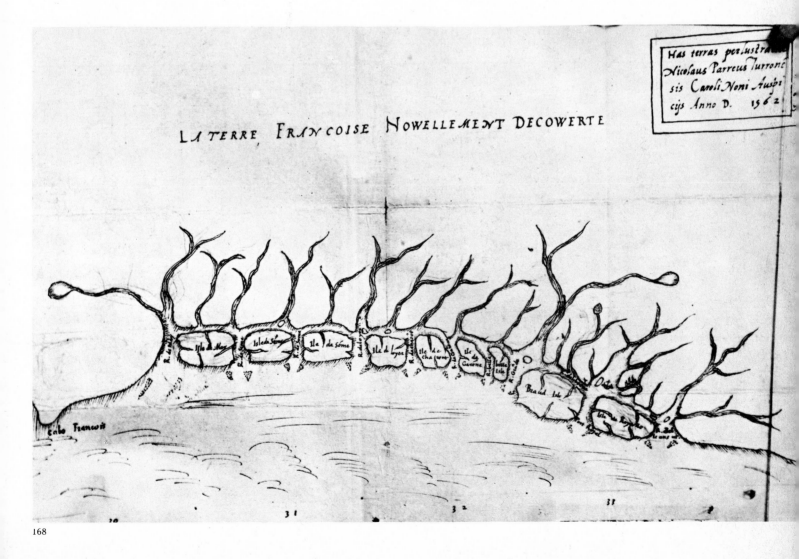

LA TERRE FRANCOISE NOWELLEMENT DECOWERTE

Has terras perlustra
Nicolaus Parreus Turrone
sis Caroli Noni Auspi
cijs Anno D. 1562

168

169

Nicotiana
inferta in-
fundibulo
ex quo hau-
riunt fumū
Indi & nau
cleri.

170

169
'The French select a place for building a fort'. Drawing by Le Moyne, engraving from T. de Bry, *America,* Part II, 1591, plate IX.
'After exploring many of the rivers in that country, it was finally decided that the River of May was the best one for an establishment, because millet and breadstuffs were most abundant there, besides the gold and silver that had been discovered there on the first voyage. They therefore sailed for that river; and, after ascending it to the neighborhood of a certain mountain, they selected a place more fit for the site of their fort than any previously observed. Next day, as soon as it was light, after offering prayers to God, and giving thanks for their prosperous coming into the province, they all went briskly to work; and, after a triangular outline had been measured out, they all began,—some to dig in the earth, some to make fascines of brushwood, some to put up the wall. Every man was briskly engaged with spade, saw, axe, or some other tool.'—Le Moyne.

170
The tobacco plant with the oldest printed picture of a pipe, from Pierre Rena and M. de l'Obel, *Stirpium adversaria nova,* London, 1570–1.
Jacques Cartier at Hochelaga (Montreal) on his second voyage observed the Indians inhaling smoke through elbow pipes. His reactions are recorded in John Florio's translation, *A short and briefe narration of two navigations,* London, 1580.
'There groweth also a certain kind of Herb, whereof in Sommer they make greate provision for all the yeare, making great accompt of it, and only men use of it, and first, they cause it to be dryed in the Sunne, they weare it aboute their necke wrapped in a little beastes skin made like a little bagge, with a hollow peece of stone or wood like a pipe [=musical instrument]; then when they please they make a pouder of it, and then put it in one of the endes of the sayd Cornet or pipe and laying a cole of fire uppon at the other ende smoke so long that they fill their bodies full of smoke, till that cometh out of their mouthes and nostrils, even as out of the Tonnel of a chimny. They say that this doth kepe them warm and in good health; they never go without some of it about the[m]. We ourselves tryed the same smoke, and having put it in our mouthes, it seemed that they had filled it with Pepper dust, it is so hote.'

171
'Hunting deer.' Drawing by Le Moyne, engraving from T. de Bry, *America*, Part II, 1591, plate XXV.
'The Indians have a way of hunting deer which we never saw before. They manage to put on the skins of the largest which have before been taken, in such a manner, with the heads on their own heads, so that they can see out through the eyes as through a mask. Thus accoutred, they can approach close to the deer without frightening them. They take advantage of the time when the animals come to drink at the river, and, having their bow and arrows all ready, easily shoot them, as they are very plentiful in those regions. It is usual, however, to protect the left arm with the bark of the branch of a tree, to keep it from being grazed by the bow-string,—a practice which they have learned naturally enough. They know how to prepare deer-skins, not with iron instruments, but with shells, in a surprisingly excellent manner.'—Le Moyne.

in Florida. As Ribaut was in prison in England, Coligny put Laudonnière in command of three ships, one a man-of-war of three hundred tons, and three hundred men on this second expedition. Two months after leaving Le Havre they reached the Florida coast in the vicinity of Matanzas Inlet on 22 June 1564.[27] Across that inlet, which Laudonnière called the River of Dolphins, hundreds of Frenchmen crossed to their death fifteen months later. At the beginning, however, all went well. The ships sailed north along the shore until they reached St Johns River, which they recognized from their visit in 1562. Here the Indians greeted them with welcoming fires and showed them the stone column engraved with the royal arms and *fleur-de-lys*, which Ribaut had placed there in act of French possession. Laudonnière decided to establish his colony on the St Johns and immediately began building a fort

on the south bank about fifteen miles from the sea. Fort Caroline, named in honor of Charles IX, was located near St Johns' Bluff on land that has since been washed away. *Isabella,* the large man-of-war, having accomplished its purpose as protective convoy, soon returned to France with a few presents gathered for the royal court and with glowing reports of gold and silver mines already located.

Laudonnière was not, however, a good administrator, and conditions in the new colony soon deteriorated under his ineffective leadership. He was eager to make friends with all the neighboring tribes and promised their chiefs military support against their enemies. The tribes, however, were at war with each other. When he attempted conciliation between them or procrastinated with diplomatic evasions, they felt betrayed and deceived; when he allowed his troops to fight for one side, he gained inveterate enemies among the tribes whose warriors had been slaughtered. Within the colony itself malcontents, disappointed in their expectations of quick wealth, were furious that he limited their exploitation of the natives and forbade piracy against the Spaniards. They imprisoned Laudonnière aboard one of the ships and forced him to sign permission for use of two vessels; on 8 December 1564 the mutineers set out on a series of marauding exploits. Most of them were eventually captured and killed by the Spanish. A few survivors returned to Fort Caroline on 25 March 1565; Laudonnière had four of the ringleaders shot. The colonists, composed of soldiers and a few mechanics and servants but no farmers, had improvidently planted no crops; they expected provisions from France, which did not come,

172

172
'Ceremonies at the death of a chief or of priests.' Drawing by Le Moyne,
engraving from T. de Bry, *America*, Part II, 1591, plate XL.
'When a chief in that province dies, he is buried with great solemnities;
his drinking-cup is placed on the grave, and many arrows are planted in
the earth about the mound itself. His subjects mourn for him three whole
days and nights, without taking any food. All the other chiefs, his friends,
mourn in like manner; and both men and women, in testimony of their love
for him, cut off more than half their hair. Besides this, for six months
afterwards certain chosen women three times every day, at dawn, noon, and
twilight, mourn for the deceased king with a great howling. And all his
household stuff is put into his house, which is set on fire, and the whole
burned up together.'—Le Moyne.

and from the Indians grain, which had been exhausted.
With only ten days' food left for the settlement, Laudonnière,
who had climbed up a little hill 'much tormented in mind',[28]
saw four ships approaching. They were the fleet of John
Hawkins, looking for fresh water on their return voyage to
England. Hawkins, a founder of the English slave trade, had
captured negroes on the Guinea coast and sold them to the
Spanish in the West Indies. He was as generous to the French
in their extremity as he had been heartless in the business
transactions of his voyage. He presented Laudonnière with
food, with shoes for his barefoot soldiers, and with one of his
small ships in return for artillery and powder which the
French, determined to abandon the colony and return to
France, offered him. Hawkins, who stayed several days at
Fort Caroline, reported with interest a fascinating custom
which his hosts had acquired from the Indians; 'the Floridians',
he noted, 'have a kinde of herb dried, who with a cane and an
earthen cup in the end, with fire, and the dried herbs put
together, doe sucke thorow the cane the smoke thereof,
which smoke satisfieth their hunger . . . and this all the
Frenchmen used for this purpose: yet do they holde the
opinion withall, that it causeth water and flame to void from
their stomacks.'[29]

173
'Ceremonies performed by the Saturioua before going on an expedition
against the enemy.' Drawing by Le Moyne, engraving from T. de Bry,
America, Part II, 1591, plate XI.
'It is mentioned in the account of the second voyages that the French made a
treaty of friendship with a powerful chief of the vicinity, named Saturioua,
with agreement that they were to erect a fort in his territory, and were to be
friends to his friends, and enemies to his enemies. He assembled his men,
decorated, after the Indian manner, with feathers and other things, in a level
place, the soldiers of Laudonnière being present; and the force sat down in a
circle, the chief being in the middle. A fire was then lighted on his left,
and two great vessels full of water were set on his right. Then the chief,
after rolling his eyes as if excited by anger, uttering some sounds deep down
in his throat, and making various gestures, all at once raised a horrid yell;
and all his soldiers repeated this yell, striking their hips, and rattling their
weapons. Then the chief, taking a wooden platter of water, turned toward
the sun, and worshipped it; praying to it for a victory over the enemy,
and that, as he should now scatter the water that he had dipped up in the
wooden platter, so might their blood be poured out. Then he flung the
water with a great cast up into the air; and, as it fell down upon his men,
he added, "As I have done with this water, so I pray that you may do with
the blood of your enemies." Then he poured the water in the other vase
upon the fire, and said, "So may you be able to extinguish your enemies,
and bring back their scalps." Then they all arose, and set off by land up the
river, upon their expedition.'—Le Moyne.
174
'Order of march observed by Outina on a military expedition.' Drawing by
Le Moyne, engraving from T. de Bry, *America*, Part II, 1591, plate XIV.
'When Saturioua went to war, his men preserved no order, but went along
one after another, just as it happened. On the contrary, his enemy Holata
Outina, whose name, as I now remember, means "king of many kings,"
and who was much more powerful than he as regards both wealth, and
number of his subjects, used to march with regular ranks, like an organized
army; himself marching alone in the middle of the whole force, painted red.
On the wings, or horns, of his order of march were his young men, the
swiftest of whom, also painted red, acted as advanced guards and scouts for
reconnoitring the enemy. These are able to follow up the traces of the enemy
by scent, as dogs do wild beasts; and, when they come upon such traces,
they immediately return to the army to report. And, as we make use of
trumpets and drums in our armies to promulgate orders, so they have
heralds, who by cries of certain sorts direct when to halt, or to advance, or
to attack, or to perform any other military duty. After sunset they halt,
and are never wont to give battle.'—Le Moyne.

173

174

R. Holata Outina.

175

175
'Outina, going at the head of his army against the enemy, consults a sorcerer on the event.' Drawing by Le Moyne, engraving from T. de Bry, *America*, Part II, 1591, plate XII.
'Laudonnière, having received some of the men of the chief, Holata Utina, or Outina, living about forty miles south from the French fort, and who had been taken in a previous expedition by his enemy Saturioua, sent them back to their chief, upon which a solemn league was made, and mutual friendship promised. This treaty was made for the reason that the only road, whether by land or by the rivers, to the Apalatcy Mountains, in which gold, silver, and brass [*æs*] are found, was through the dominions of this chief; and it was in his friendship, now of scarcely a year's standing, that the French trusted to obtain free access to those mountains. As this friendship, however, was as yet existing, he asked Laudonnière for some arquebusiers, as he wished to make war on an enemy; on which twenty-five were sent him, under D'Ottigny, Laudonnière's lieutenant. At length they reached the enemy's territories, when the chief halted his force, and summoning an aged sorcerer, more than a hundred and twenty years old, directed him to report what was the state of affairs with the enemy. The sorcerer accordingly made ready a place in the middle of the army, and, seeing the shield which D'Ottigny's page was carrying, asked to take it. On receiving it, he laid it on the ground, and drew around it a circle, upon which he inscribed various characters and signs. Then he knelt down on the shield, and sat on his heels, so that no part of him touched the earth, and began to recite some unknown words in a low tone, and to make various gestures, as if engaged in a vehement discourse. This lasted for a quarter of an hour, when he began to assume an appearance so frightful that he was hardly like a human being; for he twisted his limbs so that the bones could be heard to snap out of place, and did many other unnatural things. After going through with all this, he came back all at once to his ordinary condition, but in a very fatigued state, and with an air as if astonished; and then, stepping out of his circle, he saluted the chief, and told him the number of the enemy, and where they were intending to meet him.'—Le Moyne.
176
'How they declare war.' Drawing by Le Moyne, engraving from T. de Bry, *America*, Part II, 1591, plate XXXIII.
'A chief who declares war against his enemy does not send a herald to do it, but orders some arrows, having locks of hair fastened at the notches, to be stuck up along the public ways; as we observed when, after taking the chief Outina prisoner, we carried him around to the town under his authority, to make them furnish us provisions.'—Le Moyne.

177
'Trophies and ceremonies after a victory.' Drawing by Le Moyne, engraving from T. de Bry, *America*, Part II, 1591, plate XVI.
'After returning from a military expedition, they assemble in a place set apart for the purpose, to which they bring the legs, arms, and scalps which they have taken from the enemy, and with solemn formalities fix them up on tall poles set in the ground in a row. Then they all, men and women, sit down on the ground in a circle before these members; while the sorcerer, holding a small image in his hand, goes through a form of cursing the enemy, uttering in a low voice, according to their manner, a thousand imprecations. At the side of the circle opposite to him, there are placed three men kneeling down, one of whom holds in both hands a club, with which he pounds on a flat stone, marking time to every word of the sorcerer. At each side of him, the other two hold in each hand the fruit of a certain plant, something like a gourd or pumpkin, which has been dried, opened at each end, its marrow and seeds taken out, and then mounted on a stick, and charged with small stones or seeds of some kind. These they rattle after the fashion of a bell, accompanying the words of the sorcerer with a sort of song after their manner.'—Le Moyne.

Upon the departure of Hawkins the colonists hurriedly loaded aboard two seaworthy ships their remaining provisions and by 28 August 1565 were waiting only for favorable winds to abandon the settlement. Unknown to the dispirited group, powerful naval and military forces which had left their European ports months before were converging on them, one in support and the other intent on their destruction. That very day a French fleet of seven ships, carrying hundreds of new colonists, including women and children, and soldiers with military equipment and provisions, reached the mouth of the river. Jean Ribaut, who had escaped his English prison, was in charge, with orders from Coligny to replace Laudonnière as commander of the French colony. Under his firm and able leadership, the French began to repair the dismantled fort and build new houses, leaving only a skeleton crew aboard the ships.

176

R. Holata Outina.

177

178

'The Promontory of Florida, at which the French touched; named by them the French Promontory'. Drawing by Le Moyne, engraving from T. de Bry, *America*, Part II, 1591, plate I. *New York Public Library*.
'The French, on their first voyage to Florida, touched at a headland, not very high, as the coast in that vicinity is level, but heavily wooded with very lofty trees. This their commander named French Cape (Promontorium Gallicum) in honor of France. It is about thirty degrees from the equator. Coasting thence to the northward, they discovered a broad and beautiful river, at whose mouth they cast anchor in order to examine it in more detail next day. On landing on the shore of this river, our men saw many Indians, who came on purpose to give them a most kind and friendly reception, as their actions proved; for some of them gave their own skin-garments to the commander, and promised to point out to him their chief, who did not rise up, but remained sitting on boughs of laurel and palm which had been spread for him. He gave our commander a large skin, decorated all over with pictures of various kinds of wild animals drawn after the life.'—Le Moyne.

179

'The French reach Port Royal'. Drawing by Le Moyne, engraving from T. de Bry, *America*, Part II, 1591, plate V. *New York Public Library*.
'Resuming their voyage as before, they discovered a river which they called Bellevue [St Helena Sound]; and, after sailing three or four miles farther, they were informed that not far off was another river, surpassing all the rest in size and beauty. When they had reached this, they found it so magnificent and great a stream that they named it Port Royal. Here they took in sail, and came to anchor in ten fathoms. The commander, on landing with some soldiers, found the country very beautiful, as it was well wooded with oak, cedar, and other trees. As they went on through the woods, they saw Indian peacocks, or turkeys, flying past, and deer going by. The mouth of this river is three French leagues, or miles, wide, and is divided into two arms, one turning to the west, the other to the north. These two branches are two full miles wide, and midway between them is an island [Parris] whose point looks toward the mouth of the river. Shortly after, embarking again, they entered the arm making to the northward, in order to examine its advantages; and, after proceeding about twelve miles, they saw a company of Indians, who, on perceiving the boats, immediately took to flight, leaving a lynx's whelp which they were roasting; from which circumstance the place was called Lynx Point.'—Le Moyne.

180

'How they set on fire an enemy's town'. Drawing by Le Moyne, engraving from T. de Bry, *America*, Part II, 1591, plate XXXI. *New York Public Library*.
'For the enemy, eager for revenge, sometimes will creep up by night in the utmost silence, and reconnoitre to see if the watch be asleep. If they find every thing silent, they approach the rear of the town, set fire to some dry moss from trees, which they prepare in a particular manner, and fasten to the heads of their arrows. They then fire these into the town, so as to ignite the roofs of the houses, which are made of palm-branches thoroughly dried with the summer heats. As soon as they see that the roofs are burning, they make off as fast as possible, before they are discovered, and they move so swiftly that it is a hard matter to overtake them; and meanwhile also the fire is giving the people in the town enough to do to save themselves from it, and get it under.'—Le Moyne.

181

'Six other rivers discovered by the French'. Drawing by Le Moyne, engraving from T. de Bry, *America*, Part II, 1591, plate IV. *New York Public Library*.
'Sailing hence about six miles farther on they discovered another river which was called the Loire [Brunswick]; and subsequently five others, named the Charente [Altamaha], Garonne [Sapelo], Gironde [Midway], Belle [Ogeechee], and Grande [Savannah], respectively. Having carefully explored all these, and having discovered along these nine rivers, within the space of less than sixty miles, many singular things, but still not being contented, they proceeded still farther north, until they arrived at the River Jordan, which is almost the most beautiful river of the whole of this northern region.'—Le Moyne.

182

'Picture of Fort Caroline'. Drawing by Le Moyne, engraving from T. de Bry, *America*, Part II, 1591, plate X. *New York Public Library*.
'Thus was erected a triangular work, afterwards named Caroline. The base of the triangle, looking westward, was defended only by a small ditch, and a wall of sods nine feet high. The side next the river was built up with planks and fascines. On the southern side was a building after the fashion of a citadel, which was for a granary to hold their provisions. The whole was of fascines and earth, except the upper part of the wall for two or three feet, which was of sods. In the middle of the fort was a roomy open space eighteen yards long, and as many wide. Midway on the southern side of this space were the soldiers' quarters; and on the north side was a building which was higher than it should have been, and was in consequence blown over by the wind a little afterwards. Experience thus taught us that in this country, where the winds are so furious, houses must be built low.

On another side stood the residence of Laudonnière, looking out upon the river, and with a piazza all round it. The principal door of this opened upon the larger open space; and the rear door, upon the river. At a safe distance from the works, an oven was erected; for, as the houses were roofed with palm-branches, they would very easily have caught fire.'—Le Moyne.

183

'Outina, with the help of the French, gains a victory over his enemy Potanou'. Drawing by Le Moyne, engraving from T. de Bry, *America*, Part II, 1591, plate XIII. *New York Public Library*.
'This report so terrified the chief that he began to consider not how to come up with the enemy, but how to get safe back again. But D'Ottigny, greatly vexed at the idea of making such exertions only to return without bringing any thing to pass, threatened to consider him a base chief, and of no courage, if he should not risk an action; and, by force of reproaches and some threats too, brought him to order an attack. He, however, put the French in the advance, as they were quite willing to have him do; and indeed, unless they had sustained the whole brunt of the battle, killing very many of the enemy, and putting to flight the army of the chief Potanou, there is no question but Outina would have been routed; for it became evident that the sorcerer had made a true report of the facts, and he must certainly have been possessed by a devil. Outina, however, quite contented with the flight of the enemy, recalled his men, and marched for home, to the great wrath of D'Ottigny who wished to follow up the victory.'—Le Moyne.

A few days later, on Tuesday, 4 September, as evening was approaching, eight war ships appeared, sailed between the four French vessels remaining outside the river bar, and dropped their anchors. It was the armada of Pedro Menéndez de Avilés, admiral of Spain, former captain-general of the treasure fleets, and recently appointed Governor of Florida. Astute, courageous, fanatic of the faith, and an exceptionally able seaman and commander, he was commissioned by Philip II to destroy the French and to occupy Florida.

'What are you doing here?' asked Menéndez from his flagship *San Pelayo*.

'We are from France, bringing supplies for a fort which the King of France has in this country.'

'Catholics or Lutherans?'

'Lutherans'

'The King of Spain has sent me to burn or hang the Lutheran French found here.'

On the ships during this exchange was 'a stillness such as I never heard since I came into the world,' wrote Grajales, Menéndez's chaplain and biographer.[30]

'Surrender.'

'I will die first,' came from the French flagship, the *Trinity*.

'Draw your swords and board,' commanded Menéndez. But in the confusion following his order, the French cut their cables and escaped into the evening haze.[31] The pursuing Spaniards lost them and without attempting further attack sailed southward. All four French ships returned to the river's mouth the next morning and reported to Ribaut. He realized the immediate peril to his colony from Menéndez and the increased danger should he allow the Spanish to establish their position and add to their forces. Against the advice of Laudonnière, who warned him of the storms and 'houragans' prevalent at that season, Ribaut embarked most of the fighting force on his fleet and sailed south into a terrible hurricane that drove his ships ashore south of Matanzas Inlet. The vessels were wrecked and the provisions lost. Some men drowned, the Indians killed others, and the rest began the terrible march back toward Fort Caroline

Between them and the fort were the Spanish. Before the hurricane struck, Menéndez had put his troops and supplies safely ashore at an inlet he named St Augustine, on the north end of Anastasia Island. Overcoming the rebellious opposition of his men and officers, he ordered an immediate attack on the French settlement. After three days' march in the rain,

178

181

179

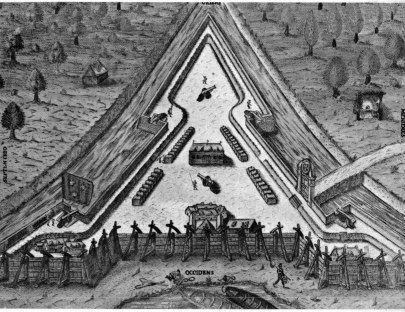

182

180

183

184

185

186

184

'Mode of drying fish, wild animals, and other provisions'. Drawing by
Le Moyne, engraving from T. de Bry, *America,* Part II, 1591, plate XXIV.
New York Public Library.

'In order to keep these animals longer, they are in the habit of preparing
them as follows: They set up in the earth four stout forked stakes; and on
these they lay others, so as to form a sort of grating. On this they lay their
game, and then build a fire underneath, so as to harden them in the smoke.
In this process they use a great deal of care to have the drying perfectly
performed, to prevent the meat from spoiling, as the picture shows.
I suppose this stock to be laid in for their winter's supply in the woods,
as at that time we could never obtain the least provision from them. For the
like reason their granaries, as was related, are placed close under some rock
or cliff, near a river, and not far from some deep forest, so that when
necessary they can carry a supply in canoes.'—Le Moyne.

185

'Killing crocodiles'. Drawing by Le Moyne, engraving from T. de Bry,
America, Part II, 1591, plate XXVI. *New York Public Library.*

'Their way of attacking crocodiles [alligators] is as follows: They put up,
near a river, a little hut full of cracks and holes, and in this they station a
watchman, so that he can see the crocodiles, and hear them, a good way off;
for, when driven by hunger, they come out of the rivers, and crawl about
on the islands after prey, and, if they find none, they make such a frightful
noise that it can be heard for half a mile. Then the watchman calls the rest
of the watch, who are in readiness; and, taking a portion, ten or twelve feet
long, of the stem of a tree, they go out to find the monster, who is crawling
along with his mouth wide open, all ready to catch one of them if he can;

and with the greatest quickness they push the pole, small end first, as deep
as possible down his throat, so that the roughness and irregularity of the
bark may hold it from being got out again. Then they turn the crocodile
over on his back, and with clubs and arrows pound and pierce his belly,
which is softer; for his back, especially if he is an old one, is impenetrable,
being protected by hard scales.'—Le Moyne.

186

'Flying fish.' Engraving from T. de Bry, *America,* Part IV, 1594.
New York Public Library.

Schools of flying fish, escaping their pursuers, sometimes fell aboard a ship,
where they were captured by the sailors.

187

'Solemnities at consecrating the skin of a stag to the sun.' Drawing by
Le Moyne, engraving from T. de Bry, *America,* Part II, 1591, plate XXXV.

'The subjects of the chief Outina were accustomed every year, a little before
their spring, that is, in the end of February, to take the skin of the largest
stag they could get, keeping the horns on it; to stuff it full of all the choicest
sorts of roots that grow among them, and to hang long wreaths or garlands
of the best fruits on the horns, neck, and other parts of the body. Thus

decorated, they carried it, with music and songs, to a very large and
splendid level space, where they set it up on a very high tree, with the head
and breast toward the sunrise. They then offered prayers to the sun, that he
would cause to grow on their lands good things such as those offered him.
The chief, with his sorcerer, stands nearest the tree, and offers the prayer;
the common people, placed at a distance, make responses. Then the chief
and all the rest, saluting the sun, depart, leaving the deer's hide there until
the next year. This ceremony they repeat annually.'—Le Moyne.

188

189

190

188

'First-born children sacrificed to the chief with solemn ceremonies.'
Drawing by Le Moyne, engraving from T. de Bry, *America*, Part II, 1591,
plate XXXIV.
'Their custom is to offer up the first-born son to the chief. When the day for
the sacrifice is notified to the chief, he proceeds to a place set apart for the
purpose, where there is a bench for him, on which he takes his seat. In the
middle of the area before him is a wooden stump two feet high, and as many
thick, before which the mother sits on her heels, with her face covered in
her hands, lamenting the loss of her child. The principal one of her female
relatives or friends now offers the child to the chief in worship, after which
the women who have accompanied the mother form a circle, and dance
around with demonstrations of joy, but without joining hands. She who
holds the child goes and dances in the middle, singing some praises of the
chief. The ceremonies being through, the sacrificer takes the child, and slays
it in honor of the chief, before them all, upon the wooden stump. This
offering was on one occasion performed in our presence.'—Le Moyne.
189

'The display with which a queen elect is brought to the king.' Drawing by
Le Moyne, engraving from T. de Bry, *America,* Part II, 1591, plate XXXVII.
'When a king chooses to take a wife, he directs the tallest and handsomest
of the daughters of the chief man to be selected. Then a seat is made on two
stout poles, and covered with the skin of some rare sort of animal, while it is
set off with a structure of boughs, bending over forward so as to shade the
head of the sitter. The queen elect having been placed on this, four strong
men take up the poles, and support them on their shoulders; each carrying
in one hand a forked wooden stick to support the pole at halting. Two more
walk at the sides; each carrying on a staff a round screen elegantly made,
to protect the queen from the sun's rays. Others go before, blowing upon
trumpets made of bark, which are smaller above, and larger at the farther
end, and having only the two orifices, one at each end. They are hung with
small oval balls of gold, silver, and brass, for the sake of a finer
combination of sounds. Behind follow the most beautiful girls that can be
found, elegantly decorated with necklaces and armlets of pearls, each
carrying in her hand a basket full of choice fruits; and belted below the
navel, and down to the thighs, with the moss of certain trees, to cover their
nakedness. After them come the body-guards.'—Le Moyne.
190

'The youth at their exercises.' Drawing by Le Moyne, engraving from
T. de Bry, *America*, Part II, 1591, plate XXXVI.
'Their youth are trained in running, and a prize is offered for him who can
run longest without stopping; and they frequently practise with the bow.
They also play a game of ball, as follows: in the middle of an open space is
set up a tree some eight or nine fathoms high, with a square frame woven

of twigs on the top; this is to be hit with the ball, and he who strikes it
first gets a prize. They are also fond of amusing themselves with hunting
and fishing.'—Le Moyne.

through swamps and forests and rivers, he reached the fort
at night and allowed his soldiers to rest. His attack at daybreak caught the French unprepared; the Spanish put to the
sword the entire colony with the exception of some fifty
women and children whom Menéndez spared and about
fifty Frenchmen who escaped into the surrounding woods.[32]
Twenty of these were later captured and killed; others found
their way to the Indians. Twenty-six reached the river near
some still unloaded ships left under the command of Jacques
Ribaut, the son of Jean. They were rescued and eventually
reached France. Among these were Laudonnière, who was ill
abed at the time of the attack, and Jacques Le Moyne de
Morgues the painter, whose vivid pictures of Florida form
one of the best visual records of North America during the
period of discovery.

Menéndez, fearful of an attack by Ribaut on the small
garrison he had left at St Augustine, returned there the next
day, 21 September. From the Indians he learned of the
survivors of two wrecked French vessels and marched south
to Matanzas Inlet. Huddled on a windswept sandbar across the
inlet were 140 Frenchmen, a group of the survivors of 200
sailors and 400 soldiers under Ribaut stranded or drowned in
the hurricane. After fruitless negotiations they surrendered
unconditionally; bringing them over in boatloads of ten,
Menéndez had their hands bound behind them and marched
them one by one behind a dune to a line he had drawn in the
sand. There they were beheaded. Twelve days later he heard
that Ribaut himself, with 200 more survivors, was near
Matanzas Inlet. Seventy of these, including Ribaut, surrendered and were murdered in the same day; the rest

191

192

'How sentinels are punished for sleeping on their posts.' Drawing by Le Moyne, engraving from T. de Bry, *America*, Part II, 1591, plate XXXII. 'But, when the burning of a town has happened in consequence of the negligence of the watch, the penalty is as follows: The chief takes his place alone on his bench, those next to him in authority being seated on another long bench curved in a half circle; and the executioner orders the culprit to kneel down before the chief. He then sets his left foot on the delinquent's back; and, taking in both hands a club of ebony or some other hard wood, worked to an edge at the sides, he strikes him on the head with it, so severely as almost to split the skull open. The same penalty is inflicted for some other crime reckoned capital among them; for we saw two persons punished in this same way.'—Le Moyne.

192
'Proceedings of the Floridians in deliberating on important affairs.' Drawing by Le Moyne, engraving from T. de Bry, *America*, Part II, 1591, plate XXIX.
'The chief and his nobles are accustomed during certain days of the year to meet early every morning for this express purpose in a public place, in which a long bench is constructed, having at the middle of it a projecting part laid with nine round trunks of trees, for the chief's seat. On this he sits by himself, for distinction's sake; and here the rest come to salute him, one at a time, the oldest first, by lifting both hands twice to the height of the head, and saying, "Ha, he, ya, ha, ha." To this the rest answer, "Ha, ha." Each, as he completes his salutation, takes his seat on the bench. If any question of importance is to be discussed, the chief calls upon his *laüas* (that is, his priests) and upon the elders, one at a time, to deliver their opinions. Meanwhile the chief orders the women to boil some *casina*; which is a drink prepared from the leaves of a certain root, and which they afterwards pass through a strainer. They esteem this drink so highly, that no one is allowed to drink it in council unless he has proved himself a brave warrior. Moreover, this drink has the quality of at once throwing into a sweat whoever drinks it. On this account those who cannot keep it down, but whose stomachs reject it, are not intrusted with any difficult commission, or any military responsibility, being considered unfit, for they often have to go three or four days without food; but one who can drink this liquor can go for twenty-four hours afterwards without eating or drinking.'—Le Moyne.

attempted to escape and were killed or enslaved by the Indians or, later, ransomed by the Spanish. With the massacres at Matanzas, Menéndez struck a devastating and decisive blow to the French colonization of Florida. Whatever condemnation history has recorded against him, he felt justified by expediency, since feeding and controlling such a large number of prisoners would have been difficult; by religion, for he 'mercifully' did not burn the heretics; and by the official orders of Philip II, who later wrote that 'you have done this with entire justification and prudence, and [we] hold ourselves greatly served thereby'.[33] Of Ribaut's death he wrote to Philip on 15 October 1565 (three days after Matanzas), 'I had Juan Ribao, with all the rest, put to the knife . . . and I hold it very good fortune that he should be dead; for the King of France could do more with him with fifty thousand ducats than others with five hundred thousand; and he could do more in one year than another in ten, for he was the most experienced seaman and corsair known, and very skillful in this navigation of the Indies and the coast of Florida.'[34]

Back at St Augustine Menéndez was consolidating his victory. Peace and friendship with the natives he considered of prime importance at this time. When he found that the surviving Frenchmen were fomenting hatred and war against the Spanish, his policy toward them became more lenient. He ransomed those enslaved by the Indians and enticed others to surrender. He went to Havana to buy food for his settlers at St Augustine, San Mateo (the French Fort Caroline), and St Lucia, a small colony he had planted south of Cape Canaveral to rescue shipwrecked crews.

For Menéndez the year 1566 was a period of intense activity and achievement. He explored the east coast from the Cape of Florida to Santa Elena (the French Port Royal), where he built Fort Felipe. He twice explored the upper reaches of St Johns River in search of a reported passage across the peninsula. With seven vessels and five hundred men he sailed from Havana along the west Florida coast as far as Tampa Bay, where Narváez and de Soto had landed. At Charlotte Harbor he made a treaty with the treacherous and powerful Caloosa chief, Carlos, who insisted on marrying his sister to the unwilling Menéndez. Carlos said that war would result if he refused; Menéndez, already married, said he could marry only a Christian. Carlos's sister immediately embraced Christianity as Doña Antonia; Menéndez capitulated and took her back to Havana. Méras, his brother-in-law, gives an amusing account of the captain-general's unsuccessful attempts to escape his marital responsibilities.[35] He was outwitted by the skilful tactics of Doña Antonia, who sat on his bed until he received her. He finally returned her to her brother. In August 1566 he sent a vessel along the North Carolina-Virginia coast to establish a small outpost on the 'Baya de Santa Maria', with secret instructions to search for the inland passage to Canada and a strait to the Pacific which he believed extended west from the 'Salado River', probably Chesapeake Bay.[36] The ship was driven out to sea by storms and eventually reached Spain without fulfilling its mission. From the fort at Santa Elena he sent Captain Juan Pardo with a small force 'to discover and conquer the interior country from there to Mexico'![37] Pardo established and garrisoned blockhouses as far inland as the Appalachians; but by 1568 the Indians had massacred most of the scattered Spanish outposts.

The attempts of Menéndez to establish and expand the great province of which he was Governor met with constant reversals. The Spanish colonists and soldiers, disappointed in their expectations of rich booty and rapid wealth, frequently mutinied. They seized the ships sent to supply them with food and arms and sailed to the West Indies or Spain, where they spread the news of their hardships. The missions of the Dominicans and Jesuits ended in martyrdom or failure, as in the Jesuit mission of Father Segura and his companions at Axacan on the Chesapeake Bay in 1572.[38] Pirates infested the West Indies. After the death of Menéndez in 1574, when his nephew Pedro Menéndez Marqués became governor and 'captain-general' of Florida, the Spanish occupation of Florida became so weak that the very existence of the settlement at St Augustine was threatened. The need of a refuge for the crews of Spanish ships wrecked on the coast, the increasing danger of a deserted coast giving harbor to pirates, and the related fear of French or English settlements, however, caused the Spanish to continue to patrol the coast as best they could into the seventeenth century.

The fear of an English settlement on the Atlantic coast was not without foundation. England's active interest in trans-Atlantic opportunities, generally dormant since Cabot's explorations, took a rapid, even spectacular, and to the Iberian powers ominous turn in the 1560s. In the first half of the sixteenth century a steady but limited traffic to Newfoundland and the fishing banks concerned a small circle of merchants; English knowledge of navigation and of shipbuilding did not, however, keep pace with the developments in the Spanish and Portuguese schools of hydrography. No ports were open to the English west of Ireland; trade to the Indies, East or West, was zealously guarded as the sole privilege of the Iberian powers. For many years after the beginning of Elizabeth's reign in 1558, her official policy was to avoid offending the enormously powerful and religiously bigoted Philip II, ruler of Spain. However, both in her court and among her merchants interest in Spain's treasure-laden galleys and American territories was growing. In 1563 the accounts of Jean Ribaut and Nicolas Barré, then in London,

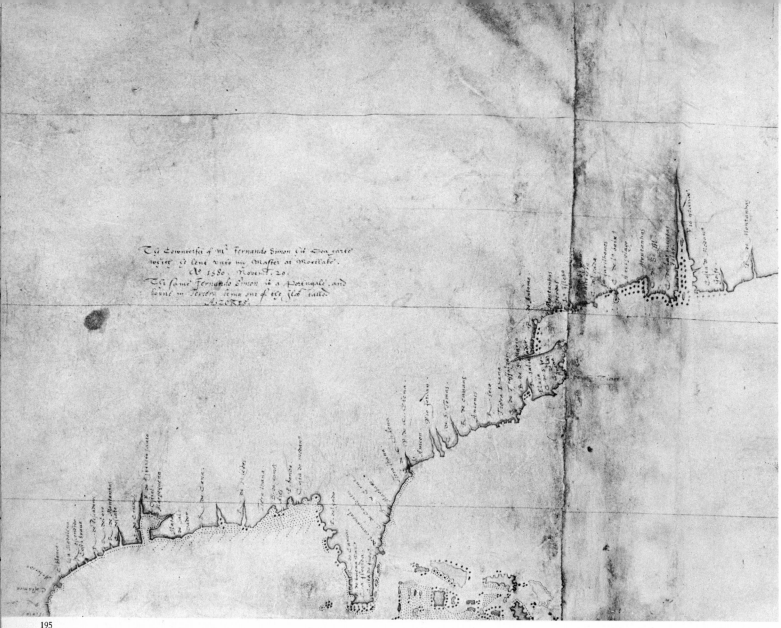

195

195

Chart of the North American coastline copied by John Dee from a chart of Simão Fernandes, 1580. *London, British Museum, Cotton Roll XIII, 48.*

The Portuguese pilot Simão Fernandes lent a chart of the continental coasts bordering the Atlantic Ocean to the famous Dr John Dee of Mortlake on 20 November 1580. Dr Dee had a 'Counterfet' of the map, apparently a Portuguese copy of an original Spanish chart, drawn on a large vellum roll about four by three feet. The section of Dee's copy here reproduced includes the coastline from Mexico to Canada. It shows graphically the probable reason for the choice of the Carolina Banks area as the location of Ralegh's colony. The only bay shown on the east coast between the Cape of Florida and New England is Bahia de Santa Maria, which on the map is placed at the latitude of Pamlico Sound. This is depicted as a large bay with two rows of three islands each across it. Fernandes played an important part in choosing the destination of the Roanoke voyages; he was master and pilot of Amadas's flagship in 1584 and of Grenville's flagship in 1585.

The bay is strategically located for preying on Spanish shipping; and for this Elizabethan sport Fernandes had almost an obsession. With its islands and with the rivers flowing into it, the bay appears on the chart to be also the best haven on the coast for concealment from Spanish counter measures.

196

'Mode of tilling and planting'. Drawing by Le Moyne, engraving from T. de Bry, *America*, Part II, 1591, plate XXI. *New York Public Library.*

'The Indians cultivate the earth diligently; and the men know how to make a kind of hoes from fishes' bones, which they fit to wooden handles, and with these they prepare the land well enough, as the soil is light. When the ground is sufficiently broken up and levelled, the women come with beans and millet, or maize. Some go first with a stick, and make holes, in which the others place the beans, or grains of maize. After planting they leave the fields alone, as the winter in that country, situated between the west and the north, is pretty cold for about three months, being from the 24th of December to the 15th of March; and during that time, as they go naked, they shelter themselves in the woods. When the winter is over, they return to their homes to wait for their crops to ripen. After gathering in their harvest, they store the whole of it for the year's use.'—Le Moyne.

197

Map of Virginia, drawn by John White, engraving from T. de Bry, *America*, Part I, 1590. *New York Public Library.*

This map of the region around Ralegh's Roanoke Colony of 1585 was the basis for most European maps of the area for over eighty years. De Bry made the engraving from a manuscript map by John White (misspelled 'With' in the small cartouche to the left), to accompany Thomas Harriot's *Briefe and true report*, Frankfurt, 1590. In the sixteenth century Wimble Shoals was apparently a more prominent cape than Hatteras. Many of the islands in the sounds here shown have since disappeared. The colonists had made a brief trip to Chesapeake Bay but did not yet know its size or shape.

198

'Floridae Americae', map drawn by Le Moyne and engraving from T. de Bry, *America*, Part II, 1591. *New York Public Library.*

This map of French Florida by Le Moyne, the artist who accompanied Laudonnière's expedition in 1564–5, was the chief basis for the maps of European cartographers for over a hundred years. The rivers along the coast have the names given by Ribaut in 1562. The lake in the central Floridian peninsula is Lake George on the St Johns River; the crescent-shaped lake to the west of Caroline, the French fort, is Okefenokee Swamp; to the north is the waterfall region of the Blue Ridge where 'In this lake the natives find grains of silver'; above that are the gold, silver and copper-bearing Appalachian Mountains bordering on what is probably Verrazzano's bay or sea, the supposed extension of the Pacific Ocean.

In preparing this map, Le Moyne added to his own knowledge information received from Laudonnière's narrative of the expedition, published in 1586. Le Moyne's map is so much more detailed and accurate than John White's general manuscript map of the area (plate 199) that it is unlikely White made use of Le Moyne's completed manuscript from which de Bry made his engraving.

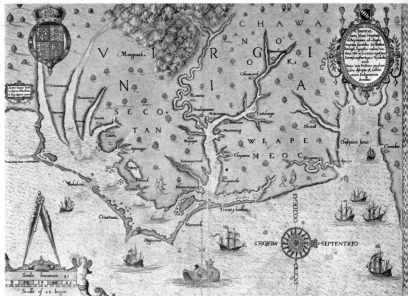

196

197

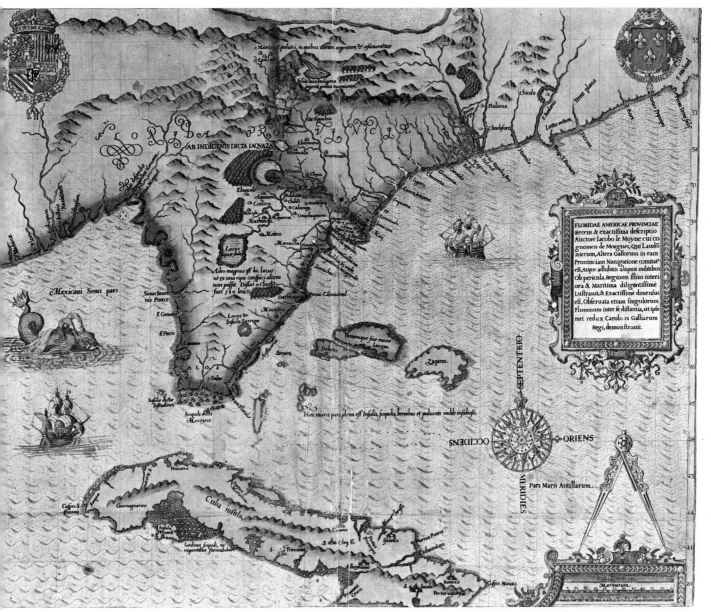

198

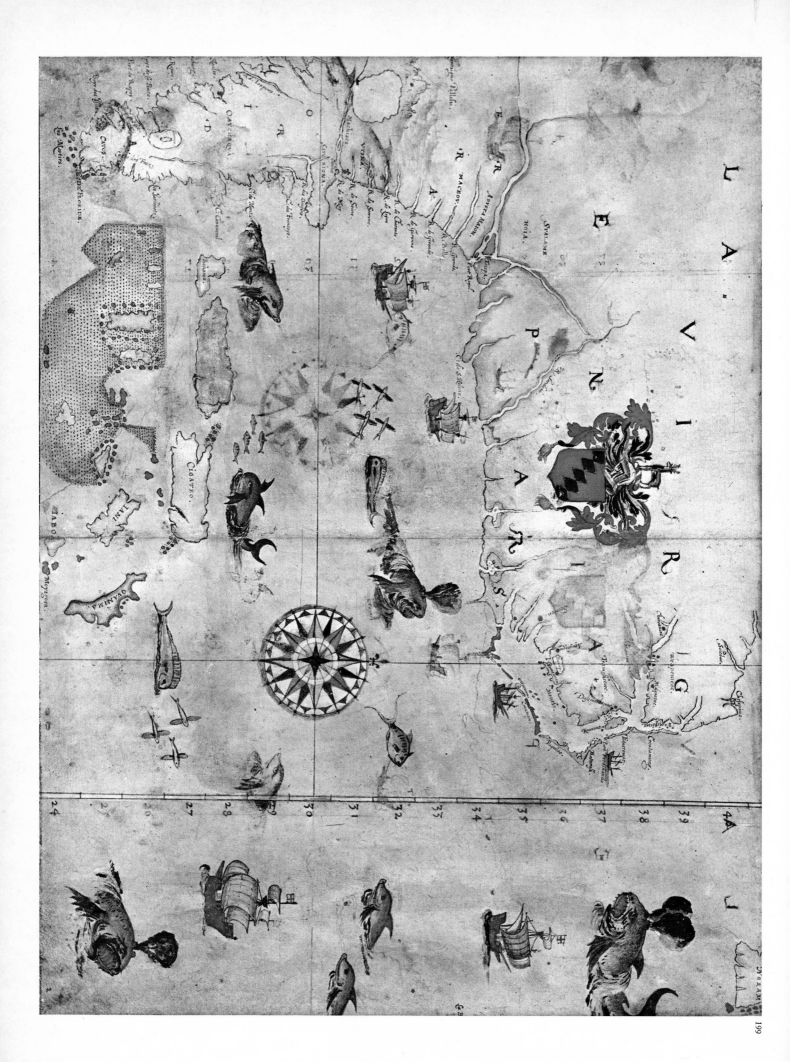

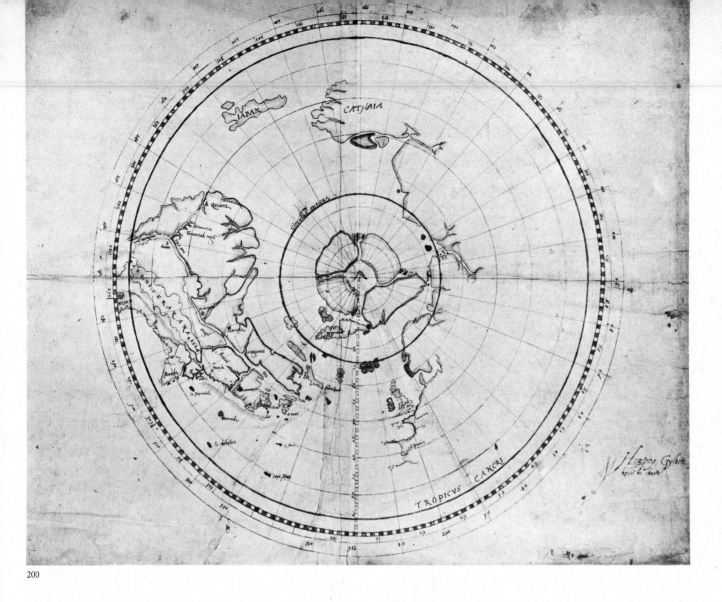

200

199
'La Virgenia Pars', map drawn by John White, c. 1585. *London, British Museum.*
White's general map of the south-eastern coast is an attempt to piece together information from several sources. The region between the Chesapeake Bay and Cape Lookout is based on the same personal explorations and surveys used by White in his more detailed map of that area (plate 213). Port Ferdinando, the entry found by the pilot Simão Fernandes and used by the English to reach Roanoke Island, is shown. At Port Royal is a strait leading to a large body of water, a geographical error influenced by current Elizabethan hopes for a seaway to the Pacific, and appearing also in the earlier Dee-Gilbert and Lok maps (plates 200 and 267). From Port Royal south the coast is derived from the explorations under Ribaut and Laudonnière; the place names are French. The differences, however, from Le Moyne's map of French Florida published by de Bry in 1591 (plate 198) are so marked that White must have used sources other than the Le Moyne manuscript which de Bry had for his engraving. White puts Fort Caroline on the north bank of the River May (St Johns), which has its source in the Okefenokee Swamp, and he has a large peninsula projecting into the Atlantic below the River May; Le Moyne's map does not have these errors. The section of the map showing the Bahamas is similar to that on a Spanish chart belonging to Simão Fernandes (plate 195).

200
Chart based on the Arctic by Dr John Dee, c. 1582. *Free Library of Philadelphia, William M. Elkins Collection of Americana, no 42.*
Dr Dee, the noted Elizabethan physician, scholar, and alchemist, whose cabalistic signs identify him as the author, made this chart for Sir Humphrey Gilbert, whose autograph is in the lower right-hand corner. Dee, as well as Gilbert, was interested in colonization and especially in a North-west Passage to the Orient. This map suggests several possible ways to reach the Pacific. Verrazzano's Sea and the great lake to its south, here shown, may be the source of these features on John White's map of Florida and Virginia.

201
Sir Humphrey Gilbert; engraving by Boissard.

201

177

uncomplicated by the political and religious dissensions, is interesting. There was an 'admiral' of the harbor chosen by rotation from among the captains, who settled disputes; a crop of peas planted ashore was ready for harvest; and on Sable Island to the south were herds providing fresh meat, which 'the Portugals (above thirty yeares past) did put into the same Island both Neat and Swine to breede, which were since exceedingly multiplied.'[43]

Nine months after Gilbert and his hopes for an American plantation vanished when the lights aboard the *Squirrel* were 'devoured and swallowed up of the sea',[44] Captains Philip Amadas and Arthur Barlowe were approaching the treacherous shoals of the North Carolina Outer Banks in two barks.

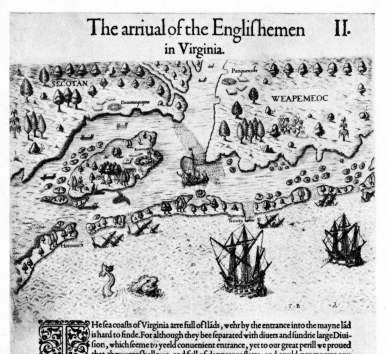

202

They had been sent out to explore the coast for a suitable colonizing site by Walter Ralegh, to whom the letters patent of his half-brother Gilbert had been transferred. On 13 July 1584, after sailing along the sandy coast for a hundred and twenty miles in search of a river or opening, they reached an inlet which led to an island in the sound which 'the Indians call Roanoak'.[45] This entrance they named Port Ferdinando after Amadas's Portuguese pilot, Simão Fernandes, who had discovered it.[46] After six weeks of exploration and trading, during which they visited the chief Wingina on Roanoke Island, they sailed for England carrying back two Indians, Manteo and Wanchese, who were to play important though divergent parts in later colonization. Barlowe's report on his return, a short but charming and favorable account of the land they saw, is a classic among the narratives of discovery. Ralegh immediately began preparations for a second expedition to establish a permanent settlement for further exploration, trade and produce, and (less openly) the establishment of a good base for privateering against the hated Spaniard. Queen Elizabeth, who had knighted Ralegh in January 1585, showed her favor by allowing the proposed colony to be named Virginia in her honor. On 9 April Sir Richard Grenville sailed from Plymouth with seven ships and, after victualing the ships in the West Indies, reached Wococon (Ocracoke Inlet) on 26 June. After exploring the sounds, Grenville left for England on 25 August, reaching Plymouth on 18 October after capturing a Spanish flagship with enormous booty. At Roanoke he left Governor Ralph Lane in charge of 108 colonists.

In this group of first settlers, besides a physician, a clergyman, a metallurgist, apothecaries, and other specialists, were Thomas Harriot, the brilliant mathematician and scientist, and John White, the painter and later governor of the 1587 colony. The extraordinary collaboration of these two is shown in White's drawings and Harriot's comments on them, many reproduced in this volume.

Although Lane's colony of 1585 was important historically as the first English colony planted in the New World and for its unrivaled records of North America as it appeared to Europeans in the sixteenth century, it was beset with difficulties from the beginning. It was plagued by antagonisms between the leaders, unruliness among the men ('as havyng,' wrote Lane to Sir Philip Sidney, 'emungst savvages, ye chardege of wylde menn of myne owene nacione'[47]), hostility

203

1.

The first v
Jean Riba

From *The whole and tru*
Ribauld . . . London . . .

Jean Ribaut sailed from
what was to be the first
Florida. He sighted lan
ward and the next d
accordingly named the
exploration and in frien
first inquiries from the
being sought by the Sp
writers who mention C
recently published, incl
Nizza or Nice, who repo

from the Indians, lack of tools to establish settlement on a secure basis, and inadequate supply of food. The familiar story repeated itself; most of the settlers were more interested in finding gold than in planting seed. Promised supplies did not arrive, and raids on Indian villages brought diminishing returns of food. By the summer of 1586 the colonists were facing famine, although Hakluyt states that they had planted a plentiful but unmatured crop.[48]

Unexpected relief appeared with the arrival of the fleet of Sir Francis Drake on his return from plundering the West Indies. Drake generously offered Ralegh's colony ships, food, supplies and men. But a hurricane scattered his fleet, and the colonists, discouraged, decided to return with him to England.

refused to transport them further, 'saying that the summer was farre spent'[52] (for privateering). The colony consisted of about a hundred and ten, including seventeen women and eleven children.[53] White, finding no trace of the fifteen men left by Grenville but the destroyed fort and a few overgrown huts, set the colonists to work 'repayring houses and building new ones'. He made contact with the friendly Croatoan Indians, and christened Manteo as 'Lord of Roanoke', thus appointed Ralegh's native ruler of the area. Five days after Manteo's christening, on 18 August 1587, a baby girl was born to Ananias Dare, one of the twelve 'assistants' of the colony, and Elenor Dare, White's daughter. She was christened Virginia on the following Sunday, the first child of English

The manner of makinge their boates. XII.

He manner of makinge their boates in Virginia is verye wonderfull. For wheras they want Instruments of yron, or other like vnto ours, yet they knowe howe to make them as handsomelye, to saile with whear they liste in their Riuers, and to fishe with all, as ours. First they choose some longe, and thicke tree, accordinge to the bignes of the boate which they would frame, and make a fyre on the grownd abowt the Roote therof, kindlinge the same by little, and little with drie mosse of trees, and chipps of woode that the flame should not mounte opp to highe, and burne to muche of the lengte of the tree. When yt is almost burnt thorough, and readye to fall they make a new fyre, which they suffer to burne vntill the tree fall of yt owne accord. Then burninge of the topp, and bowghs of the tree in suche wyse that the bodie of thesame may Retayne his iust lengthe, they raise yt vppon potes laid ouer crosse wise vppon forked posts, at suche a reasonable heighte as they may handsomlye worke vp-pon yt. Then take they of the barke with certayne shells: thy reserue the, innermost parte of the lenn-ke, for the nethermost parte of the boate. On the other side they make a fyre accordinge to the lengthe of the bodye of the tree, sauinge at both the endes. That which they thinke is sufficientlye burned they quenche and scrape away with shells, and makinge a new fyre they burne yt agayne, and soe they continue somtymes burninge and sometymes scrapinge, vntill the boate haue sufficient bothowmes. This god indueth thise sauage people with sufficient reason to make thinges necessarie to serue their turnes.

204

The Marckes of sundrye of the XXIII.
Cheif mene of Virginia.

He inhabitats of all the cuntrie for the most parte haue marks rased on their backs, wherby yt may be knowen what Princes subiects they bee, or of what place they haue their originall. For which cause we haue set downe those marks in this figure, and haue annexed the names of the places, that they might more easelye be discerned. Which industrie hath god indued them withal although they be verye simple, and rude. And to confesse a truthe I cannot remember, that euer I saw a better or quietter people then they.

The marks which I obserued amonge them, are heere put downe in order folowinge.
The marke which is expressed by A. belongeth tho Wingino, the cheefe lorde of Roanoac.
That which hath B, is the marke of Wingino his sisters husbande.
Those which be noted with the letters, of C. and D. belonge vnto diverse chefe lordes in Secotam.
Those which haue the letters E. F. G. are certaine cheefe men of Pomeiooc, and Aquascogoc.

205

Scarcely had they sailed when the supply ship promised by Ralegh reached Roanoke, found to its surprise no colony, and returned. Later in the summer a squadron, with some 400 men under Sir Richard Grenville, arrived.[49] From a captured Indian Grenville learned of Lane's departure. With inexplicable bad judgement, he left a small holding force of fifteen men, who were attacked by the Indians and did not survive; this was the first 'lost colony'.

In April 1587 Ralegh sent out yet another colony under John White as Governor, to establish 'the Cittie of Ralegh in Virginea'.[50] Ralegh's instructions were to establish the settlement on Chesapeake Bay,[51] which had been briefly explored by Lane's men the previous year; but Simão Fernandes, the master of the flagship, whose chief interest was in privateering, put the colonists ashore at Roanoke, and

parentage born in the New World.

After the supplies had been landed, the settlers petitioned and 'constrayned' White to return to England 'for the better and sooner obtaining of supplies, and other necessaries for them'.[54] On 28 August the flyboat, which he boarded, sailed for England; he never saw the colonists again. The England in which he landed needed to keep every ship it had at home against the now threatened Spanish invasion. A squadron under Grenville which Ralegh had planned to send to the Virginia colony was told peremptorily by the Privy Council to await the imminent arrival of the Spanish Armada. In April 1588, however, White managed to leave Bideford with supplies and additional colonists on two small vessels; neither reached Virginia. The *Brave*, on which he sailed, was captured and looted by a ship from Rochelle; the French captain allowed the

179

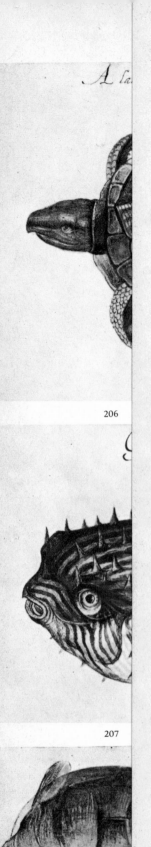

that is, the children of his children up to the fifth generation. After causing us to be seated under a bay tree which was near him, he made a sign to us of *Tymangoua,* just as the others had. They are, moreover, the greatest thieves in the world for they stole as well with their feet as with their hands, and this in spite of the fact that they have only skins before their secret parts and are all painted in black in very beautiful designs [tattooing]. The women have all around them a certain very long white [Spanish] moss covering their breasts and secret parts. They are very obedient to their husbands. They are not thieves like the men but are very fond of rings and collars to hang around their necks.

One day, having sounded the said river, they found it to be deep enough for the ships but not as commodious as the river of May. Consequently, Seigneur de Laudonnière returned on board and deliberated with Captain Vasseur about going back to the river of May. The following Tuesday we hoisted anchor to return and reached there Friday. We went ashore immediately and were received with honor by the savages as before. They conducted us to the very spot where now we have built our fort, called the Fort of Carreline because Charles is the name of [our] king. You can see the sketch enclosed.

This fort is on the river of May about six leagues up river from the sea. In this short time we have fortified it so well that it can be defended. It has good conveniences, even with water

211

211
Plan of Fort Caroline published in *Coppie d'une lettre venant de la Florida,* Paris, Norment and Bruneau, 1565. *Providence, John Carter Brown Library.* This 'portraict' of Fort Caroline, built on the St Johns River by the French under Laudonnière in 1564, was drawn by the young soldier on the expedition. It was enclosed with a letter to his father and sent to France by ship soon after their arrival. The fort bears an obvious though sketchy resemblance to the more careful drawing by Le Moyne, published by T. de Bry in 1591 (see plate 182).

The structure in this pictorial view is placed incorrectly on the north bank of the St Johns; as the course and source of the river, as well as the hills and terrain surrounding the fort, bear no resemblance to the actual topography, they were probably details added to the drawing in France.
212
René de Laudonnière; engraving in Crispin de Passe, *Effigies Regum,* Cologne, 1598.
213
'La Virginea Pars', map drawn by John White, *c.* 1585. *London, British Museum.*
This detailed map of the region between Chesapeake Bay and Cape Lookout is based on the careful surveys of the mathematician Thomas Harriot and John White. It is the chief contemporary authority on the inlets and contours of the Outer Banks in the sixteenth century, as well as on the location of Indian settlements and the place names of the area. The map was probably compiled from a large number of sheets drawn on different surveying trips and from verbal reports; it is, however, surprisingly accurate and remains the best chart of as large an area in North America made before the seventeenth century. Although the manuscript volume in which this map is found is dated 1585, some details may incorporate information gathered by White on later voyages.

De Bry used a modified drawing by White of the map of the same area for his stylized engraving in the first volume of his *America* (1590), which contains Harriot's *A briefe and true report* and Harriot's descriptive text under the engravings of White's paintings. De Bry's maps of Virginia by White and of Florida (1591) by Le Moyne were the prototypes of maps of the South-East made by European geographers for almost a hundred years.

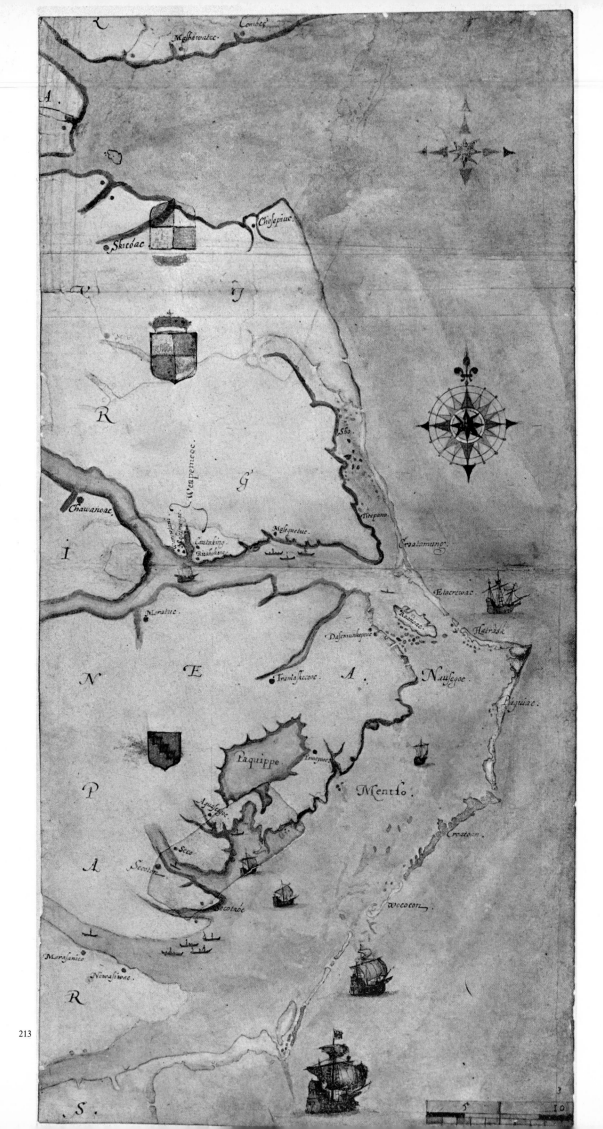

214
'The famouse W
track-chart pub
settlements capt
to illustrate Wa
1588; the five p
Virginia, Paul M
The chart was c
cartographer res
Drake's return f
in June 1586 at
them John Whit
and the four tov
engraver has ins
by White. The '
Trigger-fish.
215
'Mode of collect
Drawing by Le
plate XLI.
'A great way fro
called in the Ind
three great river
brass, mixed tog
into which the s
they collect it o
collect again wh
the great river v
the sea. The Spa
thus obtained.'–

213

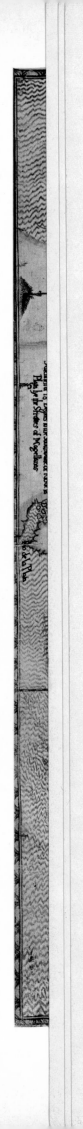

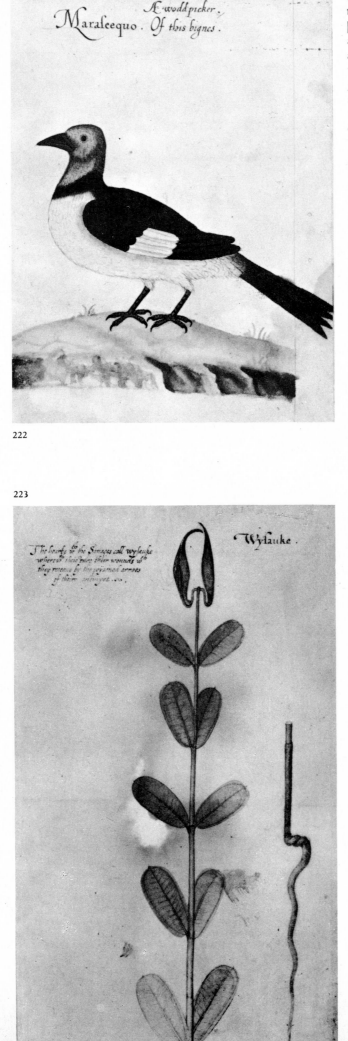

Maraleequo. Æ woddpicker. Of this bignes.

222

223

thence wee behelde the Sea on both sides to the North, and to the South, finding no ende any of both waies. This lande [the Outer Banks] laye stretching it selfe to the West, which after wee founde to be but an Island of twentie leagues long, and not above six miles broade. Under the banke or hill, whereon we stoode, we behelde the vallies replenished with goodly Cedar trees, and having discharged our harquebushot, such a flocke of Cranes (the most part white) arose under us, with such a crye redoubled by many Ecchoes, as if an armie of men had showted all together.

This Island had many goodly woods, full of Deere, conies [cottontail rabbits], hares [marsh rabbits], and Fowle, even in the middest of Summer, in incredible aboundance. The woodes are not such as you finde in Bohemia, Moscovia, or Hyrcania, barren and fruitlesse, but the highest, and reddest Cedars of the world, farre bettering the Cedars of the Açores, of the Indies, or of Lybanus, Pynes, Cyprus, Sassaphras, the Lentisk, or the tree that bearesth the Masticke [?sweet gum], the tree that beareth the rinde of blacke Sinamon, of which Master Winter brought from the Streights of Magellane[1], and many other of excellent smell, and qualitie. We remained by the side of this Island two whole daies, before we sawe any people of the Countrey: the third daye we espied one small boate rowing towards us, having in it three persons: this boate came to the landes side, foure harquebushot from our shippes, and there two of the people remaining, the thirde came along the shoare side towards us, and we being then all within boord, he walked up and downe upon the point of the lande next unto us: then the Master, and the Pilot of the Admirall, Simon Ferdinando, and the Captaine Philip Amadas, my selfe, and others, rowed to the lande, whose comming this fellowe attended, never making any shewe of feare, or

222
A Red-headed Woodpecker. Dr Hans Sloane manuscript. *London, British Museum.*
A seventeenth-century copy of a lost original by John White.
223
Milkweed. Drawing by John White, 1585. *London, British Museum.*
'There groweth in that part of Virginia, or Norembega, where our English men dwelled (intending there to erect a Colony) a kind of Asclepias, or Swallow woort, which the Savages call Wisanck: there riseth up from a single crooked roote one upright stalke a foote high, slender, and of a grennish colour: whereupon do growe faire broade leaves sharp pointed, with many ribs or nerves running through the same, like those of Ribwoort or Plantaine, set together by couples at certaine distances. The flowers come foorth at the top of the stalks, which as yet are not observed, by reason the man that brought the seeds and plants heereof did not regard them: after which, there come in place two cods (seldome more) sharpe pointed like those of our Swallowe woort, but greater, stuffed full of most pure silke, of a shining white colour: among which silke appeareth a small long toong (which is the seede) resembling the toong of a birde, or that of the herbe called Adders toong. The cods are not onely full of silke, but every nerve or sinewe wherewith the leaves be ribbed are likewise most pure silke; and also the pilling of the stems even as Flaxe is torne from his stalks. This considered; beholde the justice of God, that as he hath shut up those people and nations in infidelitie and nakednes; so hath he not as yet given them understanding to cover their nakednes, nor matter wherewith to do the same; notwithstanding the earth is covered with this silke, which daily they tread under their feete, which were sufficient to apparell many kingdomes if they were carefully manured, and cherished.'—Harriot.
224
The taking of St Augustine, Florida, by Drake on 7 June 1586. Engraved plan, probably by Baptista Boazio. *Upperville, Virginia, Paul Mellon Collection.*
St Augustine, the oldest European settlement in the United States, had been established in 1565 by Pedro Menéndez de Avilés. After taking in supplies for Ralegh's colonists and burning the town and fort, Drake sailed north to Roanoke (see plate 214).
In the bottom left-hand corner, the draftsman or engraver introduces a dolphin, crudely copied from a drawing by John White (see plate 58).

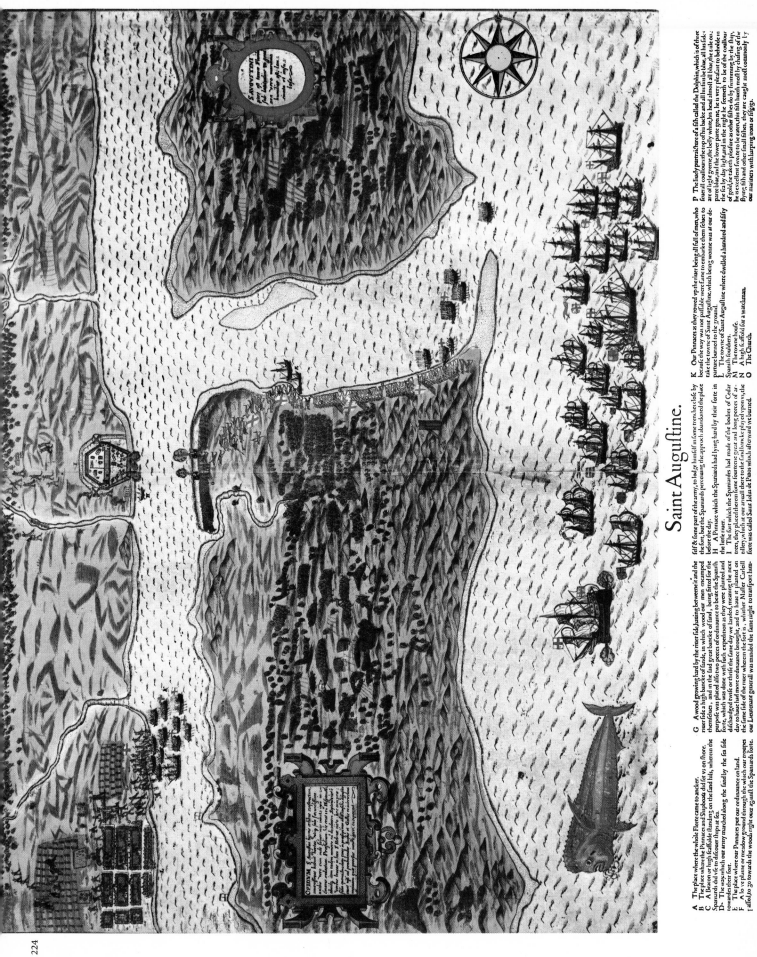

Saint Augustine.

A The place where the whole Fleete came to ancker.
B The place where the Pinnace and Shipboate did set vs on shore.
C A Beacon or high scaffolde standing on the sand hill, whereon the Spaniards did vse to discouer ships at sea.
D The way, which our army marched along the sand by the sea side towards their fort.
E The place where our Pinnaces put our ordinance on land.
F A lowe plaine or meadow ground through the which our troupes passed, so to go towards the woods right ouer against the Spaniards forte.

G A wood growing hard by the riuer side, hauing betweene it and the riuer side a high bancke of sande, in which wood our men encamped themselues, and in the sand great bancke of sand, being fitted for the purpose was placed also two peeces of ordinance to beate the Spanish forte, which was done with such expedition as they were planted and discharged twife or thrife the same day we landed, meaning the next day to haue had more ordinance brought, and to haue it planted on the same side of the riuer wherein the fort is, whither Master Carleill our Lieutenant generall was marked Saint John at Sea port him-felf & some part of the army, to lodge himself in some trenches close by the fort, but the Spaniards perceiuing the approch abandoned the place before the day.

H A Pinnace which the Spaniards had lying hard by their forte in the little riuer.

I The fort which the Spaniardes had made of the bodies of Cedar trees, they placed therein some fourteene great and long peeces of artillery, which at our assault there to the fund bancke played vpon vs, the forte was called Saint John de Pinos which afterward we burned.

K Our Pinnaces as they rowed vp the riuer being all full of men, who because the way was not passable were fane to embarke them selues to take the towne of Saint Augustine, which being wonne was at our departure burned to the ground.

L The towne of Saint Augustine where dwelled a hundred and fifty Spanish souldiers.

M The towne house.
N A high scaffold for a watchman.
O The Church.

P The liuely pourtraicture of a fish called the Dolphin, which is of three seuerall coullours the top of his backe and all his finne be blue, all his sides are of light greene, the belly white, his head almost all blue, the taile coulpure blue, and the lower parte grene, he is very pleasant to beholde in the fea by day light, and in the night he seemeth to be of the coullour of gold, he taketh pleasure as other fishes do by swimming by the ship, he is excellent fweete to be eaten, this fish lueth moft by chasing of the flying fish and other small fishes, they are caught moft commonly by our mariners with harping irons or fliggs.

225

227

The towne of Pomeiock and true forme of their howses, couered
and enclosed some wth matts, and some wth barcks of trees. All compassed
abowt wth smale poles stuck thick together in stedd of a wall.

226

The manner of their fishing.

228

196

225

Frobisher's men in a skirmish with Eskimos at Bloody Point, 1 August 1577.
Dr Hans Sloane drawing after John White. *London, British Museum.*
The Englishmen, two of them firing arquebuses, are in a ship's boat at the
foot of a low cliff from which Eskimos are shooting arrows at them.
Other Eskimos flourishing bows and arrows are seen on a point in the
middle distance; and the kayaks in the inlet beyond recall Frobisher's
observation of 'a number of small things fleeting in the sea afarre off,
whyche hee supposed to be porposes or seales . . . but coming nearer, he
discovered them to be men in small boates made of leather'. On the left is an
encampment of the sealskin tents occupied by the Eskimos in summer.
In the foreground is an Eskimo with double-bladed paddle in a kayak.
During this skirmish, the Eskimos stood their ground until all their arrows
were used, and 'five or six' of them were killed. The particularity of detail
in the drawing suggests the work of an eyewitness; it is supposed that the
artist John White was among Frobisher's company on his voyage of 1577.

226

'Their danses which they use at their hyghe feastes'. Drawing by John White,
1585. *London, British Museum.*
'At a Certayne tyme of the yere they make a great and solemne feaste
[green corn ritual]. The place where they meete is a broade playne, abowt
the which are planted in the grownde certayne posts carved with heads like
to the faces of Nonnes covered with theyr vayls. Then beeing sett in order they
dance singe, and use the strangest gestures that they can possiblye devise.
Three of the fayrest Virgins, of the companie are in the midds, which
imbrassinge one another doe as yt wear turn abowt in their dancinge.
All this is donne after the sunne is sett for avoydinge of heate.'
The comment is by Thomas Harriot published in T. de Bry, *America,*
Part I, 1590.

227

'The towne of Pomeiock'. Drawing by John White, 1585. *London, British
Museum.*
The Indian village of Pomeiooc was one of the first visited by the Roanoke
colonists after their arrival. It is situated between the present Lake Landing
and Wyesocking Bay and is shown on White's maps. He probably made the
drawing while visiting it in July 1585. The village with its enclosing
palisade and eighteen houses, has an interesting example of the Algonkian
long house.

228

'The manner of their fishing'. Drawing by John White, 1585. *London,
British Museum.*
'They have likewise a notable way to catche fishe in their Rivers. for whear
as they lacke both yron, and steele, they faste unto their Reedes or longe
Rodds, the hollowe tayle of a certain fishe like to a sea crabbe in steede of a
poynte, wehr with by nighte or day they stricke fishes, and take them opp
into their boates. They also know how to use the prickles, and prickes of
other fishes. They also make weares, with settinge opp reedes or twigges in
the water, whiche they soe plant one within a nother, that they growe still
narrower, and narrower, as appeareth by this figure. Ther was never seene
amonge us soe cunninge a way to take fish withall, wherof sondrie sortes
as they fownde in their Rivers unlike unto ours. Which are also of a verye
good taste. Dowbtless yt is a pleasant sighte to see the people, somtymes
wadinge, and going somtymes sailinge in those Rivers, which are
shallowe and not deepe, free from all care of heapinge opp Riches for their
posteritie, content with heir state, and livinge frendlye together of those
thinges which god of his bountie hath given unto them, yet without
givinge hym any thankes according to his desarte.'—Harriot (1590).
   In the foreground at the shore edge are two shells with hermit crabs
and a specimen of the horseshoe crab, with the tail of which the Indians
pointed their fishing spears. Between the shore and the 'Cannow' is a
hammer-headed shark, and another can be seen beyond the dugout.
There are no contemporary references to bark canoes in this area. The
fish-trap by the weir contains several fish, including a barndoor skate.
The two Indians are spearing trigger-fish; a nearby fish is probably a
sturgeon. At the top left is a brown pelican and below are two
trumpeter swans.

229

A woman of Pomeiooc carrying a child. Drawing by John White, 1585.
London, British Museum.
'In the towne of Dasemonquepeuc distant from Roanoac 4. or 5. milles, the
woemen are attired, and pownced, in suche sorte as the woemen of
Roanoac are, yet they weare noe worathes upon their heads, nether have
they their thighes painted with small pricks. They have a strange manner of
bearing their children, and quite contrarie to ours. For our woemen carrie
their children in their armes before their brests, but they taking their sonne
by the right hand, bear him on their backs, holdinge the left thighe in their
lefte arme after a strange, and conuesnall fashion, as in the picture is to bee
seene.'—Harriot (1590).

230

Fire-flies and a gadfly. Drawing by John White, 1585. *London, British
Museum.*

The wyfe of an Heruuon of Pomeiooc

229

A fire which in the night semeth a flame of fyer.

A dangerous biting flye.

230

doubt. And after he had spoken of many things not understoode by us, we brought him with his owne good liking, aboord the shippes, and gave him a shirt, a hatte, and some other things, and made him taste of our wine, and our meate, which he liked very well: and after having viewed both barkes, he departed, and went to his owne boate againe, which he had left in a little Cove, or Creeke adjoyning: as soone as hee was two bowe shoote into the water, he fell to fishing, and in lesse then halfe an howre, he had laden his boate as deepe, as it coulde swimme, with which he came againe to the point of the lande, and there he devided his fishe into two partes, pointing one part to the shippe, and the other to the Pinnesse: which after he had (as much as he might,) requited

232
An Indian woman. Drawing by John White, 1585. *London, British Museum*.
'Virgins of good parentage are apparelled altogether like the woemen of Secota above mentionned, saving that they weare hanginge abowt their necks in steade of a chaine certaine thicke, and rownde pearles, with little beades of copper, or polished bones, betweene them. They pounce their foreheads, cheeckes, armes and legs. Their haire is cutt with two ridges above their foreheads, the rest is trussed opp on a knott behinde, they have broade mowthes, reasonable fair black eyes: they lay their hands often uppon their Shoulders, and cover their brests in token of maydenlike modestye. The reste of their bodyes are naked, as in the picture is to bee seene. They deligt also in seeinge fishe taken in the rivers.'—Harriot (1590).
    According to Harriot, this is 'a younge gentill woeman dougter of Secotan'. Harriot's identification is probably correct.

231

231
Detail of a canoe from an engraving in T. de Bry, *America*, Part I, 1590, plate XIII. The complete drawing from which this engraving is taken is shown in plate 228.

the former benefits receaved, he departed out of our sight.

The next day there came unto us divers boates, and in one of them the Kings brother, accompanied with fortie or fiftie men, very handsome, and goodly people, and in their behaviour as mannerly, and civill, as any of Europe. His name was Granganimeo, and the King is called Wingina,[2] the countrey Wingandacoa, (and nowe by her Maiestie, Virginia,)[3] the manner of his comming was in this sorte: hee left his boates altogether, as the first man did a little from the shippes by the shoare, and came along to the place over against the shippes, followed with fortie men. When hee came to the place, his servants spread a long matte upon the grounde, on which he sate downe, and at the other ende of the matte, foure others of his companie did the like: the rest of his men stoode round about him, somewhat a farre off: when wee came to the shoare to him with our weapons, he never mooved from his place, nor any of the other foure, nor never mistrusted any harme to be offered from us, but sitting still, he beckoned us to come and sitte by him, which we perfourmed: and beeing sette, hee makes all signes of joy, and welcome, striking on his head, and his breast, and afterwardes on ours, to shewe we were all one, smiling, and making shewe the best hee could, of all love, and familiaritie. After hee had made a long speech unto us, wee presented him with divers thinges, which hee receaved very joyfully, and thankefully. None of his companye durst to speake one worde all the tyme: onely the foure which were at the other ende, spake one in the others eare very softly.

233
An old man of Pomeiooc in winter clothing. Drawing by John White, 1585. *London, British Museum*.
'The aged men of Pommeioocke are covered with a large skinne which is tyed uppon their shoulders on one side and hangeth downe beneath their knees wearing their other arme naked out of the skinne, that they maye be at more libertie. Those skynnes are Dressed with the hair on, and lyned with other furred skinnes. The yonnge men suffer noe hairr at all to growe uppon their faces but assoone as they growe they put them away, but when th[e]y are come to yeeres they suffer them to growe although to say truthe they come opp verye thinne. They also weare their haire bownde op behynde, and, have a creste on their heads like the others. The contrye about this plase is soe fruit full and good, that England is not to bee compared to yt.'—Harriot (1590).

The common Indians showed extreme reverence to the king's family and their noble entourage. After spending some days in such friendly exchanges, Barlowe, and seven companions, visited Granganimeo's village on Roanoke Island. Barlowe's account of their reception gives a vivid impression of the domestic surroundings of the Carolina Indians, and the hospitality offered to guests.

. . . at the North ende thereof, was a village of nine houses, built of Cedar, and fortified round about with sharpe trees, to keepe out their enemies, and the entrance into it made it like a turne pike very artificially [artfully]: when we came towards it, standing neere unto the waters side, the wife of Grangyno, the Kings brother, came running out to meete us very cheerefully, and friendly, her husband was not then in the village: some of her people she commanded to drawe our boate on the shoare, for the beating of the billoe: others shee appointed to carry us on their backes to the dry ground, and others to bring our oares into the house, for feare of stealing.

235

Indian medicine man. Drawing by John White, 1585. *London, British Museum.*

'They have comonlye conjurers or juglers which use strange gestures, and often contrarie to nature in their enchantments. For they be verye familiar with devils, of whome they enquier what their enemys doe, or other suche thinges. They shave all their heads savinge their creste which they weare as other doe, and fasten a small black birde above one of their ears as a badge of their office. They weare nothinge but a skinne which hangeth downe from their gyrdle, and covereth their privityes. They weare a bagg by their side as is expressed in the figure. The Inhabitants give great credit unto their speeche, which oftentymes they finde to bee true.'—Harriot (1590).

232

233

235

234

A weroance or chief. Drawing by John White, 1585. Possibly Wingina of Roanoke. *London, British Museum.*

'The cheefe men of the yland and towne of Roanoac [raise] the haire of their crounes of theyr heades cutt like a cokes combe, as thes other doe.
The rest they wear longe as woemen and truss them opp in a knott in the nape of their necks. They hange pearles, stringe copper [on] threed att their eares, and weare bracelets on their armes of pearles, or small beades of copper or of smoothe bone called minsal, nether paintinge nor powncings of them selves, but in token of authoritye, and honor, they weare a chaine of great pearles, or copper beades or smoothe bones abowt their necks, and a plate of copper hinge upon a stringe. They cover themselves before and behynde, from the navel unto the midds of their thighes as the woemen doe with a deers skynne handsomely dressed, and fringed, Moreover they fold their armes together as they walke, or as they talke one with another in signe of wisdome. The yle of Roanoac is verye pleisant, ond hath plaintie of fishe by reason of the Water that environeth the same.'—Harriot (1590).

When we were come into the utter roome, having five roomes in her house, she caused us to sitte downe by a great fire, and after tooke off our clothes, and washed them, and dried them againe: some of the women pulled off our stockings, and washed them, some washed our feete in warme water, and shee her selfe tooke great paines to see all thinges ordered in the best manner shee coulde, making great haste to dresse some meate for us to eate.

After we had thus dried ourselves, shee brought us into the inner roome, where shee set on the boord standing along the house, some wheate like furmentie, sodden Venison, and roasted, fishe sodden, boyled, and roasted, Melons [pumpkins] rawe, and sodden, rootes of divers kindes, and divers fruites:

Their fitting at meate. XVI.

 Heir manner of feeding is in this wife. They lay a matt made of bents one the grownde and fett their meate on the mids therof, and then fit downe Rownde, the men vppon one fide, and the woemen on the other. Their meate is Mayz fodden, in fuche forte as I defcribed yt in the former treatife of verye good tafte, deers flefche, or of fome other beafte, and fifhe. They are verye fober in their eatinge, and trinkinge, and confequentlye verye longe liued becaufe they doe not opprefs nature.

236

237

236
'Their sitting at meate.' Drawing by John White, engraving from T. de Bry, *America*, Part I, 1590, plate XVI. The comment is by Harriot.
237
Indian method of boiling in an earthenware pot. Drawing by John White, 1585. *London, British Museum.*
'Their woemen know how to make earthen vessells with special Cunninge and that so large and fine, that our potters with lhoye [their] wheles can make no better: ant then Remove them from place to place as easelye as we condoe our brassen kettles. After they have set them vpon an heape of erthe to stay them from fallinge, they putt wood vnder which being kindled one of them taketh great care that the fire burne equallye Rounde about. They or their woemen fill the vessel with water, and then putt the[m] in fruite, flesh, and fish, and lett all boyle together like a galliemaufrye, which the Spaniarde call, olla podrida. Then they putte it out into disches, and sett before the companye, and then they make good cheere together. Yet are they moderate in their eatinge wher by they avoide sicknes. I would to god wee would followe their exemple. For wee should bee free from many kynes of diseasyes which wee fall into by sumptwous and vnseasonable banketts, continuallye devisinge new sawces, and provocation of gluttonnye to satisfie our vnsatiable appetite.'—Harriot (1590).

their drinke is commonly water, but while the grape lasteth, they drinke wine,[4] and for wante of caskes to keepe it all the yeare after, they drinke water, but it is sodden with Ginger in it and blacke Sinamon, and sometimes Sassaphras, and divers other wholesome, and medicinable hearbes and trees. We were entertained with all love, and kindnes, and with as much bountie, after their manner, as they could possibly devise. Wee found the people most gentle, loving, and faithfull, void of all guile, and treason, and such as lived after the manner of the golden age. The earth bringeth foorth all things in aboundance, as in the first creation, without toile or labour. The people onely care to defend them selves from the cold, in their short winter, and to feede themselves with such meate as the soile affoordeth: their meate is very well sodden, and

they make broth very sweete: their dishes are woodden platters of sweete timber: within the place where they feede, was their lodging, and within that their Idoll,[5] which they worship, of which they speake uncredible things. While we were at meate, there came in at the gates, two or three men with their bowes, and arrowes, from hunting, whome when we espied, we beganne to looke one to wardes another, and offered to reach our weapons: but as soone as she espied our mistrust, she was very much mooved, and caused some of her men to runne out, and take away their bowes, and arrowes, and breake them, and withall beate the poore fellowes out of the gate againe. When we departed in the evening, and would not tarry all night, she was very sorie, and gave us into our boate our supper halfe dressed, pots, and all, and brought us to our boates side, in which wee laye all night, remooving the same a pretie distance from the shoare: shee perceiving our jealousie, was much grieved, and sent divers men, and thirtie women, to sitte all night on the bankes side by us, and sent us into our boates fine mattes to cover us from the rayne, using very many wordes to intreate us to rest in their houses . . .

Barlowe went on to give a somewhat vague description of the settlements on the mainland. He recorded a tale of Europeans shipwrecked on the Banks some twenty-six years before, and commented on the constant bloody wars which disrupted the tribes of the coast. He concluded his account with what is the best contemporary description of the Carolina Banks and the Sounds behind them.

Beyond this Island, called Croonoake, are many Islands, very plentifull of fruites and other naturall increases, together with many Townes, and villages, along the side of the continent, some bounding upon the Islands, and some stretching up further into the land.

When we first had sight of this Countrey, some thought the first lande we sawe, to be the continent: but after wee entred into the Haven, wee sawe before us another mightie long Sea: for there lieth along the coast a tracte of Islands, two hundreth miles in length, adjonyning to the Ocean sea, and betweene the Islands, two or three entrances: when you are entred betweene them (these Islands being very narrowe, for the most part, as in most places sixe miles broad, in some places lesse, in fewe more,) then there appeareth another great Sea, containing in bredth in some places, fortie, and in some fiftie, in some twentie miles over, before you come unto the continent: and in this inclosed Sea, there are about a hundreth Islands of divers bignesses, whereof one is sixteene miles long, at which we were, finding it to be most pleasant, and fertile ground; replenished with goodly Cedars, and divers othr sweete woods, full of Currans [small grapes], of flaxe, and many other notable commodities, which we at that time had no leasure to view. Besides this Island, there are many, as I have saide, some of two, of three, of foure, of five miles, some more, some lesse, most beautifull, and pleasant to behold, replenished with Deere, Conies, Hares, and divers beastes, and about them the goodliest and best fishe in the worlde, and in greatest aboundance.

Text used: D. B. Quinn, The Roanoke Voyages, *London: The Hakluyt Society, Ser. II, Vol. 104, 1955, I, pp. 91-116.*

5.

Harriot describes Virginia and its inhabitants, 1585

From *A briefe and true report of the New Found Land of Virginia,* by Thomas Harriot. London: [Robert Robinson], 1588.

Thomas Harriot, mathematician, astronomer, scientist, a member of the English settlement on Roanoke Island, 1585–6, devotes the first section of his work to a discussion of the commercial possibilities of the region. He then turns his attention to the foodstuffs afforded by the area. Native plantations yielded the maize, peas, beans, pumpkins, squashes, and sunflower seeds which, stewed or pounded into bread, formed the basis of most Indian dishes. Harriot gives the following detailed account of Indian methods of horticulture.

All the aforesayd commodities for victuall are set or sowed, sometimes in groundes apart and severally by themselves, but for the most part together in one ground mixtly: the manner thereof, with dressing and preparing of the ground, because I will note unto you the fertilitie of the soile; I thinke good briefly to describe.

The ground they never fatten with mucke, dounge, or any other thing, neither plow nor digge it as we in England, but onely prepare it in sort as followeth. A few daiyes before they sowe or set, the men with wooden instruments, made almost in forme of mattockes or hoes with long handles; the women with short peckers or parers, because they use them sitting, of a foote long and about five inches in breadth: doe onely breake the upper part of the ground to rayse up the weedes, grasse, & olde stubbes of corne stalks with their rootes. The which after a day or twoes drying in the Sunne, being scrapte up into many small heapes, to save them labour for carrying them away; they burne into ashes. (And whereas some may thinke that they use the ashes for to better the ground, I say that then they would either disperse the ashes abroade, which wee observed they do not, except the heapes bee to great: or else would take speciall care to set their corne where the ashes lie, which also wee finde they are carelesse of.) And this is all the husbanding of their ground that they use.

Then their setting or sowing is after this maner. First for their corne, beginning in one corner of the plot, with a pecker they make a hole, wherein they put foure graines, with that care they touch not one another (about an inch asunder) and cover them with the moulde againe: and so through out the whole plot, making such holes and using them after such maner: but with this regard, that they bee made in rankes, every ranke differing from other halfe a fadome or yarde, and the holes also in every ranke as much. By this meanes there is a yard spare ground betwene every hole: where according to discretion here and there, they set as many Beanes and Peaze; in divers places also among the seedes of *Macócqwer*[6], *Melden*[7], and Planta solis.[8]

Indian fields were sown between March and June. Harriot goes on to describe the cultivation and use of tobacco amongst the Carolina Algonkians. The clay smoking pipes, noted by the author and imported into England by the colonists, became the model for pipe manufactures, and set the fashion for pipe smoking in the home country.

There is an herbe which is sowed apart by it selfe & is called by the inhabitants *uppówoc:* In the West Indies it hath divers names, according to the severall places & countreys where it groweth and is used: The Spaniardes generally call it Tobacco. The leaves thereof being dried and brought into pouder, they use to take the fume or smoke thereof by sucking it thorough pipes made of claie, into their stomacke and heade; from whence it purgeth superfluous fleame other grosse humors, openeth all the pores & passages of the body: by which meanes the use thereof, not only preserveth the body from obstructions; but also if any be, so that they have not beene of too long continuance, in short time breaketh them: wherby their bodies are notably preserved in health, & know not many greevous diseases wherewithall wee in England are oftentimes afflicted.

This *Uppówoc* is of so precious estimation amongst them, that they thinke their gods are marvelously delighted therwith:

X X.

The Tovvne of Secota.

Heir townes that are not inclosed with poles aire common-lye fayrer. Then suche as are inclosed, as appereth in this fi-gure which liuelye expresseth the towne of Secotam. For the howses are Scattered heer and ther, and they haue garde-in expressed by the letter E. wherin groweth Tobacco which the inhabitants call Vppowoc. They haue also groaues whe-rin thei take deer, and fields vherin they sowe their corne. In their corne fields they builde as yt weare a scaffolde wher on they sett a cottage like to a rownde chaire, signiffied by F. wherin they place one to watche. for there are suche nomber of fowles, and beasts, that vnless they keepe the better wat-che, they would soone deuoure all their corne. For which cause the wat-cheman maketh continual cryes and noyse. They sowe their corne with a certaine distance noted by H. otherwise one stalke would choke the growthe of another and the corne would not come vnto his rypeurs G. For the leaues therof are large, like vnto the leaues of great reedes. They haue also a seuerall broade plotte C. whear they meete with their neighbours, to celebrate their cheefe solemne feastes as the 18. picture doth declare: and a place D. whear af-ter they haue ended their feaste they make merrie togither. Ouer against this place they haue a rownd plott B. wher they assemble themselues to make their solemne prayers. Not far from which place ther is a lardge buil-dinge A. wherin are the tombes of their kings and princes, as will appere by the 22. figure likewise they haue garden notted bey the letter I. wherin they vse to sowe pompions. Also a place marked with K. wherin the make a fyre att their solemne feasts, and hard without the towne a riuer L. from whence they fetche their water. This people therfore voyde of all couetousnes lyue cherfullye and att their harts ease. Butt they solemnise their feasts in the nigt, and therfore they keepe verye great fyres to auoyde darkenes, ant to testifie their Ioye.

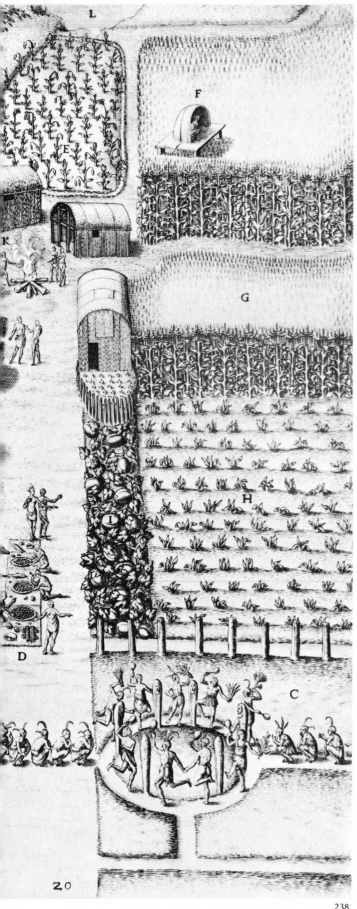

238
'The Towne of Secota.' Drawing by John White, engraving from T. de Bry,
America, Part I, 1590, plate XX. The comment is by Harriot.
The Indian town of Secota was on the Pamlico River. This is the earliest
printed picture of tobacco fields.
239
Woodcut of tobacco smoking as a cure for disease, from Girolamo Benzoni,
La historia del Mondo Nuovo, Venice, 1565.

239

Wherupon sometime they make hallowed fires & cast some
of the pouder therein for a sacrifice: being in a storme uppon
the waters, to pacifie their gods, they cast some up into the
aire and into the water: so a weare for fish being newly set up,
they cast some therein and into the aire: also after an escape
of danger, they cast some into the aire likewise: but all done
with strange gestures, stamping, sometime dauncing, clapping
of hands, holding up of hands, & staring up into the heavens,
uttering therewithal and chattering strange words & noises.[9]

The author then lists the various roots and fruits which, cooked or
raw, supplemented the Indian diet. Deer, rabbit and other game were
plentiful. The report contains the following interesting account of
bear hunting.

Squirels, which are of a grey colour, we have taken and eaten.
Beares which are all of blacke colour. The beares of this
countery are good meat; the inhabitants in time of winter do
use to take & eate manie, so also sometime did wee. They are
taken commonlie in this sort. In some Ilands or places where
they are, being hunted for, as soone as they have spiall of a
man they presently run awaie, & then being chased they clime
and get up the next tree they can, from whence with arrowes
they are shot downe starke dead, or with those wounds that
they may after easily be killed; we sometime shotte them
downe with our callevers.

The third and final section of his work Harriot devotes to discussion of
the building materials available to colonists in Virginia, and of the
customs of its inhabitants. He describes the settlements of the Indians
thus:

Their townes are but small, & neere the sea coast but fewe, some contining but 10. or 12. houses: some 20. the greatest that we have seen have bene but of 30. houses: if they be walled it is only done with barks of trees made fast to stakes, or els with poles onely fixed upright and close one by another.

Their houses are made of small poles made fast at the tops in rounde forme after the manner as is used in many arborcries in our gardens of England, in most townes covered with barkes, and in some with artificiall mattes made of long rushes, from the tops of the houses downe to the ground. The length of them is commonly double to the breadth, in some places they are but 12. and 16. yardes long, and in other some we have seene of foure and twentie.[10]

Ther Idol Kivvasa. XXI.

THE people of this cuntrie haue an Idol, which they call KIWASA: yt is carued of woode in lengthe 4. foote whose heade is like the heades of the people of Florida, the face is of a flesh colour, the brest white, the rest is all blacke, the thighes are also spottet with whitte. He hath a chayne abowt his necke of white beades, betweene which are other Rownde beades of copper which they esteeme more then golde or siluer. This Idol is placed in the temple of the towne of Secotam, as the keper of the kings dead corpses. Somtyme they haue two of thes idoles in theyr churches, and somtine 3. but neuer aboue, which they place in a darke corner wher they shew terible. Thes poore soules haue none other knowledge of god although I thinke them verye Desirous to know the truthe. For when as wee kneeled downe on our knees to make our prayers vnto god, they went abowt to imitate vs, and when they saw we moued our lipps, they also dyd the like. Wherfore that is verye like that they might easelye be brongt to the knowledge of the gospel. God of his mercie grant them this grace.

240
'Ther Idol Kiwasa.' Drawing by John White, engraving from T. de Bry, America, Part I, 1590, plate XXI. The comment is by Harriot.

In some places of the country one onely towne belongeth to the government of a *Wiroans* or chiefe Lorde: in other some two or three, in some sixe, eight, & more; the greatest *Wiroans* that yet we had dealing with had but eighteene townes in his government, and able to make not above seven or eight hundred fighting men at the most. The language of every government, is different from any other, and the further they are distant the greater is the difference.[11]

Indian warfare consisted of surprise attacks rather than pitched battles. European scientific knowledge and weapons were immeasurably superior, yet Harriot had a shrewd conviction that the natives were intelligent enough to adapt quickly to a different culture. He continues with a discussion of their religious beliefs.

In respect of us they are a people poore, and for want of skill and judgement in the knowledge and use of our things, doe esteeme our trifles before thinges of greater value: Notwithstanding in their proper manner considering the want of such meanes as we have, they seeme very ingenious; for although they have no such tooles, nor any such craftes, sciences and artes as wee; yet in those things they doe, they shewe excellencie of wit. And by howe much upon due consideration shall finde our manner of knowledges and craftes to exceede theirs in perfection, and speed for doing or execution, by so much the more is it probable that they shoulde desire our friendships & love, and have the greater respect for pleasing and obeying us. Whereby may bee hoped if meanes of good gouvernment bee used, that they may in short time be brought to civilitie, and the imbracing of true religion.

Some religion they have alreadie, which although it be farre from the truth, yet beyng as it is, there is hope it may bee the easier and sooner reformed.

They beleeve that there are many Gods which they call *Montoác*,[12] but of different sortes and degrees; one onely chiefe and great God, which hath bene from all eternitie. Who as they affirme when hee purposed to make the worlde, made first other goddes of a principall order to bee as meanes and instruments to be used in the creation and government to follow; and after the Sunne, Moone, and Starres as pettie gods, and the instruments of the other order more principall. First they say were made waters, out of which by the gods was made all diversitie of creatures that are visible or invisible.[13]

For mankinde they say a woman was made first, which by the working of one of the goddes, conceived and brought foorth children:[14] And in such sort they say they had their beginning. But how many yeeres or ages have passed since, they say they can make no relation, having no letters nor other such meanes as we to keepe recordes of the particularities of times past, but onely tradition from father to sonne.

They thinke that all the gods are of humane shape, & therefore they represent them by images in the formes of men, which they call *Kewasówak* one alone is called *Kewás*, them they place in houses appropriate or temples, which they call *Machicómuck*; Where they worship, praie, sing, and make manie times offerings unto them. In some *Machicómuck*; we have seene but on *Kewás*, in some two, and in other some three; The common sorte thinke them to be also gods.

They beleeve also the immortalitie of the soule, that after this life as soone as the soule is departed from the bodie, according to the workes it hath done, it is eyther carried to heaven the habitacle of gods, there to enjoy perpetuall blisse and happinesse, or els to a great pitte or hole, which they thinke to bee in the furthest partes of their part of the worlde toward the sunne set, there to burne continually: the place they call *Popogusso*.[15]

For the confirmation of this opinion, they tolde mee two stories of two men that had been lately dead and revived againe, the one happened but few yeres before our coming into the countrey of a wicked man which having beene dead and buried, the next day the earth of the grave being seene to move, was taken up againe; Who made declaration where his soule had beene, that is to saie, very neere entring into *Popogusso*, had not one of the gods saved him and gave him leave to returne againe, and teach his friends what they should doe to avoid that terrible place of torment.

The other happened in the same yeere wee were there, but in a towne that was three score miles from us, and it was tolde mee for a straunge newes that one beeing dead, buried and taken up againe as the first shewed that although his bodie had lien dead in the grave, yet his soule was alive, & had travailed farre in a long broade waie, on both sides whereof grewe most delicate and pleasaunt trees, bearing more rare and excellent fruites, than ever hee had seene before or was able to expresse, and at length came to most brave and faire houses, neere which hee met his father, that had beene dead before, who gave him great charge to goe backe againe and shew his friendes what good they were to doe to enjoy the pleasures of that place, which when he had done he should after come againe.[16]

Their inability to understand the strange weapons and instruments used by their European visitors convinced the Indians of the superior strength of the English god. The mysterious epidemics which decimated the villages after contacts with the English caused the natives to believe that the intruders could kill at will, and seriously to doubt whether they were mortal. Harriot concludes his account with a reiteration of the potential of the new land, in hopes of encouraging settlement there.

Text used: D. B. Quinn, The Roanoke Voyages 1584–1590. *London: Hakluyt Society, Ser. II, Vol. 104, 1955, I, 341-2, 344-5, 356, 369-70, 371-4.*

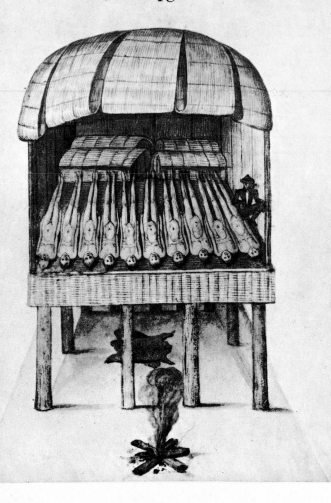

241
An ossuary temple. Drawing by John White, 1585. *London, British Museum.* 'The Tombe of their Cherounes or chief personages, their flesh clene taken of from the bones save the skynn and heare of their heads, which flesh is dried and enfolded in matts laide at theire feete, their bones also being made dry, are covered with deare skynns not altering their forme or proportion. With theire Kywash, which is an Image of woode keeping the deade.'— Harriot (1590).

6.
The voyage of Captain Vincente González to Chesapeake Bay, 1588

From *Relacion de los Martires . . . de la Florida,* by Luis Jerónimo de Oré.

In May 1588 Captain Vincente González was despatched with thirty men from the Spanish fort at St Augustine, Florida, with orders to reconnoitre northwards as far as Chesapeake Bay. He was to search for traces of English settlement in the area. Only very brief first-hand accounts of this mission have survived. Father Oré's narrative, printed here, summarizes the now missing report written by Juan Menéndez Marqués, sergeant major on the expedition.

Finally, they arrived at the bay of Madre de Dios del Jacan [Chesapeake Bay] in the month of June in the year 1588.

The mouth of this bay is about three leagues wide, without shoals or reefs and is more than eight fathoms deep at its entrance. It runs N.W.-S.E. and forms a larger circular gulf. Between the entrance and the place where one reaches the mainland it extends westward and north-westward for about three leagues. On the mainland, and in an east-west direction with the mouth, is a good harbour which has at its entrance a depth of three fathoms [entrance to Elizabeth River at Norfolk]. Rather less than two leagues from there and to the north-west is another harbour [Hampton Roads; ?Newport News] . . .

Captain González had landed a Jesuit mission to the Chesapeake at the latter haven in 1570, destroyed by the Indians.

Thereupon they departed from the said harbour, coasting along the mainland shore towards the north where they discovered another haven which seemed to be a good one and of great depth [Yorktown]. On shore there was abundance of large stones while the cape of land to the north formed a high headland [Gloucester Point on York River]. These three harbours can be seen at one glance from the mouth of the bay, the last, however, only faintly.

As they continued to sail northwards the land from the east jutted into the bay. It narrowed so much that at one point, from the western shore towardes the eastern side, it was only two leagues wide [actually 14 miles wide or more]. After that they discovered coves and inlets, as well as rivers, along the western shore. Then they came upon a large, fresh-water river which, where it entered the bay, was more than six fathoms deep. To the north of it there was very high land, with ravines, but without trees, cleared and like a green field and pleasant to behold. On the southern shore of this river the beach is very calm and it is covered with tiny pebbles. Farther up on the south bank of the same river appeared a delightful valley, wooded, with pleasant land, apparently

Map of North America by Cornelis de Jode, in *Speculum orbis terrarum*, Antwerp, 1593.

This is one of the earliest maps to represent the south-east coast in accordance with the conceptions of John White and Le Moyne, as reflected in their maps published by T. de Bry in 1590 and 1591 (plates 197 and 198). The engraved maps of de Bry have supplied the cartographer with his outlines and place names in 'Virginia' and Florida and with two long legends on the attempt at colonization by the French in 1562–5 and by Ralegh in 1585–6. The vignette (bottom right), representing Indians of 'Virginia', copies engravings by de Bry after White's drawings (see plates 229 and 232).

The following day Indians came down to the beach. The Spaniards seized one youth and took him with them.

Advancing further, they discovered many other harbours and rivers carrying much water which entered the bay from the western shore until they came to latitude 35° [?39°], where they saw mountain ridges, very high, running S.W.-N.E. Still more rivers were found and soon, in the middle of the bay, a small island. Along the western shore the depth began to diminish so much that they could go no further, so they turned eastwards. Opposite the island the land was high, broken and well-wooded, while nearby on the eastern side there were shoals of greater or lesser depth. Sailing closer to the mainland on the east they found a channel of great depth.

fertile and suitable for stock-breeding and husbandry. This river [Potomac] was located in latitude 38°. They named it San Pedro.

They continued to sail north along the western shore and passed the night in a small inlet under the protection of high and well-shaded land.

Still further north they found that the hills began to close in the view.

In different places they found mouths of rivers and coves, while, where this bay ends in a semi-circle, it is about as wide as Cadiz harbour. More than two or three leagues before they reached the head of the bay they found that the water was

243
Detail from the map of the east coast of North America from the Vaz
Dourado *Atlas, 1580. Munich, Bayerische Staatsbibliothek, fo 4.*
Fernão Vaz Dourado, the foremost Portuguese artist-cartographer in the
latter half of the sixteenth century, produced a series of magnificently
drawn atlases. The atlas of 1580, in which this map is found, is the latest
in date of his known works.

fresh. That evening they were on the point of entering a river,
west-north-west between some high hills and crags [Susque-
hanna River]. At high tide the mouth was more than three
fathoms deep, but because night was falling they anchored
about a quarter of a league inside. At dawn there was low tide,
and it was almost a miracle that the bark avoided great rocks
by which the river was enclosed from one side to the other.

With great difficulty the Spaniards navigated the river mouth safely.
It was named by them St John of the Rocks.

They went up on the ridge at a level place and saw on the
other side another river [?Octoraro Creek] and with it ranges
of hills and rolling land. Below, in the fold of this range there
was a fair valley with trees and with fertile and pleasing land.
From latitude 38° up to the end of the bay there is to be
found a great quantity of chestnuts and large walnuts, as well
as wild vines with swollen grapes. And the same day they left
the river and went some distance from the coast and the shore
towards the east for a good while. There they discovered a very
agreeable inlet, with thick woods where many deer appeared.
They entered it towards the north, and sailed as far as its
extremity.

There they landed on a pleasant beach, below some small
gullies. At that end of the little bay there was a quiet and
pleasant valley, with trees but without any craggy places.
In it they found many deer. They killed one of these and made
a feast of it on the day of the grace-giving St John the Baptist
[June 24].

Leaving the end of the bay, González sailed back southwards along
the western shore, and down the coast. He discovered a slipway for
small vessels and casks sunk for wells, traces of English occupation,
at Port Ferdinando Inlet on the Carolina coast, but they did not find
Roanoke Island. Oré implies that he thought the English had occupied
Chesapeake Bay since 1587. The expedition reached St Augustine
in July 1588.

This expedition of exploration and discovery, from start to
finish, they made in a little less than a month and a half,
according to the report, as exact as it is detailed, by the said
sergeant-major, Juan Menéndez who is now the royal treasurer
in the city of San Agustin.

Because the description of the bay of Madre de Dios and of
the harbours, with the observations and bearings of their
course, is so trustworthy and so necessary for the time when
your majesty may be pleased to command that the bay be
cleared of the robbers who have occupied and fortified it for
thirty years, it seemed well that I should dwell on it at some
length.

*The text was probably published in Madrid in 1617. Text used: D. B.
Quinn,* The Roanoke Voyages 1584–1590. *London: Hakluyt Society,
Ser. II, Vol. 105, 1955, II, 805-6, 806-7, 807-8, 808-9, 811-12.*

Blue Jay. Dr Hans Sloane manuscript. *London, British Museum.*
A seventeenth-century copy of an original by John White.

245
Eastern Cardinal. Dr Hans Sloane manuscript. *London, British Museum.*
A seventeenth-century copy of an original by John White.

246
Timucuan woman of Florida. Drawing by John White, 1585. *London, British Museum.*
White's copy of a lost Jacques Le Moyne drawing.

247
Indian in war paint for hunting or for a solemn feast. Drawing by John White, 1585. *London, British Museum.*
'The Princes of Virginia are attyred in suche manner as is expressed in this figure. They weare the haire of their heades long and bynde opp the ende of the same in a knot under their eares. Yet they cutt the topp of their heades from the forehead to the nape of the necke in manner of a cokscombe, stirking a faier longe pecher [feather] of some berd att the Begininge of the creste uppon their foreheads, and another short one on bothe seides about their eares. They hange at their eares ether thicke pearles, or somwhat els, as the clawe of some great birde, as cometh in to their fansye. Moreover They ether pownes, or paynt their forehead, cheeks, chynne, bodye, armes, and leggs, yet in another sort then the inhabitantz of Florida. They weare a chaine about their necks of pearles or beades of copper, wich they much esteeme, and ther of wear they also braselets ohn their armes. Under their brests about their bellyes appeir certayne spotts, whear they use to lett them selves bloode, when they are sicke. They hange before them the skinne of some beaste verye feinelye dresset in suche sorte, that the tayle hangeth downe behynde. They carye a quiver made of small rushes holding their bowe readie bent in on hand, and an arrowe in the other, radie to defend themselves. In this manner they goe to warr, or tho their solemne feasts and banquetts. They take muche pleasure in huntinge of deer wher of ther is great store in the contrye, for yt is fruit full, pleasant, and full of Goodly woods. Yt hathe also store of rivers full of divers sorts of fishe. When they go to battel they paynt their bodyes in the most terible manner that their can devise.'—Harriot (1590).

248
An Indian man of Florida. Drawing by John White, 1585. *London, British Museum.*
Since there is no record of White's being in Florida, this figure of a Timucuan Indian of the St Johns River region is almost certainly drawn from a lost original by Jacques Le Moyne. Le Moyne and White were both in the employ of Sir Walter Ralegh.

249
The wife of the chief of Pomeiooc and her eight or ten year old daughter, who is carrying an English doll and a rattle which had been given to her. Drawing by John White, 1585. *London, British Museum.*
'About 20. milles from that Iland, neere the lake of Paquippe, ther is another towne called Pomeioock hard by the sea. The apparell of the cheefe ladyes of that towne differeth but litle from the attyre of those which lyve in Roanoac. For they weare their haire trussed opp in a knott, as the maiden doe which we spake of before, and have their skinnes pownced in the same manner, yet they weare a chaine of great pearles, or beades of copper, or

smoothe bones 5. or 6. fold about their necks, bearinge one arme in the same, in the other they carye a gourde full of some kinde of pleasant liquor. They tye deers skinne doubled about them crochinge hygher about their breasts which hange downe before almost to their knees, and are almost altogither naked behinde. Commonlye their yonge daugters of 7. or 8. yeares olde doe wayt upon them wearinge about them a girdle of skinne, which hangeth downe behinde, and is drawen under neath betwene their twiste and bownde above their navel with mose of trees betwene that and their skinnes to cover their priviliers withall. After they be once past 10. yeares of age, they wear deerskinnes as the older sorte doe. They are greatlye Deligted with puppetts and babes which wear brought oute of England.'—Harriot (1590).

250-3 *Overleaf*
'The Demonstration of the Fordes, Rivers, and the Coast': four manuscript charts of the west coast of Greenland drawn by James Hall, pilot of the Danish expedition in 1605. *London, British Museum, Royal Ms. 17.A.XLVIII, fos. 7 to 10.*
The expedition of three ships under the command of a Scot, Captain William Cunningham, was despatched by King Christian IV to search for the old Norse colonies in southern Greenland and to bring back some of the natives. One ship parted company before reaching Greenland, as recorded in Resen's map (plate 272); the other two under Cunningham, in whose ship Hall was pilot, sailed north-west up Davis Strait, sighting Baffin Island, before turning east to find a passage through the 'pester of yce' to the Greenland coast in 66°N. In 'King Christian's Fjord' (Itivdlek Fjord) they lay for a month, and Hall explored the coast northward in the pinnace to 68½°N, naming capes and bays.

Hall's general chart illustrates his boat survey northward; the other three charts depict, on a larger scale, the fjords where they anchored and landed. The general chart is remarkable for its indication of soundings, in fathoms. The charts are illustrated by little drawings, evidently from observation, of whales, walrus, seals, narwhal, and Eskimos with their kayaks, summer tents and weapons.

Of Florida.

Of Florida.

The manner of their attire and
painting them selues when
they goe to their generall
huntings or at theire
Solemne feasts.

A cheife Heroroans wyfe of Pomeoc.
and her daughter of the age of. 8. or.
10 yeares.

209

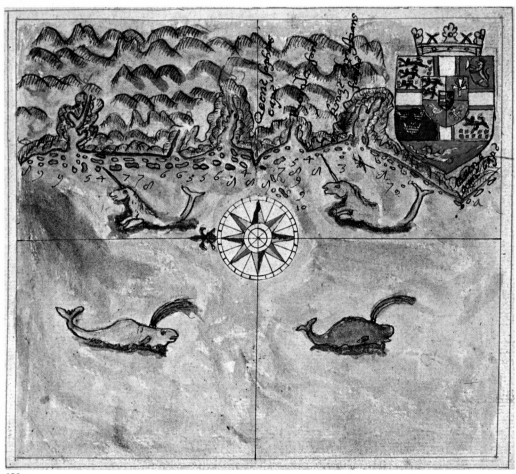

250

251

210

252

Cvninghams forde

The names of such places
as we found in this forde

a. the first place of ancoring in this forde
b. Catt sovnd or weike
c. greete sovnd or weike
d. mvsle sovnde

Brade kansens forde

the name of places within
this forde

A. shovlde wike
B. henriks pas
C. cliffe road

5 THE SEARCH FOR A NORTH-WEST PASSAGE

From its rediscovery by John Cabot to the establishment of permanent settlements, and long after, North America was visualized by Europeans as a stage in the westward course to Asia. The legendary wealth of Cathay, the islands where the spices grew, the rich trade of China and India were in turn powerful magnets which attracted expeditions to discover a physically and commercially viable sailing route by the west or the north. The nations of northern Europe, who during the sixteenth century were denied the seaways south of Africa and of Patagonia pioneered by Portugal and Spain, were to search for water passages through or round North America for over three centuries after Cabot's discovery.

The continuity of the Atlantic coast of North America, from Florida to the St Lawrence, was foreshadowed by an inspired guess of Martin Waldseemüller in his world map of 1507. It was demonstrated by Verrazzano in 1524, though the 'narrow neck of land' across which he looked west from his ship over the North Carolina Banks was to foster English illusions of easy access to 'the oriental sea . . . about the extremity of India, China and Cathay'. Nor did the St Lawrence lead Cartier to 'Asia on its western side', as his promoters believed.[1]

As men came to realize that Columbus and John Cabot had not attained the shores of East Asia, and that North America stood as a great barrier across the seaway westward, the dream of outflanking it in high northern latitudes was born. Medieval ideas about the distribution of land and water round the North Pole were inherited by Renaissance geographers and fortified by the authority of Mercator (plate 257)[2]; and wishful thinking added the Strait of Anian (where Bering Strait lies) as the final link in a navigable sea-route leading from the Atlantic into the Pacific by the north of Asia or of America.

An English propagandist, in 1527, urged on his countrymen 'one way to discover, which is into the North',[3] and during the sixteenth and seventeenth centuries, expeditions were despatched from England, from the Netherlands and from Denmark to discover a north-west passage, or a north-east

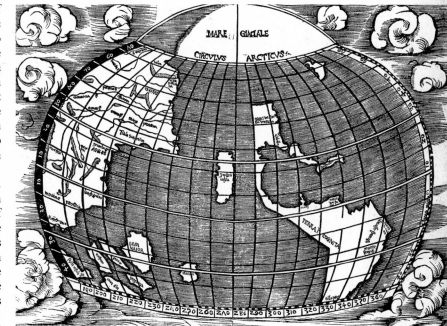

255

passage, or a passage across supposedly open sea at the pole. From globes and maps on polar projections it could be shown that these routes provided a shorter way to the Spice Islands than that by the Cape of Good Hope or Magellan Strait (see plates 257 and 258). The seamen who attempted them discovered, by bitter experience, only the unpredicted difficulties of navigation in high latitudes—the immense power of pressure ice, the great rise and fall of tides, the enormous range of compass variation. The geographical information which these voyages contributed to the world map was hardly won.

After John Cabot's voyage of 1498, from which he did not return, there was in London 'no more talk of Asia as lying on the other side of the ocean'.[4] His son Sebastian was the first to test the possibility of outflanking 'the New Land' to the north. The story of his voyage in 1509, as he told it later in Spain, suggests that he passed through Hudson Strait to the mouth of Hudson Bay, which (as he believed) offered an open seaway 'towards Eastern Cathay'.[5]

This 'secret of nature' was carried with him by Cabot on his flight from Spain into England in 1547. The Muscovy Company's failure, in various attempts between 1553 and 1580, to find a navigable route to the north of Asia convinced the English 'that the passage by the Northwest is more commodious for our traffick, then the other by the East'. The first expedition led by Martin Frobisher, in 1576, was promoted by his associates, the leader of whom was Michael Lok, on a very modest scale; his ship *Gabriel* was of only twenty tons, and

254
Photograph of an ice field.
255
The Western Hemisphere; woodcut map in Joannes de Stobnicza, *Introductio in Ptholemei Cosmographiam*, Cracow, 1512, copied from an inset of Martin Waldseemüller's world map of 1507.
By an inspired guess, Waldseemüller laid down the lands of North and South America, of which only discontinuous sections had been discovered, as an uninterrupted continental coastline from 50°N lat. to the foot of the map; the rectilinear drawing of the west coasts indicates their conjectural character. The German geographer thus prefigured the Pacific Ocean six years before Balboa set eyes on it from 'a peak in Darien'. In the ocean, the island of 'Zipangri' (Japan) is placed ten degrees west of the American coast.

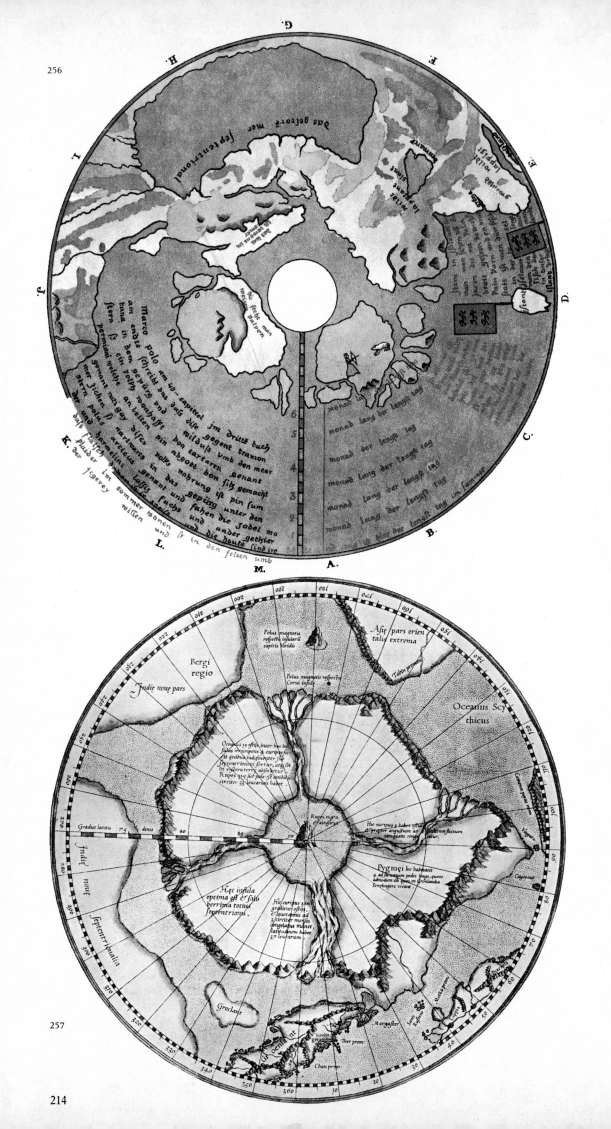

256

The Arctic, in the terrestrial globe of Martin Behaim, 1492. *Nuremberg, Germanisches Museum.*

The representation of islands separated by channels flowing into a polar ocean was probably derived by Behaim from a lost tract, *Inventio Fortunata,* apparently describing the visit of an English Minorite friar to the Eastern Settlement in Greenland about 1360. Through Behaim, and subsequently Mercator, this medieval Scandinavian concept of the North was incorporated into European cartography.

257

The Arctic; inset of Gerard Mercator's world map of 1569. *Rotterdam, Maritiem Museum Prins Hendrik.*

The version of polar geography here adopted by Mercator was found by him in the lost fourteenth-century tract, *Inventio Fortunata,* a transcript of which (also now lost) had come into his hands. The concept of 'indrawing seas' pouring into a circumpolar ocean between large islands reflects

medieval Norse geographical ideas. A legend on one of the islands refers to 'pygmies 4 feet tall, said to be like the Skrælings of Greenland', on the east coast of which 'Screlingers' are also marked. By this date Mercator was convinced of the navigability of sea passages by the north of America and of Asia; and this 'strange plat of the Septentrionall Ilands', which aroused the curiosity of Dr John Dee in 1477, strongly influenced English projectors and the maps which served them as propaganda.

258

Sebastian Cabot's 'secret of nature': the passage to Cathay which he supposed himself to have discovered in 1509, as depicted in the terrestrial globe of Gemma Frisius and Mercator, completed at Louvain in 1537. *Vienna, Österreichische Nationalbibliothek.*

This globe and other maps and globes derived from it were known in England, where they encouraged belief in a North-west Passage and projects for its discovery.

258

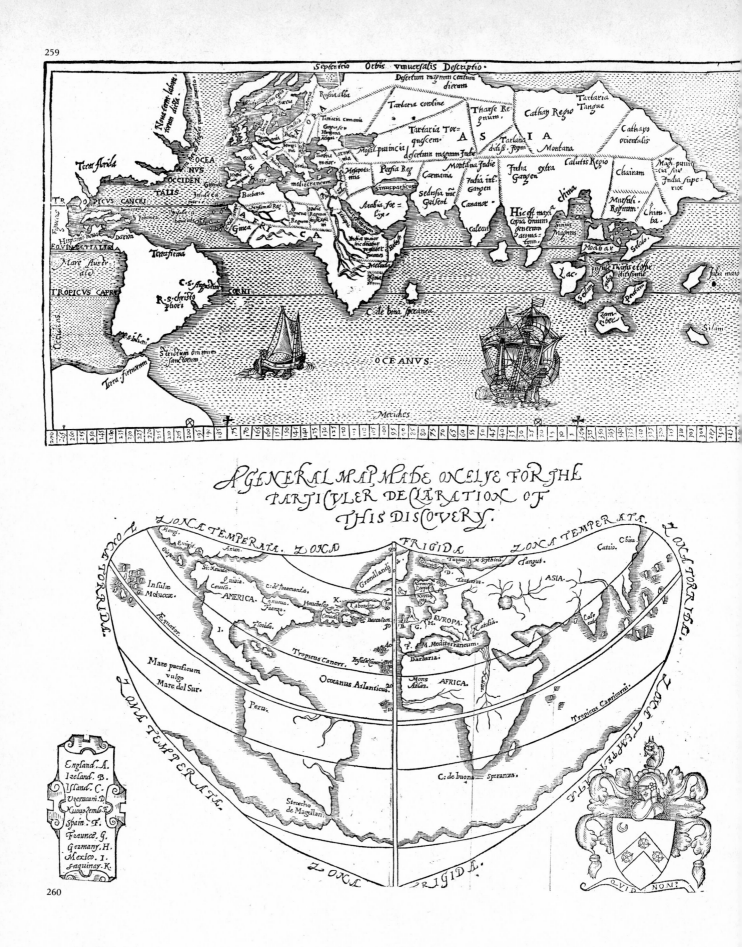

In 1527 Robert Thorne, an English merchant trading in Seville, sought to arouse the interest of King Henry VIII in oceanic trade, the fruit of which Spain and Portugal already enjoyed by virtue of geographical discovery. The magnet was Cathay and the Spice Islands, 'the most richest londes and ilondes in the worlde'. The manuscript 'book and card of the viage to Cataia' which Thorne addressed to the King in 1527 were printed in 1582, as propaganda for a North-west Passage, in Richard Hakluyt's *Divers voyages touching the discoverie of America*.

If the woodcut reproduces Thorne's manuscript of 1527, this is the earliest post-medieval map known to have been drawn by an Englishman. It is not a very original compilation. The design for the Old World is substantially copied from a map published by a German geographer in 1515; that of the New World from a Spanish map drawn after 1522 to which (although a 'classified' document) Thorne had obtained access. In only one detail has he seriously modified his prototype. Since his purpose was to demonstrate 'ye short way to the spicerie by our Seas' (by 'sayling Northward and passing the Pole'), he has redrawn the Moluccas, as revealed by Magellan's circumnavigation, with special prominence in the south-east of the map. The sentence written off the mainland of North America, claiming its first discovery by the English, was perhaps added by Hakluyt. The map is graduated in latitude and longitude; in the sixteenth century, problems of world trade and international politics had to be discussed in terms of mathematical geography.

Sir Humphrey Gilbert, in a tract entitled *A discourse of a discoverie for a new passage to Cataia* (written in 1566, printed in 1576), argued that a passage into the Pacific by the north-west was 'more commodious' than that by the north-east. The woodcut map illustrating his thesis is the earliest surviving world map printed in England. It is a simplified copy of Ortelius' world map of 1564 (plate 77), and the heart-shaped projection emphasizes the shortness of the north-west route to the Moluccas, by comparison with the southern routes by Magellan Strait and the Cape of Good Hope. The passage, derived from Sebastian Cabot's discovery in 1509, is shown in temperate latitudes, while that to the north of Asia lies within the Arctic Circle.

The 'navigation chart of Nicolò and Antonio Zeno who were in the North in the year 1380'; engraved map in the *Commentarii* edited by their descendant Nicolò Zeno, Venice, 1558.

The narrative of the voyages of the Zeni brothers in the north and west Atlantic in 1380–7 is largely apocryphal; but the map which accompanies it was copied (as the Venetian compiler says) from 'a chart which I found among the ancient things in our home, all rotten and many years old.' This was evidently a version of Claudius Clavus' map of the North, similar to that of Henricus Martellus (see plate 30). To it the sixteenth-century editor added features illustrating the geography of the Zeni narrative— the Atlantic islands of Estland, Frisland (a doublet of Iceland), Icaria and others, and the western lands of Estotiland and Drogeo. The only other serious modification which he made is in the location of the southern point of Greenland (Cape Farewell); Henricus Martellus, following Clavus, put it in $62\frac{1}{2}°$N (already over three degrees north of the true latitude), and in the Zeni map it is moved further north still, to 65° 40'.

The representation of the North Atlantic and of Greenland in the Zeni map was given authority and widespread diffusion by its adoption by Mercator in 1569. Frobisher's officers carried not only Mercator's world map, but also the original Zeni map and the *Commentarii*. George Best, describing 'Frisland' (Greenland) as observed in the voyage of 1577, thought 'Nicholaus and Antonius Genua' to have been 'the first knowen Christians that discovered this lande'; and, sailing, along it, he compared 'their carde with ye coast', finding it 'very agreeable'.

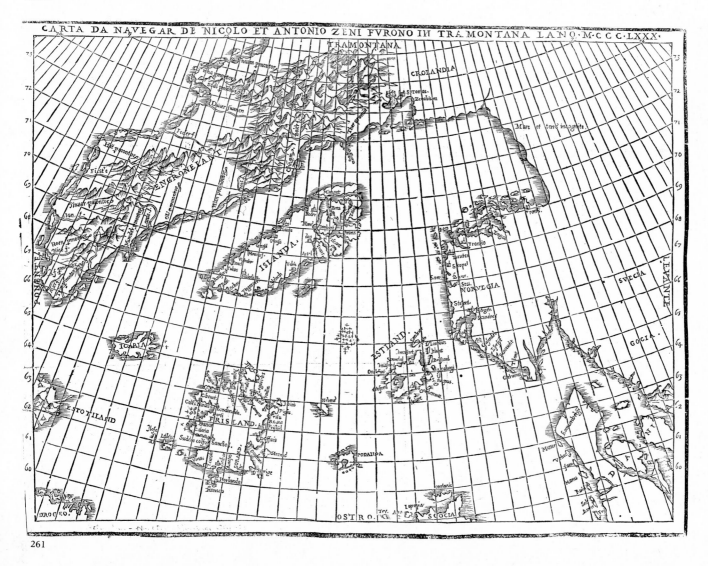

her consort, which turned back in a storm off Greenland, of twenty-five tons. Frobisher carried with him Mercator's printed world map of 1569 (plate 263), and he interpreted his landfalls in the light of its delineation of the North Atlantic, with some fictitious geography which Mercator had found in a map, published at Venice in 1558, illustrating a supposed

262

'A marvellous huge mountaine of yce, which surpassed all the rest that ever we sawe.' An iceberg seen off Baffin Island, 2 July 1578, and sketched by Thomas Ellis, a seaman in Frobisher's ship, the *Aid*. Woodcut in Thomas Ellis, *A true report of the third and last voyage into Meta Incognita*, London, 1578.

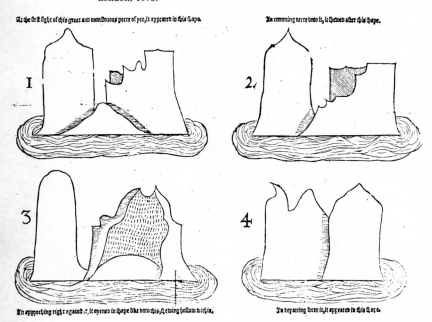

westward voyage made by the Zeno brothers in the late fourteenth century. So Frobisher's American landfalls on Baffin Island, north of Hudson Strait, came to be laid down on maps, for nearly two centuries, in southern Greenland.[6] Reports on his three voyages were published by his lieutenant George Best, with rough maps, and by others.[7]

On 1 July 1576 Frobisher 'hadde sighte of a highe and ragged lande'; this was the Greenland coast near Cape Farewell, which he took to be the imaginary island of Friesland laid down in the same latitude, though ten degrees further east, in the Zeni map (plate 261), but he 'durste not approche the same by reason of the greate store of ise that lay alongst the coast, and the greate mistes'. Alone in the *Gabriel*, Frobisher drove on north-west to the coast of Baffin Island, later to be named by the Queen 'Meta Incognita' (the Unknown Goal). After beating up and down along the ice-edge, he was able to sail up the broad opening of 'Frobisher's Straits [Frobisher Bay], supposing Asia to lie to starboard and America to port, and 'the great open [sea] betwene them . . . by reason of the great tydes of flood . . . comming owt of the same . . . to be the West Sea, whereby to pas to Cathay and to the West India'.

Frobisher brought back to England in October 1576 a captured Eskimo, who died 'of colde' after the return, and a sample of glittering black stone, probably marcasite, which London assayers pronounced to contain gold. In this expectation, backers were found for two further and better-equipped expeditions, in which the search for a passage was subordinated to the lading of 'gold ore'. In 1577, after touching at the Orkneys, Frobisher's three ships 'traversed these Seas by

the space of 26 dayes, without sight of any land, and met with much drift woode and whole bodyes of trees' borne south by the East Greenland Current. On 4 July land was sighted in 60½°N and identified as Friesland, or West Friesland, by reference to the printed narrative of Nicolò and Antonio Zeno, 'for so much of this land as we have sayled amongst, comparing their carde [map] with ye coast, we find it very agreeable'. This again was southernmost Greenland, 'a ragged and high lande, having the mountaynes almost covered with snow alongst the coast full of drift ise'. The seamen noted with wonder 'of what great bignesse and depth some ilandes of ise be heere, some seventy some eighty fadome under water, besides that which is above, seemyng ilands more than half a mile in circuit'; and, finding 'none of these islands of ise salt in taste', they concluded (wrongly) that the icebergs were formed only on land, of fresh water or frozen snow, and that 'ye maine sea freeseth not'. Drift ice prevented landing, and on 16 July Frobisher, by accurate navigation, 'made the North Forlande perfite' where, at the mouth of Frobisher Bay, ore had been found in the previous year. While the men were loading the ships, Frobisher went ashore, took a view of the country, which seemed 'barren and full of ragged mountains, in most parts covered with snow', and established friendly relations with the Eskimos. An attempt to capture a 'salvage' as interpreter led to a skirmish, in which Eskimos drove the English to their boats, wounding Frobisher 'in the buttocke'. On 29 July Frobisher came to an anchorage at Countess of Warwick Island, thirty leagues within Frobisher Bay. Here a search was made for the boat's crew lost on the previous voyage and the loading of the ships continued. Best made further observations of Eskimo life, supposing them to be 'a dispersed and wandering nation, as the Tartarians, and live in hords and troupes, withoute anye certayn abode'. At a place named 'the Bloody Point', there was a desperate fight with Eskimos who resisted the landing of the English 'manfullye . . . so long as theyr arrows and dartes lasted'.[8] On 23 August, as 'ye ise began to congeale and freese about our ships sides a night', Frobisher sailed for home with 200 tons of 'ore' and a captive Eskimo man, woman and child, of whom, before their death a month after arrival in England, John White made drawings (see plates 225, 285 and 286).

In 1578 Frobisher led a squadron of fifteen ships, with equipment for wintering. Touching on 20 June at Greenland, where they thought themselves 'the fyrste knowen Christians . . . that ever set foote upon that ground',[9] they found traces of Eskimo habitations. The observation that these people were 'in all sortes, very like those of Meta incognita' led to the conjecture that 'West England' (as Frobisher renamed West Friesland) was connected in the north with the land on the west side of Davis Strait discovered on the two earlier voyages. Ice conditions in Davis Strait were very bad this year, and the ships were in much danger from large floes which 'open and shutte together . . . wyth the tydes and sea-gate, that whilest one shippe followeth the other wyth full sayles, the ise wyche was open unto the foremoste will joyne and close togyther before the latter can come to followe the fyrste'. There were many icebergs, and a bark of 100 tons 'received such a blowe with a rocke of ise, that she sunke downe therewith, in the sight of the whole fleete'. After many similar lessons in ice-navigation, Frobisher took his ships in July along the north shore of Hudson Strait, which he took to be 'Frobisher's Straits', sailing up it sixty leagues in thick fog and snow, so that no sun-sights could be taken to ascertain the latitude. When the error was discovered, a channel was found west of 'Queen Elizabeth's Foreland' (Resolution Island), so named on the first voyage, to take the ships into Frobisher Bay.

263
Greenland and north-eastern North America, in Mercator's world map of
1569. *Rotterdam, Maritiem Museum Prins Hendrik.*

This was the 'great mappe universall of Mercator in prente' purchased for
Frobisher in 1576 (for £1 6s 8d) and carried by him on his first voyage.
Mercator followed the Zeni map in his delineation of Greenland and
location of its southernmost point about six degrees too far north, in
65° 40′N. When in 60½°N (by his estimation) Frobisher fell in with land,
he accordingly thought it to be the island of 'Frislant' shown on the
Zeni map in about this latitude, though somewhat to the east of his supposed
position. In Lok's map (plate 267), an attempt is made to reconcile
Frobisher's observed latitude with the Zeni map, by drawing 'Frisland' with
the Zeni outline (but no north coast) and terminating in about 59°N, thus
providing an alternative position for Greenland. The Zenian names
Estotiland and Drogeo are placed by Mercator in the position of Baffin
Island and northern Labrador respectively.

264

Frobisher would gladly have followed the 'Mistaken Straits' westward, believing that they might lead 'to the south sea' [the Pacific] and provide 'the passage which we seeke to find to the rich countrey of Cathaya'. This opinion was sustained by the ice-free condition of Hudson Strait this year, the 'marvellous great indrafte' with 'nine houres flodde to three ebbe' (due in fact to the Labrador Current), and the 'great course of flouds and currant, so highe swelling tides with continuance of so deepe waters'. But he had to put first 'the charge and care he had of ye fleete and fraughted shippes'; and at Countess of Warwick Island he reassembled his ships, reopened the mines, and loaded ore in 'unconstant weather', fierce snowstorms alternating with sunshine of 'a marvellous force of heate'. Reconnaissances up the 'strait' led Frobisher to think the land to the north 'not firme [mainland], as it was first supposed, but all broken ilandes'. On 31 August the fleet sailed for home. At its return, the bubble was pricked; the 'gold ore' was found worthless, and the principal investor ruined.

On the Innuit Eskimos of Baffin Island, their first encounter with Europeans left a deep impression. Nearly three hundred years later, in 1862, their descendants were able to communicate to an American explorer, C. F. Hall, accurate reports of Frobisher's three visits, of his digging in the ground, and of the fate of his lost boat-crew; and they led Hall to the mine workings and to the site of the stone house built by the English.[10]

Frobisher knew nothing of the Norsemen and their Atlantic colonies, and was unaware that he had rediscovered the country which they named Helluland. From Greenland and from Baffin Island he and his men brought back the earliest detailed accounts of the Eastern and Central Eskimos and their habitat to be received in Europe, where they aroused profound interest. John White and other artists drew portraits of the captured Eskimos; and the illustrations made on the voyages and printed in German, French and perhaps English tracts (see plate 265) became the standard representations of Eskimo manners, reappearing for many years in travel books and as vignettes of maps.[11] They fostered belief in the Mongolian character of the Eskimos, which, though historically correct, was delusive in its suggestion of Asia.

To the original purpose of the expeditions Frobisher made no contribution beyond pointing to the possibility of a western passage through Hudson Strait. Like later explorers, he was willingly deceived by supposed signs of a seaway between ocean and ocean—a strong westward current, great tidal range and depth of water, an ice-free channel—in a region notoriously subject to varying conditions of ice and weather from one season to another. To his successors however he

264
The Northern Hemisphere, in a manuscript atlas prepared by the Flemish cartographer Christian Sgrooten for Philip II, King of Spain. *Madrid, Biblioteca Nacional.*
Although the atlas was completed in 1592, the representation of North America is considerably older. In outline and nomenclature Mercator's world map of 1569 was the model for the east coast and the interior, but Sgrooten draws the north coast ten degrees further south than Mercator, below the Arctic Circle, though fringed by a frozen sea ('Mare congelatum'). In the ocean northward, Sgrooten's geography is peculiar to himself. The islands round the Pole are laid down as in the inset of Mercator's map; but the southern tip of Greenland is in 73°N, with Iceland (wrongly oriented) east of it and north of the British Isles. Frobisher's discoveries of 1576–8, marked as 'NOVA ANGLIA' and with English place names, are represented by 'Fresland' and (twenty degrees further west) two islands named as 'Hasles Isle' and 'Queenes Foreland', separated by 'Streight'. These lie off the north coast of North America, in about the longitude of Mexico City, thus some forty degrees west of the true position of Baffin Island—and by so much nearer to China!

265
Eskimos hunting sea-birds. Woodcut, probably after a drawing by John White, in a German version of Dionyse Settle's report on Frobisher's second voyage, *Beschreibung der Schiffart des Haubtmans Martini Forbissher . . . im Jar 1577,* Nürnberg, 1580.
In the foreground, an Eskimo in a kayak using a three-pronged spear. In the background, on shore, (left) a summer camp of sealskin tents and a dog drawing a sledge shaped like a kayak; (right) another Eskimo man carrying a kayak and bow, and an Eskimo woman with child in a bag on her back. This illustration was copied, with variations, as a vignette on maps (see plate 272).
266
Martin Frobisher, from H. Holland, *Herwologia,* London, 1620.

265

266

bequeathed not only the continuing hope of a passage but also, and more usefully, a detailed report on the physical conditions to be met by ships in high latitudes and (virtually) a manual of Arctic seamanship.

John Davis, a sea-captain of Sandridge near Dartmouth, no less competent a commander than Frobisher and a more scientific navigator, sought the passage 'unto China' both farther north and farther south than Frobisher.[12] On each of

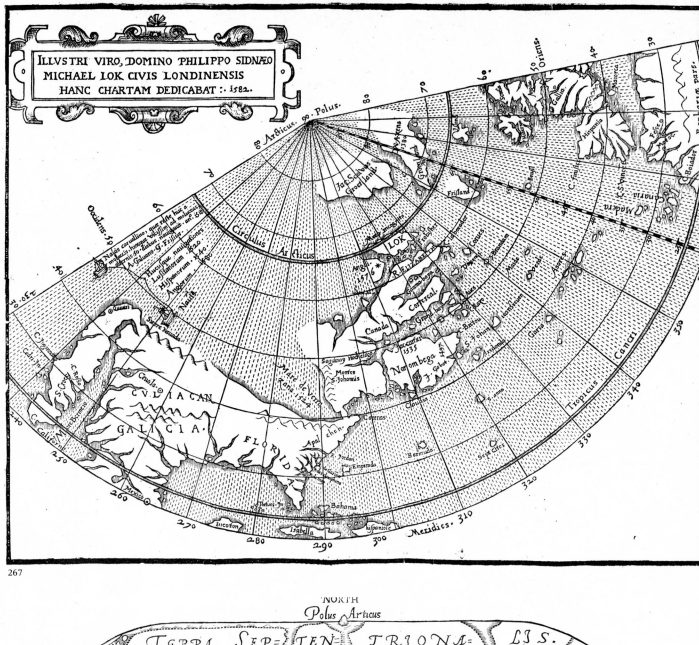

267

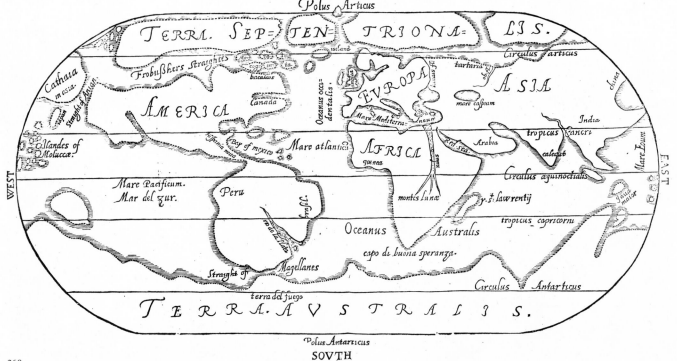

268

222

his three voyages, in 1585, 1586 and 1587, he landed in Godthaab Fjord in south-west Greenland, in the area (though unknown to him) of the Icelanders' Eastern Settlement; on an island one of his officers found 'a grave with a crosse layd over'. Davis noted the climatic contrast between the south-east coast of Greenland, which he named the 'Land of Desolation'—'the most deformed rocky and mountainous land that ever we sawe . . . the tops altogether covered with snowe, and the shoare beset with yce a league off into the Sea'—and the west coast, which they found 'utterly voyde of the pester of yce, and very temperate', and inland 'tenne miles within the snowy mountains, a plaine champion countrey, with earth and grasse, such as our moory and waste grounds of England are'.

With the Greenland Eskimos, Davis's men established good relations, seeing in them 'a very tractable people, voyde of crafte or double dealing, and easie to be brought to any civilitie or good order', though 'marvellous theevish, especially for iron'. They were 'of good stature, well in body proportioned, with small slender hands and feet, with broad visages, and small eyes, wide mouthes, the most part unbearded, great lips, and close toothed'. Communication was not difficult, and Davis collected a vocabulary of forty Eskimo words, observing that 'they pronounce theyr language very hollow, and deep in the throat'. To Davis are due 'the first ethnological notes of any consequence made about the Greenlanders'.[13]

On his first voyage, Davis took his two small ships, of fifty and thirty-five tons, from Greenland across Davis Strait to the Cumberland Peninsula, on Baffin Island. In Cumberland Sound, which he penetrated in August 1585 for sixty leagues, he found 'the sea navigable, voyd of yse, the ayre tollerable,

267
Map of the northern hemisphere drawn by or for Michael Lok and published by Richard Hakluyt in *Divers voyages touching the discoverie of America*, London, 1582, to support English claims to North America and to illustrate access routes from the North Atlantic into the Pacific.
Lok, a London merchant, was the principal investor in Frobisher's expeditions of 1576–8, by which he was ruined. His map is an anthology of discoveries in North America since the end of the fifteenth century, with some even older elements such as the mythical Atlantic islands of Brasil and St Brendan and the representation of Greenland derived through Mercator and the Zeni map from Claudius Clavus. Names of discoverers and dates of discovery are noted: for instance, in the St Lawrence region Corte-Real and Cartier, for California the Portuguese in 1520 (an apocryphal voyage), the Spanish in 1540 (Cabrillo) and the English in 1580 (Drake, 1579).
In this propaganda map, the significant features are 'Norombega' and the 'Mare de Verrazana'. Norumbega (located in the present State of Maine) was the objective of Sir Humphrey Gilbert's planned colony, and its discovery is ascribed in the map to John Cabot in 1497. The Sea of Verrazzano, with the 'little necke of lande' in 40°N separating the Atlantic from the Pacific by an easy portage, was to make a deep impression on the minds of Englishmen who projected colonization further south.
In this map, almost for the last time until the nineteenth century, Frobisher's discoveries are placed in their true positions. 'Frisland' is a duplicate representation of southern Greenland, correctly located in latitude from Frobisher's landfalls and observations in 1576 and 1577. The Baffin Island discoveries, with Frobisher's Strait dividing 'Lok' from 'R. Elizabeth', are laid down to the north of Labrador.
268
Oval world map illustrating Frobisher's voyages, published in George Best, *A true discourse of the late voyages of discoverie*, London, 1578.
This woodcut map (the second surviving world map printed in England) may be from a drawing by James Beare, who is recorded by Best to have 'drawne out the cardes of the coast' on Frobisher's expeditions.
A continuous navigable passage from the Atlantic to the Pacific is represented by 'Frobusshers Straightes' and the Strait of Anian. The map, as graphic propaganda for the North-west Passage, is intended to demonstrate that this offered a shorter route to Cathay, Japan and the Spice Islands than the North-east Passage (also shown as open) or than the Spanish and Portuguese seaways by the south of America and Africa.

and the waters very depe'; and on his return in October he reported 'that the north-west passage is a matter nothing doubtfull, but at any tyme to be passed'. On the second expedition, in 1586, Davis took four ships, the largest of 120 tons, to his Greenland anchorage. Sailing north, along the coast, he was surprised to find the coast of Davis Strait, which he had found 'free and navigable' the year before, jammed with 'a most mighty and strange quantity of ice, in one intyre masse, so bigge as that we knew not the limits thereof'. At an anchorage in 66° 33', whence he sent his largest ship home, they 'found it very hot, and . . . were very much troubled with a flie called Musketa, for they did sting grievously'. In the *Sunshine* of fifty tons, Davis crossed to his former landfall on Baffin Island and coasted southward to Labrador, passing but failing to recognize the mouths of Frobisher Bay and Hudson Strait, and taking 'great abundance of cod' which they cured and brought home, with 500 seal skins.

On Davis's return he expressed the view that the passage 'must be in one of foure places, or els not at all'. Three were westward leads—Cumberland Sound, Hudson Strait, and Hamilton Inlet, found by Davis in 1586; to test the fourth possibility, north up Davis Strait, was the objective of his third voyage, in 1587. Sailing north from his old Greenland base, he followed the eastern shore of the strait for nine days to a high headland in 72° 12'N which on 30 June he named Hope Sanderson after his patron. Here, in the southern part of Baffin Bay, the winter ice had dispersed and Davis, finding 'the Sea all open, and forty leagues between land and land', concluded that 'the passage was free and without impediment toward the North'. He was forced into a westerly course by head winds, and into a southerly by the ice of the middle pack; not until 14 July was he able to round the pack and set course for Baffin Island. Cumberland Sound was examined to its head, and a compass variation of thirty degrees west noted. Crossing the opening of Frobisher Bay, which he named Lumley's Inlet, Davis 'passed by a very great gulfe, the water whirling and roring'; this was Hudson Strait, to be charted by Davis as 'the furious overfall'.[14] Naming Cape Chidley, he continued south to 51°N before setting course for home.

Davis's own journals and those of his supercargo John Janes record the voyages succinctly; Davis's charts are lost, but (as he wrote later), 'how far I proceeded and in what forme this discovery lieth' was drawn on the globe completed in 1592 by Emery Molyneux (plate 269), who had perhaps sailed with Davis, at the expense of William Sanderson, Davis's patron. Three years later, in a tract entitled *The worldes hydrographicall discription*, Davis set out his arguments 'to prove a passage by the Norwest, without any land impediments to hinder the same'. After demonstrating 'that America is an Iland, and may be sayled round about', he quoted his own observations in the Arctic as proof 'that the Sea fryseth not', 'that the ayre [climate] in colde regions is tollerable' for human life, and that 'curious lyned globes to the right use of Navigation' enabled the seaman to lay course on a bearing in high latitudes despite the convergence of the meridians, for which the 'ordenarie sea chart' did not allow, and the 'quicke and uncertayne variation of the Compasse'. So Davis expounded the theoretical basis for navigation in the polar seas.[15]

The investors in the voyages of Frobisher and Davis had already shown signs of hedging their bets, and recovering their costs, by immediate profits from the natural wealth of the north-west Atlantic and its shores. On Davis's last expedition, two of his three ships were instructed to bring back cargoes of cod. Since the Cabot voyages, and perhaps earlier, fishermen of western Europe—English, Basque, Breton, Portuguese—had frequented the Newfoundland Banks,

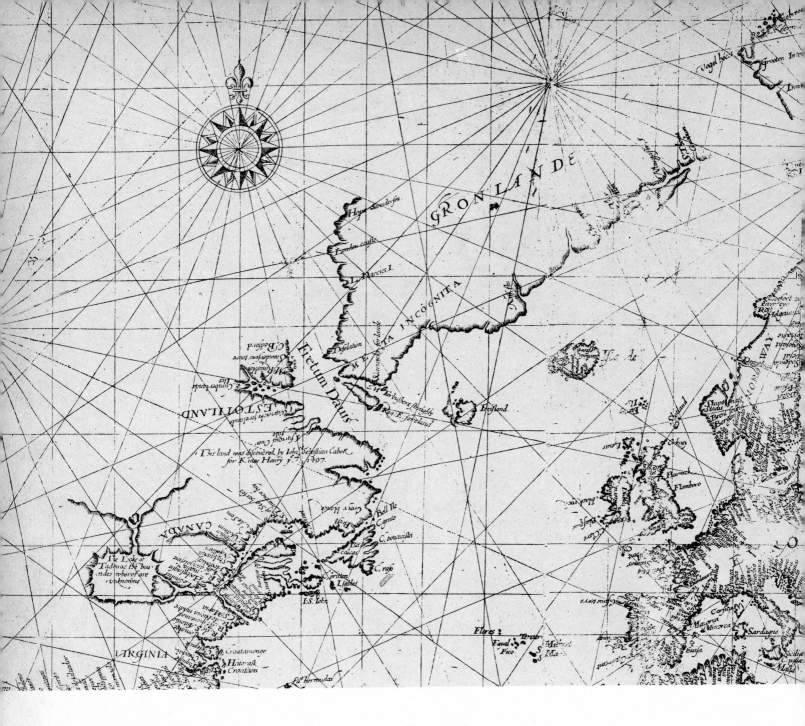

269
John Davis's discoveries recorded in the world map published by Richard
Hakluyt in *The principal navigations . . . of the English nation,* vol. I,
London, 1598.

The charts made by Davis and brought back from his three voyages for a
North-west Passage (1585–7), though mentioned by him and by later
explorers, have not survived. His discoveries were mapped with authority
in the large terrestrial globe (the first to be made in England) prepared by
Emery Molyneux and engraved in 1592 at the expense of William
Sanderson. Sanderson, married to Sir Walter Ralegh's niece, was a London
merchant who had promoted Davis's expeditions; and there is reason to
believe that Molyneux had sailed with Davis, who (as he tells us)
recommended him to Sanderson for the making of the globe. The world map
on Mercator's projection, probably prepared by Molyneux and the
mathematician Edward Wright, and published by Hakluyt in 1598,
reproduces that of the globe, with some updating from recent discovery.

The cartographer has been careful to depict only lands actually discovered,
allowing himself no conjectural outlines. The difficulty of reconciling the
recorded landfalls of Frobisher and of Davis, and both with the geography
of the Zeni map (plate 261), has however introduced an extraordinary error
in the mapping of Greenland which, beginning with the globe of 1592,
was to persist in cartography until the middle of the nineteenth century.
It must be assumed that the interpretation of the data exhibited in the globe
and in the Hakluyt map originated with Davis himself.

In the map, 'Freisland' (located as in Lok's map of 1582) represents
Frobisher's landfalls in southern Greenland. Davis also touched at south-
east Greenland ('Desolation' in the map) on each of his three voyages;
unlike Frobisher and Lok, he did not identify it with 'Frisland' of the Zeni
map, perhaps because of the difference—a good ten degrees—in longitude.
On his first two voyages, Davis traversed the coasts of Baffin Island without
recognizing them as those previously visited by Frobisher, as the new
names in the map, bestowed by Davis, demonstrate. His third voyage took
him from 'Desolation' in 60°N up the east shore of Davis Strait to 'Hope
Saunderson' in over 72°N, thus far to the north of the southernmost cape of
Greenland as laid down (in 65° 40′N) by the Zeni map and by Mercator.
These observations, taken together, convinced Davis (correctly) that
Greenland extended nearly six degrees further south than earlier maps had
indicated and (incorrectly) that Frobisher, sailing westward from 'Freisland',
must have made his next landfall on Greenland (not on Baffin Island).
Hence, on the globe of 1592, followed by the map of 1598, Frobisher's
discoveries are located and named in south-west Greenland, where we see
Meta Incognita, Frobisher's Straits, and Queen Elizabeth's Foreland.

Nevertheless, Davis's scrupulous indication of unexamined channels or
gulfs, as illustrated in this map, served as a program for future exploration.
He was, as Foxe remarked, to 'light Hudson into his Strait', the mouth of
which is marked as 'A furious Overfale' in the map; and his report on Davis
Strait was to lead William Baffin north into Baffin Bay.

though they left few records and made no maps. Whaling in northern waters had been practised from a far more remote past. The primitive technique of driving whales ashore or into enclosed waters was extended, during the Middle Ages, by hunting them in the open sea with specially built ships and harpooning from boats. The Basques were specially active in taking the right whales at their feeding grounds in the ocean; they cut the blubber from the floating carcasses and took it ashore to render, or 'try out', the train-oil. John Davis observed 'great store of whales' in Davis Strait; and in July 1587, off the Labrador coast, he met a ship which he supposed to be 'a Biskaine . . . a fishing for whales, for . . . we saw very many'. The vast number of right whales which Henry Hudson saw about Spitsbergen in 1607 encouraged his employers, the Muscovy Company of London, to enter the whaling industry in those waters, with Basque harpooners; and they were followed by the Dutch.[16] Later in the century, as whales and whalers moved farther afield, the rich Greenland fishery was developed.

The joint-stock companies of English merchants who promoted voyages to the north-west in the early seventeenth century were aware of the quick returns to be expected from the harvest of the sea—dried or salted fish, whale oil, seal skins, bear skins, ivory from walrus or narwhal tusks. But their

270

270
Flensing a whale on land. Woodcut in Olaus Magnus, *Historia de gentibus septentrionalibus*, Rome, 1555.

271
The harvest of the northern seas. The vignettes illustrate the techniques of catching and flensing whales and trying out the blubber, and of hunting polar bears and walrus. A map compiled for the Muscovy Company of London, published in *Purchas his pilgrimes*, London, 1625, and republished in Edward Pelham, *God's power and providence*, London, 1631.

271

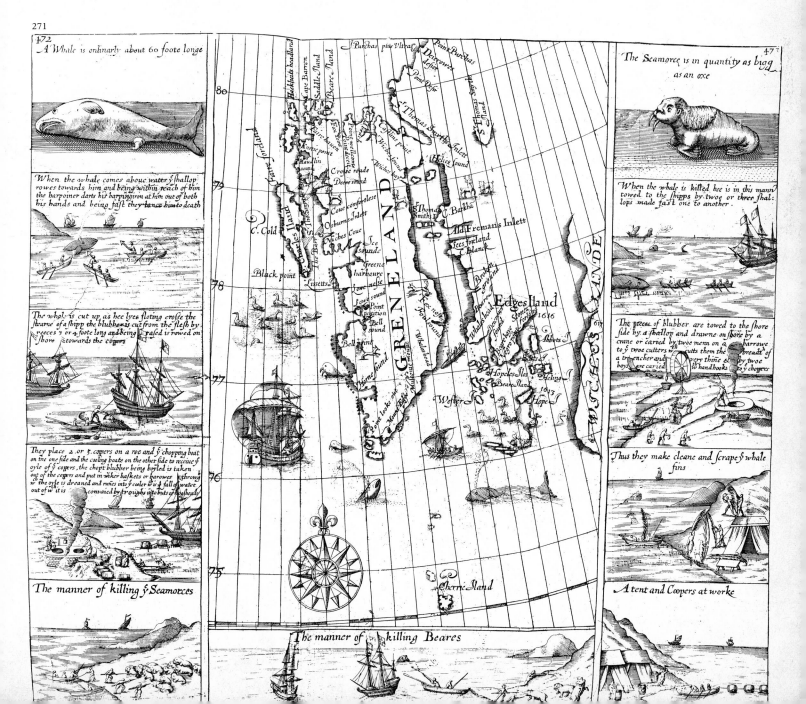

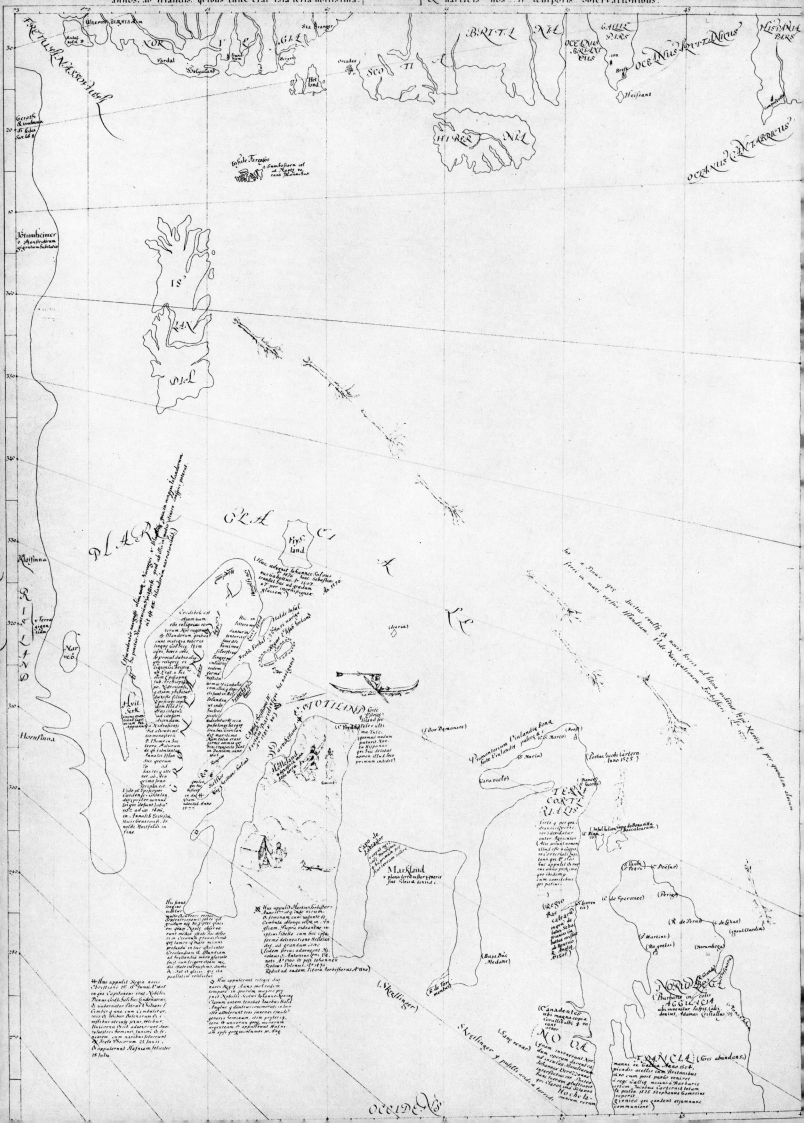

272
Map of the North Atlantic drawn by Bishop Hans Poulson Resen for presentation to King Christian IV of Denmark, 1605. *Copenhagen, Kongelige Bibliotek.*

In the title of his map, which is drawn with east to the top, Resen refers to his sources: first, 'an ancient map rudely drawn centuries ago by Icelanders, to whom that land [Greenland] was then well-known'; and second, 'the observations of seamen in our day'. The survival of any medieval Icelandic map is doubtful, and Resen's map—like those drawn by Icelanders about this time (plates 32 and 34)—is another attempt to adjust the geography of the Norse voyages, as deduced from Icelandic literature, to recent printed cartography of Greenland and North America based on sixteenth-century exploration. In spite of its larger scale, greater elaboration, and wealth of written annotation, Resen's geographical representation is identical with that in the map of Sigurdur Stefánsson drawn about ten years earlier (plate 32). In both, Greenland has the same orientation and outline; the mainland southward has three gulfs forming two broad peninsulas ('Helleland' and 'Markland'); and the 'Promontorium Vinlandiæ', with a deep bay to the west, has exactly the same shape and location, in 50°N. To this base-map Resen has added American coastal place-names from Mercator's world map of 1569 (plate 263) and numerous notes on later exploratory voyages, especially Frobisher's.

The occasion of the map was the search for the lost Greenland colonies, promoted by King Christian in 1605–7. On the north-east coast of Greenland Resen shows the landmark of Hvitserk 'ex Islandorum narrationibus' (see plate 33), and on the south-west coast 'Erics fjord' and 'Vesterbygds fiord', i.e. the Eastern and Western Settlements. Further up Davis Strait (wrongly oriented ESE–WNW, with a note on Davis's voyages of 1585–6), two symbols ǂǂ and ◊ are explained in notes as indicating the points on the west Greenland coast reached by the three ships of the Danish expedition of 1605, in which James Hall sailed as pilot. Frobisher's Strait, with other features named by him in Baffin Island (namely Queen Elizabeth's Foreland and Hall's Island, from his pilot Christopher Hall), are, exceptionally, located in south-west Greenland, near 'Erics fjord'.

Yet Resen also associates Frobisher's discoveries with 'Helleland' (identified as 'Estotiland', as by the Zeni map and by Mercator), which can only be Baffin Island. A symbol ⊠ and note record Frobisher's taking of a man, woman and child hence to England in 1577; and the three little drawings of Eskimo life are plainly copied from the woodcut in Dionyse Settle's account of the 1576 voyage (see plate 265). Best's report on the 1577 voyage is cited by Resen as his authority for the representation of tree-trunks drifted from America across Denmark Strait to Iceland.

Allowing for simplification and distortion of outlines and for some licence in the distribution of 'modern' place-names, it cannot seriously be doubted that Resen located Helluland in Baffin Island, Markland in Labrador, and Vinland in northern Newfoundland.

273
Map of Greenland and picture of a Greenland Eskimo; insets of John Speed's map of America, engraved at Amsterdam in 1626, and published in *A prospect of the most famous partes of the world,* London, 1627.

dominant motive was still the discovery of a seaway to East Asia. Of the alternative routes enumerated by Davis, the search was now concentrated on Hudson Strait and Davis Strait.

The northward route up Davis Strait, although it leads to the eastern entrance by which the North-west passage was eventually to be navigated, was the first to be discredited by the reports of seventeenth-century explorers. The three expeditions prepared by King Christian IV of Denmark in 1605, 1606 and 1607 attempted vainly to locate the lost Norse colonies in Greenland; but their chief pilot, the Englishman James Hall of Hull, had previous experience, presumably gained on Davis's voyages, of the coasts further north.[17] In 1605 he took one ship up to the fjords south of Disco Bay and surveyed the coast from 66° to 68°N, where he noted deposits of 'silver ore'. The most useful fruits of these voyages were Hall's description and charts of the West Greenland coast (plates 250-3). In 1612, backed by some merchants, he took two ships to the supposed silver mines. The events of this expedition were recorded by the quartermaster John Gatonbe and the pilot William Baffin. As they bartered with Eskimos, 'our master, James Hall, being in the boate, a savage with his dart strooke him a deadly wound upon the right side'; and Baffin conjectured that the murderer was a brother or kinsman of the Eskimos carried off by the Danes seven years before.

In 1612 the powerful 'Company of the Merchants of London, Discoverers of the North-West Passage' (or North-West Company) received a royal charter. Its first three voyages were directed to Hudson Strait. Baffin had piloted the third, in 1615, and on his return he advised that 'the mayne [passage] will be upp fretum Davis [Davis Strait]'. In the following year, under the same captain, Robert Bylot, he set out to examine this route, with instructions from the Company to sail north to 80°, then west and south to 60° (the latitude of Hudson Strait), 'then direct your course to fall in with the land of Yedzo [Japan].'[18] By the end of May, they had passed Davis's farthest north at Hope Sanderson, a month earlier in the season than Davis. At the Baffin Islands, in 74°N, summer habitations of the Eskimos were found to be still unoccupied. Failing to make way westward through the middle pack, they continued north up Baffin Bay to Cape Dudley Digges, in 76°N, Whale Sound (so named for the 'great numbers of whales') and 'Sir Thomas Smith's Sound' (Smith Sound), where Baffin was astonished to find 'the greatest variation of the compasse of any part of the world known'. The North Water of Baffin Bay which they had crossed is, for complex oceanographic reasons, almost ice-free throughout the year—a characteristic which was to become known to later whalers and to nineteenth-century advocates of an 'open polar sea'.[19] Forced west by weather, they crossed the opening of 'Alderman Jones's Sound', between Ellesmere and Devon Islands, and of 'Sir James Lancaster's Sound', which was to lead explorers of the nineteenth and twentieth centuries through the North-west Passage. As they sailed south, the 'hope of a passage' was frustrated by the ice-bound coast, and they returned by Baffin Island and Greenland.

To his employers Baffin reported discouragingly on the

273

prospect of a passage 'in the north of Davis Streights', which he thought 'no other then a great Bay'; but, writing with earlier experience of the Spitzbergen whale fishery, he offered them a 'probabilitie or hope of profit' in the catching of whales, of which he had seen 'great numbers . . . easie to be strooke', besides walrus and narwhal.

Hudson Strait had been vainly reconnoitred by George Waymouth in 1602.[20] At the entrance of 'Lumley's Inlet', in fog and snow, he discerned that 'a great current setteth to the west, the greatest hope of a passage this way', with 'no ground in 120 fathom'. Beating north and then south to clear the ice, and with 'his roapes and sailes all frozen', his men mutinied and, after watering from an iceberg which cracked like thunder

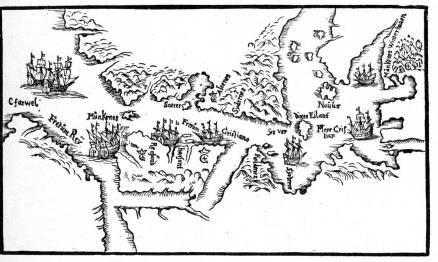

274

274

Jens Munk's passage of Hudson Strait ('Fretum Cristiano') and Bay ('Mare Cristian'), 1619–20; woodcut map in Munk, *Navigatio septentrionalis*, Copenhagen, 1624. South is at the top.

From Cape Farewell Munk, crossing Davis Strait to Frobisher's Inlet, worked round Resolution Island ('Munkenes') and along the north shore of the Strait before crossing to the south shore and examining Ungava Bay. His anchorages are indicated by ships, and the points where he set up King Christian IV's arms by a crown and the symbol C4. By Mansel Island ('Dixes Eilant') and Coats Island ('Nouum') Munk crossed the mouth of Hudson Bay to his wintering place at Port Churchill, drawn in the map to a much larger scale and with two forks. The openings north of this, noticed on his return in the sloop in the spring of 1620, probably represent the mouths of Chesterfield Inlet and of Foxe Channel, with Southampton and Salisbury Islands. Since Gerritsz' map (see plate 294), which Munk knew, shows only the eastern part of Hudson Bay, Munk's is the earliest surviving map of the whole Bay.

275

Map of North America by Henry Briggs, illustrating his 'Treatise of the North-west Passage to the South Sea, through the Continent of Virginia, and by Fretum Hudson', published in *Purchas his pilgrimes*, London, 1625.

In his tract and map, Briggs advanced the hypothesis—to be tested six years later by his friend Captain Luke Foxe—that Hudson Strait and Button Bay offered 'a faire entrance to ye nearest and most temperate passage to Japa & China'. He criticized 'our usuall Globes and Maps' for exaggerating the width of North America and for following Mercator's representation of polar channels, 'which now are found to bee all turned into a mayne Icie Sea'. Button's wintering-place of 1612–3 at Port Nelson was thought by Briggs to 'extend it selfe very neere as farre towards the west as the Cape of California, which is now found to bee an Iland'; and the map suggests a North-west Passage from 'Buttons Baie' into the head of the Gulf of California. Briggs pointed to the small tidal range in James Bay (2 feet) and Davis Strait (1 foot), 'wheras by the nearenes of the South Sea in Porte Nelson, it was constantly 15 foote or more'. The tract also expresses the 'hope that the South Sea may easily from Virginia be discovered over land' by river, citing the 'constant report of the Savages . . . of a large Sea to the Westwards'.

This is the earliest map in which the name 'Hudsons bay' appears, though Briggs applies it to James Bay and assigns the name 'Buttons Baie' to the western part of Hudson Bay.

275

Map of the Arctic published by Henricus Hondius at Amsterdam in 1636, with vignettes of whaling scenes in the corners. First included in the English-text edition of the Mercator-Hondius *Atlas*, 1636, perhaps in recognition of English enterprise in seeking a North-west Passage. The map reflects the state of geographical knowledge following the expeditions of Foxe and James in 1631–2. Its sources are revealed by the forms of place-names: French in the St Lawrence region, Dutch on the coasts of east Greenland and Labrador, where whalers from Netherlands ports were active, English in all the coasts and waters west of Greenland disclosed by sixty years of exploration. Frobisher's discoveries of 1576–7 are located in south-east Greenland. The coasts of Davis Strait and of Baffin Bay are laid down from the voyages of John Davis in 1585–7 and of William Baffin in 1616; the shores of Hudson Strait from Henry Hudson's discovery in 1610, and those of Hudson Bay and James Bay from the expeditions of Thomas Button in 1612–3, Luke Foxe in 1631 and Thomas

James in 1631–2. For Hudson Strait and Bay and the channels leading from them, Hondius' immediate sources are the map of James (1633, plate 305), from which the details of James Bay are copied, and that of Foxe (1635, plate 304). The map graphically expresses Foxe's conclusion that there was no westward lead out of Hudson Bay; the islands in the north-west of the Bay were thought to be part of the mainland, and only the entrance of Foxe Channel had been examined. But the cartographer recognizes (if conjecturally) the insular character of Baffin Island and, farther north, the possibility of passages through Jones Sound and Lancaster Sound, by which the North-west Passage was eventually, over two and a half centuries later, to be traversed.

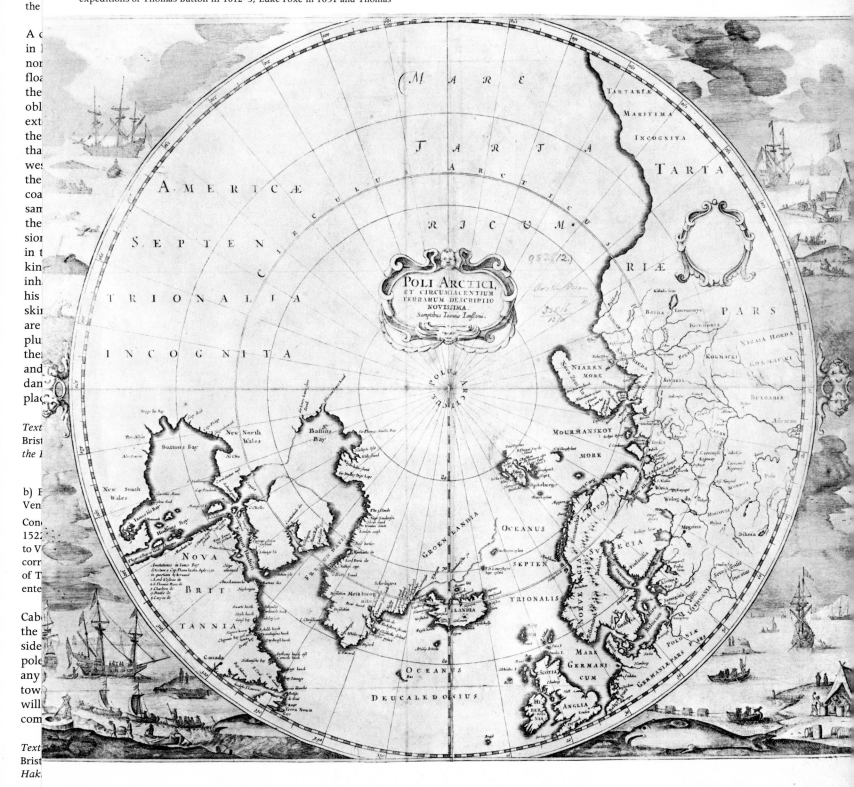

278
'Meta Incognita': view looking south across Frobisher Bay toward the
Grinnell Glacier. Woodcut in C. F. Hall, *Life with the Esquimaux,* New York,
1864.

gutte had continuance, and whether he mighte carrie himselfe
through the same into some open sea on the backe syde,
whereof he conceyved no small hope, and so entred the same
the one-and-twentieth of July, and passed above fyftie
leagues therein, as hee reported, having upon eyther hande a
greate mayne or continent; and that land uppon hys right
hande as hee sayled westward, he judged to be the continente
of Asia, and there to bee devided from the firme of America,
whiche lyeth uppon the lefte hande over against the same.

This place he named after his name Frobishers Streytes,
lyke as Magellanus at the south-weast ende of the worlde
having discovered the passage to the South Sea (where
America is devided from the continente of that lande whiche
lyeth under the south pole), and called the same straites
Magellanes Streightes . . .

In this place he saw and perceyved sundry tokens of the
peoples resorting thither, and being ashore upon the toppe
of a hill, he perceived a number of small things fleeting in
the sea afarre off, whyche hee supposed to be porposes or
seales, or some kinde of strange fishes; but coming nearer,
he discovered them to be men in small boates made of leather.
And before he could descende downe from the hyll certain
of those people had almost cut off his boate from him, having
stollen secretly behinde the rocks for that purpose, where he
speedily hasted to his boate and bente himselfe to his holberte,
and narrowly escaped the daunger and saved his bote. Afterwards he had sundry conferences with them, and they came
aborde his ship, and brought him salmon and raw fleshe and
fishe, and greedily devoured the same before our mens faces.

Frobisher led a second expedition, in 1577, to collect the 'gold ore'
(apparently marcasite) of which a sample had been brought back in
the *Gabriel.* In Frobisher Bay, a skirmish was fought with the natives
at 'Bloody Point'; an Eskimo man and a woman with her child were
taken and brought back to Bristol, where they survived for a month.

Having now got a woman captive for the comfort of our men,
we brought them both togither, and every man with silence
desired to beholde the manner of their meeting and entertain-
ment, the whiche was more worth the beholding than can
be well expressed by writing. At theyr first encountering,
they behelde each the other very wistly a good space,

withoute speeche or worde uttered, with greate change of
colour and countenance, as though it seemed the greefe and
disdeyne of their captivitie had taken away the use of their
tongues and utterance: the woman of the first verie suddaynely,
as though she disdeyned or regarded not the man, turned away
and beganne to sing, as though she minded another matter:
but being agayne broughte togyther, the man brake up the
silence first, and with sterne and stayed countenance beganne
to tell a long solemne tale to the woman, whereunto she gave
good hearing, and interrupted him nothing till he had finished,
and, afterwards being growen into more familiar acquaintance
by speech, were turned togither, so that (I think) the one would
hardly have lived without the comfort of the other. And, for so
muche as we could perceive, albeit they lived continually
togither, yet did they never use as man and wife, though the
woman spared not to do all necessarie things that apperteyned
to a good huswife indifferently for them both, as in making
cleane their cabin, and every other thing that apperteyned to
his ease: for when hee was seasicke, shee would make him
cleane, she would kill and flea [skin] ye dogges for their eating
and dresse his meate. Only I thinke it worth the noting the
continencie of them both; for the man would never shifte himselfe, except he had first caused the woman to depart out of his
cabin, and they both were most shamefast least anye of their
privie parts should be discovered, eyther of themselves or any
other body.

On Frobisher's third voyage, in 1578, after a difficult navigation
through ice, he made the entrance to Hudson Strait before turning
north to his former landfall.

The seaventh of July, as men nothing yet dismayed, we cast
about towards the inward, and had sighte of lande, which rose
in forme like the northerlande of the straytes, which some of
the fleete, and those not the worst marriners, judged to be the
north forlande: howbeit, other some were of contrary opinion.
But the matter was not well to be discerned, by reason of the
thicke fogge, whiche a long time hung uppon the coast, and
the newe falling snowe which yearely altereth the shape of the
land, and taketh away oftentimes the marriners markes. And
by reason of the darke mists, whiche continued by the space
of twenty dayes togither, this doubt grew the greater and the
longer perillous. For wheras indeede we thought our selves
to be upon the northeast side of Frobishers straytes, we were
now carried to the southwestwards of the Queenes forlande,
and being deceyved by a swift currant comming from the
northeast, were brought to the southwestwards of our sayd
course, many miles more than we dyd thinke possible could
come to passe . . .

Here we made a poynt of land, which some mistooke for a
place in the straytes, called Mount Warwicke: but howe we
shoulde be so farre shotte up so suddaynely within the sayde
straytes, the expertest mariners began to marvell, thinking
it a thing impossible, that they coulde be so farre overtaken
in their accompts, or that any currant coulde so deceyve them
heere, whiche they had not by former experience proved and
found out. Howbeit, many confessed, that they founde a
swifter course of floud than before time they had observed.
And truly it was wonderfull to heare and see the rushling and
noyse that the tydes do make in thys place, with so violente
a force that our shippes lying a hull, were turned sometimes
rounde aboute even in a momente, after the manner of a
whirlpool, and the noyse of the streame no lesse to be hearde
a farre off, than the waterfall of London Bridge.

After Frobisher's third voyage to Baffin Island, in 1578, his lieutenant
George Best describes the country.

The Countries, on
and roughe stonie m
thereon. There is v
except a little, whic
on soft-ground, such
all. To be briefe, the
of man, which that
forth: Howbeit, th
skinnes are like unt
exceed, as wel in le
partes or Countrie:
oxens, whiche we
breadth. There are

Sea foule of sundri
    As the Countrie
and of no capacit
but are contented
with rawe flesh a
panches, whiche i

Text used: V. Stefa
London, 1938, pp. 19

First therefore concerning the topographicall description of the place. It is nowe founde in the last voiage that Queen Elizabeths Cape, being situate in latitude of [62] degrees and a halfe, whiche before was supposed to be parte of the firme land of America. And also all the rest of the south side of Frobishers Straytes, are all severall ilands and broken land, and likewise so will all the north side of the said straytes fall out to be, as I thinke. And some of our company being entred about 60 leagues within the mistaken straytes, in the third booke mentioned, thought certaynely that they had descryed the firme lande of America towards the south, which I thinke will fall out so to bee.

These broken landes and ilandes, being very many in number, do seeme to make there an archipelagus, which as they all differ in greatnesse, forme, and fashion one from another, so are they in goodnesse, couloure and soyle muche unlike. They all are very high lands, mountaynes, and in most parts covered with snow, even all the summer long. The norther lands have lesse store of snow, more grasse, and are more playne countreys; the cause may be, for that the souther ilands receive all the snow, [that] the cold winds and percing ayre bring out of the north. And contrarily the norther partes receive more warme blastes of milder aire from the south, whereupon may grow the cause why the people covet and inhabit more upon the north partes, than the south, as farre as we can yet by our experience perceive they doe. These people I judge to be a kinde of Tartar, or rather a kind of Samowey, of the same sort and condition of life [that] the Samoweides be to the northeastwards, beyond Moscovy.

Text used: Richard Collinson, The three voyages of Martin Frobisher, London, Hakluyt Society, 1867, pp. 72-3, 144-5, 239-40, 281.

b) From *A true reporte of the laste voyage by Capteine Frobisher,* by Dionyse Settle, London, 1577.

A report on the Eskimos and their culture is given by Dionyse Settle, a gentleman who sailed in Frobisher's second expedition.

They are men of a large corporature, and good proportion: their colour is not much unlike the Sunne burnte Countrie man, who laboureth daily in the Sunne for his living.

They weare their haire somethinge long, and cut before, either with stone or knife, very disorderly. Their women weare their haire long, and knit up with two loupes, shewing forth on either side of their faces, and the rest foltred [plaited] up on a knot. Also, some of their women race [slash] their faces proportionally, as chinne, cheekes, and forehead, and the wristes of their handes, whereupon they lay a colour, which continueth darke azurine.

They eate their meate all rawe, both fleshe, fishe, and foule, or something perboyled with bloud & a little water, whiche they drinke. For lacke of water, they wil eate yce, that is hard frosen, as pleasantly as we will doe Sugar Candie, or other Sugar.

If they, for necessities sake, stand in neede of the premisses, such grasse as the countrie yeeldeth they plucke uppe, and eate, not deintily, or salletwise, to allure their stomaches to appetite: but for necessities sake, without either salt, oyles, or washing, like brutish beasts devoure the same. They neither use table, stoole, or table cloth for comelinesse: but when they are imbrued with bloud, knuckle deepe, and their knives in like sort, they use their tongues as apt instruments to licke them cleane: in doeing whereof, they are assured to loose none of their victuals.

They franck [eat] or keep certeine doggs, not much unlike

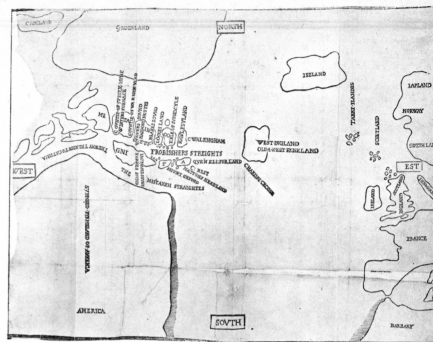

279
Frobisher's discoveries on his three voyages for a North-west Passage, 1576–8. Woodcut map, in George Best, *A true discourse,* London, 1578. The map crude though it be, illustrates Frobisher's interpretation of his discoveries in the light of Zenian geography of the North Atlantic. His landfalls in southern Greenland, in about 60°N, are identified as 'Frisland' of the Zeni map (here 'West Ingland olim West Friseland'); and Greenland is laid down, as on the Zeni map, much further north and west immediately above his named discoveries in Baffin Island. These are represented as 'broken landes and ilandes' forming the archipelago of Meta Incognita along the north side of 'Frobisshers Streights'. To the south, 'The Mistaken Straightes' (Hudson Strait, entered by Frobisher in 1578), like 'Frobisshers Streights', lead into a western channel 'trending to Cathaia'.

Wolves, whiche they yoke together, as we do oxen and horses, to a sled or traile: and so carrie their necessaries over the yce and snowe, from place to place: as the captive, whom we have, made perfecte signes. And when those Dogges are not apt for the same use: or when with hunger they are constreyned, for lacke of other victuals, they eate them: so that they are as needefull for them, in respect of their bignesse, as our oxen are for us.

They apparell themselves in the skinnes of such beastes as they kill, sewed together with the sinewes of them. All the fowle which they kill, they skin, and make thereof one kinde of garment or other, to defend them from the cold.

They make their apparell with hoods and tailes, which tailes they give, when they thinke to gratifie any friendshippe shewed unto them: a great signe of friendshippe with them. The men have them not so syde [loose] as the women.

The men and women weare their hose close to their legges, from the wast to the knee, without any open before, as well the one kinde as the other. Uppon their legges, they weare hose of lether, with the furre side inward, two or three paire on at once, and especially the women. In those hose, they put their knives, needles, and other thinges needefull to beare about. They put a bone within their hose, whiche reacheth from the foote to the knee, whereupon they drawe their said hose, and so in place of garters, they are holden from falling downe about their feete.

They dresse their skinnes very softe and souple with the haire on. In cold weather or Winter, they weare ye furre side inward: and in Summer outward. Other apparell they have none, but the said skinnes.

233

in al respects like the dung of an horse, wherein we might very plainely see the very strawes . . .

We saw a raven upon mount Raleigh. We found withies also growing lowe like shrubs, and flowers like primroses, in the sayd place. The coast is very mountaynous, altogether without wood, grasse or earth, and is only huge mountaines of stone, but the bravest stone that ever we sawe. The ayre was very moderate in this country.

The 8 we departed from mount Raleigh, coasting along the shoare, which lyeth south southwest, and north northeast . . .

The eleventh we came to the most southerly cape of this lande, which we named the Cape of Gods mercy: as being the place of our first entrance for the discovery. The weather being very foggie we coasted this Northland: at length, when it brake up, we perceived that we were shotte into a very fayre entrance or passage, being in some places 20 leagues broade, and in some 30, altogether voyde of any pester of yce, the weather very tollerable, and the water of the very colour, nature, and qualitie of the mayne ocean, which gave us the greater hope of our passage. Having sayled Northwest sixtie leagues in this entrance wee discovered certaine Islandes standing in the middest thereof, having open passage on both sides. Whereupon our shippes devided themselves, the one sayling on the North side, the other on the south side, of the sayde Isles, where wee stayed five dayes, having the winde at Southeast very foggie and foule weather.

The 14 we went on shoare and found signes of people, for we found stones layde up together like a wall, and saw the skull of a man or a woman . . .

The 17 we went on shoare, and in a litle thing made like an oven with stones, I found many smal trifles, as a small canoa made of wood, a piece of wood made like an image, a bird made of bone, beads having small holes in one end of them to hang about their necks, and other small things. The coast was very barbarous, without wood or grasse. The rockes were very faire, like marble full of vaynes of diverse coulors. We found a seale which was killed not long before, being fleane and hid under stones.

Our Captaine and master searched still for probabilities of the passage, and first found, that this place was all Islands, with great sounds passing betweene them.

Secondly, the water remained of one coulour with the mayne ocean without altering.

Thirdly, we saw to the west of those Isles, three or foure Whales in a skul [school], which they judged to come from a westerly sea, because to the Eastward we saw not any whale.

Also as we were rowing into a very great sound lying southwest, from whence these whales came, upon the suddayne there came a violent counter checke of a tide from the southwest against the flood which we came with, not knowing from whence it was maintayned.

Fiftly, in sayling 20 leagues within the mouth of this entrance we had sounding in 90 fathoms, faire gray osie [oozy] sand, and the further we ran into the westwards, the deeper was the water, so that hard abord the shoare among these yles we could not have ground in 330 fathoms.

Lastly it did ebbe and flowe 6 or 7 fathome up and downe, the flood comming from diverse parts, so as we could not perceive the chiefe maintenance thereof.

On his second voyage, in 1586, Davis with part of his squadron made his old landfall in Gilbert Sound, in south-west Greenland. Failing in his attempt to penetrate the pack-ice which this year blocked Davis Strait north of 63°, he took one ship across to Exeter Sound and followed the coast of Baffin Island and Labrador southward for seventeen days (20 August to 6 September), as far as a gulf, probably Hamilton Inlet, before returning home.

We coasted this land till the eight and twentith of August, finding it still to continue towards the South, from the latitude of 67 to 57 degrees: we found marvellous great store of birds, guls and mewes, incredible to be reported; wherupon, being calme weather, we lay one glasse upon the lee, to prove for fish, in which space we caught 100 of cod, although we were but badly provided for fishing, not being our purpose.

This eight and twentith, having great distrust of the weather, we arrived in a very fayre harbor in the latitude of 56 degrees, and sailed ten leagues into the same, being two leagues broad, with very fayre woods on both sides: in this place we continued untill the first of September, in which time we had two very great stormes. I landed and went six miles by ghesse into the country, and found that the woods were firre, pine, apple, alder, yew, withy, and birch: heere we saw a blacke beare: this place yeeldeth great store of birds, as fezant, partridge, Barbary hennes or the like, wilde geese, ducks, blacke birds, jeyes, thrushes, with other kindes of small birds. Of the partridge and fezant, we killed great store with bowe and arrowes: in this place, at the harborough mouth, we found great store of cod . . .

The fourth of September, at five a clocke in the afternoone, we ankered in a very good road among great store of Isles, the countrey low land, pleasant, and very full of fayre woods. To the North of this place eight leagues, we had a perfect hope of the passage, finding a mighty great sea passing betweene two lands West. The South land, to our judgement, being nothing but Isles, we greatly desired to go into this sea, but the winde was directly against us.

282
'The draughte by Robarte Tindall of virginia', 1608. *London, British Museum, Cotton Ms. Aug. I.ii.46.*
This, the first extant map of Virginia drawn by a Jamestown colonist, is of historical importance because it shows with an unusual degree of accuracy the location of Indian villages on the James and York Rivers observed on the expeditions of Captain Newport in the summer of 1607 and the spring of 1608. Tindall, a gunner in the service of Prince Henry, who was a patron of the Virginia Company, listed fourteen names on the James and five on the York on this now faded manuscript. He accompanied Newport.
    The west is at the top of the map, with the entrance to Chesapeake Bay and Cape Henry to the left. Near Cape Comfort at the mouth of 'King James his River' is the Indian settlement of Chechotanke (Kecoughtan); farther up the James is Jamestown, with its peninsula location, now an island, clearly indicated. Several Indian settlements are marked and named between Chickahominy River and Poetan (Powhatan) below the falls at the present site of Richmond. Below and to the north are 'Prince Henneri His River' and 'Mobjack Bay'; at the head of the York River is the confluence of its two unnamed branches, Pamunkey and Mattaponi.
283
Route chart of William Baffin's voyage through Hudson Strait in 1615, drawn by him in his log-book. *London, British Museum, Add. Ms. 12206, fo 6.*
The 'red prickle lyne' indicates Baffin's track along the north shore of the Strait and his penetration of Foxe Channel, with names given by him to capes and islands; a red cross (or flag) marks 'every place wheare we came on shore (to make tryall of the tyde)'. Coasts examined by Baffin are outlined in green, those not seen by him—and sketched in from earlier maps— in brown.
284 *Overleaf*
The Western Hemisphere from the Sanches planisphere, 1623. *London, British Museum, Add. Ms. 22874.*
Antonio Sanches, a Portuguese cartographer whose work survives in ten other charts besides this planisphere, shows technical skill but adds little to earlier sixteenth-century Spanish and Portuguese maps. None of the recent French and English explorations and settlements is shown.
Lower California is still a peninsula and the coast stretches north-west to the Strait of Anian (not shown in this detail) without a break.

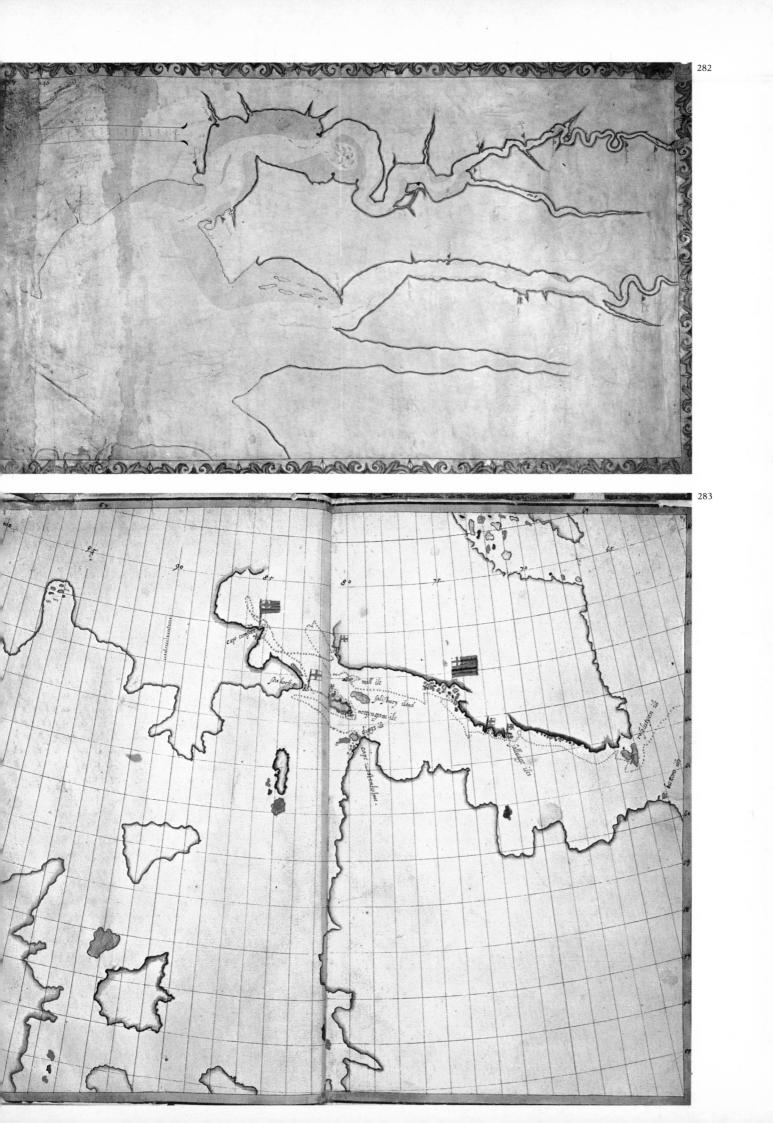

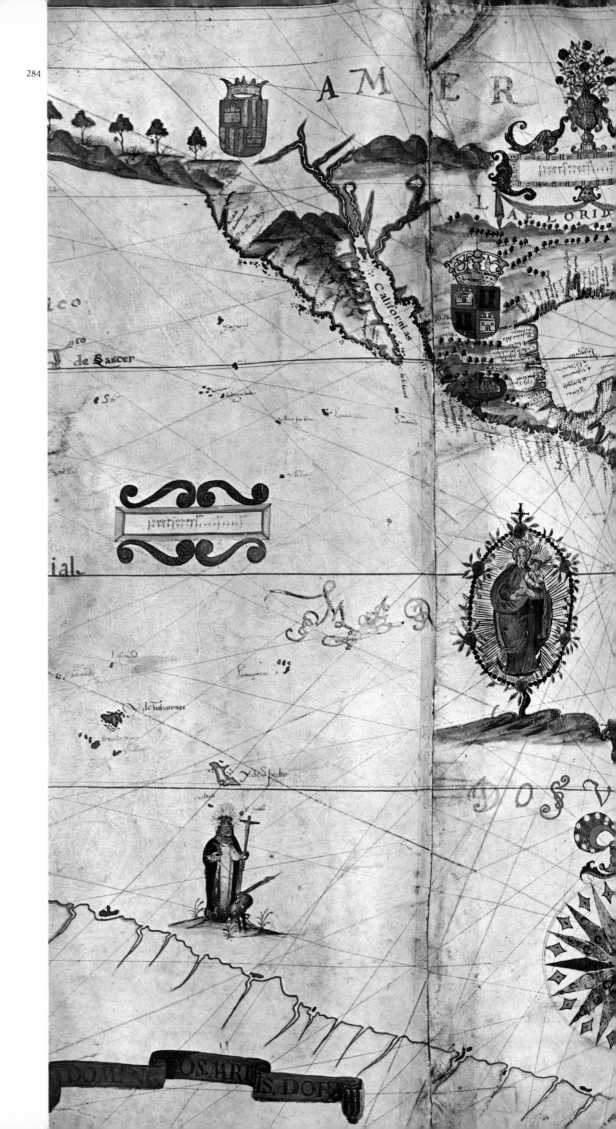

M.R. OSEANO

Estreito de magalhani

estreito de cuicente

239

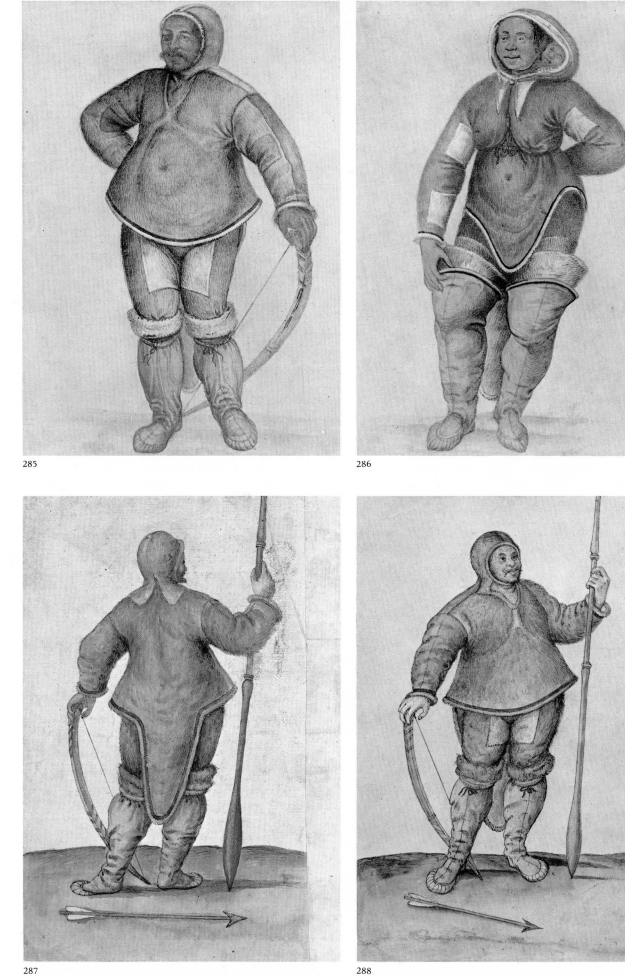

285

286

287

288

285 and 286

Eskimo man and woman with a child, brought back to England by Frobisher in 1577. Drawing by John White, 1585. *London, British Museum.* If the artist John White accompanied Frobisher on his second expedition, these careful drawings may have been made on board ship during the voyage home. They illustrate the physical characteristics and clothing of the Central Eskimos of Baffin Island, as described by the voyagers and by eye-witnesses in England: broad-faced, full-bodied but short in the leg, sallow of complexion, 'much like [as Lok wrote] . . . to the Tartar nation, whereof I think he was', and clad in hooded jackets, trousers and boots of sealskin. The woman is tattooed in blue round the eyes.

287 and 288

Eskimo man, back and front view. Copy of a drawing by John White, *London, British Museum.*

These two views of an Eskimo man by White are in Dr Hans Sloane's volume of drawings in the British Museum. The man holds a paddle with a narrow pointed blade and a round carved staff; the bow, between two and three feet long, is bound at top and bottom by sinews; and the arrow, fletched with two feathers showing, has a barbed grey point, probably of metal.

289

John Davis's 'London Coast', traversed on his third voyage, in 1587.

(above)

Views on the west coast of Greenland, between latitudes 60°N and 74°N. Engraving, after drawings made by Midshipman John Bushnan in 1818, published in John Ross, *A voyage of discovery . . . for the purpose of exploring Baffin's Bay*, London, 1819.

(below)

Disco Island, in 70°N, with icebergs. Engraving, after a drawing made by Midshipman A. M. Skene in 1818, published in John Ross, *A voyage of discovery*, London, 1819.

In 1587, Davis took his ships up the Greenland coast on the east side of Davis Strait to a latitude of 72° 12′, 'finding the sea all open and forty leagues betweene land and land'. Here John Janes describes the middle pack of Baffin Bay observed by Davis before he turned back.

Now having coasted the land, which we called London coast, from the 21 of this present till the 30, the sea open all to the Westwards and Northwards, the land on starboord side East from us, the winde shifted to the North, whereupon we left that shore, naming the same Hope Sanderson, and shaped our course West, and ran 40 leagues and better, without the sight of any land.

The second [of July] we fel with a mighty banke of Ice West from us, lying North and South, which banke we would gladly have doubled out to the Northwards, but the winde would not suffer us, so that we were faine to coast it to the Southwards, hoping to double it out that we might have run so farre West till wee had found land, or els to have bene thorowly resolved of our pretended purpose.

289

4.
Reports on north-west Greenland, 1605

a) From James Hall's report to King Christian IV on the Danish expedition of 1605.

James Hall, a native of Hull in Yorkshire, was chief pilot to the three Danish expeditions sent in search of the lost Norse colonies in Greenland in the years 1605–7. He wrote reports for the King of Denmark on the first two expeditions, with remarks on the land and its people, illustrating that of 1605 with 'land-sights' (coastal views) and four charts. He went, in 1605, as far north as Disco Bay in 69°N lat., and his observations describe the fjord coasts immediately south of it. In 1612 Hall led an English expedition in search of silver to the same area, with William Baffin as a pilot and John Gatonbe as quartermaster. Hall was killed in Grampus Road (an inlet off Itivdlek Fjord, in 66° 30′), and Gatonbe brought back a journal and chart of the voyage.

In June 1605, in the *Lion,* Hall sailed north up Davis Strait, 'costing longst a great banke of yce . . . in the mid streeme betweene America and Groineland' (the middle pack), to make a landfall at Mount Kakatsiak, in 66° 38′N.

Beinge a verye hie ragged land, haveinge the toppes of the hilles all covered with snowe, the forme and ffashon of which is heare sette downe to youre Majesties vewe, betweene two Cape or hadlandes; betweene which 2 capes, we first fell withall, they lyinge one of the other s. b. w. and n. b. e., about 18 english leages. The southermost of which capes or Headlandes we names Queene anns Cape, after the name of youre Majesties Queene;

290

A profile showing, as is indicated, Mount Cunningham from the manuscript drawn by James Hall, pilot of the Danish expedition under Captain William Cunningham of 1605 (see plates 250 to 253). *London, British Museum, Royal Ms. 17.A.XLVIII, fo 4.*

and the northermost of the said Headelandes we called Queene Sophias Cape, after the name of youre Majesties mother. This daye, at noone, we came into a verye great Baye, which which we did suppose to be a great rever, and therefore named it youre Majesties ford. At the mouth or entrye in of this Baye, on the north side, standeth a great mounte or hill, riseinge in forme of a suger loafe, the which mounte is the best marke for this place that maybe; the which I called Cunningehams mounte, after the name of my Captaine.

291

Cape Christian, south-west Greenland, in 59° 50′N, as seen by James Hall, pilot of one of Captain Cunningham's ships, on 30 May 1605. 'This Head-land wee named after the Kings Maiesties of Denmarke, because it was the first part of Greenland which we did see'. *London, British Museum, Royal Ms. 17.A.XLVIII, fo 2.*

The original of this report is British Museum Royal Ms. 17.A.XLVIII, *and is printed by C. C. A. Gosch,* Danish Arctic expeditions, 1605 to 1620, *London, Hakluyt Society, 1897, Vol. I, pp. 9-10, 36-7.*

b) From another journal of the 1605 expedition, written by James Hall.

From King Christian's Fjord, just to the north, they explored and mapped the coasts in their pinnace, encountering parties of Eskimos. Hall describes the kayaks.

Moreover, by their houses, there did lye two great Boates, being covered under with Seale skins, but aloft open, after the forme of our Boates, being about twentie footie in length, having in each of them eight or ten tosts [thwarts] or seates for men to sit on; which Boates, as afterwards I did perceive, is for the transporting of their Tents and baggage from place to place; and, for a saile, they have the guts of some beast, which they dresse very fine and thin, which they sow together. Also the other sorts of their Boates are such as Captaine Frobisher and Master John Davis brought into England, which is but for one man, being cleene covered over with Seale skins artificially dressed, except one place to sit in, being within set out with certaine little ribs of Timber, wherein they use to row with one Oare more swiftly than our men can doe with ten; in which Boates they fish, being disguised in their Coates of Seale skinnes, whereby they deceive the Seales, who take them rather for Seales then men; which Seales or other fish they kill in this manner :- They shoot at the Seales or other great fish with their Darts, unto which they use to tye a bladder, which doth boy up the fish in such manner that, by the said means, they catch them.

292

A kayak from John Gatonbe's journal of James Hall's 1612 expedition to west Greenland, printed in Churchill's *Collection of voyages and travels,* vol. vi, 1732.

Hall's 'Topographicall Description of the Land'.

The Land of Groenland is a very high, ragged, and mountainous Country, being, all alongst the Coast, broken Ilands, making very goodly Sounds and Harbours, having also in the Land very many good Rivers and Bayes, into some of which I entred, sayling up the same the space of ten or twelve English leagues, finding the same very navigable, with great abundance of fish of sundrie sorts. The Land also, in all places whereso-ever I came, seemed to be very fertile, according to the Climate wherein it lyeth; for betweene the Mountaynes was most pleasant Plaines and Valleyes, in such sort as, if I had not seene the same, I could not have beleeved that such a fertile Land in shew could bee in these Northerne Regions. There is also in the same great store of Fowle, as Ravens, Crowes, Partridges, Pheasants, Sea-mewes, Gulles, with other sundry sorts. Of Beasts, I have not seene any, except blacke Foxes, of which there are many. Also, as I doe suppose, there are many Deere, because that, comming to certaine places where the people

The land did rife thus full of fnow. The cape 7 leagues off.
N. N. W.

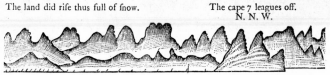

This land is the foutbermoft point in Greenland, *the heighth of the pole there being* 59° 15'.

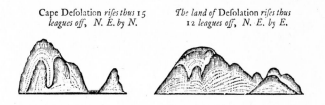

This land fo called by captain Davids, *it being fo defolate and comfortlefs, with huge mountains of fnow lying upon it, fuch as he had never feen, nor any of his men before him.*

Cape Defolation *rifes thus* 15 leagues off, N. E. by N.   *The land of* Defolation *rifes thus* 12 leagues off, N. E. by E.

E. N. E.   E.

Cape Comfort *rifes thus, the heighth of the pole being* 62° 33', *the fmootheft land, and, beft to look to of all the country of* Greenland ; *yet we could not come near it for ice.*

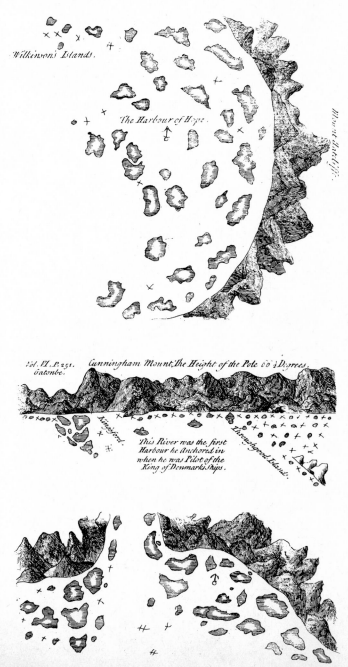

Wilkinfons Iflands.

The Harbour of Hope.

Cunningham Mount, The Height of the Pole 66 ½ Degrees.
Fol. VI. P. 251.
Gatonbe.

This River was the first Harbour he Anchored in when he was Pilot of the King of Denmarks Ships.

Kingsford.

Throughgoend Iflands.

293

Chart of the North Atlantic by John Gatonbe, quartermaster on Captain James Hall's expedition to west Greenland in 1612. Gatonbe's journal, charts and drawings (the originals of which are not known) were printed in Churchill's *Collection of voyages and travels,* vol. VI, 1732, pp. 244-56, from which these reproductions are made.

The apparent objective of Hall's expedition, which was backed by a group of 'Merchant Adventurers of London', is indicated by the legend 'Silver Mine supposed', in 69½°N, where on the Danish voyage of 1605 Hall had noticed (as he thought) silver-bearing ore.

The two ships sailed west from the Orkneys direct to Cape Farewell (the southernmost point of Greenland) and tacked along the ice to Cape Desolation (south-west Greenland) and thence northward to 'Cape Comfort'; this name and the five following it to the north on Gatonbe's chart were bestowed by Hall on this voyage. In the 'Harbour of Hope' (Davis's Gilbert Sound, i.e. Godthaab Fjord) they came to anchor, bartered with the Eskimos who paddled to the ships in their kayaks, and assembled a pinnace. Sailing north to the coast discovered by Hall under the Danish flag in 1605 and 1606, they lay in an inlet which they named Grampus Road, off 'the King's-ford' (King Christian's Fjord of the 1605 voyage). From here Hall took his smaller ship with the pinnace north to the 'silver mine'. After his death at the hands of the Eskimos in 'Ramblaford' (Ramels Fjord, Amerdlok Fjord), his men rowed in the pinnace to the mine and collected ore, pronounced by their goldsmith to be 'of no value'.

had had their Tents, we found very many Harts Hornes, with the bones of other beasts round about the same. Also, going up into the Land, wee saw the footing and dunging of divers beasts, which we did suppose to be deere, and other beasts also, the footing of one which wee found to be eight inches over; yet, notwithstanding, we did see none of them; for, going some two or three miles from the Pinnasse, we returned againe to goe aboord. Moreover, in the Rivers, we found sundry sorts of Fishes, as Seales, Whales, Salmons, with other sorts of Fishes, in great abundance. As concerning the Coast: all alongst it is a very good and faire Land, having very faire shoalding of the same; for, being three English leagues off the same, I found very faire shoalding in fifteene fathomes; and, comming neerer the same, fourteene, twelve, and tenne fathomes, very faire sandie ground. As concerning the people: they are (as I doe suppose) a kinde of Samoites, or wandring Nation, travelling in the Summer time in Companies together, first to one place, and, having stayed in that place a certayne time in hunting and fishing for Deere and Seales with other fish, streight they remove themselves with their Tents and baggage to another. They are men of a reasonable stature, being browne of colour, very like to the people of the East and West Indies. They be very active and warlike, as we did perceive in their Skirmishes with us, in using their Slings and Darts very nimbly. They eat their meate raw, or a little perboyled, either with bloud, Oyle, or a little water, which they doe drinke. They apparell themselves in the skinnes of such beasts as they kill, but especially with Seales skins and fowle skins, dressing the skins very soft and smooth, with the haire and feathers on, wearing in Winter the haire and feather sides inwards, and in Summer outwards. Their Weapons are Slings, Darts, Arrowes, having their Bowes fast tied together with sinewes; their Arrowes have but two feathers, the head of the same being for the most part of bone, made in manner and forme of a Harping Iron. As concerning their Darts: they are of sundry sorts and fashions. What knowledge they have of God, I cannot certainly say; but I suppose them to bee Idolators, worshipping the Sunne. The Country (as is afore-said) seemeth to be very fertile; yet could I perceive or see no wood to grow thereon. Wee met all alongst this Coast much Drift-wood, but whence it commeth I know not.

The above two extracts are printed in Samuel Purchas, *Hakluytus posthumus or Purchas his pilgrimes, London, 1625, III, iv, pp. 817-20.*

5.
Henry Hudson's last voyage, 1610

From Samuel Purchas, *Purchas his pilgrimes,* London, 1625, III, iv, p. 817.

On his fourth and last voyage for a northern sea route in 1610, Henry Hudson returned to the purpose of his unsuccessful second voyage of 1608, 'to make triall' of the westward opening called by Davis 'the furious overfall', namely the entrance of Hudson Strait. The course of the voyage, in which Hudson penetrated the Strait and followed the eastern shore of Hudson Bay to winter in James Bay, with the ensuing mutiny and return of the ship in the summer of 1611, are briefly told in an abstract made by Samuel Purchas from papers of Hudson and other participants.

In the yeare 1610, Sir Tho. Smith, Sir Dudley Digges, and Master John Wostenholme, with other their friends, furnished out the said Henry Hudson, to try if, through any of those inlets which Davis saw but durst not enter, on the westerne side of Fretum Davis, any passage might be found to the other ocean called the South Sea. There barke was named the Discoverie . . .

They raised Gronland the fourth of June, and Desolation after that; whence they plyed north-west among ilands of ice, whereon they might runne and play, and filled sweet water out of ponds therein: some of them aground in sixe or seven score fadome water, and on divers of them beares and patriches. They gave names to certaine ilands, of Gods mercy, Prince Henries Forland, K. James his Cape, Q. Annes Cape. One morning, in a fogge, they were carried by a set of the tide from N.E. into one of the inlets above mentioned, the depth whereof and plying forward of the ice made Hudson hope it would prove a through-fare. After he had sailed herein by his computation 300 leagues west, he came to a small strait of two leagues over, and very deepe water, through which he passed betweene two headlands, which he called, that on the south Cape Wostenholme, the other to the N.W. Digges Iland, in deg. 62,44′ minutes, into a spacious sea, wherein he sayled above a hundred leagues south, confidently proud that he had won the passage.

But finding at length by shole water that he was embayed, he was much distracted therewith, and committed many errours, especially in resolving to winter in that desolate place, in such want of necessarie provision. The third of November he moored his barke in a small cove, where they had all undoubtedly perished, but that it pleased God to send them several kinds of fowle: they killed of white partridges above a hundred and twentie dozen. These left them at the spring, and other succeeded in their place, swan, goose, teale, ducke, all easie to take; besides the blessing of a tree, which in December blossomed, with leaves greene and yellow, of an aromaticall savour, and being boyled yeelded an oyly substance, which proved an excellent salve, and the decoction being drunke proved as wholesome a potion, whereby they were cured of the scorbute, sciaticas, crampes, convulsions, and other diseases, which the coldnesse of the climate bred in them. At the opening of the yeere also, there came to his ships side such abundance of fish of all sorts, that they might therewith have fraught themselves for their returne, if Hudson had not too desperately pursued the voyage, neglecting this oportunitie of storing themselves with fish, which hee committed to the care of certaine carelesse dissolute villaines, which in his absence conspired against him; in few dayes the fish all forsooke them. Once a savage visited them, who for a knife, glasse, and beades given him, returned with bevers skins, deeres skins, and a

294

Chart of Henry Hudson's discoveries in 1610–1, engraved by Hessel Gerritsz, probably after an original by Hudson himself, and published in *Descriptio ac delineatio geographica detenctionis freti,* Amsterdam, 1612. To the geographical representation of the north-west inherited by Hudson from preceding explorers, is added his mapping of Hudson Strait, the opening of Hudson Bay, and James Bay where he wintered. There are names from Frobisher (Frisland, Buss, Queen Elizabeth's Foreland), and his discoveries on Baffin Island are laid down on the east coast of Greenland. All the names on the west coast, except one, are those introduced by James Hall in 1605. On the far shore of Davis Strait, 'Lomles Inlet' (Frobisher Bay on Baffin Island) was the starting-point selected by Hudson for his exploration; as he wrote at the end of his north-east voyage in 1608, 'I resolved . . . to make triall of that place called Lumleys Inlet, and the furious overfall by Captaine Davis [Hudson Strait]'. The names in the Strait are those bestowed by Hudson in his traverse of it in 1610, for members of the English royal family or for subscribers to his voyage. The chart illustrates his confidence that, in the 'wide sea' (Mare Magnum) discovered by him, 'he had won the passage'. In the south-east of James Bay, as noted in the chart, Hudson wintered and was abandoned by the mutineers in the following spring.

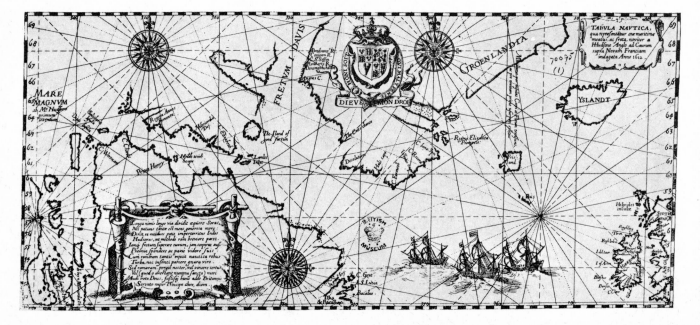

sled. At Hudsons returne, they set sayle for England. But in a few dayes, their victuals being almost spent, and hee, out of his despaire, letting fall some words of setting some on shore, the former conspirators (the chiefe whereof was Hen. Greene, none of their allowed company, but taken in by Hudson himselfe; and one Wilson) entred his cabin in the night, and forced him the master, together with his sonne John Hudson, Tho. Widowes, Arn. Ludlo, Sidrach Faner, Ad. Moore, Hen. King, Mic. Bute, to take shallop and seeke their fortune . . .

A few dayes after, [the mutineers'] victuals being spent, the ship came aground at Digges Iland, and so continued divers houres, till a great floud (which they by this accident tooke first notice of) came from the westward and set them on flote. Upon the cliffes of this Island they found aboundance of fowles tame, whereof they tooke two or three hundred and seeing a great long boat with forty or fifty savages upon the shore, they send on land; and for some of their toyes had deeres skinnes well dressed, morse-teeth, and some few furres. One of our men went on land to their tents, one of them remaining for hostage, in which tents they lived by hoords, men, women, and children; they are bigge bones, broad faced, flat nosed, and small footed, like the Tartars: their apparell of skinnes, but wrought all very handsomely, even gloves and shooes. The next morning Greene would needs goe on shore with some of his chiefe companions, and that unarmed, notwithstanding some advised and intreated him the contrary. The savages entertained him with a cunning ambush, and at the first onset shot this mutinous ringleader into the heart (where first those monsters of treacherie and bloodie crueltie, now payed with the like, had beene conceived) and Wilson, his brother in evil, had the like bloody inheritance, dying swearing and cursing: Perse, Thomas, and Moter dyed a few dayes after of their wounds. Every where can Divine Justice find executioners . . .

Being got aboord with a small weake and wounded company, they made from this island unto the northerne continent, where they saw a large opening of the sea northwestward, and had a great floud, with such a large billow, as they say, is no where but in the ocean. From hence they made all possible haste homewards.

Some of their men were starved, the rest all so weake, that onely one could lye along upon the helme and steere. By God's great goodnesse, the sixth of September 1611, they met with a fisherman of Foy, by whose meanes they came safe into England.

6.
William Baffin and the probing of Davis Strait, 1616

From Baffin's journal in *Purchas his pilgrimes,* London, 1625, III, iv, pp. 847, 843.

In 1615 and 1616, William Baffin made and recorded two voyages, as mate to Robert Bylot, a survivor of Hudson's last expedition, in search of a passage in the service of the North-West Company of London. The first, through Hudson Strait and north into Foxe Channel, was checked by thick ice and 'the smale showe of any tyde'. Baffin's conclusion that 'the mayne [passage] will be upp fretum Davis' was to be tested by the expedition of 1616. After passing Davis's farthest north at Hope Sanderson and failing to break through the middle pack, Bylot and Baffin made a circuit round the head of Baffin Bay, reaching a latitude of 78°. The openings of Smith Sound, Jones Sound and Lancaster Sound were crossed, and they followed the coast of Baffin Island southward before returning to Greenland and home.

In the icebound opening of Lancaster Sound, on 12 July, Baffin failed to recognize the only navigable entry to the North-west Passage and had to put out into the open sea.

On the twelfth day we were open of another great Sound, lying in the latitude of 74°20', and we called it Sir James Lancaster's Sound; here our hope of passage began to be lesse every day then another, for from this Sound to the southward wee had a ledge of ice betweene the shoare and us, but cleare to the seaward, we kept close by this ledge of ice till the fourteenth day in the afternoon, by which time wee were in the latitude of 71°16', and plainely perceived the land to the southward of 70°30': then wee having so much ice round about us, were forced to stand more eastward, supposing to have beene soone cleare, and to have kept on the off side of the ice untill we had come into 70°, then to have stood in againe.

295
Views of the coasts of Baffin Bay, traversed by Robert Bylot and William Baffin in 1616. Engraved after drawings made by Midshipman John Bushnan in 1818 and published in John Ross, *A voyage of discovery,* London, 1819.

View of Cape York, in Latitude 75.55. Longitude 68.33. bearing N 18. 39.W. about 7 miles distance.

D° Bearing S.W.

Buchanan's Isle, Prince Regents Bay, Lat. 76.04 Long 65.25.

But this proved quite contrary to our expectation, for wee were forced to runne above three score leagues through very much ice, many times so fast that wee could goe no wayes, although we kept our course due east; and when wee had gotten into the open sea, wee kept so neere the ice that many times wee had much adoe to get cleare, yet could not come neere the land till we came about 68°, where indeede we saw the shoare, but could not come to it by eight or nine leagues for the great abundance of ice.

Writing after the voyage to one of the 'adventurers', Baffin reported on its geographical results and on the commercial possibilities of Baffin Bay. He comments on the formation of icebergs, on the quantity of whales and walrus, on the season for whaling, and on the great range of compass variation.

I entend to show the whole proceeding of the voyage in a word: as namely, there is no passage nor hope of passage in the north of Davis Straits. We having coasted all, or neere all the circumference thereof, and finde it to be no other than a great bay, as the voyage does truely show . . .

Neither was Master Davis to be blamed in his report and great hopes, if he had anchored about Hope Sanderson, to have taken notice of the tydes. For to that place, which is 72°12', the sea is open, and of an unsearchable depth, and of a good colour: onely the tydes keepe a certaine course, nor rise but a small height, as eight or nine foote; and the flood cometh from the southward; and in all the bay beyond that place the tyde is so small, and not much to be regarded. Yet by reason of snow melting on the land, the ebb is stronger than the floud; by means whereof, and the windes holding northerly the fore part of the yeere, the great iles of ice set to the southward, som into Fretum Hudson, and other into Newfoundland: for in all the channell where the sea is open, are greate quantities of them driving up and downe; and till this yeere not well known where they were bred.

Now that the worst is known (concerning the passage) it is necessarie and requisite your worship should understand what probabilitie and hope of profit might here be made hereafter, if the voyage might bee attempted by fitting men. And first, for the killing of whales; certain it is, that in this bay are great numbers of them, which the Biscayners call the Grand Bay whales, of the same kind as are killed at Greeneland, and as it seemeth to me, easie to be strooke, because they are not used to be chased or beaten. For we being but one day in Whale Sound (so called for the number of whales we saw there sleeping, and lying aloft on the water, not fearing our ship, or ought else); that if we had beene fitted with men and things necessarie, it had beene no hard matter to have strooke more than would have made three ships a saving voyage; and that it is of that sort of whale there is no fear. I being twise at Greeneland took sufficient notice to know them againe; besides a dead whale we found at sea, having all her finnes (or rather all the rough of her mouth), of which with much labour we got one hundred and sixtie the same evening we found her: and if that foule wether and a storme the next day had not followed, we had no doubt but to have had all, or the most part of them: but the winde and sea rising, she broke from us, and we were forced to leave her ther. Neither are they onely to be looked for in Whale Sound, but also in Smith's Sound,

Wolstenholme's Sound, and others etca.

For the killing of sea-morse [walrus] I can give no certaintie, but onely this: that our bote being but once a shore in all the north part of this bay, which was in the entrance of Alderman Jones his Sound; at their returne our men told us they saw many morses alonge by the shore on the ice; but our ship being under sayle, and the wind comming faire, they presently came aboord without further search: besides, the people inhabiting about 74°, tould us by divers signes, that toward the north were many of those beasts, having two long teeth; and showed us divers peeces of the same.

As for the sea-unicorn [narwhal], it being a great fish, having a long horne or bone growing forth of his forehead or nostrils

297

296

'The fynding of an unicornes horne'. George Best's drawing of a narwhal horn, 'wreathed and strayte' and 'two yards long', found ashore by Frobisher's men in July 1577 and brought home 'to be seene and reserved as a jewel, by the Queenes majesties commandment in hir wardrop of robes'. From G. Best, *A true discourse of the late voyages of discoverie*, London, 1578.
297
Whaling in Disco Bay in the eighteenth century from Hans Egede, *A description of Greenland*, 1745.
In 1719 the Norwegian Hans Egede, the 'apostle of Greenland', formed a company in Bergen for the establishment of a mission and for whaling in Davis Strait, hitherto mainly practised by the Dutch. During his fifteen years in Greenland (1721–36), Egede founded the settlement at Godthaab and thoroughly explored the west coast. He was the first European to identify Norse ruins of the Eastern Settlement and to appreciate that Frobisher's discoveries were to be located on the east coast not of Greenland but of Baffin Island. This map was published by his son Poul Egede in 1741.

(such as Sir Martin Frobisher, in his second voyage, found one), in divers places we saw of them: which, if the horne be of any good value, no doubt but many of them may be killed . . .

And seeing I have briefly set downe what hope there is of making a profitable voyage, it is not unfit your worship should know what let or hindrance might be to the same. The chiefest and greatest cause is, that som yeere it may happen by reason of the ice lying between 72 and a halfe and 76 degrees, no minutes, that the ships cannot com into those places till toward the middest of July, so that want of time to stay in the countrey may be some let: yet they may well tarry till the last of August, in which space much businesse may be done, and good store of oyle made. Nevertheless, if store of whales come in (as no feare to the contrarie) what cannot be made in oyle, may be brought home in blubber, and the finnes will arise to good profit. Another hinderance will be, because the bottome of the sounds will not be so soone cleere as would bee wished; by means whereof, now and then a whale may be lost. (The same case sometimes chanceth in Greenland.) Yet I am perswaded those sounds before named will all be cleere before the twentieth of July: for we, this yeere, were in Whale Sound the fourth day, amongst many whales, and might have strooke them without let of ice . . .

And I dare boldly say (without boasting) that more good discoverie has not in shorter time (to my rememberance) beene done since the action was attempted, considering how much ice we have passed, and the difficultie of sayling so neere the pole (upon a traverse). And above all, the variation of the compass, whose wonderfull operation is such in this bay, increasing and decreasing so suddenly, and swift, being in some part, as in Wolstenholme Sound and in Sir Thomas Smith's Sound, varied above five points or 56°, a thing almost incredible and matchlesse in all the world beside; so that without great care and good observations, a true description could not have beene had.

but how it lyeth may be better seene in the mapp then heare nominated with writinge. Heare driving to and fro with the ice most parte of this daye till 7 or 8 a clocke, at which time the ice began somewhat to open and separate. Then we set sayle and havinge not stood past an houer: but the ice came driving with the tyde of floud from the south east with such swiftnesse, that it overwent our shippe, havinge all our sayles abroad and a good gale of winde, and forced her out of the streame into the eddy of these iles.

The iland or iles, lying in the middle of the channell, having many sounds runninge through them, with dyvers points and headlands, encountering the force of the tyde, caused such a rebounde of water and ice, that unto them that saw it not is almost incredible. But our ship being thus in the pertition, between the eddy which runne on waye, and the streame which runne another, endured so great extremytie, that unless the Lord himselfe had been on our side we had shurely perished; for sometymes the ship was hoysed aloft; and at other tymes shee havinge, as it were, got the upper hand, would force greate mighty peeces of ice to sinke downe on the on side of hir, and rise on the other.

Baffin draws his inference from the observations of tides made in Foxe Channel and Foxe Basin.

Doubtles there is a passadge. But within this strayte, whome is called Hudson's Straytes, I am doubtfull, supposinge the contrarye. But whether there be, or no, I will not affirme. But this I will affirme, that we have not beene in any tyde then that from Resolutyon Iland, and the greatest indraft of that commeth from Davis Straytes; and my judgment is, if an passadge within Resolution Iland, it is but som creeke or in lett, but the mayne will be upp fretum Davis.

Text used: Clements R. Markham, The voyages of William Baffin, *London, Hakluyt Society, 1881, pp. 126-7, 137.*

7.

In search of a western outlet from Hudson Strait, 1612–15

From Baffin's journal printed with additions from the version in *Purchas his pilgrimes,* London, 1625, III, iv, pp. 837-43.

Thomas Button's observation in the north of Hudson Bay, in 1612, suggested a search north-north-west from Nottingham Island, at the west end of Hudson Strait. This was the objective of the voyage by Bylot and Baffin in 1615.

Having traversed the north shore of the Strait, they forced a passage through the ice jammed in Foxe Channel.

The first of July close, haysie weather, with much raine, the winde at south south east. By noone this daye we weare some 3 leagues from Salisbury Island; but havinge much ice by the shore stood alonge to the northward; and the next morninge we weare fayre by another smale ile (or rather a many of small ilandes), which we afterward called Mill Island by reason of the greate extremetye and grindinge of the ice, as this night we had proofe thereof. At noone beinge close by this ile we took the latytude thereof, which is near to 64.00′,

8.

Wintering in Hudson Bay, 1619–20

From *Navigatio septentrionalis,* by Jens Munk, Copenhagen, 1624.

The Danish expedition led by Jens Munk in 1619 for the discovery of a North-west passage had difficulty in beating through the ice of Hudson Strait ('Freto Christiano'), where he noted a tidal range of thirty feet. They landed, bartered with Eskimos, and shot reindeer.

On the 13th of July, towards evening, we were in the greatest distress and danger, and did not know what counsel to follow, because we could not advance any further by tacking, the ice pressing us hard on all sides . . .

While we thus drifted forwards and backwards in the ice, in great danger of our lives, the ice displaced a large knee in the ship, which was situated under the peg of the head of the ship, and fastened with six large iron bolts; wherefore I set all my carpenters to work to set that knee straight again. But it was too big for them, so that they could do nothing with it in that place. I therefore had the ship swung and turned, so that the side to which the knee had come into a crooked position drifted against the ice, and then ordered the rudder to be worked so

Jens Munk encounters Eskimos; woodcut in Munk, *Navigatio septentrionalis*, Copenhagen, 1624.

In July 1619 Munk lay at two harbors on the north shore of Hudson Strait, or south coast of Baffin Island, near Jackman Sound in 68°E. The illustration depicts his meeting with Eskimos at the first anchorage and the shooting of a reindeer at the second, which he accordingly named 'Ren Sound'. Here he set up the royal arms of Denmark, and his ships were caught fast in the ice.

299

A ship lifted by pressure ice. Engraving in Gerrit de Veer's narrative of William Barents's last voyage 1596–7, *Waerachtige Beschryvinghe*, Amsterdam, 1598.

298

299

as to turn against the ice in order that the knee in a measure might right itself again, which also was effected as perfectly as if 20 carpenters had been engaged in refitting it. Afterwards, the carpenters adjusted the bolts which had become bent . . .

On the 22nd of July, towards evening, finding that none of the natives would come to me, I made ready to sail from there, and caused His Royal Majesty's Arms and Name, Christianus

Quartus, to be set up there; and I named the said harbour Rin Sund, because in that place we shot some reindeer. Wherever we found the fishing nets of the natives lying, we deposited near them various kinds of our goods, such as knives and all sorts of iron tools, after which we set sail. The same harbour is a very good one, because one may lie there in safety from any wind whatever.

On the 23rd of July, in the morning early, when it became day, we found ourselves entirely surrounded by ice on all sides, so that we could not get away from it on either bow or in any direction . . .

In the night next following, the ice pressed on us so hard, and we were so firmly fixed in the ice, particularly to leeward, that we could not give way on either side, and the ice crushed four anchors to pieces on the bow of the sloop. At the same time, the ice forced itself underneath the keel of *Lamprenen*, so that one might pass one's hand along the keel from stem to stern . . .

On the 26th of July, we found ourselves entirely hemmed in by ice on all sides, so that we could nowhere manage to get an anchor in the ground, nor could we get any hawser on shore. The ship, however, remained in the same place all day, drifting neither outwards nor inwards, so that we were now in the greatest distress and danger.

Emerging from the Strait on 10 August, Munk crossed Hudson Bay to Port Churchill where he wintered in rigorous conditions, losing most of his crew from scurvy and dysentery. When the spring thaw came, he returned home in the sloop with only two men of his original complement of sixty-five.

On the 3rd of December, the weather being very mild, I went out into the middle of the estuary, with some of the men, in order to ascertain how thick the ice was in the middle of the channel; and we found that the ice was seven Seeland quarters [3 foot 7 inches] thick; and this thickness is retained until long after Christmas, whether the frost was more or less severe. But, in quiet standing water, the ice became much thicker than seven quarters. As regards much of the drift-ice which floats forwards and backwards in the sea, and exhibits very great thickness: this ice comes out of the many large rivers and bays, and owing to the great force of the wind and the current, by which it is shoved together, it attains such great thickness, and thus floats away. Amongst this ice, there occur large masses rising quite twenty fathoms above the water; and some such masses of ice, which I myself have had examined, stood firm on the sea-bottom in more than 40 fathoms, which, perhaps, may seem incredible, but, nevertheless, is so in truth. Concerning such deep and high masses of ice as I have found: it is my opinion that, where many high and steep mountains are found, there is also very deep water. All the snow which is driven on to the mountains, having great weight, slides down by degrees; and, as soon as the snow comes into the water, in such cold places, it is at once converted into ice. Being every day in such wise increased, it at last becomes so thick and high; because, generally, where such high lands and mountains are found, there also such large and thick masses of ice occur . . .

May 28th. During these days, there was nothing particular to write about, except that we seven miserable persons, who were still lying there alive, looked mournfully at each other, hoping every day that the snow would thaw and the ice drift away.

As regards the symptoms and peculiarities of the illness which had fallen upon us: it was a rare and extraordinary one. Because all the limbs and joints were so miserably drawn

Jens Munk at Port Churchill; woodcut in Munk, *Navigatio septentrionalis*, Copenhagen, 1624.
In September 1619 Munk took his ship and sloop up Port Churchill and secured them for the winter. His crew wintered, and most of them died of scurvy, in the ships, and not (as suggested by the illustration) in houses on shore, which were perhaps shelters for the sick.

301
Interior of the hut built for wintering. Engraving in de Veer's narrative of Barents's last voyage, *Waerachtige Beschryvinghe,* Amsterdam, 1598.

together, with great pains in the loins, as if a thousand knives were thrust through them. The body at the same time was blue and brown, as when one gets a black eye, and the whole body was quite powerless. The mouth also was in a very bad and miserable condition, as all the teeth were loose, so that we could not eat any victuals . . .

June the 8th. As I could not now any more stand the bad smell and stench from the dead bodies, which had remained in the ship for some time, I managed, as best I could, to get out of the berth . . .

I spent that night on the deck, using the clothes of the dead. But, next day, when the two men who were on shore saw me and perceived that I was still alive—I, on my part, had thought that they were dead long ago—they came out on the ice to the ship, and assisted me in getting down from the ship to the land, together with the clothes which I threw to them; for the ship was not farther from the shore than about twelve or fourteen fathoms. For some time, we had our dwelling on the shore under a bush, as may be seen on the accompanying plate; and there we made a fire in the day time. Later on, we crawled about everywhere near, wherever we saw the least green growing out of the ground, which we dug up and sucked the main root thereof. This benefited us, and as the warmth now commenced to increase nicely, we began to recover . . .

On the 16th of July, which was Sunday, in the afternoon, we set sail from there in the name of God. At that time, it was as warm in that country as it might have been in Denmark, and the cloudberries were in bud. There was such a quantity of gnats that in calm weather they were unbearable. A quantity of rain also fell every day at this time of the year . . .

And I have called the same harbour after myself, *Jens Munckes Bay.* All that has happened here is found depicted in this plate.

Text used: Translation in C. C. A. Gosch, Danish Arctic expeditions, *1605 to 1620, London, Hakluyt Society, Vol. II, 1897, pp. 11-6, 47-51.*

9.
Hudson Bay circumnavigated, 1631–2

a) Captain James's account of Hudson Strait.

From *The strange and dangerous voyage of Captain Thomas James,* London, 1633.

The two English expeditions of Captain Luke Foxe and Captain Thomas James sent out in 1631 by rival companies had alike instructions to probe north-west of Nottingham Island and to seek an opening along the west coast of Hudson Bay. Both made hazardous passages of Hudson Strait, in difficult ice conditions; and between them they completed the map of the southern shore of the Bay (see plate 305).

But, before I proceed further, it were not amisse in some manner to describe the Straight, which begins at the Iland of Resolution, and ends here at Digges Iland. If you goe downe into the Bay, the Straight is about 120 leagues long, and trends W.N.W. and E.S.E. generally. In the entrance, it is about 15 leagues broad; and then on the Southward side is a great Bay. About the middle it is likewise about 15 leagues broad, and then the Land opens something wider; so that betwixt

b) Captain Foxe describes his experience of ice in the Strait.
From *North-West Fox*, London, 1635.

Now this prodigious thing we call Ice is of two sorts; as mountainous ice, which is a huge peece, compact, of a great quantity, some of more, some of lesse [size]; but, in this Freet [strait], you seldome have any bigger than a great Church, and the most therof lesse, being of severall formes, as some 20, some 30, some 40 yards above the superficies of the water, but farre more under; of these, you may tell sometimes 7 or eight in sight, so that they are no hindrance to us.

The other [sort] is smaller, and that we call masht or fleackt ice. Of this you shall [there] have numbers infinite, some of the quantity of a Rood, some a Pearch, $\frac{1}{2}$ an acre, some 2 acres, but the most is small and about a foot or 2 or more above the water, and 8 or 10 or more under the water; and those are they which doe inclose you, so as, in much wind, from the topmast head, you shall hardly see any water for them; but, whilst you lie amongst them, it is so smooth as you shall not feele the ship stirre. Onely, if it be much wind, make the ship snugge; and, at returne of the Tydes, when the

303

ice doeth loozen, have all care to the Rudder. At shift of wind, the ice will make way one from another; in the meane time, have patience; and, in trailing of ice on sterne, if the ship doe touch but against it with the stemme, so that the stroke sodainely stay her way, then have care to keep the helme in midships, for your traile, with its way, will come presently at the backe of the Rudder, and it, lying on either side, is in danger to breake or set it on wry . . .

I came by one peece of Ice something higher than the rest, whereupon a stone was, of the Contents of 5 or 6 Tonne weight, with divers other smaller stones and mudde thereon. It seemeth to condescend with reason that these peeces of ice are ingendred upon the Winter's snow, which, falling in drifts by the forcing & wheeling of the wind, condensing and compacting a great quantity together over the steepe brow of some high mountaine, cleaving thereto untill [the] dissolving time of the yeare, when the earth receives her naturall warmnesse, [are] then inforced by their weight to tumble into the Sea, carrying with them all such trees or stones as they have formerly inclosed. God be thanked, the [blocks of] Ice begun to thinne and separate; this hot weather doth fast dissolve them.

The country about Churchill River, where Munk had wintered, was observed by Foxe in August 1631 (see plate 304).

This land bore from me to the S.E. by E., and was gentlie descending down to the Seaside, the greenest & best like I have seene since I came out of the river of Thames, and as it

302
Greenland ice: (*above*) coastal pack, (*below*) heavy ice-floes with ice blink; lithographs in G. W. Manby, *Journal of a voyage to Greenland*, London, 1827.
303
A large iceberg off the west coast of Greenland, in 66° 30′N, seen at midnight. Drawing made in H.M.S. *Isabella*, 7 June 1818. (*Hydrographic Department, British Ministry of Defence, 'Coastal Views: Arctic', vol. II.*)

Digges Iland and Cape Charles, it is about 20 leagues broad; betwixt which two stands Salisbury Iland and Nottingham Iland. If it be cleere weather, you may see both the South and the North shoares; ordinarily, the depth in the middle of the Straight is 120 faddomes, white sand. A certaine tyde runnes in it, and no current. The North shoare is the straightest, and the cleerest from Ice too. Along the North shoare, you have many low small Ilands, which cannot be seene farre off from the land; and, in many places, the land makes as if it had small sounds into it. The Maineland on both sides is indifferent high land. And so much for discourse may suffice; referring you to the Plot [chart] for the particulars.

Text used: Miller Christy, The Voyages of Captain Luke Foxe and Captain Thomas James, *London, Hakluyt Society, Vol. II, 1894, p. 475.*

were inclosed with thick rowes of Trees between one meadowe and another, distinct as it were Barn Elmes, neare London, and at sight hereof I did think of them; and if there be any keeping of tame Deere or other beasts, or tillage, in all that countrey, I should think it to be there; for certainly there must, by those burials, be great store of people, for it is not to be thought that they will bring or carry their dead farre to buriall; and it cannot be thought also but that we were seene by them, although they were not seene by any of us, for we stayed not but in the night; all day wee made as much way as sailes would drive forward, so as, if they would have come to us, wee were gone before they could make ready; and although they might see us, whether they durst come or no, I know not, having, as I suppose, never seene ship in their lives before; as Hudson who sought after them in his Bay (though far distant from hence), they set their woods on fire hard by him, and yet would not come to him although he was but in his Shallop.

Traversing the southern shore of the Bay east of Port Nelson, the two explorers met on 29 August, as recounted by Foxe.

I was well entertained and feasted by Captain James, with varietie of such cheere as his sea provisions could aford, with some Partridges; we dined betwixt decks, for the great cabin was not bigg enough to receive our selves and followers; during which time the ship, but in 2 courses and maine bonnet, threw in so much water as wee could not have wanted sause if wee had had roast Mutton.

Whereat I began to ponder whether it were better for his

304
Captain Luke Foxe's 'Polar Map or Card', with his emblem, published in *North-West Fox*, London, 1635.
Foxe's track in 1631 is indicated by a dotted line. The names on the west and south shores of Hudson Bay are those bestowed by Foxe. He concluded that, if there were a passage out of the Bay to the west, it must lie by way of 'Sir T. Roes Welcom' in 65°N; and the inlet named 'Ne ultra' (go no farther) in Henry Briggs's map of 1625 (plate 275) is accordingly renamed on Foxe's map 'ut ultra' (go farther). Like Briggs, Foxe gives the name 'Buttons bay' to the west part of Hudson Bay, while James Bay is named 'hudsons bays'.

Unlike James, but following the model of Briggs's map, Foxe illustrates the possibility of a Pacific outlet, to the north of California, for the westward passage from Hudson Bay.

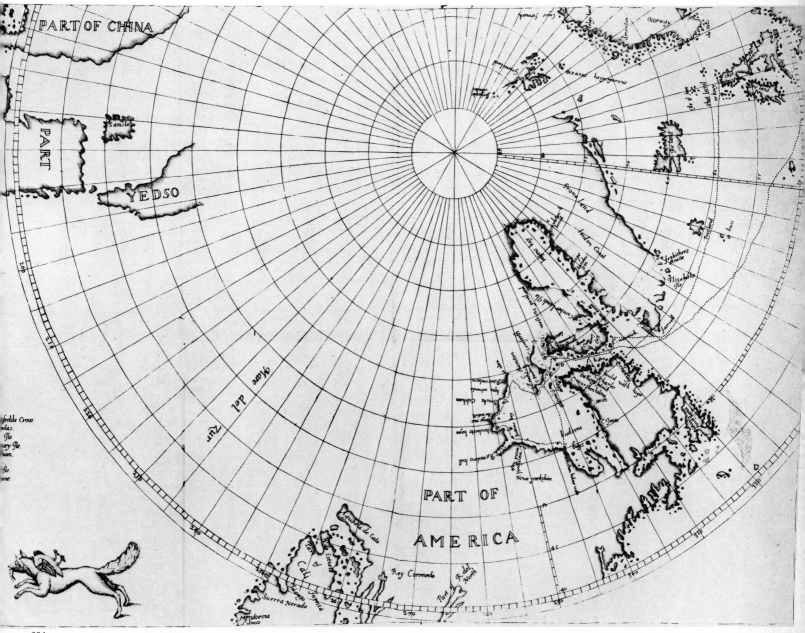

company to bee impounded amongst Ice, where they might be kept from putrifaction by the piercing ayre; or in open Sea, to be kept sweete by being thus daily pickled. However, they were to be pittied; the ship taking her liquor as kindly as our selves, for her nose was no sooner out of the pitcher, but her nebe [beak], like the Ducks, was in't againe. The Gentleman could discourse of Arte (as observations, calculations, and the like), and showed me many Instruments, so that I did perceive him to be a practitioner in the Mathematicks; but when I found that hee was no Seaman, I did blame those very much who had councelled him to make choyce of that shippe for a voyage of such importance . . .

And (being demanded), I did not thinke much for his keeping

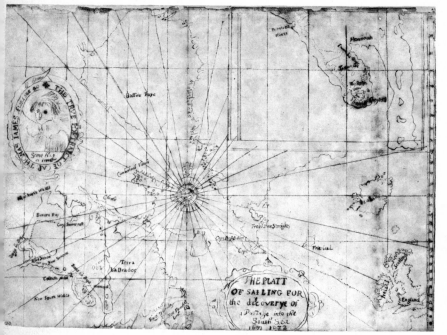

305
Captain Thomas James's chart of his voyage to Hudson Bay in 1631–2, with his portrait. Inset: chart of James Bay, on a larger scale. *London, British Museum, Add. Ms. 5415.G.1.*
The map indicates, by dotted or continuous lines, James's outward track across Hudson Bay to 'Briggs his Bay' and Port Nelson, along the south shore of the Bay, and his homeward track by the same route. The inset shows his winter quarters on Charlton Island in James Bay. The map illustrates James's conclusion that it was 'most probable that there is no passage'. The name 'Buttons Bay' is here confined to the north-west part of Hudson Bay; Coats Island, with Button's landfall of 1612 at 'Cary Swans nest', is drawn as a peninsula; and the name 'New Wales' applied by Button to the west shore of Hudson Bay, is altered by James to 'New North Wales'. All the other names in the Bay, given on the map, are those bestowed by James.
The engraved version of this map was published in *The strange and dangerous voyage of Captain Thomas James*, London, 1633.

out his flagg . . . To this was replide, that hee was going to the Emperour of Japon, with letters from his Majestie, and that, if it were a ship of his Majesties of 40 Peeces of Ordnance, hee could not strike his flag. 'Keepe it up then,' quoth I, 'but you are out of the way to Japon, for this is not it.' Hee would have perswaded mee to take harbour to winter in, telling mee that Sir Thomas Button tooke harbour the 14 of this instant. Quoth I, 'hee is no precedent for mee. I must paralell my poverty with poore Hudson's, who tooke no harbour before the first of November; and that then I durst not take harbour untill the midst of the same.'

Foxe returned north and penetrated Foxe's Basin to 'Foxe his farthest' in 66° 47′N, whence he returned home.

I doe account this Cape to lie some mi. within the Arctick Cirkle. It stretches E.-wards as before, which, in hazie weather, as in the night, is easie to discerne in those parts, for the land lying hid in snow, doth cause a white reflexe in the Ayre all night, as though it were dawning or twi-light, before and after sunset. This Cape I named my Lord Weston's Portland.

Text used for above four extracts: Miller Christy, The Voyages of Captain Luke Foxe and Captain Thomas James, *London, Hakluyt Society, Vol. II, 1894, pp. 288-9, 292-3, 336-7, 358-9.*

c) Captain James examines James Bay.
From *The strange and dangerous voyage of Captain Thomas James,* London, 1633.

James continued east and explored James Bay where he wintered. He records the cold of the Arctic winter in February 1632 and his men's suffering from scurvy.

The cold was as extreme this moneth as at any time we had felt it this yeere, and many of our men complained of infirmities; some of sore mouthes, all the teeth in their heads being loose, their gums swollne, with blacke rotten flesh, which must every day be cut away. The paine was so sore on them that they could not eate their ordinary meat. Others complained of paine in their heads and their brests; some of weakness in their backs; others of aches in their thighs and knees; and others of swelling in their legges. Thus were two thirds of the company under the Chirurgions hands. And yet, neverthelesse, they must worke daily, and goe abroad to fetch wood and timber, notwithstanding the most of them had no shooes to put on. Their shooes, upon their comming to the fire, out of the snow, were burnt and scorcht upon their feete, and our store-shooes were all sunke in the Ship.

The spring thaw and the aspect of his wintering place are noted by James before sailing for home in July 1632.

In the woods, wee found the Snow partly wasted away, so that it was passable. The ponds were almost unthawd, but the Sea from any place we could see all firme frozen.

The snow does not melt away here with the Sunne or raine, and so make any land-floods, as in England; but it is exaled up by the Sunne, and suckt full of holes, like honeycombs, so that the land whereon it lyes will not be at all wetted. The like observation we also had: that, let it raine ever so much, you shall see no land-floods after it . . .

This Iland, and all the rest (as likewise the maine), is a light white sand, covered over with a white mosse, and full of shrubs and low bushes, excepting some bare hils and other patches. In these bare places, the sand will drive with the wind like dust. It is very full of trees, as Spruce and Juniper; but the biggest tree I saw was but a foote and a halfe over. At our first comming hither, we saw some Deare, and kild one; but never any since. Foxes, all the winter, we saw many, and kild some dozen of them; but they went all away in May. Beares we saw but few, but kild none: we saw some other little beasts. In May there came some fowle, as Duckes and Geese, of which we kild very few. White Partridges we saw, but in small quantities; nor had we any shot to shoot at them. Fish we could never see any in the Sea, nor no bones of fish on the shoare side, excepting a few Cockle-shels, and yet nothing in them neither.

Text used for above two extracts: Miller Christy, The Voyages of Captain Luke Foxe and Captain Thomas James, *London, Hakluyt Society, Vol. II, 1894, pp. 534-5, 550, 565-6.*

6 THE EARLY SEVENTEENTH CENTURY: THE FIRST SETTLEMENTS

To the establishment of permanent settlements in North America the sixteenth century was prologue; the seventeenth century saw the unfolding drama of successful colonization on the eastern seaboard. Although conditions were not favorable for effective planting of colonies before the uneasy peace between Spain and England in 1604, both French and English seamen were active along the entire coast during the decades before permanent settlement. The Spanish governors of the small but tenacious garrison at St Augustine, founded in 1565, sent vessels northward along the coast periodically to support the struggling and impermanent missions of their Church, as well as to report on and attempt to discourage foreign intrusions. English and French privateers made depredations on these mission outposts, and their pilots learned the harbors suitable for retreat, for water, and for repairing their vessels.[1]

Before the end of the sixteenth century many ships, ranging in size from a few tons to whaling vessels of 400 tons, made their way annually to the fishing areas, especially around Newfoundland. For over 600 miles along the Terra Nova coast, Anthony Parkhurst wrote Hakluyt in 1578, 'above 100. saile of Spaniards . . . come to take Cod . . . besides 20. or 30. more that come from Biskaie to kill whale for traine [oil] . . . Of Portugals there are not lightly above 50. saile . . . Of the French nation and Britons, are about one hundred and fifty sailes,'[2] and during Parkhurst's voyages there in the past four years, he said that English ships had increased from thirty to fifty. Usually they sailed with little more government supervision than did the local fishing fleets along their own coasts. The later reaction of the Indians to explorers and colonizers, sometimes friendly and at other times extremely hostile, often reflected their treatment by motley crew members, sometimes hardened criminals released from prisons, in search of food or barter or shipwrecked on the coast.[3]

In the northern latitudes the cold winters and methods of fishing and trade did not encourage or make necessary the establishment of permanent settlements for the fishers. Two methods of fishing and preparing cod were in practice. The Bretons and the French and Spanish Basques characteristically fished from their ships, cleaned and salted the fish, which they then piled into barrels and thoroughly pressed. This was called the 'green-cod' method. The English, who did not have the large quantity of salt necessary for this process, more frequently used the 'dry-cod' method. They built stages on which to land and dress the cod in harbors where timber was readily accessible, and flakes or scaffolds on which to spread the fish, turning them over in the sun every few hours to dry until ready to pack in barrels. They usually anchored their ships near the shore and went out in small boats to catch the fish, which they brought in to the drying stages.[4]

Other activities beside cod fishing had long interested the French, and later the English, taking them beyond Newfound-

A View of a Stage & also of ý manner of Fishing for, Curing & Drying Cod at NEW FOUND LAND.
A. The Habit of ý Fishermen. B. The Line. C. The manner of Fishing. D. The Dressers of ý Fish. E. The Trough into which they throw ý Cod when Dressed. F. Salt Boxes. G. The manner of Carrying ý Cod. H. The Cleansing ý Cod. I. A Press to extract ý Oyl from ý Cods Livers. K. Casks to receive ý water &Blood that comes from ý Livers. L. Another Cask to receive the Oyl. M. The manner of Drying ý Cod.

306

Curing and drying cod in Newfoundland, inset to the map of North America, by H. Moll, London, 1720.
An accurate portrayal of methods and staging procedures already practised by English cod fishermen in the sixteenth century.

land. Whaling increased; walrus, inhabiting the smaller islands of the Gulf of St Lawrence in great numbers, were especially valuable for 'train-oil', used in making soap without a fishy smell, and for their tusks. Trade in furs with the Indians, however, which had begun as an incidental but profitable sideline for the fishing fleets, became a major factor in the development of trans-Atlantic commerce and a powerful factor in colonization schemes. Most valuable were the beaver skins; in the latter half of the sixteenth century European felt makers found that the fur of beavers made the best hats.[5]

It is curious that New England, destined to become the site of the second English settlement and one of the most vigorous of the early colonial centres in North America, was until the beginning of the seventeenth century almost unknown to Europeans, except as a coast can be known from the sea. Many had sailed along its shores, from Verrazzano and Gomes

Pinus maritima major prima mathioli.

Pinus sylvestris montana tertia.

Pinus sylvestris altera **Tab: LXXXIX**
Dodonei

307
Whale hunting off Newfoundland. Detail from Petrus Plancius' map 'Nova Francia', 1592–4.
308
Varieties of pines, from J. T. de Bry, *Florilegium renovatum et auctum*, Frankfurt, 1641.

Pinus maritima major altera.

Pinaster II. Hispanicus Clusy.

Pinus maritima major prima Dodonei

Pinus Conis erectus.

Pinus maritima minor

Pinus maritima major altera Mathioli:

to fishermen and fur hunters in the late sixteenth century. Many knew it by its early name of Norumbega. How then did this known but unknown land appear, that it remained uninvaded so much longer than Canada, Virginia, Florida and the south-west?

To the captain of a ship, to the navigator as yet without a chart, the coast of New England must have appeared hostile and dangerous. The rocky reefs of Maine, the headlands of Cape Ann were scarcely more formidable than the tricky 'sholdes' off Cape Cod. The harbors and the mouths of the small rivers were hidden behind pebble-ringed islands, thick with pine and fir. It was not easy from the sea to see the 'champion land', the cultivable fields like those which bordered the St Lawrence; much of what was later cultivated was wrung from the grip of forest and rock. Granite was everywhere, and thick, dark woods, to the very edge of the sea. Great storms and 'houracanes' beat along that coast, and an icy cold came early and stayed late, a fiercer cold than any known to Frenchmen or Englishmen. Of fish and fur there was clearly wealth for the taking, but there seemed no sign of gold. The Indians were few, and often unwelcoming.

In the year 1602, however, there began a series of English voyages to the New England coast, still 'the north part of Virginia', which were a prelude to colonization. Though none of these penetrated far inland, they did much more than sail past; lingering at least to collect a cargo, they have left in their accounts a small series of vivid initial impressions of this land. The first voyage was made by 'Captaine Bartholowmew Gosnold, Captaine Bartholowmew Gilbert [not the son of Sir Humphrey], and divers other gentlemen'; they sailed from Falmouth on 20 March 1602 with thirty-two people, aboard the *Concord*.[6] One was John Brereton, author of the *Briefe and true relation of the discoverie of the north part of Virginia*, one of the earliest English writings to deal with New England.

This voyage pioneered also in the route taken. Instead of coming to New England in the usual way, south from New-foundland or north from the West Indies, Gosnold steered straight across from the Azores, making landfall on 14 May on the coast of Maine, probably about Casco Bay, 'very stony or rocky'. Evidence came quickly that others had fished that coast; on the first day, 'six Indians, in a Baske-shallop with mast and saile, an iron grapple, and a kettle of copper, came boldly aboard us, one of them apparelled with a waistcoat

Detail of a shoal of fish off Cape Cod added to the engraving of John
Smith's chart of New England, originally drawn in 1614, in 1635.
In 1497 Cabot, according to Soncino, a contemporary, found the
Newfoundland Banks 'swarming with fish, which can be taken not only
with the net, but in baskets let down with stone'. Captain John Smith,
117 years later, wrote with a promoter's pen of fishing off Cape Cod and the
New England shore: 'You shall scarce find any Baye, shallow shore, or Cove
of sand where you may not take many Clampes, or Lobsters, or both at your
pleasure . . . a little Boye might take of Cunners and Pinacks and such
delicate fish at the ships sterne, more then sixe or tenne can eate in a daie;
but with a casting Net, thousands . . . Cod, Cuske, Holybut, Mackerell,
Scate or such like, a man may take with a hooke or line what he will . . .
no River where there is not plenty of Sturgion, or Salmon or both: all of
which are to be had in abundance.'

310
Newfoundland fishing and elk hunting, from T. de Bry, *America*, Part XIII,
1634, page 15.

311
The Sassafras tree, valued for the supposed curative potency of its bark
especially for venereal disease. From N. Monardes, *Joyfull newes out of the
newe founde world*, Englished by J. Frampton, London, 1577.

310

and breeches of blacke serdge, made after our sea-fashion,
hose and shoes on his feet; all the rest (save one that had a
paire of breeches of blue cloth) were all naked'.[7] Sailing south,
standing somewhat out to sea, 'in the morning we found
ourselves embayed with a mightie headland'.[8] Thus many later
explorers saw the great sweep of Cape Cod, 'a white sandie
and very bolde shore'; but these named it, according to
Archer, another diarist of the voyage, because 'in five or six
hours . . . we had pestered our ship so with Cod fish, that we
threw numbers of them over-board again'. Rounding the great
Cape, they came among the offshore islands of Nantucket,
Martha's Vineyard, and others which they explored. Trees,
berries, and birds delighted them, and 'a great standing lake
of fresh water, neere the sea side . . . which is maintained with
the springs running exceedingly pleasantly thorow the
woodie grounds which are very rockie'.[9] And they marvelled
at 'stones . . . glistering and shining', and 'huge bones and
ribbes of Whales'.[10]

Finally they landed on Cuttyhunk, which they called
Elizabeth's Isle, the name now given to the whole group of
islands. There they found a little island in the midst of a
freshwater lake, which they fortified, and made their home.
Brereton's description of this small refuge, and of the mainland near it, is so lyrical that it has given rise to the speculation

311

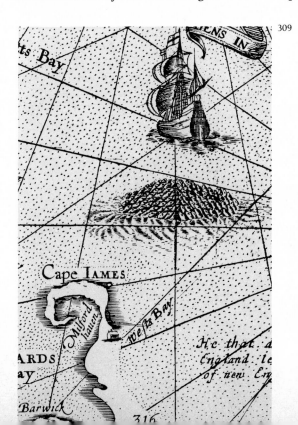

309

that Shakespeare, friend of the Earl of Southampton, one of
the patrons of the voyage, might have had it in mind when he
created Prospero's magic isle in *The Tempest*.[11] From hence
they gathered their sassafras, that 'sovereign remedy for the
French poxe', and traded successfully with the Indians for
skins. Abandoning an idea of splitting their small company
to leave a colony, they sailed for England with a laden ship
on 18 June and put in at the riverside village of Exmouth,
Devon, on 23 July 1602.[12]

In the next year some merchants of Bristol, not to be outdone
by their southern competitors, sent another voyage to seek
for sassafras along the coast of 'the North part of Virginia'.
This was commanded by Martin Pring, a young captain of
twenty-three. In 1603, his little fleet consisted of the *Speedwell*
and the *Discoverer*. He also used the direct route from the
Azores to the coast of southern Maine, where he sailed up one
or two rivers; put in at Gosnold's Savage Rock [probably
Cape Ann]; and, finding no sassafras, 'bare into that great gulf

which Captaine Gosnold overshot the yeare before'.[13] Scanning the shores of Massachusetts Bay, Pring selected Plymouth Harbor, with its 'pleasant Hill thereunto adjoyning',[14] made a 'small barricado', and stayed seven weeks. During this time the crew gathered sufficient sassafras to lade both ships, and also planted 'Wheate, Barley, Oates, Pease, and sundry sorts of Garden Seeds',[15] which grew rapidly. Pring catalogs trees, animals and fish with fervor, names the berries they could eat, and gives an excellent description of a birch-bark canoe, 'in proportion like a Wherrie of the River Thames', holding nine men, and 'rowed' very swiftly by 'Oares . . . flat at the end like an Oven peele [baker's wooden shovel]'.[16]

Pring's company had with them two great mastiffs, one of

312
Martin Pring's 'barricado', from Pieter van der Aa's book of voyages, *De Aanmerkenswaardigste en alomberoemde zee- en landreizen,* Leyden, 1706. In 1603, seventeen years before the Pilgrims, Martin Pring landed with his two ships in Plymouth Harbor, built a 'small barricado', and stayed seven weeks, loading sassafras. One of his seamen played the 'gitterne' which so attracted the Indians that they came in large numbers to dance to the music.

whom could carry a half-pike in his mouth, and a youth who played the 'gitterne'; the latter charmed the Indians into dancing to his music, and the former frightened them away when they became threatening.[17] Pring reached home in October 1603. He was a good forerunner, encouraging both the Sagadahoc Colony and the Pilgrims by his delightful descriptions of their future sites.

Two years later, another Devonshire captain, George Waymouth, set sail on a voyage with a more definite purpose of exploration for a colony in New England than those before. His patrons were, again, the Earl of Southampton, and also Sir Thomas Arundell, a Roman Catholic, who had sent along James Rosier, a graduate of Cambridge University, possibly a Catholic, with instructions to observe and to write.[18]

Waymouth sailed from London down the Thames, with twenty-nine seamen in the *Archangel.* They had hoped to bear farther south than the other discoverers of 'the northern part of Virginia', but the wind persistently pushed them north. Rosier gives with great vividness the excitement and dismay

of suddenly finding themselves in shoal water, with the 'whitish sandy cliff' of the eastern end of Nantucket rising up ahead, and many whales in sight.[19] Since they were 'embaied with continuall showldes and rocks in a most uncertaine ground', they abandoned with relief the land they had so longed to see, and allowed the wind to take them north and east. They found their 'sea-charts very false, putting land where none is';[20] but, after standing out to sea all night in a gale, they managed to anchor safely alongside Monhegan Island off the coast of Maine, and go ashore for desperately needed wood and water. Working their way among the islands toward the mainland, where they could see the Camden Mountains, they came to anchor in an excellent harbor which they called Pentecost Harbor for the day, the present St George's Harbor under Allen's Island. Of this island, Rosier describes in glowing terms the 'pleasant fruitfulnesse'. They found 'very great egge shells bigger than goose egges', 'excellent clay for bricke', 'a well of good and holesome cleare water', 'great Cod, Haddock, Thorneback', and the Lucullan joys of Maine lobsters. They planted 'peaze and barley', which grew eight inches in sixteen days. They listed many trees and their products, including 'Oke very great and good', and 'Turpentine in . . . marvellous plenty'; they found pearls and mother of pearl. They 'set up a crosse on the shore side upon the rocks',[21] which was found two years later by the Popham Colonists.

At first the relations of Waymouth's company with the Indians were as friendly as any described, with much 'drinking' of tobacco together (the Indians used a pipe made of a lobster claw), trading, and exchange of overnight visits. But on one of these, a seaman named Griffin found 283 savages, with bows and arrows, dogs and tame wolves, and nothing to trade, who 'would have drawen us up further into a little narrow nooke of a river'.[22] We detect a slight relief at this evidence of contemplated treachery, for Waymouth had determined already to take some Indians back with him. This being effected by very real treachery, 'we shipped five Salvages, two canoas, with all their bowes and arrowes'.[23] These Indians were kindly treated, instructed in English, and most of them returned as guides on later expeditions. But at the moment, they were hidden below decks while Waymouth, in the 'light horseman', explored harbor islands, and sailed three-score miles up a beautiful river (the St George) and on the first voyage to claim to penetrate that far the interior of New England. It is most unfortunate that the 'perfect Geographicall Map' made by Waymouth, whose instruments are carefully listed by Rosier, has disappeared.[24] Up the river they found the 'champion land', the gentler, grassy New England, bordering a great stream leading inland they knew not how far; Rosier's relation becomes a promotion tract indeed, of one ravished with 'variety of pleasantnesse'. He gives a final catalog of flora and fauna, a spirited description of the Indians' method of killing whales, and reports that they reached Dartmouth Haven on 18 July laden with fish, captive Indians, and good news.

Waymouth's voyage and Waymouth's Indians caused a great stir in England, and it was not long after his return that another patron, Sir John Zouche, possibly a Roman Catholic, proposed to take him back to 'Virginia', and set him up as a sort of feudal lord over a colony.[25] But the time had come when England, increasing in commercial prosperity, was to realize that private enterprise was not a valid basis for colonization, even with royal acquiescence; that what was needed to launch, equip, continuously supply, and profit from the labor and trade of a lasting colony was a cooperative organization of business men. Thus the famous English companies came into existence, and developed in various ways to produce the most effective kind, the joint-stock company. They alone made early colonization possible, and were the link between private adventure and the forms of colonial government and policy which later evolved. In this instance, the first of such companies to deal with America was formed to forestall the plan of Sir John Zouche. Waymouth's discovery was fully used, but he himself, unsympathetic, was pensioned off and did not participate.

The leaders in this new form of enterprise were Sir John Popham, Lord Chief Justice of the King's Bench, who represented London commercial interests, and Sir Ferdinando Gorges, Governor of the fort of Plymouth, who represented those of the outports, Bristol, Plymouth, and Exeter. Associated with them were eight other men of substance, all concerned with discovery and adventure: such men as Sir Thomas Gates, later Governor of Virginia; Richard Hakluyt, of the *Principall Navigations*; and Ralegh Gilbert, son of Sir Humphrey, nephew of Ralegh. These petitioned the king for a charter incorporating the Virginia Company, in two parts, one of London, the other of Plymouth. The patent, issued 10 April 1606, was for the part of America north of the Cape Fear River, at 34°N, and south of 45°, which is a little above Bangor in present Maine.[26] This was judged to be 'outside the possession of any Christian prince'; the fact that neither Spain, France, nor Holland agreed was to cause later complications. Non-Christian princes of course did not count.

The land around Chesapeake Bay was well known; Ralegh had hoped to move his ill-fated colony there. The climate was far kinder than that of New England, and it is not at all surprising that it was the London, or South Virginia, Company which planted the first successful permanent English settlement in that region. Popham and Gorges, however, impressed by an enthusiastic account of the river of Sagadahoc (the Kennebec in Maine), and by their conversations with his imported Indians, also made an attempt. In May 1607, shortly after the London Company vessels had set out for the founding of Jamestown, the *Gift of God* and the *Mary and John*, commanded by George Popham, kinsman of the Chief Justice and a member of the Plymouth Company, and Ralegh Gilbert, set sail with 120 settlers for the coast of Maine, carrying two of Waymouth's Indians, trained to be interpreters and guides.

Our account of this expedition and brief colony is in an unsigned manuscript discovered in 1875 in the Lambeth Palace Library and thought to be by James Davies, navigator of the *Mary and John*.[27] It breaks off abruptly, but is supplemented by a passage in William Strachey's *The historie of travell into Virginia Britania*;[28] he had apparently used the former account when it was complete. They made landfall near Halifax Harbor, and also encountered Indians in a 'bisken shallop', and others who knew some French words. They came south along the coast, marvelling at the abundance of fish. 'Thear at Lo wattr,' writes this quaintly-spelling seaman, 'in an hower kild near 50 great lopsters. You shall see them whear they ly in shold wattr nott past a yeard deep and wth a great hooke mad faste to a staffe you shall hitch them up.'[29] They admired the Bay of Fundy. Finally, winding in among the densely wooded, rocky islands, they came in sight of the 'three heigh mountains that lye in upon the mainland near unto the ryver of Penobskot'.[30] (The text is interspersed with useful little profile drawings of shoreline.) To their delight, they found Waymouth's cross on the island alongside which they anchored. They made contact with the local Indians and their chief Nahanada, through their interpreter Skidwarres, the Indian they had brought, whom they allowed to come and go freely to his own people. On Sunday, 9 August, they landed,

and at the cross, 'we heard a sermon delyvred unto us by our preacher',[31] Rev. Richard Seymour, which was the first of many interminable ones to be listened to in New England.

The mouth of the Sagadahoc, or Kennebec, was difficult to enter, but once in, they were delighted with the terrain and its safety. They soon 'mad choies of a place for our plantation whch ys at the very mouth or entry of the Ryver of Sagadehocke on the West Syd of the Ryver being almoste an Illand of a good bygness'. Here at Sabino, everyone labored hard at the building of a fort. The plan of this, discovered in the Royal Archives of Spain (plate 313), shows some twenty-five buildings, houses and a church; quite a complete small community.[32] They explored up the river, finding, like Pring in 1606, 'a gallant Champion Lande and exceedinge fertill', with grapes of a 'mervellous deepe red'. They went up to modern Augusta, where 'ys a great downfall of wattr the wch runeth by both sydes of this illand very swyfte and shallow . . . wth a stronge rope made fast to our bott and on man in her to gyde her against the swyfte stream we pluckt her up throwe ytt pforce',[33] and went even farther inland. They explored Casco Bay.

Here the manuscript breaks off, but Strachey supplements briefly. The colonists sent the *Mary and John* back for supplies, and built a pinnace, the *Virginia*. What happened during that New England winter we do not know in detail, but it seems probable that 'the wynter proved . . . extreme unseasonable and frosty'[34] was a great understatement. In the spring Captain Davies returned in the *Mary and John*, bearing the sad news that Gilbert's brother had died, and he was needed at home. Davies found George Popham dead at Sabino, and although, as Strachey reports, 'all things' were 'in good forwardness' in the colony, no mines had been discovered, and the settlers, bereft of leaders and exhausted by the cold, were more than ready to return. This they did in the *Mary and John* and the *Virginia*, probably the first New England built ship to sail the Atlantic.[35] Thus with the abandonment of the Popham Colony, organized English settlement of 'the north part of Virginia' was postponed for some years.

In southern Virginia, the London Company had succeeded in establishing the first permanent English colony in America at Jamestown in 1607. Three ships under Captain Christopher Newport, 'a Marriner well practised',[36] sailed from London on 20 December 1606, and after a slow voyage by the West Indies reached Chesapeake Bay. One hundred and forty-four colonists, including four boys, were in this first group. They were a somewhat ill-assorted mixture of gentlemen, artisans, laborers, and two or three professional men, united chiefly in the desire to better their own fortunes.[37] George Percy, eighth son of the Earl of Northumberland and later President of the Council in Virginia, describes their landing: 'The six and twentieth day of Aprill [1607], about foure a clocke in the morning, wee descried the Land of Virginia: the same day wee entred into the Bay of Chesupioc directly, without any let or hindrance.'[38] After putting together a shallop from prepared lumber carried on one of the ships, they discovered Point Comfort at the mouth of the James River, and raised a cross near their landing place at Cape Henry. They then proceeded up the James, which, a little later, Percy described in these terms: 'This River which wee have discovered is one of the famousest Rivers that ever was found by any Christian, it ebbes and flowes a hundred and threescore miles where ships of great burthen may harbour in safetie. Wheresoever we landed upon this River, wee saw the goodliest Woods as Beech, Oke, Cedar, Cypresses, Wal-nuts, Sassafras and Vines in great abundance, which hang in great clusters on many Trees, and other Trees unknowne, and all the grounds bespred

Drawing of St George's Fort, Sagadahoc Colony, 1607. *Archivo General de Simancas.*

This fort at Sabino, an island just within the mouth of the Kennebec River in Maine, was built in the summer and fall of 1607 by a group of colonists under Captain George Popham and Captain Ralegh Gilbert. The plan shows a complete community, with numerous houses, a church, a 'kitchin generall', a running stream, defenses, and, outside the walls, the 'Garden place'. Here the colonists spent the winter of 1607–8, suffering greatly from extreme cold. The English made no further attempt to colonize 'the north part of Virginia' until the Plymouth Pilgrims arrived in 1620. Zuñiga, the Spanish ambassador in London, obtained this plan and sent it to Philip III in 1608; it was discovered in the Royal Archives of Simancas by J. L. M. Curry, United States Minister to Spain.

mouth of the James on a swampy, mosquito-infested, malarial peninsula, poorly protected from the Indians. By the year's end, half the settlers were dead from Indian attacks, starvation, and disease. The colonists were also instructed to search for a passage up the rivers to the 'East India Sea', to look for precious minerals and mines, and to seek for survivors of the Roanoke Colony. The search for the Roanoke survivors was half-hearted and unsuccessful. That for gold was too vigorously prosecuted. John Smith, who knew more important things needed doing, wrote contemptuously that there was 'no talke, no hope, nor worke, but dig gold, refine gold, load gold'.[41] The ore which they sent to England proved valueless. Captain Newport went up the James River to the

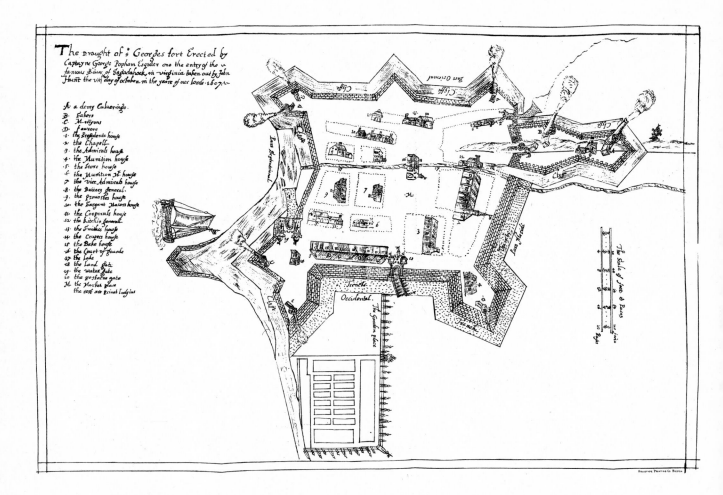

with many sweet and delicate flowres of divers colours and kindes. There are also many fruites as Strawberries, Mulberries, Rasberries and Fruits unknowne, there are many branches of this River, which runne flowing through the Woods with great plentie of fish of all kindes, as for Sturgeon all the World cannot be compared to it. In this country I have seene many great and large Medowes having excellent good pasture for any Cattle. There is also great store of Deere both Red and Fallow. There are Beares, Foxes, Otters, Bevers, Muskats, and wild beasts unknowne.'[39]

All was not easy for the colony, however. The 'Instructions' which they carried, signed with the royal seal, advised them to settle and fortify a place, 'a hundred miles from the River's mouth; neither must you plant in a low and moist place.'[40] These and other orders were only partly followed; Jamestown, whose site was selected at the insistence of the President of the Council, Wingfield, was little over thirty miles from the

314

Captain John Smith's map of Virginia, engraved by William Hole and published in *A map of Virginia*, Oxford, 1612.

Captain Smith's 'Virginia' is one of the important documents of early colonial history. It is the first map to depict with reasonable accuracy the Chesapeake Bay with its tributaries. In 1607 Smith examined the James River up to the present site of Richmond; during the summer of 1608 he explored the Bay to its head and marked on the map with crosses the distance of his ascent up the rivers that flow into it. He gave the location of nearly two hundred Indian settlements; this information has been of major ethnological value, and its accuracy and detail have been invaluable in archaeological research in the region.

William Hole, who engraved the map, used Smith's description in the text of *A Map of Virginia* to supplement Smith's manuscript chart. For the inset of Powhatan at top left, he turned to de Bry's engraving of John White's drawings. He skillfully combined the figure of Kiwasa, 'ther Idol' (plate 240) for the figure of Powhatan, with 'The Tombe of the Cherounes' (see plate 241) as a setting; for the large figure of the Susquehanna chief, he used the figure of an Indian in war paint (see plate 247). The reproduction of the map given here is of its first state.

Falls (present Richmond, Virginia) where he found only negative or ambiguous reports about the South Sea. He met Powhatan, emperor of the great Indian confederation that included present-day Tidewater Virginia and part of the Piedmont. Newport followed too conscientiously the instructions 'that all just, kind, and charitable courses shall be holden'[42] with the natives. The wily Powhatan maintained from the beginning an unrelenting policy, even when diplomatically concealed: kill the English when possible and drive the invaders from the land.

The dense and seemingly inexhaustible forest which came down to the very water's edge, except for tidal marshes, depressed the early settlers because it prevented easy planting of crops and because of their belief that it generated disease. Yet they also realized its potential value as timber for European trade and shipbuilding. John Smith wrote: 'All the country is overgrowne with trees. The wood that is most common is Oke and Walnut: many of their Okes are so tall and straight, that they will beare two foot and a half of good timber for 20 yards long . . . There is a kinde of wood we called Cypress . . . of those trees there are some neere 3 fadome [18 feet] about at the root, very straight, and 50, 60, or 80 foot without a branch.'[43] William Strachey, secretary of the colony, wrote about the same time that there were 'pynes infinite by the Sea-coast',[44] and that the *Starre*, a ship of 300 tons sent to Virginia especially equipped to transport pine masts, was unable to

handle forty of the eighty prepared pines without cutting them shorter.

The early reports abound in descriptions of the animals and fowl available for food. Most commonly found were wild turkey, '40. in a Company', quail, geese and ducks, squirrels and rabbits. Strachey wrote that, 'Bears there be towardes the Sea-coasts, which the Indians hunt most greedily, for indeed they love them above all other flesh'. Farther up the rivers deer was plentiful: 'our people have seene 200. 100. and 50. in a heard'. Animals new to the Europeans naturally interested them. 'A smaller beast they have,' Strachey commented, 'which the Indians call *Assapanick*, not passing so big as a Ratt, but we call them flying Squirrels, because spreading

315

315

Pocahontas saving the life of Captain John Smith, from T. de Bry, *America*, Part XIII, 1634, page 37.
316
An Indian chief from Johan de Laet, *Nieuwe Wereldt ofte beschrijvinghe van West-Indien*, Leyden, 1630.
A portrait of a Susquehanna Indian chief of huge size whom Captain John Smith met at the head of Chesapeake Bay in August of 1608. This figure is derived from an engraving in Smith's map of Virginia (plate 314).

their leggs from whence to either showlder runs a flappe or Fynne much like a Batts wing, and so stretching the largnes of their skyns, they have bene seene to make a pretty flight from one tree to another sometymes 30. or 40. yardes.

'An Oppusum is a beast as big as a pretty Beagle of grey cullor, yt hath a head like a swyne, eares, Feet, and Taile like a Ratt, she carryes her young ones under her belly in a piece of her owne Skynn, like as in a bagge, which she can open and shutt, to lett them out or take them in as she pleases, and doth therein lodge, carry, and succle her young, and eates in taste like a Pig.'[45]

The rivers and the bay teemed with life. 'In sommer,' wrote John Smith, 'no place affordeth more plenty of Sturgeon, nor in Winter more abundance of fowle, especially in time of frost.

There was once taken 52 Sturgeon at a draught, at another 68 . . . Young Sturgeon of 2 foot or a yard long. From thence [July] till the midst of September them of 2 or three yards and fewe others; in 4 or 5 hours with one nette were ordinarily taken 7 or 8. In small rivers all the year there is good plenty of small fish.'[46] The oyster beds rimmed the banks of the tidal rivers and proved later to be one of the easiest and most certain sources of food in time of scarcity. Shortly after reaching Virginia, Percy wrote that near Point Comfort, 'we got good store of Mussels and Oysters, which lay on the ground thick as stones: we opened some, and found in many of them Pearles'.[47]

Yet with all nature's plenty, starvation threatened the existence of the colony. The expectation that the Indians could and would supply them with 'corne and flesh', the old illusion that had so often proved disastrous to colonists in the sixteenth century, combined with the unwillingness of the gentlemen to do manual labor, afflicted the Jamestown settlers.[48] Lack of food, sickness, and Indian attacks left only 38 alive of the original 144 colonists when Captain Newport returned on 8 January 1608, with 120 reinforcements; in October he brought 70 more. In September of that year, Captain John Smith took over the control of the colony as President, ending a régime of inefficiency, shortsightedness, and bitter internal dissension under Wingfield and Ratcliffe. Smith's measures were stern and prompt: 'he that will not worke shall not eate'. Powell and Todkill, two of the settlers, wrote: 'Till this present, by the hazard and endeavor of some 30 or 40, this whole number had ever been fed. Wee had more Sturgeon then could be devoured by dogge and man. But such was the strange condition of some 150, that had they not beene forced nolens volens perforce to gather and prepare their victuall, they would all have starved, and have eaten one another.'[49] Under Smith's vigorous command, only seven or eight died while he remained in the colony, except for those drowned in a boating accident.[50]

Smith made contributions to the survival of the colony in other ways. He was quick to act and decisive in moments of danger. He believed strongly that the best defense was offense. When he found himself treacherously surrounded by several hundred Indians with thirty arrows drawn to the notch

316

against him, he seized the Indian chief Opecancanough, pressed a pistol to his chest, and ordered the Indians 'to cast downe their armes' and bring supplies of food for the settlers.[51] They did. Smith knew more about the nature of the Indians, how to meet their duplicity, and how to barter for food, than did any other early leader. He was a realist; he was quick to anger, real or simulated, but was just, and did not harbor malice or revenge.

During the summer of 1608, Smith made two exploratory voyages up Chesapeake Bay and recorded his discoveries in a map (1612) that gave Europeans the first good delineation of Tidewater Virginia (plate 314). It has been referred to as a 'canoe survey', but Smith's map is much better than such a name implies. Already he had furnished information for a rough sketch of the region, possibly aided by Robert Tindall, including the reported location of two groups of survivors from the Roanoke colony, a copy of which was made and sent to Spain by Zuñiga, the Spanish ambassador in London. After he had explored the Bay, he probably sent to his friend Henry Hudson a more finished map of the east coast from Virginia to New England. Barbour, the best biographer of Smith, suggests that he had acquired, before leaving for Virginia, some knowledge of surveying and mapmaking from Hudson.[52]

In 1609 Smith, injured by a gunpowder pouch explosion against his thigh, sailed for England, never to return to Virginia. The winter after he left was called 'the starving time'; of 490 persons, only 60 survived, 'most miserable and poore creatures . . . preserved for the most part, by roots, herbes, acornes, walnuts, berries, now and then a little fish'; toward the end they ate 'one another boyled and stewed with roots and herbs'.[53]

The arrival of Lord De La War in June 1610, with new settlers and support barely saved the colony from extinction. John Rolfe began to cultivate tobacco in 1612; within a few years this commodity became the chief export.[54] Bitter as were the attacks against the 'sotweed' from King James and many others, it proved to be the financial salvation of the colony. Rolfe's marriage to Pocahontas, Powhatan's beloved daughter, established a peace with the Indians which was seriously broken only by the Indian massacre of 1622 (plate 319), fomented by Powhatan's brother Opecancanough. The population of the colony, after the temporary reversal caused by the massacre, rapidly increased. In 1634 the first settlers for a new plantation, Lord Baltimore's Maryland, arrived and purchased land north of the Potomac River from the Indians. It was too late for the Indians to win back their land; it was too late for the Spanish to regret the attitude of Philip II years before, who refused the advice of his ministers to take action because he considered that 'the English were wasting money on a worthless region; he was well pleased to see them do so'.[55]

While the English in the Chesapeake area were establishing themselves solidly and securely, far to the north the French were making repeated efforts to settle the 'river of Canada', and even sending tentacles southward to the New England coast. In France, as in England, the early years of the seventeenth century saw conditions ripening for colonizing projects, with the end of the civil wars and the triumph of Henry of

317
Pocahontas taken captive, from T. de Bry, *America*, Part X, 1618, plate VII.
Captain Argall, who had sailed up the Potomac early in April 1613 to trade for corn, learned that Pocahontas was nearby. Although friendly to the English, she had not visited Jamestown since Captain John Smith's departure in 1609. Bribed by Argall, Iapassus and his wife persuaded Pochahontas to visit Argall's ship with them; in the scene depicted above, the three Indians are in the foreground. Argall then kept Pocahontas aboard and sailed back to Jamestown.
318
Two sons of Powhatan visit their sister, from T. de Bry, *America*, Part X, 1618, plate VIII.
Powhatan, informed that his daughter was hostage for the return of prisoners and goods, remained belligerent. Governor Dale with a hundred and fifty armed men sailed up the York River; the burning of the Indian village, shown in the preceding plate, took place then and not on the Potomac at the time of Pocahontas's abduction some months earlier.
A wary truce was arranged after two sons of Powhatan were allowed to visit their sister, whom they found well treated and unharmed. Permanent peace, except for the outbreak of 1622, came to the colony in 1614 with the marriage, approved by both Powhatan and Governor Dale, of Pocahontas and John Rolfe.

318

Indian massacre of the English at Jamestown, 22 March 1622, from
T. de Bry, *America*, Part XIII, 1634, opposite page 28.
320
'Nova Terrae-Mariae tabula', Lord Baltimore's map, 1635.
This, the first separate map of Maryland, is of historical importance
because of its delineation of the boundary lines between Maryland and her
neighbors, Pennsylvania and Virginia. The northern (Pennsylvania) line at
the 40th parallel and the dotted line along the southern bank of the
Potomac River were subjects of later boundary disputes.

Navarre and his adherents. Conflicts arose between powerful
merchant interests of St Malo, Honfleur, and other ports,
which were concerned primarily with increasing trade, and
military and naval supporters of the court, who were concerned
with territorial aggrandizement as well as with profit. These
conflicting forces coalesced in a joint effort when two former
naval captains turned merchants, Pierre de Chauvin de
Tonnetuit and his partner François Gravé du Pont, sailed from
Honfleur early in 1600 with four ships. They took as a
passenger Pierre du Gua de Monts, later to be the Governor
of Acadia (Nova Scotia). Against the protests of Gravé and
de Monts, who wanted wisely to go further up the St Lawrence,
Chauvin anchored at the mouth of the Saguenay River. There,
on the left bank, he built the first known trading post and
house in Canada at Tadoussac, where for fifty years Indians
had bartered skins with French crews.[56] 'The habitation of
Capt. Chauvin in 1600,' as Champlain described it later, 'was
twenty-five feet long by eighteen wide and eight feet high,
covered with boards with a fireplace in the middle.'[57] Of

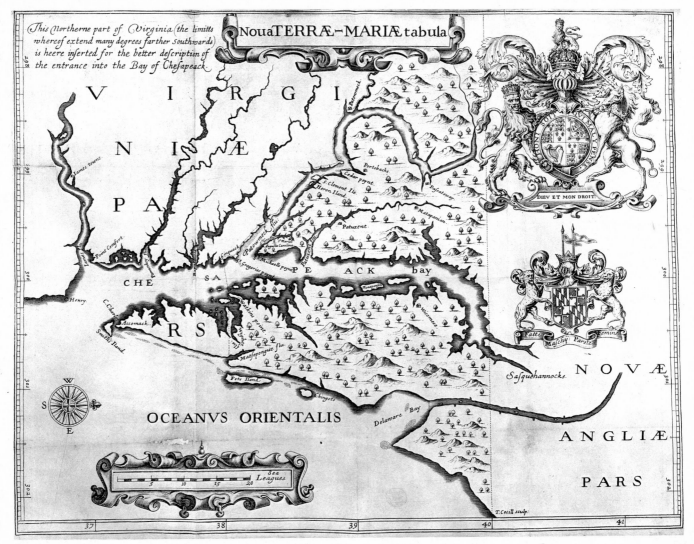

320

321

Port au Mouton, Nova Scotia, from Champlain's *Voyages,* Paris, 1632.
The French under de Monts reached the Acadian coast on 8 May 1604.
'Coasting and exploring the shore', wrote Lescarbot, 'they came to another very fine harbour which they called Port Mouton because a sheep which was drowned was brought back again and eaten as a fair prize. They built huts, as do the savages, while waiting news of the other ship. In this harbour they waited for a month.'

322

Île Sainte-Croix (Dochet Island, Maine), from Champlain's *Voyages,* Paris, 1632.
The French colony under de Monts spent the bitterly cold winters of 1604 and 1605 plagued by scurvy, at a settlement built on a small island at the mouth of the Sainte-Croix River off the Maine coast. The houses where, according to an accompanying legend, de Monts (A) lived and Champlain with two companions (P) lived were well built; but the engraver probably exaggerated the details of Champlain's sketch, since the buildings could not have been much more than log structures.

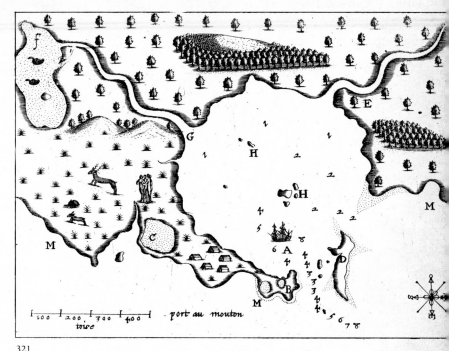

321

sixteen men Chauvin left there, only five survived the winter: 'if there is an ounce of cold forty leagues up the river, there will be a pound here.'[58] Chauvin's hopes and plans ended with his death early in 1603. A kaleidoscopic series of alliances and political controls which had begun in the sixteenth century continued for another generation; their complicated history profoundly influenced the schemes of colonization, but cannot be given here in detail.

Upon Chauvin's death the fur monopoly passed to a new alliance which included Gravé du Pont. He sailed in command of a ship to find a more suitable place for settlement than Tadoussac. On the ship as an observer was Samuel de Champlain, who had been to the West Indies but who was making his first voyage to the region where he achieved fame and where his abilities were to be brilliantly employed. When Gravé reached Tadoussac on 26 May 1603, Champlain began the explorations and the gathering of information from and about the Indians that were to enlarge so greatly for Europeans the knowledge of Canada. He ascended the Saguenay for twelve leagues; he learned from the natives of a salt-water sea to the north and inferred, seven years before Hudson reached the Bay, the existence of 'some gulf of this our sea, which overflows in the north into the midst of the continent'.[59] For years he was to seek a way there; he never succeeded. With Gravé he ascended the St Lawrence to the rapids beyond Hochelaga (Montreal) and learned from the Indians of great rapids ahead, including vague reports of Niagara Falls beyond a great freshwater lake. He also explored the Richelieu River south as far as the Saint-Ours Rapids, but on this trip did not reach the lake that bears his name.

Upon the return of Gravé's ship to France in September, Champlain reported his discoveries to the king and published in November *Des sauvages,* a brief account of what he had seen and learned. The following year de Monts, now a powerful member of the trading monopoly, sailed with three ships from Le Havre. Champlain, authorized by the king to act as geographer but still without an official position, had apparently convinced de Monts and others that Acadia would be a more suitable site for a colony than the St Lawrence.[60] They sighted Nova Scotia on 8 May 1604, and five days later landed in a small harbor named Port-au-Mouton. A few weeks later, in a small bark, de Monts and Champlain explored Baie Française (the Bay of Fundy) to its head, found a small subsidiary bay which Champlain named Port Royal (now Annapolis Royal, N.S.), and chose the Île Sainte-Croix (Dochet Island in the Ste Croix River) for their winter quarters.[61] While the colony was raising buildings, Champlain began an exploration along the coast of 'Norumbegue' or New England. At the mouth of the Penobscot River, he was impressed by Mount Desert:

322

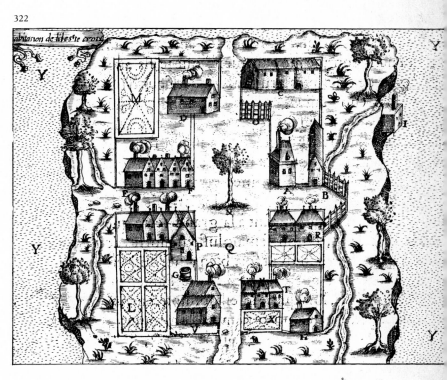

'an island about four or five leagues long, in the neighbourhood of which we just escaped being lost on a little rock on a level with the water, which made an opening in our barque near the keel. It is very high, notched in places, so that there is an appearance to one at sea, as of seven or eight mountains extending along near each other. The summit of most of them is destitute of trees, as there are only rocks on them. I named it Isle des Monts Déserts.'[62] The Penobscot River Champlain identified as the great river of Norumbega mentioned by 'several pilots and historians';[63] he sailed up it twenty-five

323

Mallebarre (Nauset Harbor), from Champlain's *Voyages*, Paris, 1632.
De Monts and Champlain left Sainte-Croix on 17 June 1605 in an
unsuccessful search for a place to settle. The southernmost harbor they
investigated was the present-day Nauset Harbor on the outer shore of Cape
Cod, which Champlain called Cap Blanc.

324

Port St Louis (Plymouth Bay, Massachusetts), from Champlain's *Voyages*,
Paris, 1632.
Champlain visited and drew this map of Plymouth Bay on 18 July 1605,
fifteen years before the Pilgrims landed there. He made a sketch hastily
from a single viewpoint (G on the map), the dunes at the north end of
Long Beach.

323

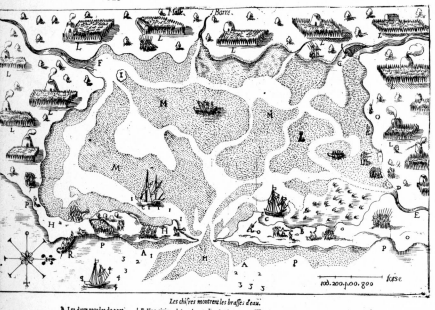

Les chiﬀres montrent les braﬀes d'eau.

A Les deux entrées du port.	E Vne riuiere deſcendant audit	I Iſle à la pointe des dunes	P La coſte de la mer.
B Dunes de ſable ou les ſauua-	port.	L Les mattons & habitatiōs des	Q La barque du ſieur de Poi-
ges tuerent vn Matelot de la	F Ruiſſeau.	ſauuages qui cultiuent la terre	trincourt quand il y fut deux
barque du ſieur de Mons.	G petite riuiere où on prend	M Baſſs & bancs de ſable tant	aus aprés le ſieur de Mons.
C les lieu où fut la barque du	cantité de poiſſon.	à l'entrée que dedãs ledit port.	R Deſſente des gens du ſieur de
ſieur de Mons audit port.	H Dunes de ſable où il y a vn	O Dunes de ſable.	Poitrincourt.
D Fontaine ſur le bort du port.	petit bois & force vignes.		

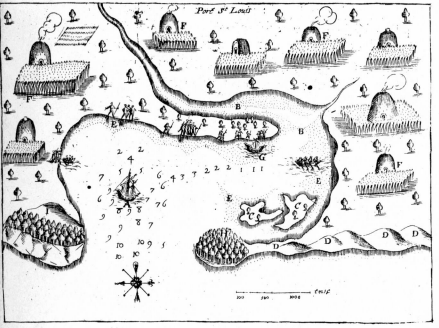

Port St Louis

324

leagues to the present site of Bangor. Descending the river he
made friends with two local Indian chiefs; then bad weather
forced him to return to Sainte Croix.

The winter began with snow in early October. By spring of
1605 thirty-five of the seventy-nine colonists had died of
scurvy; Champlain, with an exceptionally robust physique,
seems neither then nor later to have succumbed to the dread
affliction. In the summer of 1605 he again explored the coast
with de Monts, this time as far south as Nauset Harbor on the
outer shore of Cape Cod. He described Boston Harbor and
Charles River; off Plymouth Harbor, which he named Port
St Louis, 'there came to us two or three canoes, which had
just been fishing for cod and other fish, which are found there
in large numbers. These they catch with hooks made of a
piece of wood, to which they attach a bone in the shape of a
spear, and fasten it very securely. The whole has a fang-shape,
and the line attached to it is made out of the bark of a tree.
They gave me one of their hooks, which I took as a curiosity.'[64]
Champlain drew plans of Port de Cap St Louis and other places
visited; on this and later voyages along the New England and
Nova Scotia coasts, he gathered information for the maps
which show his exceptional skill as geographer and cartographer. Upon their return de Monts moved the colony to
Port Royal, where it remained for another two years. In 1607
de Monts sent word from France that his charter had been
revoked; the settlers returned to France.

Under Poitrincourt in 1610 Port Royal was again settled,
and the following year the Marquise de Guercheville, a
wealthy and devout Roman Catholic, gave generous financial

325

Map of Chesapeake Bay to Penobscot Bay by Adriaen Block, 1614.
The Hague, Algemeen Rijksarchief.
This is the first map to show as a separate island the land of the 'Manhates'
Indians. Adriaen Block, a Dutch fur trader who arrived in 1611, began a
coasting trip in the spring of 1614 on which he gathered information for his
map. He sailed in his ship *Onrust* (the first boat built on Manhattan Island)
'through Hellegat [East River] into the great bay [Long Island Sound] and
explored all the places thereabout'. The territories of the 'Mahicans',
'Pequats', and other Indian tribes, soon to be well known to colonial
settlers, are here shown; the 'Meer Vand Irocoisen' (Lake Champlain)
appears far east of the Connecticut River. Block Island was named after
Adriaen Block.

326 *Overleaf*

Map of the East Coast of North America (the 'Velasco' map), 1611.
Simancas, Archivo General de Simancas, Estado. Leg. 2588, fo 22.
This map was sent by Don Alonso de Velasco, the Spanish ambassador in
London, to King Philip II in 1611. It apparently accompanied a letter in
cipher dated March 22, 1611, in which Velasco writes that he is enclosing
a copy of a map made by a surveyor who was sent by James I to survey the
English province in America.

This large map ($31\frac{1}{2}$ x $43\frac{5}{8}$ inches), in color on four sheets, extends from
Cape Fear to Labrador; the unknown surveyor gathered his information
from many sources, some of it not elsewhere recorded. For the Ralegh colony
region he used John White's maps but has new names like Cape Kenrick
(Wimble Shoals), Port Grenvil, and Port Lane, which he may have obtained
orally from Harriot; other details he may have learned from expeditions
south from Jamestown, sent by Captain John Smith. Chesapeake Bay is
exceptionally detailed in its rivers and Indian names; W. Hole, the engraver
of Smith's map of Virginia (1612) may have had the original of this map
before him as well as Smith's draft. Hudson River, which connects with
Lake Ontario, is unnamed but has by it 'Manahata' and 'Manchotin', Indian
tribal names which appear here for the first time on a map. North of Cape
Charles the mapmaker apparently had the careful charts of Captain Argall
(1610), now lost, and for New England possibly also surveys by other
explorers like Pring and Gosnold. The map shows no knowledge of Long
Island and Long Island Sound. Nova Scotia, Newfoundland, and the
St Lawrence have both French and English names, and indicate detailed
knowledge of bays, rivers, capes, and islands. 'F. Sta. Croix' and 'Po Riall'
in the Bay of Fundy show that the English were well aware of current
French colonizing activities.

Virginia

Dewyck van chesapeack

NOVÆ FRANCIÆ PARS

Canada

De Groote Revier can

De Groote Riviere van niev Nederlandt

NIEDERLANDT

Het Maerlandt eilen

De Zuyder Zee

De Noord Zee

Staten bay

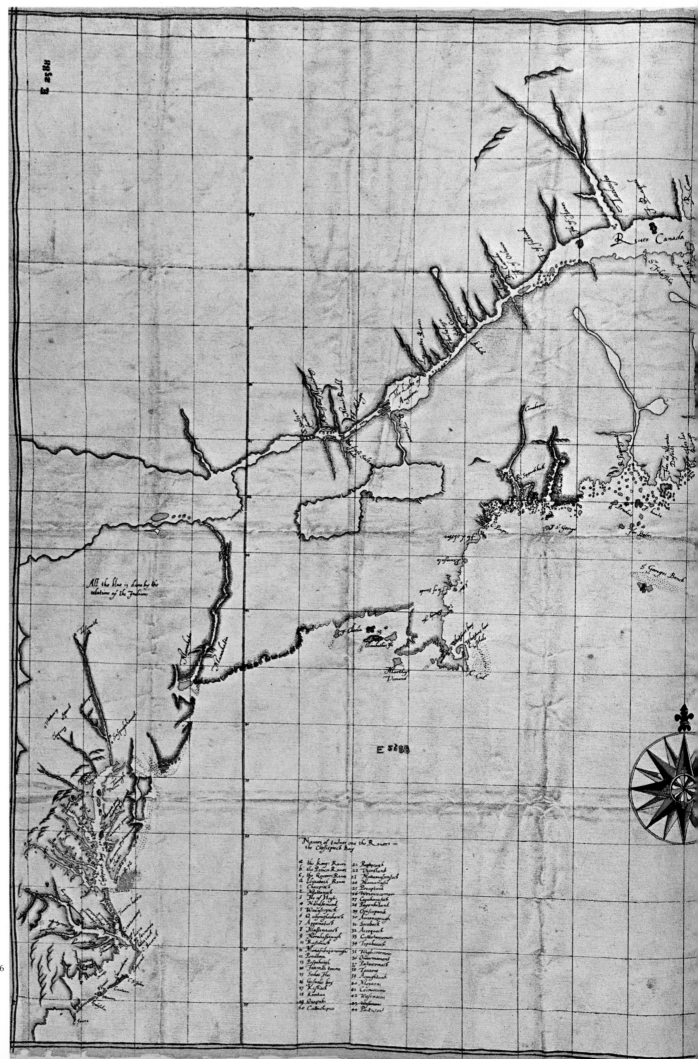

The Sea of China and the Indies.

Sir Francis Drake
was on this sea and landed
An⁹ 1577 in 37 deg: where hee tooke
Poſſeſſion in the name of Q:
Eliza: Calling it new Albion.

Scala Miliarum

A mapp of Virginia diſcouered to ye Hills, and
in its Latt: From 35. deg: & ¼ neer
Florida, to. 41. deg: bounds of new England.

327
'Ould Virginia, 1584, now Carolana, 1650, New Virginia, 1606, New
England, 1606', map by John Farrer, 1650. *New York Public Library*.
This roughly drawn manuscript map in water colors is inserted in John
Farrer's own copy of Edward Williams' *Virgo Triumphans: or, Virginia richly
and truly valued* (London, 1650); it is the original drawing for the printed
map by Farrer which appeared in the third edition of Williams's book
published in 1651 (see plate 328).
Williams in his 'To the Reader' acknowledged that 'The whole substance
of it . . . was communicated to me by . . . Mr. John Farrer of Geding in
Huntingdonshire'; in the margin of his copy of *Virgo Triumphans* Farrer
wrote 'But a map had binn very proper to this Book. For all men love to see
the country as well as to heare of it.' A comparison with the engraved map
shows the evolution from Farrer's first sketch to the elaborately augmented
and detailed engraving produced the following year.

328
Map of Virginia by John Farrar, 1651. *New York Public Library,
I. N. Phelps Stokes Collection, Addenda Map 9*.
John Farrer, official of the Virginia Company in England, shows in this
map a combination of recent knowledge about the coastal settlements and
misconceptions of the continent west of the Appalachian Mountains.
The Pacific Ocean, and Drake's New Albion, Farrer states, is only ten days'
march from 'the head of Jeames River'; many Englishmen, including the
colonists, still hoped to make Virginia an overland transportation point for
commerce between the Orient and Europe. To the north (right on the map)
Hudson River and the St Lawrence ('Canada flu:') join to form a waterway
to the 'Sea of China'; on this fourth state of the map, probably revised in
1652, is an isthmus, lacking in the earlier states, which has been drawn
across a 'great Lake'.
   Along the coastal plain fantasy gives way to informed details found on no
earlier map: the Swedish settlement on the Delaware is south of the Dutch
'Fort Orang' on the Hudson; county divisions and many place names in
Maryland and Virginia appear for the first time; and the placing on the map
of 'Carolana', Heath's undeveloped grant of 1629 from Charles I, indicates

awareness of an attempt to settle this territory around 1650. There are many
charming pictures of native animals, birds, and trees.
   Farrer's manuscript map in Williams's *Virgo Triumphans: or Virginia
richly and truly valued* (London, 1650), is reproduced opposite.

assistance to the enterprise and sent two Jesuit priests, Biard
and Massé, to convert the Indians. They later moved their
mission to Mount Desert Island. Unfortunately, the French
settlements were within the territory, from 34° to 45°N,
which James I had granted the Virginia Company in 1606,
ignoring the colony of de Monts already established in 1605
under his letters patent from Henry IV for the land between
40° and 46°. Jamestown had been sending fishing vessels
north each summer which furnished information concerning
the French settlements; Sir Samuel Argall, already experienced
in New England navigation by a northern voyage in 1610,
was despatched to expel the French from the Company's
territory. This he did in two voyages in 1613. He razed the
settlements and brought some of the colonists, including the
two Jesuits, back to Jamestown as prisoners. The Acadian
Peninsula, with the new name of Nova Scotia, James I in 1621
granted to the Scot Sir William Alexander under another
conflicting charter. For the next century and a half a tragic
struggle for ownership of the region was to continue.

allies with Champlain, it was an impressive victory over a
dreaded enemy. For Champlain and the French the decision
to make a trade and military alliance with the Hurons instead
of the Iroquois seemed wise; it was, however, a misfortune for
the colonists and ended in the extermination of the Huron
nation by the Iroquois. Neither Champlain nor the French,
of course, had had any desire to make the Iroquois their
enemies. The immediate result of Champlain's journey was to
add greatly to the geographical knowledge shown on his later
maps and to open a strategic route southward toward the great
river which Hudson sailed up only a month later.

For another ten years, Champlain continued to explore,
with indomitable energy and tireless curiosity, the land of
Canada to the north, south and west of the St Lawrence:
he canoed up the rivers and portaged the falls; he penetrated
the forests; he reached Lake Huron by the Ottawa River; and
he recorded his increasing knowledge in a series of maps that
culminated in the draft of 1632 (plate 357). He published a
series of accounts of his voyages, illustrated by his own vivid
and well-drawn pictures of Indian life and warfare (plates 333,
336/7, 355/6). In 1635 he died.

In 1610, Champlain had placed a young French lad,
Étienne Brulé, with the Indian chief Iroquet in order for him
to learn the Algonkian language, observe the rivers, and
explore the mines;[66] Brulé became the first of a new kind of
trader, the *coureur de bois,* who lived and traveled among the

335
Indians of Canada, from Johan de Laet, *L'histoire du Nouveau Monde,*
Leyden, 1640.
a) Huron Indian war equipment; b) Huron mother with her child.
These illustrations are taken directly from Champlain's drawings made after
visiting the Huron Indians.
336
Huron dancing ceremony to cure sickness, from Champlain, *Voyages et
descouvertures,* Paris, 1620.
The Ogui, or medicine man, when summoned by a member of the tribe who
is ill, gathers a large group of Indians, young and old. These take part in a
dancing ceremony in which the patient is urged to join, thus demonstrating
that he is cured.
337
Huron burial ceremonies from Champlain, *Voyages et descouvertures,*
Paris, 1620.
'They take the body of the deceased, wrap it in furs, cover it very neatly
with tree-bark, then lift it up on four posts on which they build a cabin
covered with tree-bark as long as the body. Others they put into the
ground . . . about eight or ten years (later) they take up all the bones of the
dead which they cleanse and make quite clean, saying that as their bones are
collected in one place they should be united in friendship and harmony.
They dig a great pit ten fathoms square, in which they place these said
bones.'—Champlain.

336

335a   335b

337

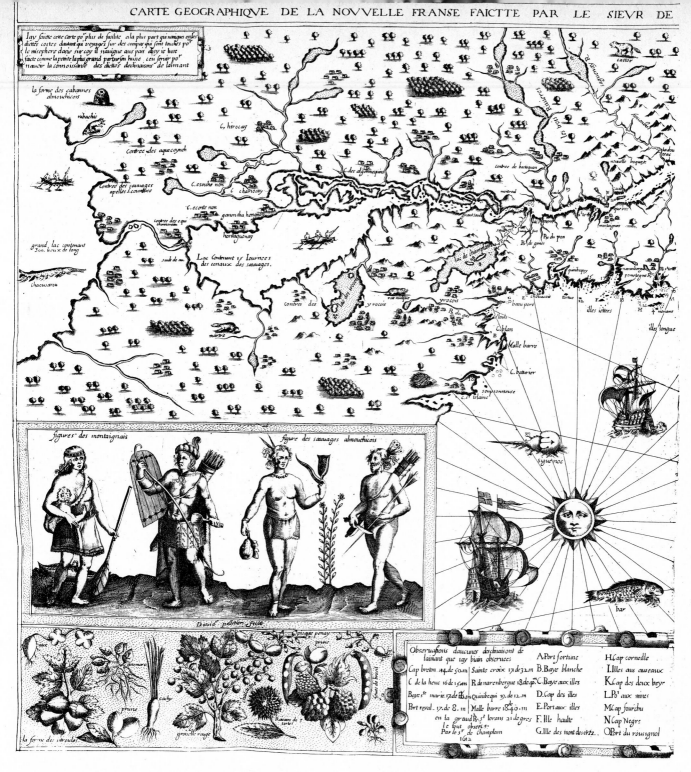

338
Map of New France by Champlain, in *Voyages*, Paris, 1612.
This section of a large map of New France was made by Champlain in 1612, 'for the satisfaction of sailors'. It shows the upper part of the Ottawa River newly discovered by him; a small Lake Ontario flows northward into Lake Huron, and the composition of the Great Lakes system is still unknown.

Of the two kinds of Indians pictured, the Montagnais, who were allies of the Algonkians against the Iroquois, lived on both sides of the Saguenay River; the Almouchiquas lived in Acadia. Champlain found the latter inland in present Maine when he made his voyage up the Kennebec River; he was impressed by their corn, vegetables, and their language, which was quite different from that of the St Lawrence Indians.

Champlain's drawing of the edible plants that interested him include three kinds of grapes, plums, chestnuts, Brazilian beans, pumpkins, and currants.

Indians and became a major intermediary in the fur trade. From Brulé and other *coureurs de bois* as well as their counterparts the English Indian traders and the Dutch *boschloopers*, European geographers as well as local settlers learned much about the vast interior of the continent. But even more was learned from the written records of the missionaries.

In 1625, three Jesuit priests, Massé, who had survived Argall's attack on Mont Désert, Charles Lalemont, and Jean de Brébeuf arrived in Quebec as missionaries to the Indians. They were followed by others of the Order, like Father Paul le Jeune who arrived in 1632. They lived among the Indians, and endured hardship, privation, torture, and, not infrequently, death in their efforts to 'save the unbaptized from eternal damnation'. 'The life of a Montagnais missionary,' wrote one of them, Father François de Crepieul, 'is a long and slow martyrdom, a truly penitential and humiliating life, especially in the cabins and on journeyings with the savages. The cabin is made of poles and birch-barks, and fir-branches are placed around it to cover the snow and the frozen ground. He eats from a dish that is very seldom clean or washed, and in most cases is wiped with a greasy piece of skin or is licked by the dogs.'[67] The Jesuit missionary made reports to his superior in Montreal or Quebec, who in turn edited them for

Carte geographique de la Nouuelle franse en fon uray meridien

GROENLANDIA

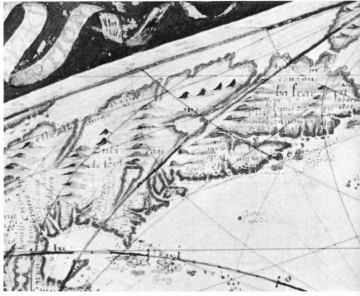

10 Maton-ouëscariny.	V Cap des deux bayes.	R Port au mouton.	11 Mantane.	4 Riuiere des Ethechemins.	9 Isle aux lieures.	C Isle percée.	N Port Royal.
∞ Ouëscariny.	H Baye Françoise.	S Port du roslignol.	A Tadoussac.	5 Saule.	E Islea aux gros yeux.	6 Lac sainct Pierre.	M Menane.
∞ Quenongebin.	P Isle Longue.	T Sesambre.	B Lesquemain.	3 Isle aux coudres.	D Baye de Chaleur.	7 Riuiere des Yroquois.	I Islesaux Oiseaux.
L Riuiere des Etechemins.	Q Cap fouschu.	SS Lac de medicis.	4 Saincte Croix.	10 Riuiere platte.	8 Galpay.	40 Cap saincte Marie.	Pour la page 161. X

160

an annual report to France. The accounts, usually written by perceptive and highly trained men, contain a great body of information about the frontiers of Canada. In France the reports were published annually for many years as *Relations des Jésuites*; that the authors could write under the circumstances with charity and often with humor is a tribute to their stamina and their character.

Between the struggling colony in Virginia and the coast of New England, already frequented by fishing fleets, lay a land still almost as unknown as when Verrazzano had sailed along it in 1521. On a September morning in 1609 the captain who stood on the deck of a flat-bottomed, two-masted vlie had lost one of the great gambles of his life. He had found that the magnificent river up which he had sailed was not the hoped-for strait to the Pacific Ocean. He had, nevertheless, made one of the important discoveries in the New World. The harbor where the ship lay anchored was deep and wide. On the west bank rose high palisaded cliffs; to the east was a heavily timbered shore, with scores of small creeks and rivulets running into the harbor. It was without a sign of human habitation, although on that island of Manhatta, three centuries later, would rise some of the tallest buildings in the world. Henry Hudson, an English navigator now in the service of the Dutch, who had an obsession for discovering a northern route to Cathay, had sailed on 11 September 1609 through the narrows between two headlands into this great bay, and continued up a wide, tidal body of water which he hoped was a strait leading to the South Sea on the other side of the continent.[68] He passed magnificent mountains rising several thousand feet from the water's edge; the forests on either side were of high timber, and the country was rich in beaver and other skins, as barter with the Indians they encountered showed. But the banks

339
Map of New France, from Champlain's *Voyages*, Paris, 1613. Champlain shows on this map his impressive achievements as explorer in the ten years since his first voyage to New France in 1603. Although by the end of 1612 he had not yet reached any of the Great Lakes, he had spent three years examining the coasts of Acadia and New England, had discovered and named Lake Champlain, and had gained a generally accurate conception of the St Lawrence River valley. He was always an intelligent and curious observer; *Les Voyages*, in which this map appeared, greatly increased his reputation in France.

340
Planisphere by Jehan Cossin, 1570. *Paris, Bibliothèque Nationale, No. 17784.* On this world map is shown for the first time an (unrecorded) exploration of the area about New York Harbor, shown in this detail.

grew closer and the water shallower; finally, anchored just below the present site of Albany, New York, he had sent the ship's boat to explore what was ahead. They reported that the shallowness increased; it was a river, and unnavigable. Hudson returned to the mouth of the river, and sailed eastward to Europe.

He had begun his voyage in the *Half Moon* with hopes of finding a north-*east* passage to Cathay. But the ice encountered after reaching Nova Zembla made his crew fearful and mutinous. They agreed, however, to sail westward. Hudson already had told Hondius and Plancius, Dutch geographers and mapmakers, that he was interested in exploring a western route; Emanuel van Meteren, a Dutch contemporary living in London, wrote: 'This idea had been suggested to him by some letters and maps which his friend Captain John Smith had sent him from Virginia, and by which he informed him that there was a sea leading into the western ocean, by the north of the southern English colony. Had this information been true (experience goes as yet to the contrary), it would have been of great advantage.'[69] After crossing the Atlantic in the *Half Moon,* Hudson had reached Newfoundland, where he turned south. Along the New England coast he landed several times, replacing a foremast that he had lost in a storm, catching many cod and lobsters, and trading warily with Indians who came aboard to barter beaver skins. By 24 August he reached the latitude of the Outer Banks of North Carolina, near Nag's Head; then without landing he turned back north, this time keeping close to the shore. He did not visit his friend Captain John Smith and the Jamestown settlement, although he may have entered Chesapeake Bay; perhaps he was wise, since he was in the employ of a foreign power. He did, however, note the entrance to the Delaware River, which the Dutch later called the South River and tried unsuccessfully to colonize. Hudson's exploration of the North River, soon called Hudson River, and his report that it was not a strait to the South Sea, may have been disappointing to his backers in the Netherlands. But the Dutch were interested in the fur trade and wanted to get a foothold before commercial rivals pre-empted the land. In a year or two their ships began to enter the harbor; in 1614 the States-General granted a three-year monopoly for trade to a company of merchants and named the region New Netherlands. They built a fort and trading house at 'Fort Nassau' on Castle Island near present Albany.[70] In 1613–4 Adriaen Block explored the southern New England coast and made a map which was sent to the States-General (see plate 325). On this basis the Dutch also laid claim to that region. Despite increasing protests from the English, they established trading posts; in June 1633 they bought land from the Pequot Indians on the Connecticut River where Hartford now stands and built a fort there.[71] The English at Plymouth in turn sailed farther up the river, and established a trading post to catch the Indians who were descending the river with their furs before they could reach the Dutch. By 1626 there was a Dutch fort and small settlement at the southern end of Manhattan Island; Peter Minuit, commissioned Director General by the Dutch West India Company, had arrived and made his famous purchase of the island from the Indians for the equivalent of twenty-four dollars in goods. New Amsterdam became a thriving center of trade and shipping.

Between the expulsion of the French and the coming of the Pilgrims, activity along the shores of 'the north part of Virginia' took the form of fishing, fur trading, and coastal exploration. A few hardy souls camped out from time to time, but there was no colony. Sir Ferdinando Gorges, who considered himself the chief promoter of the region, was inclined to be pessimistic about permanent settlement because of the

terrible cold. Relations with the Indians were given a set-back by the action of one Hunt, whom the Council for New England, which had superseded the Plymouth Company, described in its 'Relation' of those years as 'a worthlesse fellow of our Nation, set oute by certaine Merchants for love of gaine',[72] and who basely kidnapped twenty-four of the savages, carried them to Malaga, and sold as many as he could for slaves, until the friars rescued the rest. This dastardly act aroused enmity and suspicion among the Indians of New England which plagued the English for years; it also furnished them with a few Indian friends and trained interpreters, notably Squanto, one captured by Hunt who returned to help the Pilgrims. It ruined the exploratory expedition of Captain

341

342

341 and 342
The New Amsterdam fort on Manhattan Island from Joost Hartgers, *Beschrivinghe van Virginia, Nieuw Nederlandt, Nieuw Engelandt,* Amsterdam, 1651. *New York Public Library.*
'Nieu Amsterdam,' anonymous print, 1643.
Soon after the Dutch established themselves at the southern tip of Manhattan Island, *boschloopers* penetrated the wilderness for trade with the Indians, the padroons founded their estates up the Hudson River, and Indians came in their dugouts and canoes with food and fur in exchange for European goods. Peter Minuit, one of the directors of the Dutch West India Company, to whom the development, government, fortification, and trade of the New Netherlands had been granted by the States-General, arrived in 1626. He bought Manhattan Island from the Indians and founded New Amsterdam; his engineers soon constructed the fort there, which was destined to be the major bulwark of Dutch power in North America. Commerce and shipping flourished, with a rapid increase in population. The first print shows the fort and settlement as they appeared in the earliest years of the colony; in the second published in 1643, New Amsterdam is thriving on commerce and shipping, with a rapid increase in population.

Hobson in 1611, who found the natives so aroused that he had to return.

In 1614, however, the New England coast was explored, adequately mapped, and at last named, by that incurable optimist and colonial expert, Captain John Smith. The Company sent him out, with Captain Dermer, to 'lay the foundation of a new Plantation'.[73] He was instructed to hunt whales, look for traces of gold, and ship fish and fur. While his shipmates engaged in these activities, he explored the coast in an open boat, making his careful surveys. His *Description of New England* was published in 1616, with his famous map (plate 343), the names on which, some still in use, were given by Prince Charles, afterwards Charles I. Smith was

343

Smith's map of New England, 1616 [1614].

In April 1614 Captain John Smith reached New England, where '37 [men] did fish; myself with eight others ranging the coast, I took a plot of what I could see.' This 'plot' of the coast from Cape James [Cape Cod] to Penobscot Bay, of extraordinary correctness considering Smith's primitive equipment and stay of only six weeks, was published in 1616, with names given by young Prince Charles. Of these only three names survive in the location given on the map: Plimouth, Cape Anna, and the River Charles. The Pilgrims knew Smith's map, and retained the name when they settled at Plymouth in 1620.

a promoter with a large view of what 'Virginia', and indeed America, should be; his vision of this northern region was almost as dear to him as that of Jamestown, his creation as much as that of any man. New England was beginning to appear in terms other than a granite shore, dense forest, and ice cold: terms of timber and game, masts, furs and fish, whale oil and ambergris and pearl. At the end of the 'Relation', the Council expresses itself in 1622 as having 'dispatched some of our people of purpose, to dyve into the bowels of the Continent, there to search and finde out what Port, or Place, is most convenient to settle our mayne Plantation'.[74]

Although by 1620 the potentialities of New England were beginning to be more fully realized and the hazards to appear less insuperable, the latter were great enough to require a special combination to plant a permanent settlement there:

a determined group of strong people in great need of a home, and an adequate backing of organized commercial enterprise. This was found in a little group of separatists originating in the village of Scrooby, Nottinghamshire, and transplanted to the city of Leyden in Holland. These people were convinced that they were directly under God, whose will for them could be known by prayer and study of the Bible. What was all-important to them was not so much to convert others as to obey, themselves. Their duty was to come out, to separate, and to maintain their corporate life in obedient purity. Therefore they fled, first the coercions of the English bishops, and second the more insidious corruptions of the tolerant city of Leyden. They expected hardship in this world, believing all mankind to have deserved it, and were psychologically equipped to bear it patiently. They believed in the right of the individual to choose his leaders, but that God guided the choice, and, once chosen, leaders were to be obeyed and the unity of the group maintained. They had exceptionally strong leaders in Elder Brewster, William Bradford their often-elected Governor, Edward Winslow, Captain Miles Standish, and a handful of others. Although of the one hundred and one members of the *Mayflower*, only thirty-five were of the Leyden group, thanks to this leadership the colony neither fell apart, as so many had, nor deviated from its purpose. Also many of them were country people, used to the land, to farming, to simple living. They had in addition been trained in commerce and trade in Leyden. None of these factors, however, would have preserved them, or even gotten them to America, if it had not been for the body of entrepreneurs which was found to send and support them. It was a joint-stock arrangement, in which the planters, some of whom held stock also, were to pay the merchant adventurers for transportation and supply by their daily labor in sending back profitable cargoes. On board the *Mayflower*, the colonists drew up a solemn agreement, the Mayflower Compact, binding themselves to obey whatever laws their elected governor and his assistants should make.[75] It is often referred to as the first document in the history of American political democracy.

These, then, were the people who, in 1620, braved a stormy voyage in a small, over-crowded ship, and in November, as Bradford tells us, 'fell with that land which is called Cape Cod'. They tried to push south, having planned to reach Captain Hudson's great sheltered river, but 'fell among dangerous shoulds and roring breakers . . . and the wind shrinking upon them with all, they resolved to bear up again for the Cape'.[76] At first the calm of the great bay seemed wonderful, but when they had waded ashore through freezing water on the bleak sands of present Provincetown, they began to realize their perilous condition. Nevertheless, while their shallop was being put together, Captain Standish, with a few of the men, set out to explore inland for the best place to settle. Cape Cod was then 'compassed about to the verie sea with Oakes, Pines, Juniper, Sassafras, and other sweete Wood'.[77] They found it to be a neck of land composed of sandhills, with 'excellent black earth', 'a Spits depth' under the sand. They saw their first Indians, with a dog; these ran from them. They made a fire and spent the night out; 'marched thorow Boughes and Bushes, and under Hils and Vallies, which tore our verie Armour in peeces'; found at last springs and a freshwater lake, and 'sat us downe and drunke our first New England Water, with as much delight as ever we drunke drinke in our lives'. The most important find of all was a store of Indian corn of divers colors which they took back to be kept for seed, 'purposing so soone as we could meete with any of the Inhabitants of that place, to make them large satisfaction'. This corn doubtless saved lives the next summer.

Then began the explorations in the shallop. It was now December. 'It blowed and did snow all that day and night, and froze withall; some of our people that are dead took the originall of their death here.'[78] They found Indian graves with elaborate contents, and houses; deer, and a deer trap, in which Bradford was unexpectedly hoisted up; they fought their first battle with Indians attacking in the night. A baby was born aboard the *Mayflower*. Finally, in a storm, they anchored their shallop under the lee of some land, and in the morning found it to be an island. Plymouth Harbor opened out before them, 'a most hopeful place', with four or five brooks running into the sea, timber, herbs, fish, clay, and a high hill for a fort. On 23 December they started to build, and on Christmas Day drank on the *Mayflower* the last of their English beer.

The story of the first years of the Pilgrims at Plymouth is that of a small band of frontiersmen exploring and wrestling with a most intransigent land. The primary sources of our knowledge are the writings of Bradford and Winslow. They tell of the dividing of land, planting and building. Illness caused by poor food, cold, and exhaustion took a terrible toll the first winter; over half of them died, including Carver, the first Governor. The Indians greeted them with arrows tipped with brass and eagle's claws.[79] They were Nausets and Massasoits; the Nausets were especially hostile because Hunt had carried out his kidnapping in this very region, Patuxet. They had also been recently decimated by a terrible plague. At last, on 16 March, 'there presented himself a savage, . . . very boldly . . . all alone',[80] who spoke to them in English. This was Samoset, from Monhegan in Maine, friend of English fishermen. He gave them much information, and soon brought to them Squanto, or Tisquantum, a Patuxet native who had escaped from Hunt in London. Squanto became their invaluable companion and interpreter; probably the most important thing he taught them was to plant their corn with a dead fish in every hill, which assured a good yield.[81] Finally, he brought King Massasoit himself, 'a very lusty man, in his best yeares, an able body, grave of countenance, and spare of speech'.[82] With him they concluded a treaty of peace which was kept unbroken for fifty years, the Pilgrims dealing justly with the Indians, and often helpfully. Guided by Squanto, Winslow and Hopkins went to visit Massasoit, taking him a red horseman's coat; there 'he laid us on the bed with himself and his wife, they at the one end and wee at the other'; but sleep was scarce, because 'they use to sing themselves asleepe'.[83] They improved their terms with the Nausets, and explored their high land on the other side of the Cape, seeking a boy who had wandered off, and whom they found 'behung with beades'.[84]

Slowly, the Plymouth colony climbed away from its beginnings to a better life. In November 1621, the *Fortune* brought them thirty-five new people.[85] By May 1630, they numbered three hundred. They moved away from collective farming to individual ownership, and the yield bettered. Still, there were desperate times. Once Winslow was sent to Monhegan in Maine to beg food from the fishermen, which was generously granted. The Narragansett Indians sent a snake-skin challenge; the settlers built and equipped a fort on their hill, but real war was avoided. In spite of all these difficulties, the Plymouth colonists managed in 1627 to dissolve their partnership with the merchant adventurers in London, and in 1628 to pay off their debt to them. After that, they were a phenomenon in America: as Jernigan says, 'a free and independent political and economic unit'.[86] Nor had they modified their religious position. They set up trading stations on the Kennebec in Maine, at Manomet across Cape Cod for trade with the Dutch and Indians (the Dutch introduced them to the value

344

344

English sporting life in the New World, from T. de Bry, *America,* Part X, 1618, plate XI.
English knights in Virginia are hunting and fishing in this imaginary scene, which de Bry based upon the narratives which he published.
345

Englishmen giving Indians beads and knives, from T. de Bry, *America,* Part XIII, 1634, page 7.

of 'wampum' or 'sewan', made of shells and much prized by the Indians); and, far inland, on the Connecticut River at present Windsor. Except for evil doers, like the notorious Thomas Morton of Merrie Mounte, who even erected a may-pole, they got on well with their increasing neighbors. On this beginning New England was founded.

With the exception of this small foothold on Cape Cod, the land of New England lay almost empty of settlers for another decade after 1620. The great forests and rivers of Maine stretched away inland undisturbed by the white man; the clear lakes and high white and green mountains of New Hampshire and Vermont lay undiscovered; in Massachusetts, only a few hardy mavericks began to have homes around

346

Boston Harbor, and not even the Charles River had been followed to the pleasant inland country. The Dutch and the Pilgrims had looked into Narragansett Bay, but no one lived in interior Rhode Island; and the Connecticut River, with its broad and fertile valley, was only just beginning to attract attention as an area for trade. The Plymouth Company for Northern Virginia had given way to the Council for New England, incorporated in 1620; their charter was the founda-tion of many later grants. In 1635, the Council surrendered its patent to the King; Sir Ferdinando Gorges was given a royal charter to the Province of Maine.[87]

It was from a small fishing settlement on Cape Ann, the northern tip of the great bay of which Cape Cod is the southern,

that the next important colony, after that at Plymouth, took root. This small group, sponsored by the Dorchester Fishing Company, moved along the bay to Naumkeag, later the sea-faring port of Salem. A patent was issued to them by the Council, from three miles north of the Merrimac River to three miles south of the Charles, and William Endicott was sent out with power to govern.[88] What a poor, rough little pioneer settlement it was can be seen from its reconstruction in modern Salem: a few hovels, and even dugouts, clinging to the narrow, rocky strip between stormy sea and dark forest. Even as late as 1630, when several hundred had come, Winthrop refers to people's 'tents' and writes, 'Finch, of Watertown, had his *wigwam* burnt and all his goods'.[89]

Now events in Old England made the time ripe for a much larger migration. Economic distress, political unrest, and especially the rise of the Puritans, who wanted to reform the Church of England and could not, made people anxious to leave and ready to venture. Under the new Massachusetts Bay Company, a body of persons undertook the settlement. They were mostly Puritans, including some men of noble birth like Isaac Johnson and his wife the Lady Arbella, and some of substantial county families like John Winthrop, repeatedly re-elected Governor. A number of the merchant adventurers themselves emigrated with the colony, which became in effect a self-governing commonwealth, theocratic in nature, demo-cratic in political practice. Twenty thousand people came to the shores of Massachusetts Bay within ten years, fanning out into numerous towns.

When the small ship *Arbella* landed at Naumkeag, or Salem, on 11 June 1630,[90] however, with the first group, this was far ahead. Several vessels were in the little fleet. The settlers in Salem were living miserably, and weakened by privation and disease. Winthrop, a tower of strength, was everywhere around the Bay and up the Maine coast, trading for corn, arranging shelter. He placed the center of his new settlement on the peninsula of Shawmut, renamed Boston, with its narrow neck and defensible position. Nevertheless, he could not prevent the first winter being hard. Many died, including the Johnsons. Wolves came into the towns and stole calves.[91] The forest, with all its hazards, was terribly close. 'The Governor, being at his farmhouse at Mistick, walked out after supper, and took a piece in his hand, supposing he might see a wolf . . . and being about half a mile off, it grew suddenly dark, so as, in coming home, he missed his path.'[92] Totally lost, he stumbled along to a little Indian hut. '(He always carried about him match and a compass, and in summer time snake-weed,) he made a good fire . . . and so spent the night . . . sometimes singing psalms.' His servants had 'shot off pieces, and hallooed in the night, but he heard them not'. The Massachusetts colonists braved the forests, and explored inland. By 1635, there were twelve settlements.

The other New England colonies were, in differing ways, born from Massachusetts Bay. While Gorges continued to be proprietor of Maine and one Mason held a royal patent for New Hampshire, both were regions of individual settlers, hunters and fishers until taken over by Massachusetts. Rhode Island owed its beginnings to the theological intransigence of Massachusetts Congregationalism, which banished Roger Williams, Anne Hutchinson and others for their heretical ideas to the wilds around Narragansett Bay. Connecticut owed its existence to the desire of the frontiersman to leave settle-ments and push into the wilderness, this time westward by a famous Indian trading path across central Massachusetts; and also to rivalry with the Indian trade begun up the Connecticut River by the Dutch and by Plymouth. Massa-chusetts men ousted them both, and founded another Bible commonwealth at New Haven, on land bought from the Indians. England, living through her civil war, interfered with these colonies very little in the middle of the century. They fought their way to an easier life through Indian wars and continual combat with a vast wilderness; by the time England was ready to attempt an imperialistic control, the habit of self-government in New England was too strong to be shaken. It had been formed by a new land.

By the 1630s, a thin circle of settlement clung to the eastern shoreline from the St Lawrence to Florida; a small finger of exploration had entered the continent up the Rio Grande, leaving an outpost; and sailors had made landings along the Pacific Coast and far to the northeast on Hudson Bay. Yet, although the French had sent their *coureurs de bois* and missionaries as far west as Lake Superior, the discovery of the Mississippi Basin and the Great Plains lay still before them; the Virginian English had not yet reached the Blue Ridge Mountains, nor had the Spanish climbed the Rockies. The vast interior of the continent lay virtually unknown.

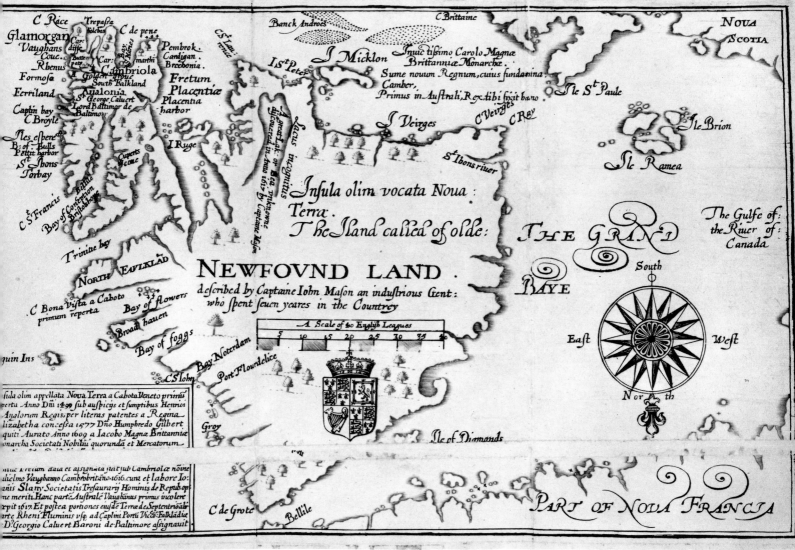

347

346
Edward Winslow, 1651. *Plymouth, Pilgrim Hall Museum.*
347
Map of Newfoundland by John Mason in W. Vaughan, *Cambrensium Caroleia*, London, 1625.
In this, the first map of Newfoundland by an Englishman, the north is at the bottom of the map. Mason, an able and honest administrator, was appointed Governor of the English settlement on Newfoundland in 1616, and explored the island from his base at Cupid's Cove (Cuperts Cove on the map).
He returned to England in the spring of 1621 and contributed a map and comments on Newfoundland to Vaughan's *Cambrensium Caroleia*. Later, in 1631, Mason founded the colony of New Hampshire with a settlement on the Piscataqua River.

1.

The first English account of New England

From John Brereton's *A briefe and true relation of the discoverie of the north part of Virginia*. London: George Bishop, 1602.

John Brereton was a member of the company of Captains Gosnold and Gilbert, who made the first brief settlement in New England in 1602 on Cuttyhunk Island off Cape Cod. He wrote an unusually charming account, the first description of New England by an Englishman. The likelihood that Shakespeare had this island in mind when he wrote *The Tempest* is enhanced by this quotation:

Ceres, most bounteous lady, thy rich leas
Of wheat, rye, barley, vetches, oats, and pease . . .

(Act IV, Sc. 1, 11. 60-1)

Some of the words of this are found in the extract from Brereton's *Relation* below.

In mid May we did sowe in this Island (as for triall) in sundry places, Wheat, Barley, Oats, and Pease, which in fourteene daies were sprung up nine inches and more: the soile is fat and lustie; the upper crust, of gray colour; but a foot or lesse in depth, of the colour of our hempe-lands in England; and being thus apt for these and the like graines; the sowing or setting (after the ground is cleansed) is no greater labour, than if you should set or sowe in one of our best prepared gardens in England. This Island is full of high timbered Oaks, their leaves thrise so broad as ours; Cedars, strait and tall; Beech, Elme, Hollie, Walnut trees in abundance, the fruit as bigge as ours, as appeared by those we found under the trees, which had lien all the yeere ungathered; Haslenut trees, Cherry trees, the leafe, barke and bignesse not differing from ours in England, but the stalke beareth the blossomes or fruit at the end thereof, like a cluster of Grapes, forty or fifty in a bunch; Sassafras trees plentie all the Island over, a tree of high price and profit; also divers other fruit trees, some of them with strange barks, of an Orange colour, in feeling soft and smoothe like Velvet: in the thickest parts of the woods, you may see a furlong or more round about. On the North-west side of this Island, neere to the sea side, is a standing Lake of fresh water, almost three English miles in compasse, in the middest whereof stands a plot of woodie ground, an acre in quantitie or not above: This Lake is full of small Tortoises, and exceedingly frequented with all sorts of fowles before rehearsed, which breed, some lowe on the banks, and others on lowe trees about this Lake in great abundance, whose young ones of all sorts we tooke and eat at our pleasure: but all these fowles are much bigger than ours in England. Also, in every Island, and almost in every part of every Island, are great store of Ground nuts, fortie together on a string, some of them as bigge as hennes egges; they grow not two inches under ground: the which nuts we found to be as good as Potatoes. Also, divers sorts of shell-fish, as Scallops, Muscles, Cockles, Lobsters, Crabs, Oisters, and Whilks, exceeding good and very great. But not to cloy you with particular rehearsall of such things as God and Nature hath bestowed on these places, in comparison whereof, the most fertil part of al England is (of it selfe) but barren; we went in our light-horsman fro this Island to the maine, right against this Island some two leagues off, where comming ashore, we stood a while like men ravished at the beautie and delicacie of this sweet soile; for besides divers cleere Lakes of fresh water (whereof we saw no

end) Medowes very large and full of greene grasse; even the most woody places (I speake onely of such as I saw) doe grow so distinct and apart, one tree from another, upon greene grassie ground, somewhat higher than the Plaines, as if Nature would shew herselfe above her power, artificiall. Hard by, we espied seven Indians; and comming up to them, at first they expressed some feare; but being emboldned by our courteous usage, and some trifles which we gave them, they followed us to a necke of land, which we imagined had beene severed from the maine; but finding it otherwise, we perceived a broad harbour or rivers mouth, which ranne up into the maine: but because the day was farre spent, we were forced to returne to the Island from whence we came, leaving the discoverie of this harbour, for a time of better leasure: of the goodnesse of which harbour, as also of many others thereabouts, there is small doubt, considering that all the Islands, as also the maine (where we were) is all rockie grounds and broken lands. Now the next day, we determined to fortifie our selves in the little plot of ground in the midst of the Lake above mentioned, where we built an house, and covered it with sedge, which grew about this lake in great abundance; in building whereof, we spent three weeks and more.

Text used: John Brereton, A briefe and true relation . . . of the North part of Virginia, *with an introductory note by Luther S. Livingston. New York: Dodd, Mead & Co., 1903. Facsimile of first edition of 1602.*

2.

Captain John Smith's exploration of Chesapeake Bay, 1608

From John Smith's *A Map of Virginia,* 1612. The narrative of the first voyages, from which the following extracts are taken, was written by Walter Russell and Anas Todkill.

Smith made two voyages of discovery up the Chesapeake Bay in 1608. On the first expedition he left Jamestown on 2 June with fourteen others in an open barge of less than three tons' burden. After crossing the Bay to Cape Charles, they explored as far north as Patapsco River, above the Potomac. On their return they went up the Potomac River past the present site of Washington, D.C. They entered numerous other rivers and inlets. In spite of initial hostility and showers of arrows from the Indians, Smith usually ended by establishing friendly relations with them and reached Jamestown without loss of a man of his company.

Leaving the Phenix at Cape-Henry we crossed the bay to the Easterne shore & fell with the Iles called Smiths Iles the first people we saw were 2. grimme and stout Salvages upon Cape-Charles with long poles like Javelings, headed with bone, they boldly demanded what we were, and what we would, but after many circumstances, they in time seemed very kinde, and directed us to Acawmacke the habitation of the Werowans where we were kindly intreated; this king was the comliest proper civill Salvage wee incountred.

Passing along the coast, searching every inlet, and bay fit for harbours & habitations seeing many Iles in the midst of the bay, we bore up for them, but ere wee could attaine them, such an extreme gust of wind, raine, thunder, and lightning happened, that with great daunger we escaped the unmercifull raging of that ocean-like water.

Finding this easterne shore shallow broken Iles, & the maine for most part without fresh water, we passed by the straights of Limbo for the weasterne shore. So broad is the bay here, that we could scarse perceive the great high Cliffes on the other side; by them wee ancored that night, and called them Richards Cliffes. 30 leagues we sailed more Northwards, not finding any inhabitants, yet the coast well watred, the mountaines very barren, the vallies very fertil, but the woods extreame thicke, full of Woolves, Beares, Deare, and other wild beasts.

348
Map of Virginia by John Smith, *The generall historie of Virginia*, London, 1624.
Episodes in Captain John Smith's *Generall historie of Virginia* are here portrayed by his friend, the engraver Robert Vaughan. [inset, top left] Captain John Smith is captured and bound by the Indians in 1607. [top right] Captain John Smith foils an ambush by seizing the werowance Opecancanough, brother of Powhatan. [bottom left] Captain John Smith defeats the king of Paspehegh in single combat, 1609. [bottom right] Captain John Smith, condemned to death by Powhatan, is saved by Pocahontas. [bottom center] Ould Virginia: Captain John Smith's map of the region south of the Chesapeake is an adaptation of White's map of Virginia engraved by de Bry in 1590 (plate 197). Smith's map, with its liberal use of the names of his family, friends and patrons for often imaginary physical features of the region, was not followed by subsequent mapmakers.

The 16 of June we fel with the river of Patawomeck [Potomac]: feare being gone, and our men recovered, wee were all contented to take some paines to knowe the name of this 9 mile broad river, we could see no inhabitants for 30 myles saile; then we were conducted by 2 Salvages up a little bayed creeke toward Onawmament where all the woods were laid with Ambuscadoes to the number of 3 or 400 Salvages, but so strangely painted, grimed, and disguised, showting, yelling, and crying, as we rather supposed them so many divels, they made many bravadoes, but to appease their furie, our Captaine prepared with a seeming willingnesse (as they) to encounter them, the grazing of the bullets upon the river, with the ecco

281

of the woods so amazed them, as down went their bowes & arrowes; (and exchanging hostage) James Watkins was sent 6 myles up the woods to their kings habitation: wee were kindly used by these Salvages, of whome we understood, they were commaunded to betray us, by Powhatans direction.

Some Otters, Beavers, Martins, Luswarts [lynx], and sables we found, and in diverse places that abundance of fish lying so thicke with their heads above the water, as for want of nets (our barge driving amongst them) we attempted to catch them with a frying pan, but we found it a bad instrument to catch fish with. Neither better fish more plenty or variety had any of us ever seene, in any place swimming in the water, then in the bay of Chesapeack, but there not to be caught with frying pans. [In this amusing episode Todkill may be poking fun at two members of the company, Keale, a fishmonger, and Profit, a fisherman.]

Having finished this discovery (though our victuall was neare spent) he intended to have seene his imprisonments acquaintance upon the river of Toppahannock [Rappahanock, where the Indians had taken Captain Smith]. But our boate (by reason of the ebbe) chansing to ground upon a many shoules lying in the entrance, we spied many fishes lurking amongst the weedes on the sands, our captaine sporting him-selfe to catch them by nailing them to the ground with his sword, set us all a fishing in that manner, by this devise, we tooke more in an houre then we all could eat; but it chanced, the captaine taking a fish from his sword (not knowing her condition) being much of the fashion of a Thornebacke with a longer taile, whereon is a most poysoned sting of 2. or 3 inches long, which shee strooke an inch and halfe into the wrist of his arme the which in 4. houres had so extreamly

swolne his hand, arme, shoulder, and part of his body, as we al with much sorrow concluded his funerall, and prepared his grave in an Ile hard by (as himselfe appointed) which then wee called stingeray Ile after the name of the fish. Yet by the helpe of a precious oile Doctour Russel applyed ere night his tormenting paine was so wel asswaged that he eate the fish to his supper, which gave no less joy and content to us, then ease to himselfe. Having neither Surgeon nor surgerie but that preservative oile, we presently set saile for James Towne.

Text used: Philip L. Barbour, ed., The Jamestown voyages under the first charter 1606–1609. Cambridge: Hakluyt Society, Ser. III, No. CXXXVII, 1969, II, pp. 400-5, passim.

3.
The Emperor Powhatan

From the Princeton University manuscript of William Strachey's *The historie of travell into Virginia Britania (1612).*

William Strachey accompanied Governor Sir Thomas Gates to Virginia in a vessel wrecked on the Bermudas. Almost a year later, in May 1610, they reached Jamestown. Strachey, secretary of the colony, collected material for his *Historie* during his stay; he returned to England in the fall of 1611. He did not complete his work until 1612 or later, for in it he used passages from Smith's *Map of Virginia,* published in that year. His criticisms of the government and conditions in the colony evidently made it unacceptable to the Virginia Company in London for publication. Strachey's observations on the country and on the Indians are valuable

The great Emperour at this tyme amongst them we Commonly call Powhatan for by that name true yt is, he was made known unto us, when we arryved in the Country first, and so indeed he was generally called when he was a young man, as taking his denomynacion from the Country Powhatan, wherein he was borne, which is above at the Falls as before mencioned, right over aneinst the Islands, at the head of our river.

The greatnes and bowndes of whose Empire by reason of his Powerfulnes, and ambition in his youth, hath lardger lymittes then ever had any of his Predicessors in former tymes: for he seemes to comaund South and North from the Mangoags, and Chawonookes, bordering upon Roanoak or South-Virginia, to Tockwogh, a towne pallisado'de, standing at the North-end of our Bay in 40. degrees or thereaboutes: South-west to Anoeg (not expressed in the Mappe) whose howses are buylt as ours, 10. dayes journye distant from us, from whence those inhabiting Weroances sent unto him of their Commodityes.

He is a goodly old-man, not yet shrincking, though well beaten with many cold and stormy wynters, in which he hath bene patient of many necessityes and attempts of his fortune, to make his name and famely great, he is supposed to be little lesse than 80. yeares old, (I dare not say how much more, others say he is). Of a tall stature, and cleane lymbes, of a sad aspect, rownd fat visag'd with gray haires, but playne and thyn hanging upon his broad showlders, some few haires upon his Chynne, and so on his upper lippe. He hath bene a strong and able salvadge, synowie, active, and of a daring spiritt, vigilant, ambitious, subtile to enlarge his dominions, for but the Countryes Powhatan, Arrohateck, Appamatuck, Pamunky, Youghtamond, and Mattapanient which are said to come unto him by Inheritaunce, all the rest of the Territoryes

349
Ralph Hamor visits Powhatan, from T. de Bry, *America,* Part X, 1618, plate X.
In 1614 Thomas Dale, the Governor of Virginia, sent his secretary, Ralph Hamor, to ask Powhatan to give Dale his favorite daughter in marriage. Hamor is here arriving on his mission. Powhatan refused but accepted the Governor's assurance of peace and friendship.

350

Captain Samuel Argall concludes a treaty with the Chickahominies, who accept James I as their King; from T. de Bry, *America,* Part X, 1618, plate IX. Sir Thomas Dale visited the Chickahominy Indians in the spring of 1614 after they made overtures of peace. Captain Argall went ashore with forty men to arrange the articles of peace, in a great assembly, here depicted in de Bry's engraving. The Indians, who wished to be protected against Powhatan's tyranny, agreed to become 'new Englishmen with a generall assent, and a great shout to confirme it'.

351

Map of Virginia by Ralph Hall, 1636.

Hall's 'Virginia', with its charming details of deer, wild boars, panther, hunting scenes, and Indian vignettes from de Bry's engravings of White's paintings, was made for the second edition of Wye Saltonstall's English translation of Mercator's *Atlas,* London, 1637. A note in the first edition of the *Atlas* (1635) promises that 'a more exact map drawing in that country whose platforme is not yet come over' is to be used for a new map; Hall apparently used this 'platforme' in indicating on his map the location of new settlements and plantations in the colony. The map otherwise provides no new geographical information of importance, however, and Chesapeake Bay is a distortion of its representation on William Hole's 'Virginia' (1612, plate 314), and Hondius' 'Nova Virginia' (*c.* 1630), on which the map is chiefly based. One addition to the place names, an eponymous 'Hall poynt' at the mouth of the Rappahanock River, is found on no other map.

before named and expressed in the Mappe, and which are all adjoyning to that River, whereon we are seated, they report (as is likewise before mencioned) to have bene either by force subdued unto him, or through feare yeilded: Cruell he hath bene, and quarrellous, as well with his owne Weroances for triffles, and that to stryke a terrour and awe into them of his power and condicion, as also with his neighbours in his younger dayes, though now delighted in security, and pleasure, and therefore standes upon reasonable condicions of peace,

350

351

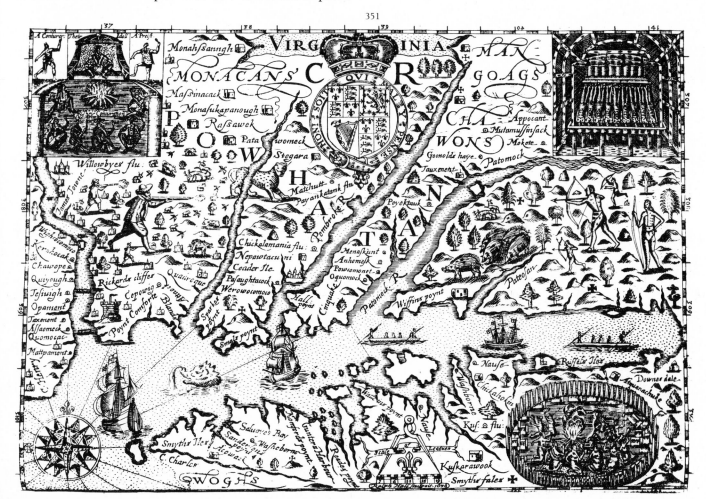

with all the great and absolute Weroances about him, and is likewise more quietly setteled amongst his owne. Watchful he is over us, and keeps good espiall upon our proceedings, Concerning which he hath his Sentinells, that at what tyme soever any of our boates, pinaces or shippes, come in, fall downe, or make up the River, give the Alarum.

Text used: Louis B. Wright and Virginia Freund, ed., The historie of travell into Virginia Britania (1612). London: Hakluyt Society, Ser. II, No. CIII, 1958, pp. 56-8.

352

352
The first printed illustration of Niagara Falls, from Louis Hennepin, *A new discovery of a large country in America,* London, 1698.
Although Champlain heard Indian reports of Niagara Falls in 1603, and Lalemont and others saw and described them in the 1640s, the first picture of them was published in a book by the Recollet Father, Louis Hennepin, in Utrecht in 1697. The engraving reproduced here is taken from the English translation of his work. Hennepin wrote that the falls, 'a vast and prodigious Cadence of Water', were 600 feet high; they are actually 193 feet. He describes a fall on the western verge which has since disappeared. Hennepin's engraving was often reproduced in books and on maps in the eighteenth century.
353
Map of New France: 'Figure de la Terre Neuve' by Lescarbot, 1611.
Lescarbot's map of New France is one of the most accurate up to that time. Marc Lescarbot, a French lawyer-poet, and the author of the *Histoire de la Nouvelle France* (1609), was a member of de Monts's colony at Port Royal from the summer of 1606 to the summer of 1607. His perceptive comments on colonization and on the Indians make a valuable supplement to Champlain's more factual narrative. The map appears in the second enlarged edition (1611) of his history.
354
Indian clothing and equipment, from Champlain, *Voyages et Descouvertures,* Paris, 1620.
A and *C.* Armaments for the war-path; the round shield in *C* is made of buffalo hide; *B.* A woman with child, canoe and paddle; *D.* An Indian on snowshoes, clothed for winter travel with mocassins and robe of deer, bear, or beaver skins; *G.* An Algonkian girl dressed for a dance; sometimes, writes Champlain, she is 'loaded and decked out with more than twelve pounds of wampum and other trifles'; *H.* A girl in ordinary dress.

4.
Champlain hears of Niagara Falls and discovers Lake Champlain

a) From Samuel Champlain's *Des sauvages: ou voyage de Samuel Champlain,* Paris, 1604. Translated by Samuel Purchas, *Purchas his pilgrimes,* London, 1625.

In 1603 Champlain, who never reached Niagara Falls, gives the following account of it, as well as of Lake Ontario and Lake Erie, which he heard from a young Indian who 'had travelled much' and whom 'wee examined very particularly'.

From thence they enter into an exceeding great Lake [Ontario], which may containe some three hundred leagues in length: when they are passed some hundred leagues into the said Lake, they meet with an Iland, which is very great; and beyond the said Iland the water is brackish: But when they have passed some hundred leagues farther, the water is yet salter: and comming to the end of the said Lake, the water is wholly salt. Farther he said, that there is a Fall that is a league broad, from whence an exceeding current of water descendeth into the said Lake. That after a man is passed this Fall, no more land can be seene neither on the one side nor on the other, but so great a Sea [Erie], that they never have seene the end thereof, nor have heard tell, that any other have seene the same.

Text used: Samuel Purchas, Hakluytus Posthumus or Purchas his pilgrimes. Glasgow: James MacLehose & Sons, 1906, VI, p. 217.

b) From Samuel Champlain's *Les voyages de Sieur de Champlain.* Paris, 1613.

In 1609 Champlain continued the exploration of the Richelieu River which he had begun on his first voyage in 1603. He discovered a great lake which he named Lake Champlain and had a victorious encounter with Iroquois Indians, of which he drew and published a picture (plate 333). He also heard of the passageway to the sea down the river which Henry Hudson was to discover from its mouth in September, a month later.

Setting out from the mouth of this river [Richelieu], which is some four hundred to five hundred paces broad, and very beautiful, running [up from the] southward, we arrived at a place in latitude 45°, and twenty-two or twenty-three leagues from the Trois Rivières. All this river from its mouth to the first fall, a distance of fifteen leagues, is very smooth, and bordered with woods, like all the other places before named, and of the same sorts. There are nine or ten fine islands before reaching the fall of the Iroquois, which are a league or a league and a half long, and covered with numerous oakes and nut-trees. The river is nearly half a league wide in places, and very abundant in fish. We found in no place less than four feet of water. The approach to the fall is a kind of lake, where the water descends, and which is some three leagues in circuit. There are here some meadows, but not inhabited by savages on account of the wars. There is very little water at the fall, which runs with great rapidity. There are also many rocks and stones, so that the savages cannot go up by water, although they go down very easily. All this region is very level, covered with forests, vines, and nut-trees. No Christians had been in

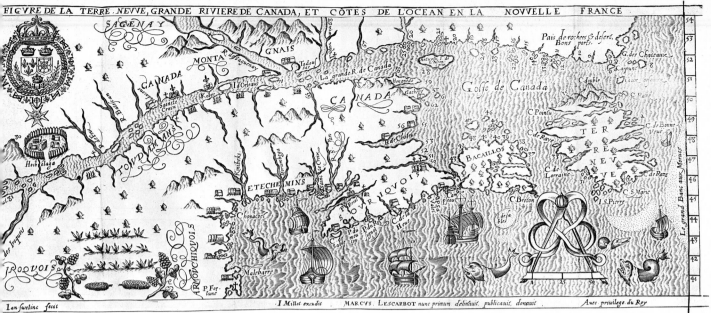

FIGVRE DE LA TERRE NEVVE, GRANDE RIVIERE DE CANADA, ET CÔTES DE L'OCEAN EN LA NOVVELLE FRANCE.

354

this place before us; and we had considerable difficulty in ascending the river with oars.

The next day we entered the lake [Champlain; he overestimates the length], which is of great extent, say eighty or a hundred leagues long, where I saw four fine islands, ten, twelve, and fifteen leagues long, which were formerly inhabited by the savages, like the River of the Iroquois; but they have been abandoned since the wars of the savages with one another prevail. There are also many rivers falling into the lake, bordered by many fine trees of the same kinds as those we have in France, with many vines finer than any I have seen in any other place; also many chestnut-trees on the border of this lake, which I had not seen before.

Continuing our course over this lake on the western side, I noticed, while observing the country, some very high mountains on the eastern side, on the top of which there was snow [probably the white limestone of the Green Mountains of Vermont]. I made inquiry of the savages whether these localities were inhabited, when they told me that the Iroquois dwelt there, and that there were beautiful valleys in these

355

356

places, with plains productive in grain, such as I had eaten in this country, together with many kinds of fruit without limit. They said also that the lake extended near mountains, some twenty-five leagues distant from us, as I judge. I saw, on the south, other mountains, no less high than the first, but without any snow. The savages told me that these mountains were thickly settled, and that it was there we were to find their enemies; but that it was necessary to pass a fall [Ticonderoga] in order to go there (which I afterwards saw), when we should enter another lake [George], nine or ten leagues long. After reaching the end of the lake, we should have to go, they said, two leagues by land, and pass through a river [Hudson] flowing into the sea on the Norumbegue coast, near that of Florida, whither it took them only two days to go by canoe.

Translation used: Charles P. Otis, Champlain's voyages. Boston: Prince Society, 3 vols, 1878-82. Text used: W. L. Grant, Voyages of Samuel de Champlain 1604–1618. New York: Barnes & Noble, Inc., 1959, pp. 154-5, 161-2.

355
Siege of an Iroquois village, from Champlain, Voyages, Paris, 1632. Champlain reached Lake Huron on an expedition in 1615; from there he went south with his Indian allies to help them attack their enemies the Iroquois. On 10 October they besieged this fortified village on Lake Onondaga in present New York state. The French constructed a cavalier or movable shelter and mantlets to protect the attackers; the Indians used wood to fire the fort. Champlain was wounded in the knee during the engagement.

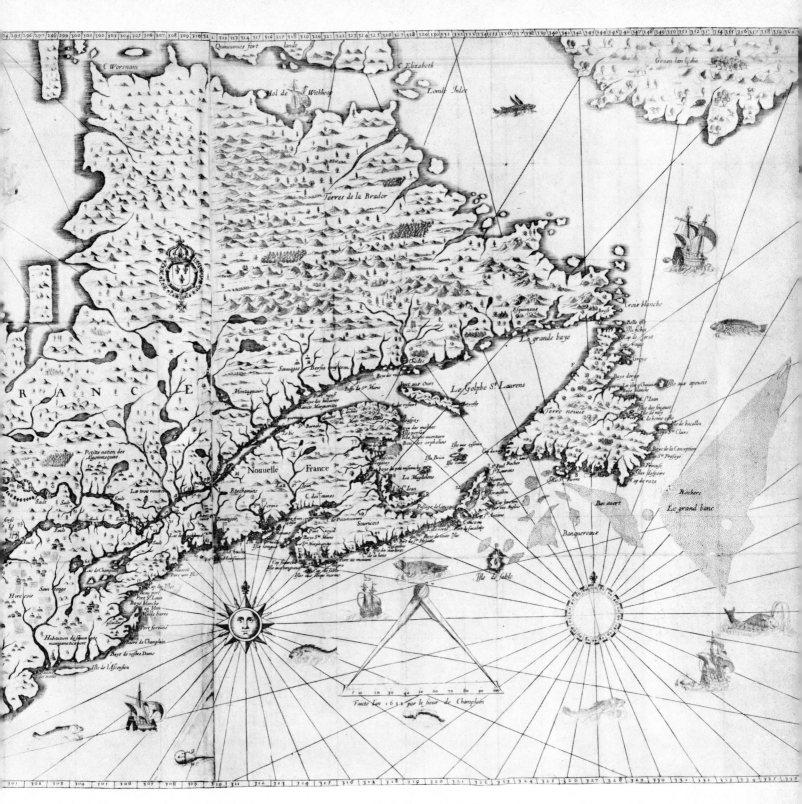

356
A Huron deer-pound, from Champlain, *Voyages et descouvertures*, Paris, 1620.

Champlain describes the Huron deer hunt shown in this drawing, in which he took part. Twenty-five Indians took ten days to build the two fences of stakes nine or ten feet high, extending about 1500 feet on each side. They then formed a line before daybreak, beating on sticks and howling like wolves to drive the deer toward the enclosure at the apex of the triangle. There they shot the deer with arrows. On thirty-eight days, driving deer into the enclosure and using traps shown to the right, the Indians captured and killed 120 deer.

357
Map of New France by Samuel de Champlain, *Voyages*, Paris, 1632.

This map, the last and greatest produced by Champlain, was the prototype of later European maps for nearly a century. It summarizes the information he gathered in his career as intrepid, tireless explorer, brilliant navigator, and expert cartographer.

For the western and northern areas, beyond his own travels, he is less accurate, although the information and misinformation he gathered from questioning of Indians and from reports of his fur traders was stimulating and valuable. There is a growing but confused knowledge of the Great Lakes: 'Lac St Louis' is Ontario; for '90' (Niagara Falls) he has a note, 'Waterfall . . . of great height, where many kinds of fish are stunned in descending'; the two small lakes above 'La nation neutre' are Erie; 'Mer douce' combines Georgian Bay and Huron; '34' (Sault Ste. Marie) he says flows from 'another extremely large lake', which he calls Grand Lac (Superior). Lake Champlain, which he discovered, he puts too far east of the Hudson, which he did not reach.

358

358
Snowshoes used in a Canadian winter hunt from A. Thevet, *Les singularités de la France Antarctique,* Paris, 1558.
359
Detail of the New York area from the figurative map of Cornelis Hendriks, 1616. *The Hague, Algemeen Rijksarchief.*

5.

Father Paul le Jeune, S.J., lives among the Canadian Indians, 1632–4

From Father Paul le Jeune's *Relation de ce qui s'est passe en la Nouvelle France en l'annee 1633.* Paris: Sebastien Cramoisy, 1634.

Father le Jeune joined the Jesuit missionaries in Canada in 1632. That same year his *Brieve relation du voyage de la Nouvelle-France* was printed in Paris and began the annual publication of reports by the Order, called the *Relations,* which continued until 1673. The *Relations* contain an unrivalled storehouse of information about events in Canada during those years, recounted with vivid detail. The following extracts, all from the early accounts of Father le Jeune, tell of his experience with snowshoes, describe the skunk and the hummingbird, and portray conditions in an Indian house in winter.

On the 3rd of December [1632] we began to change our foot-gear, and to use raquettes [snowshoes]; when I first put these great flat skates on my feet, I thought that I should fall with my nose in the snow, at every step I took. But experience has taught me that God provides for the convenience of all nations according to their needs. I walk very freely now on these raquettes. As to the Savages, they do not hinder them from jumping like bucks or running like deer . . .

On the second day of January 1633, I saw a number of Savages trying to cross the great river St Lawrence in their canoes. Usually this river does not freeze in the middle; it drifts or floats immense pieces of ice, according to the course and movement of the current. These poor fellows approached large pieces of the floating ice, sounded them with their paddles, then mounted them, and drew their canoes up after them, crossing over to reach the water on the other side of the ice. Nimble as they are, not infrequently some of them are drowned . . .

How often, when coming to a hill or a mountain which I must descend, I have rolled down to the bottom on the snow, experiencing no other discomfort than to change for a little while my black habit for a white one, and all this is done with much laughter. For if you do not stand firmly upon your raquettes, you will whiten your head as well as your feet.

How many times have I done this also upon the ice heights of the river banks along which I was going. It was a Savage who taught me this trick, known to everybody here; he went ahead of me, and, seeing that his head was in danger of reaching the river before his feet, he let himself roll the whole length of the ice, and I after him. The best of it is that you have only to do it once, in order to understand the trick. I was afraid, at first; for the rising tide, lifting up those great blocks of ice, cracks them in many places, and the water, splashing up on the banks of the river, makes a thin layer of ice over the thicker one. When you try walking upon the thin ice, it breaks under you. The first time I tried it, I thought it was all going to sink under me. But I do not believe that a cannon could crack the thickest ice. When you walk upon it in the spring, it is then that there is danger of stepping into a hole and going under . . .

[This] is a low animal, about the size of a little dog or cat. I mention it here, not on account of its excellence, but to make of it a symbol of sin. I have seen three or four of them. It has black fur, quite beautiful and shining; and has upon its back two perfectly white stripes, which join near the neck and tail, making an oval which adds greatly to their grace. The tail is bushy and well furnished with hair, like the tail of a Fox; it carries it curled back like that of a Squirrel. It is more white than black; and, at the first glance, you would say, especially when it walks, that it ought to be called Jupiter's little dog. But it is so stinking, and casts so foul an odor, that it is unworthy of being called the dog of Pluto. No sewer ever smelled so bad. I would not have believed it if I had not smelled it myself. Your heart almost fails you when you approach the animal; two have been killed in our court, and several days afterward there was such a dreadful odor throughout our house that we could not endure it. I believe the sin smelled by

359

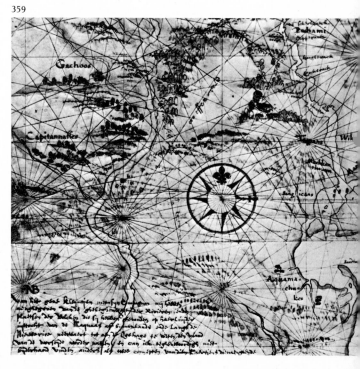

sainte Catherine de Sienne must have had the same vile odor . . .

It is called by our French the fly-bird, because it is scarcely larger than a bee; others call it the flower-bird, because it lives upon flowers. It is in my opinion one of the great rarities of this country, and a little prodigy of nature. God seems to me more wonderful in this little bird than in a large animal. It hums in flying, like the bee; I have sometimes seen it hold itself in the air and stick its bill into a flower. Its bill is rather long, and its plumage seems to be a mottled green. Those who call it the flower-bird would, in my opinion, speak more correctly if they would call it the flower of birds . . .

In order to have some conception of the beauty of this edifice, its construction must be described. I shall speak from knowledge, for I have often helped to build it. Now, when we arrived at the place where we were to camp, the women, armed with axes, went here and there in the great forests, cutting the framework of the hostelry where we were to lodge; meantime the men, having drawn the plan thereof, cleared away the snow with their snowshoes, or with shovels which they make and carry expressly for this purpose. Imagine now a great ring or square in the snow, two, three or four feet deep, according to the weather or the place where they encamp. This depth of snow makes a white wall for us, which surrounds us on all sides, except the end where it is broken through to form the door. The framework having been brought, which consists of twenty or thirty poles, more or less, according to the size of the cabin, it is planted, not upon the ground but upon the snow; then they throw upon these poles, which converge a little at the top, two or three rolls of bark sewed together, beginning at the bottom, and behold, the house is made. The ground inside, as well as the wall of snow which extends all around the cabin, is covered with little branches of fir; and, as a finishing touch, a wretched skin is fastened to two poles to serve as a door, the doorposts being the snow itself. Now let us examine in detail all the comforts of this elegant Mansion.

You cannot stand upright in this house, as much on account of its low roof as the suffocating smoke; and consequently you must always lie down, or sit flat upon the ground, the usual posture of the Savages. When you go out, the cold, the snow, and the danger of getting lost in these great woods drive you in again more quickly than the wind, and keep you a prisoner in a dungeon which has neither lock nor key. This prison, in addition to the uncomfortable position that one must occupy upon a bed of earth, has four other great discomforts,—cold, heat, smoke, and dogs. As to the cold, you have the snow at your head with only a pine branch between, often nothing but your hat, and the winds are free to enter in a thousand places. For do not imagine that these pieces of bark are joined as paper is glued and fitted to a window frame; they are often like the plant mille-pertuis, except that their holes and their openings are a little larger; and even if there were only the opening at the top, which serves at once as window and chimney, the coldest winter in France could come in there every day without any trouble. When I lay down at night I could study through this opening both the Stars and the Moon as easily as if I had been in the open fields.

Nevertheless, the cold did not annoy me as much as the heat from the fire. A little place like their cabins is easily heated by a good fire, which sometimes roasted and broiled me on all sides, for the cabin was so narrow that I could not protect myself against the heat. You cannot move to right or left, for the Savages, your neighbors, are at your elbows; you cannot withdraw to the rear, for you encounter the wall of snow, or the bark of the cabin which shuts you in. I did not know what position to take. Had I stretched myself out, the place was so narrow that my legs would have been halfway in the fire; to roll myself up in a ball, and crouch down in their way, was a position I could not retain as long as they could; my clothes were all scorched and burned.

Text used: R. G. Thwaites, ed., The Jesuit relations and allied documents. *Cleveland, 1896-1901, V, p. 127; V, p. 141; V, pp. 149-51; VI, pp. 315, 317; VII, pp. 35-9.*

6.
The *Half Moon* sails up Hudson River, 1609

From Samuel Purchas's *Hakluyt Posthumus or Purchas his pilgrimes,* London, 1625. The narrative, written by Robert Juet of Limehouse, an officer of the *Half Moon,* is a careful day-by-day report of wind, weather, latitude, soundings, and chief events from leaving Amsterdam on 25 March 1609 until the *Half Moon* reached Dartmouth, England, 7 November 1609. Purchas, in a marginal gloss, says he has Juet's manuscript journal. This manuscript is not extant.

Sailing northward along the coast, Henry Hudson reached the Navesink Hills on the New Jersey coast, noted by Verrazzano in 1524. After several days of exploration he entered the Narrows and discovered what is now New York Harbor and the Hudson River, the exploration of which is described below.

The second of September 1609 to the Northward we saw high Hils. This is very good Land to fall with, and a pleasant land to see.

Eleventh [September]. At one of the clocke in the afternoone, wee weighed and went into the River [New York Harbor]. Then wee Anchored, and saw that it was a very good Harbour for all windes, and rode all night. The people of the Countrey came aboord of us, making shew of love, and gave us Tabacco and Indian Wheat, and departed for the night; but we durst not trust them.

The twelfth [September], very faire and hot. We turned into the River two leagues and Anchored. This morning, at our first rode in the River, there came eight and twentie Canoes full of men, women, and children to betray us [!]. They brought with them Oysters and Beanes, whereof wee bought some. They have great Tabacco pipes of yellow Copper, and Pots of Earth to dresse their meate in.

The fourteenth [September]. We sayled up the River twelve leagues and came to a Streight between two Points. The River is a mile broad; there is very high Land on both sides [near Peekskill]. The land grew very high and Mountainous. The River is full of fish.

The fifteenth [September]. Wee weighed with the wind at South, and ran up into the River twentie leagues, passing by high Mountains [Catskill Mountains, rising over 3,000 feet]. At night we came to other Mountaines, which lie from the Rivers side. There wee found very loving people, and very old men: where wee were well used. Our Boat went to fish, and caught a great store of very good fish.

The Nineteenth [September] was faire and hot weather: at the floud [tide], being neere eleven of the clocke, wee weighed, and ran higher up two leagues above the Shoalds, and had no lesse water than five fathoms. The people of the Countrie came flocking aboord and brought us Grapes, and Pompions, which wee bought for trifles. And many brought us

Bevers skinnes and Otters skinnes, which we bought for Beades, Knives, and Hatchets. So we rode there all night.

Here the *Half Moon* reached its northerly limit of exploration, at or near the present site of Albany. There the officers followed a procedure which established a custom adopted by visitors to the leaders assembled in the city down to the present day.

The twentieth [September]. Our Master and his Mate determined to trie some of the chiefe men of the Countrey, whether they had any treacherie in them. So they tooke them down into the Cabbin, and gave them so much Wine and Aqua vitæ, that they were all merrie: and one of them had his wife with him, which sate so modestly, as any of our Countrey women would doe in a strange place. In the ende one of them was drunke, which had beene aboord our ship all the time we had beene there: and that was strange to them; for they could not tell how to take it.

The two and twentieth [September] was faire weather: in the morning our Masters Mate and foure more of the companie went up with our Boat to sound the River higher up. This night, at ten of the clocke, our boat returned in a showre of raine from sounding of the River; and found it to be at an end for shipping to goe in. For they had been up eight or nine leagues [to the mouth of the Mohawk River or beyond] and found but seven foot water, and unconstant soundings.

With this proof by the mate's boat crew that there was no passage through to the sea of China, Hudson sailed back down the river past the island described below, now more populous.

The second [October]. We saw a very good piece of ground: and hard by it there was a Cliffe, that looked of the colour of a white greene, as though it were either Copper or Silver Myne: and I thinke it to be one of them, by the trees that grow upon it. For they be all burned, and the other places are as greene as grasse; it is on that side of the River that is called Manna-hatta. There we saw no people to trouble us: and rode quietly all night; but had much wind and raine.

Leaving the harbor and sailing through the Narrows and past Sandy Hook, the *Half Moon* 'steered away east south-east, and south-east by east off into the mayne sea', reaching Dartmouth on the south coast of England 7 November 1609.

Text used: Samuel Purchas, Hakluyt Posthumus or Purchas his pilgrimes. *Glasgow: James MacLehose & Sons, 1906, XIII, pp. 361-73. In the above extracts, no indication is made of omissions.*

7.
The landing of the Pilgrims, 1620

From Governor Bradford's *History of Plymouth Plantation, 1606-1646.* The original manuscript is now in Lambeth Palace Library, London.

The manuscript of Bradford's *History of Plymouth Plantation*, begun by him in 1630 and coming down to 1646, was known to earlier writers and then lost for a long time. It was rediscovered in the library of the Bishop of London at Fulham in 1855, and published by the Massachusetts Historical Society in 1856. In this moving passage,

Bradford has expressed both the desolation and the courage of the little band of Pilgrims who waded ashore at Provincetown on Cape Cod in November 1620.

But hear I cannot but stay and make a pause, and stand half amased at this poore peoples presente condition; and so I thinke will the reader too, when he well considers the same. Being thus passed the vast ocean, and a sea of troubles before in their preparation (as may be remembred by that which wente before), they had now no freinds to wellcome them, nor inns to entertaine or refresh their weatherbeaten bodys, no houses or much less townes to repaire too, to seeke for succoure. It is recorded in scripture as a mercie to the apostle and his shipwracked company, that the barbarians shewed them no smale kindnes in refreshing them, but these savage barbarians, when they mette with them (as after will appeare) were readier to fill their sids full of arrows then otherwise. And for the season it was winter, and they that know the winters of that cuntrie know them to be sharp and violent, and subject to cruell and feirce stormes, deangerous to travill to known places, much more to serch an unknown coast. Besids, what could they see but a hidious and desolate wildernes, full of wild beasts and willd men? and what multituds ther might be of them they knew not. Nether could they, as it were, goe up to the tope of Pisgah, to vew from this willdernes a more goodly cuntrie to feed their hops; for which way soever they turnd their eys (save upward to the heavens) they could have litle solace or content in respecte of any outward objects. For summer being done, all things stand upon them with a wetherbeaten face; and the whole countrie, full of woods and thickets, represented a wild and savage heiw. If they looked behind them, ther was the mighty ocean which they had passed, and was now as a maine barr and goulfe to seperate them from all the civill parts of the world. If it be said they had a ship to sucour them, it is trew; but what heard they daly from the mr [master] and company? but that with speede they should looke out a place with their shallop, wher they would be at some near distance; for the season was shuch as he would not stirr from thence till a safe harbor was discovered by them wher they would be, and he might goe without danger; and that victells consumed apace, but he must and would keepe sufficient for them selves and their returne. Yea, it was muttered by some, that if they gott not a place in time, they would turne them and their goods ashore and leave them. Let it also be considred what weake hopes of supply and succoure they left behinde them, that might bear up their minds in this sade condition and trialls they were under; and they could not but be very smale. It is true, indeed, the affections and love of their brethren at Leyden was cordiall and entire towards them, but they had little power to help them, or them selves; and how the case stode betweene them and the marchants at their coming away, hath allready been declared. What could now sustaine them but the spirite of God and his grace? May not and ought not the children of these fathers rightly say: 'Our faithers were Englishmen which came over this great ocean, and were ready to perish in this willderness; but they cried unto the Lord, and he heard their voyce, and looked on their adversitie, etc. Let them therefore praise the Lord, because he is good, and his mercies endure for ever.'

Text used: W. T. Davis, ed., Bradford's history of Plymouth Plantation, *1606–1646. New York: Barnes & Noble, Inc., 1964, pp. 95-7.*

Map of the south part of New England from William Wood, *New Englands prospect*, London, 1634.
This map is the first of New England made by a resident of the country, where Wood had lived for four years before his return to England in 1633. On the map are names of the rapidly expanding new settlements between Narragansett Bay and 'Acomenticus', near present York, Maine; the crudely drawn rivers and mis-shaped bays nevertheless show a rapidly increasing topographical knowledge of the region.

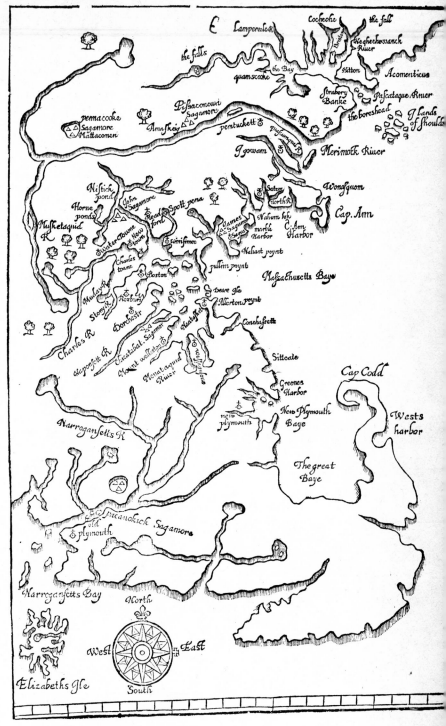

8.

The Plymouth settlers learn about and befriend Indian neighbors

From *Mourt's Relation,* London: John Bellamie, 1622; and Edward Winslow's *Good news from New England,* London: Dawson, Bladen and Bellamie, 1624.

Between the first landing and the finding of Plymouth Harbor, the Pilgrims explored inland on Cape Cod, seeking both a site for settlement and communication with the Indians, who ran from them. On 30 November they made an interesting discovery. This first account, called *Mourt's Relation*, is believed to be by Bradford and Winslow.

When we had marched five or six miles into the woods, and could find no signs of any people; we returned again another way. And as we came into the plain ground, we found a place like a grave: but it was much bigger and longer than any we had yet seen. It was also covered with boards: so as we mused what it should be, and resolved to dig it up.

Where we found first a mat, and under that a fair bow; and there, another mat; and under that, a board about three-quarters [of a yard] long finely carved and painted, with three tynes [prongs] or broaches on the top like a crown. Also between the mats, we found bowls, trays, dishes, and such like trinkets. At length, we came to a fair new mat; and under that, two bundles; the one bigger, the other less. We opened the greater, and found in it a great quantity of fine and perfect red powder; and in it the bones and skull of a man. The scull had fine yellow hair still on it; and some of the flesh unconsumed. There were bound up with it, a knife, a pack-needle, and two or three old iron things. It was bound up in a sailor's canvass cassock [blouse], and a pair of cloth breeches. The red powder was a kind of embalment; and yielded a strong, but no offensive smell. It was as fine as any flour.

We opened the less bundle likewise; and found of the same powder in it, and the bones and head of a little child. About the legs and other parts of it were bound strings and bracelets of fine white beads [wampum]. There was also by it a little bow, about three-quarters [of a yard] long; and some other odd knacks.

We brought sundry of the prettiest things away with us; and covered up the corpse[s] again.

After this, we digged in sundry like places; but found no more corn, nor any things else but graves.

There was variety of opinions amongst us about the embalmed person. Some thought, It was an Indian lord and king. Others said, The Indians have all black hair; and never any was seen with brown, or yellow hair. Some thought, It was a Christian of special note, which had died amongst

them; and they thus buried him, to honour him. Others thought, They had killed him; and did it in triumph over him.

The Plymouth colonists encountered Indian hostility, especially at first, but their early peace treaty with Chief Massasoit was kept for fifty years. Edward Winslow describes the journey which he made in March 1623, with John Hamden, a visitor from London, guided by Hobbamock, to visit and attempt to relieve Massasoit, who was at death's door.

When we came thither, we found the house so full of men as we could scarce get in; though they used their best diligence to make way for us. There were they, in the midst of their charms for him: making such a hellish noise, as it distempered us that were well; and therefore [was] unlike[ly] to ease him that was sick. About him were six or eight women, who chafed his arms, legs, and thighs; to keep heat in him. When they had made an end of their charming; one told him, That his friends the English were come to see him.

Having [his] understanding left, but his sight was wholly gone; he asked, 'Who was come?'

They told him, 'Winsnow'. For they cannot pronounce the letter *l*; but ordinarily [use] *n* in the place thereof.

He desired to speak with me.

When I came to him, and they told him of it; he put forth his hand to me, which I took. Then he said twice, though very inwardly [in a low tone], Keen Winsnow?, which is to say, 'Art thou Winslow?'

I answered, Ahhe; that is, 'Yes'.

Then he doubled [repeated] these words, Matta neen wonckanet namen Winsnow?, that is to say, 'O Winslow, I shall never see thee again.'

Then I called Hobbamock, and desired him to tell Massassowat, That the Governor [William Bradford], hearing of his sickness, was sorry for the same: and though, by reason of many businesses, he could not come himself; yet he sent me with such things for him, as he thought most likely to do him good, in this his extremity. And whereof, if he pleased to take; I would presently [at once] give him.

Which he desired. And having a confection [preparation] of many comfortable conserves &c.: on the point of my knife, I gave him some; which I could scarce get through his teeth. When it was dissolved in his mouth, he swallowed the juice of it: whereat those that were about him, much rejoiced; saying, He had not swallowed anything in two days before.

Then I desired to see his mouth, which was exceedingly furred; and his tongue [had] swelled in such a manner, as it was not possible for him to eat such meat as they had, his passage [gullet] being stopped up. Then I washed his mouth, and scraped his tongue; and got abundance of corruption out of the same.

After which, I gave him more of the confection; which he swallowed with more readiness. Then he desiring to drink; I dissolved some of it in water, and gave him thereof. Within half an hour, this wrought a great alteration in him, in the eyes of all that beheld him. Presently after, his sight began to come to him: which gave him and us good encouragement.

When the day broke, we went out, it being now March [1623], to seek herbs: but could not find any but strawberry leaves; of which I gathered a handful, and put in the same. And because I had nothing to relish it; I went forth again, and pulled up a saxafras [sassafras] root: and sliced a piece thereof, and boiled it (in the broth) till it [the broth] had a good relish; and then took it [the slice of sassafras] out again. The broth being boiled; I strained it through my [pocket] handkerchief: and gave him at least a pint, which he drank; and liked it very well. After this, his sight mended more and more: also he had three moderate stools; and took some rest. Insomuch as we, with admiration [wonderment], blessed God, for giving his blessing to such raw and ignorant means: making no doubt of his recovery; [he] himself, and all of them, acknowledging us [to be] the Instruments of his preservation.

The morning, he caused me to spend in going from one to another, amongst those that were sick in the town: requesting me to wash their mouths also, and give to each of them some of the same [that] I gave him; saying, They were good folk. This pains I took with willingness; though it were much offensive to me, not being accustomed with [to] such poisonous savours.

After dinner, he desired me to get him a goose or duck; and make him some pottage therewith, with as much speed as I could.

So I took a man with me, and made a shot at a couple of ducks, some six score paces [100 yards] off; and killed one: at which he wondered. So we returned forthwith, and dressed it: making more broth therewith, which he much desired. Never did I see a man, so low brought, recover in that measure in so short a time.

Text used: Edward Arber, ed., The story of the Pilgrim Fathers, 1606–1623. *Boston: Houghton Mifflin & Co., 1897; pp. 421-2 (Mourt's Relation); pp. 549-51, 552-3 (Good News from New England).*

9.
Massachusetts Bay colonists explore the rest of New England, 1633

From *The journal of John Winthrop,* 29 March 1630 to 14 May 1634. Governor John Winthrop of Massachusetts Bay had to plan for a large number of immigrants arriving in quick succession. Here he sends a ship to explore the lesser known parts of New England, and gathers information to help him dispute with the Dutch the possibilities for Indian trade and proliferating settlement.

October 2 [1633]. The bark Blessing, which was sent to the southward, returned. She had been at an island over against Connecticut, called Long Island, because it is near fifty leagues long, the east part about ten leagues from the main, but the west end not a mile. There they had store of the best wampampeak, both white and blue. The Indians there are a very treacherous people. They have many canoes so great as one will carry eighty men. They were also in the River of Connecticut, which is barred at the entrance, so as they could not find above one fathom of water. They were also at the Dutch plantation upon Hudson's River (called New Netherlands), where they were very kindly entertained, and had some beaver and other things, for such commodities as they put off. They showed the governour (called Gwalter Van Twilly) their commission, which was to signify to them, that the king of England had granted the river and country of Connecticut to his own subjects; and therefore desired them to forbear to build there, etc. The Dutch governour wrote back to our governour, (his letter was very courteous and respectful, as it had been to a very honorable person), whereby he signified, that the Lords the States had also granted the same parts to the West India Company, and therefore requested that we would forbear the same till the matter were decided between the king of England and the said lords.

The said bark did pass and repass over the shoals of Cape Cod, about three or four leagues from Nantucket Isle, where the breaches are very terrible, yet they had three fathom water all over.

The company of Plimouth sent a bark to Connecticut, at this time, to erect a trading house there. When they came, they found the Dutch had built there, and did forbid the Plimouth men to proceed; but they set up their house notwithstanding, about a mile above the Dutch. This river runs, so far northward, that it comes within a day's journey of a part of Merrimack called [blank], and so runs thence N.W. so near the Great Lake [Champlain], as [allows] the Indians to pass their canoes into it over land. From this lake, and the hideous swamps about it, come most of the beaver which is traded between Virginia and Canada, which runs forth of this lake; and Patomack River in Virginia comes likewise out of it, or very near, so as from this lake there comes yearly to the Dutch about ten thousand skins, which might easily be diverted by Merrimack, if a course of trade were settled above in that river.

Text used: Edmund S. Morgan, ed., The founding of Massachusetts: Historians and the sources. *Indianapolis: Bobbs-Merrill Co., 1964, pp. 268-9.*

361
Map of New Belgium and New England from Blaeu's *Novus Atlas,* Amsterdam, 1640.
This richly adorned and interesting map first appeared in the second volume of Willem and Johannes Blaeu's *Theatrum Orbis Terrarum* in the Latin, French and Dutch editions of 1635 and influenced many other European mapmakers during the remaining years of the century. Geographical details are derived from Adraien Block's manuscript map, 1614 (plate 325), and from a map in Johan de Laet's *Nieuwe Wereldt,* 1630 edition. The error of placing Lake Champlain (Lacus Irocoisiensis) in eastern New England is ultimately based on Champlain's map of New France, 1613 (plate 339).

On this map appear the typical animals and birds of the North American continent: bears, egrets, cranes, turkeys, deer, foxes, rabbits, and probably the first depiction of beavers, polecats, and, in the center, an otter with a fish in his mouth. Many of these fauna were first mentioned by Jacques Cartier just a hundred years earlier. West is at the top.

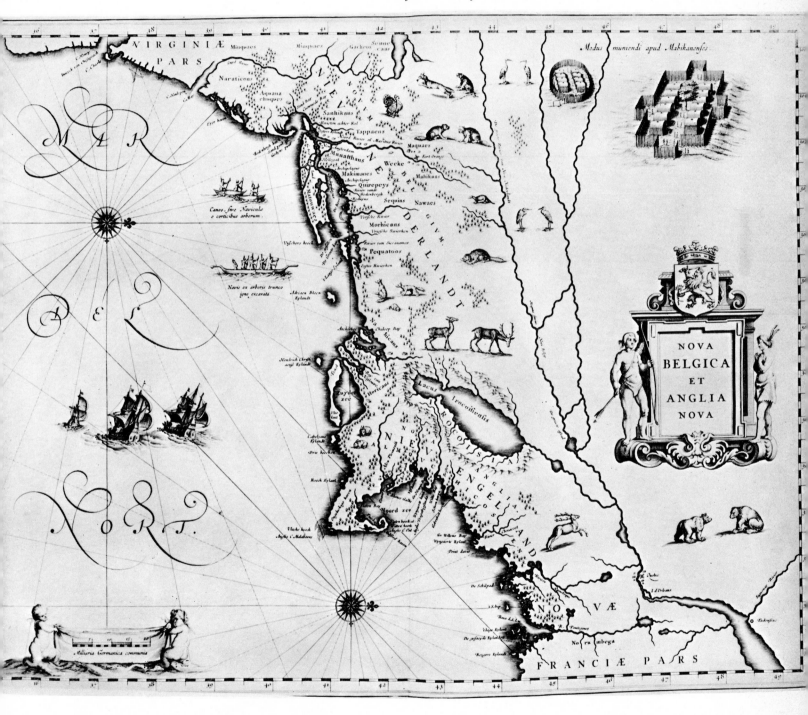

EPILOGUE

The exposure of North America to European exploration was a slow process, but one which continued from first to last to be an exciting and challenging one. It took a long time for Europeans to recognize that the landmass to the west was a new continent, not a collection of oceanic islands or the mainland shore of Asia. It took a long time, more than a century, before the eastern and western shores of the land-mass in temperate latitudes were defined with any degree of accuracy—those in the Arctic north had to wait until the twentieth century for precise definition. Great excursions were made into the interior in the sixteenth century—Hernando de Soto and Francisco de Coronado between them spanned the continent at its widest part by the middle of the sixteenth century, Cartier worked 1000 miles inland from the Strait of Belle Isle—yet the interior was to remain largely unexplored until the nineteenth century. In the early seventeenth century it was commonplace for the English to talk as if the Pacific Ocean (in spite of what the Spaniards knew) was only 300 or 400 miles from Chesapeake Bay.

Down to the time when this book ends with the closing of the first third of the seventeenth century, any voyage across the Atlantic that was not a routine operation to catch cod on or off the Newfoundland shores might turn up a new piece of shoreline, might disclose a novel plant, tree, fish or animal; might bring the travellers at their landfall into contact with the strange aboriginal people whom the Europeans were gradually coming to displace and destroy. Europeans came first to look, second to trade, and third to stay. Speculation about lands in the western ocean shades into discovery; discovery shades into exploration; exploration turns with some abruptness into settlement. The new land ceases to be a toy, a source of wonderment, a source of exotic furs and odd trinkets, and becomes a place to live in. At this point concern with the new continent becomes serious and social. It means that Europeans have to come to terms with a land where they spend not a few weeks or months but the remainder of their lives, must learn all its secrets of living, all its products, all the tricks of adopting agriculture, commerce and essential industry which will keep them alive, which will enable them to multiply, which will make them collectively into a new sort of community in a novel environment. Conquest makes men ruthless, colonization makes them implacable. All the existing creatures of the land, men, animals, fish, become objects not for curiosity or delight but objects for exploitation. A new society can arise only by the creation of a new ecological landscape.

It is this exacting process which this book illuminates by means of maps which demonstrate both what men thought and knew of the emerging America, by means of narratives which tell the story and analyze the process, by selections from what was seen by the discoverers, explorers and settlers themselves—the hard graphic words which make the maps turn into places, and finally the pictures—the significant but imperfect drawings and engravings which call back the visible world as seen through pioneer European eyes and, finally, the photographs, suggesting rather than telling us in modern terms something, but only something, of what the land looked like. Together these elements make up an interpretation, an America, the America of the first comers from the east to the west, the men whose descendants were to mould, build, and damage a large section of the earth's surface while creating a remarkable, a powerful, a frightening Republic.

362
Shipbuilding in the New World, from T. de Bry, *America*, Part IV, 1594.

NOTES

Chapter 1

1 Skelton (1964) pp.5-6, 11; Skelton (1965) pp.167-9, 174. The 'Bruges Itinerary': Hamy (1908) pp.157-216.
2 Jones (1964) pp.5-11.
3 *Íslendingabók*: Jones (1964) p.102.
4 Ashe (1962) pp.153-6.
5 *Íslendingabók*: Jones (1964) p.106.
6 Jones (1964) p.60; but, for the view that these relics were not Eskimo but Irish, Sauer (1968) pp.176-8.
7 Ashe (1962) pp.149-55; for contrary view, Sauer (1968) pp.178-82.
8 *Íslendingabók*: Jones (1964) p.102.
9 Jones (1964) pp.33-7.
10 Nansen (1911) I, pp.274-8; Jones (1964) pp.50-2; Sauer (1968) pp.104-8, 140-4.
11 *Descriptio insularum aquilonis* (c. 1070): Jones (1964) p.85.
12 Jones (1964) pp.86-7: 'while this famous sentence may help to convince us that someone made a significant observation somewhere in America, it helps not at all to determine the site of Leif's booths'.
13 Sauer (1968) pp.123-5.
14 Jones (1964) pp.91-4; Sauer (1968) pp.127-9; Jones (1968) p.304.
15 'Saga of the Greenlanders': Magnusson and Pálsson (1965) pp.65-6.
16 Jones (1964) pp.93-4.
17 Sauer (1968) pp.129-30.
18 Nansen (1911) ch. X; Sauer (1968), pp.126-32.
19 Icelandic Annals, under year 1121 (properly 1117?): Nansen (1911) II, pp.29-31.
20 Icelandic Annals, under year 1147: Nansen (1911) II, pp.36-7.
21 Skelton (1964) pp.10-11.
22 Nansen (1911) ch. XI; Sauer (1968) ch. VII; Jones (1968) pp.306-11.
23 Annals of Bishop Gisli Oddson, c. 1637 (*ad Americae populos converterunt*, 1342): Jones (1968) p.309.
24 Skelton (1965) pp.198-208.
25 Giovanni da Fontana, *Liber de omnibus rebus naturalis*, c. 1450: Skelton (1965) p.159.
26 Duarte Pacheco Pereira, *Esmeraldo de situ orbis* (ed. 1937) p.11.

Chapter 2

1 Williamson (1962) pp.209-10.
2 *Ibid*, p.208.
3 *Ibid*, pp.66-83.
4 *Ibid*, p.93.
5 *Ibid*, p.225.
6 Harrisse (1892) p.711.
7 Morison (1940) pp.62-4.
8 Hoffman (1961) p.13.
9 Morison (1940) pp.62-3.
10 Hoffman (1961) pp.13-7.
11 Biggar (1911) p.35.
12 Morison (1940) p.70.
13 Biggar (1911) pp.66-7.
14 Pasqualigo, in Markham (1893) pp.235, 237.
15 Biggar (1911) p.64.
16 Williamson (1962) p.122.
17 Cantino to Ferrara, 19 Nov. 1502, in Harrisse (1892) p.422.
18 Harrisse (1892) p.67.
19 Peter Martyr, *Opera* (1511).
20 Lowery (1901) pp. 131-2.
21 Scisco (1913) pp.721-7.
22 Lowery (1901) p.140.
23 *Ibid*, p.141; Navarrete (1825–9) III, pp.50-3.
24 Lowery (1901) pp.150-1.
25 Delanglez (1945) p.13.
26 Navarrete (1825–9) III, p.69.
27 Quattlebaum (1956) p.11 (Quexos' deposition).
28 Winsor (1886) II, p.239.
29 MacNutt (1912) p.267.
30 Oviedo, *Hist. Gen.* III, lib. xxxvii, cap. 1, p.228.
31 *Ibid*, p.628; Quattlebaum (1956) pp.126-9.
32 *Ibid*, p.630.
33 Winsor (1886) II, p.240.
34 Vigneras in *D.C.B.* I, p.342.
35 Gómara: Vigneras (1957) pp.1-19.
36 Peter Martyr, Dec. VIII Bk. 8; MacNutt (1912) pp.419-20.
37 Lanctot (1963) p.46.
38 Hall (1910) p.179.
39 Cumming, *Southeast* (1962) p.9.
40 Lanctot (1963) p.53.
41 Biggar (1930) p.42.
42 Ganong (1964) p.265.

Chapter 3

1 Wagner, *Some Imaginary California Geography* (1926) pp.85, 100 (the best condensed treatment of these legends); Clissold (1962) *passim* (Cibola).
2 Wagner (1937) I, 3.
3 Quinn (1940) I, 281-96.
4 Quinn (1966) I, 380-1; Quinn (1955) I, 4.
5 Hodge and Lewis (1907) pp.4, 18; Lowery (1901) p.177 and App. J.
6 *Ibid*, p.24.
7 *Ibid*, p.47.
8 Cleve Hallenbeck (1940) Part II, has the best study of Vaca's route.
9 Hodge and Lewis (1907) p.112.
10 *Ibid*, pp.136-7; Lowery (1901) p.211, 216.
11 *Final Report of the United States de Soto Expedition Commission* (1939) has the best analysis of de Soto's route.
12 Hammond (1946) Introd. and Ch. I.
13 *Ibid*, p.8.
14 *Final Report of the U.S. de Soto Expedition Commission* (1939) pp.137-8; Lewis (1900) pp.351-7, defends Charlotte Harbor; R. F. Schell (1966) devotes a book to an attempt to identify the landing place as Punta Rassa, Carlos Bay.
15 Hodge and Lewis (1907) pp.130-2, summarize the sources and reliability of the different relations; the *Final Report of the U.S. de Soto Expedition Commission* (1939) does it more fully.
16 *Final Report of the U.S. de Soto Expedition* (1939) pp.183, 185; Cutifachiqui was below Augusta, in South Carolina.
17 Quattlebaum (1956) pp.126-9 (location of Ayllón settlement); Lowery (1901) pp. 447-52 (App. H).
18 Hodge and Lewis (1907) pp.190 ff; *Final Report . . . de Soto Expedition* (1939) *passim.*
19 *Ibid*, p.221.
20 *Ibid*, p.236.
21 Winship (1896) p.354.
22 *Ibid*, pp.360, 475.
23 *Ibid*, pp.362-3; Cortés and Castañeda attacked, the archaeologist A. F. Bandelier (1890) defended him.
24 Bolton (1949) pp.50-2.
25 Wagner (1924) p.386.
26 Winship (1896) p.378.
27 *Ibid*, p.482.
28 *Ibid*, p.471.
29 *Ibid*, pp.519-22.
30 *Ibid*, pp.513, 525.
31 *Ibid*, pp.216-7; Joseph Krutch (1967) p.18.
32 Winship (1896) p.493.
33 Wagner, *Some Imaginary California Geography* (1926) p.85.
34 Winship (1896) p.529.
35 Wagner (1924) p.394.
36 Wagner (1929) p.319: the document is in the Archives of the Indies, Seville, 1-1-1/20, R. 23.
37 *Ibid*, p.85.
38 *Ibid*, pp. 72 ff; Wagner disagrees in some identifications with Bolton (1916) pp.6-10.
39 Wagner (1929) p.93.
40 Bolton (1916) pp.137-53.
41 *Ibid*, pp.163-95.
42 *Ibid*, p.182.
43 *Ibid*, p.179.
44 *Ibid*, p.190.
45 *Ibid*, p.194.
46 Wagner (1929) pp.105-6, 111-2.
47 *Ibid*, p.135.
48 *Ibid*, pp.141-51.
49 *Ibid*, pp.154-67.
50 Wagner, *Sir Francis Drake's Voyage* (1926) p.1.
51 *Ibid*, pp.15-27, where the objectives of the voyage are discussed.
52 Bolton, ed. *Drake's Plate of Brass*, Cal. Hist. Soc. (Special Publication No. 13)

San Francisco, 1937; Fink and Polushkin, *Drake's Plate of Brass Vindicated, Ibid*, No. 14, San Francisco, 1938.

53 Heizer (1947) p.278 (Miwok Indians) and Wagner, *Sir Francis Drake's Voyage* (1926) pp.154-69 (Trinidad Bay); Oko (1964) pp.1-24 and von der Porten (1960) pp.62-6 (argument for Drake's Estero); Power (1959) pp.M7-M11 and Starr (1962) pp.1-29 (argument for San Francisco Bay).
54 Wagner (1929) pp.175-6.
55 *Ibid*, p.234.
56 *Ibid*, p.253.
57 *Ibid*, pp.265-6.
58 *Ibid*, p.282.
59 Bolton (1916) pp.200-1.
60 Hammond and Rey (1953) p.7.
61 Bolton (1916) pp.202-3.
62 *Ibid*, p.203, n.1.

Chapter 4

1 Burrage (1906) p.65.
2 *Ibid*, p.63.
3 *Ibid*, pp.41-2.
4 *Ibid*, p.59.
5 *Ibid*, p.55.
6 *Ibid*, pp.76-7.
7 *Ibid*, pp.106-10.
8 *Ibid*, p.107.
9 *Ibid*, p.109.
10 E. G. R. Taylor (1931) pp.469-70.
11 Lanctot (1963) pp.61-5.
12 *Ibid*, p.65.
13 Biggar (1930) pp.141, 143, 162, 197, 203-4.
14 Lanctot (1963) pp.66-7.
15 Biggar (1930) pp.457-61.
16 Lanctot (1963) p.71.
17 Biggar (1924) pp.265-70.
18 Lanctot (1963) pp.76-9.
19 Cumming (1963) p.32.
20 Ribaut, ed. Connor (1927) pp.88-90.
21 Cumming (1963) pp.27-33.
22 Ribaut, ed. Connor (1927) p.91.
23 Hakluyt (1903–5) VIII, p.473.
24 Ribaut, ed. Connor (1927) p.5.
25 Hakluyt (1903–5) VIII, pp.484-6.
26 Cumming (1963) p.30.
27 *Ibid*, pp.31, 33.
28 Lowery (1905) p.89.
29 Burrage (1930) pp.125-6.
30 Grajales, ed. French (1875) p.211.
31 Lowery (1905) p.157.
32 *Ibid*, p.184.
33 Méras, ed. Connor (1923) p.122 n.6.
34 *Ibid*, pp.122-3.
35 *Ibid*, pp.189-93.
36 Vigneras (1969) pp.398-414.
37 Lowery (1905) p.275.
38 Lewis and Loomie (1953) *passim*.
39 Burrage (1906) pp.114-32.
40 Quinn (1940) I, 7, 156-8.
41 *Ibid*, I, 188-94.
42 *Ibid*, p.282.
43 *Ibid*, II, 410.
44 *Ibid*, II, 420.
45 Quinn (1955) I, 94, 106.
46 *Ibid*, I, 94, 202, 320.
47 *Ibid*, p.204.
48 *Ibid*, I, 477-8.
49 *Ibid*, I, 467; II, 787-8.
50 *Ibid*, II, 516.
51 *Ibid*, II, 523.
52 *Ibid*, II, 523.
53 *Ibid*, II, 543, for full analysis of the number of settlers.
54 *Ibid*, II, 535.
55 *Ibid*, II, 613-5.
56 *Ibid*, II, 712-6.
57 Weeks (1891) pp.107-46.
58 Barbour (1969) I, 240.

Notes for extracts in Chapter 4

1 John Winter brought back cinnamon from the Straits of Magellan in 1579; the aromatic bark aroused interest because of its supposed medicinal qualities. Barlowe may be referring to the bark of the magnolia or dogwood tree. Quinn (1955) I, 97 n.7.
2 Chief of the Roanoke tribe, who ruled one village on Roanoke Island and at least one other on the mainland.
3 For some time the name Wingandacoa was applied to the whole region of North Carolina bordering on the Sounds. The name Virginia, in honor of Queen Elizabeth, was conferred upon it sometime between December 1584 and March 1585.
4 Barlowe was in error here. The absence of deliberately fermented beverages in eastern America is well-known. Quinn (1955) I, p.108 n.7.

5 This reference to an inner shrine in a dwelling is unusual. Spelman records that Powhatan kept an idol in his house. Quinn (1955) I, p.109 n.5.
6 The Indian name, as given by Harriot, for pumpkins, squashes, and gourds.
7 An Orache or salt bush. Its leaves were used by the Indians to salt their stews.
8 The sunflower.
9 The variety *Nicotiana rustica* is native to eastern North America. Tobacco offerings were common among the Algonkian Indians. Harriot's account is important, however, for his reference to the use of dried tobacco. The myth that the Roanoke colonists of 1585–6 introduced tobacco smoking into England is a long-lasting one; its use in England and on the continent was already established.
10 The only details to survive of the size of the Algonkian long-house in its southern form. Harriot's measurements give an area ranging from 30′ x 18′ to 72′ x 36′.
11 Harriot gives the only definite reference to dialectical differences between the languages of the North Carolina Algonkian tribes: cf. Quinn (1955) I, p.370 n.5.
12 Harriot's word derives from Manito, an ordinary term in Algonkian language for a spirit, or supernatural being. The concept of a Supreme Being is basic to all Algonkian ideas of the supernatural, with other spirits regarded as inferior. Solar worship was strongest in the south-east, the concept of the sun being normally kept distinct from that of the Supreme Being by the coastal Algonkians: cf. Quinn (1955) I, p.373 n. & 3.
13 A mixture of European religious concepts and the Indian myth of origin from the underground, often by way of a lake: cf. Quinn (1955) I, p.372 n.4.
14 The myth of the woman who fell from the sky is an Iroquoian legend taken over by some coastal Algonkian peoples: cf. Quinn (1955) I, p.373 n.1.
15 Differential treatment in the after life, according to conduct on earth, is emphasized by many coastal Algonkian peoples. As a pre-Christian example of separation of good from bad, however, this is unique. Other writers have suggested a Christian influence, possibly through the Spanish Jesuit mission on Chesapeake Bay, 1570–2: cf. Quinn (1955) I, p.373 n.4.
16 These tales, both without precise parallel, appear to be connected with the belief in the transmigration of souls, where the wicked were given another chance by rebirth: cf. Quinn (1955) I, p.374 n.1.

Chapter 5

1 See Chapter 2.
2 Skelton (1965) p.180-2.
3 Robert Thorne: Hakluyt (1582), sig. B2; facs. ed., p.23.
4 Williamson (1962) p.106.
5 The documents on Cabot's voyage are printed by Williamson (1962) pp.265-91.
6 Skelton (1965) pp.192, 198.
7 George Best, *A true discourse of the late voyages of discoverie for finding of a passage to Cathaya* (London, 1578); Dionyse Settle, *A true reporte of the laste voyage by Capteine Frobisher* (London, 1577). Best's book is reprinted, with other documents, by Collinson (1867); and, with Settle's narrative and other journals and documents, by Stefansson (1938).
8 This fight was depicted by John White: Hulton and Quinn (1964) p.144 and pl.85(b).
9 In making this comment, Best betrays his ignorance of the Norse settlement, and overlooks the supposed visit of the Zeno brothers.
10 C. F. Hall (1865) pp.77-80; Stefansson (1938) vol. II, pp.240-7.
11 Hulton and Quinn (1964) pp.43-7, 141-5, and pls.62-3, 84-5, 146-7.
12 Davis's journals, letters and published works are printed by Markham (1880).
13 Dodge (1961) p.96.
14 It is so named in the Molyneux globe.
15 Waters (1958) pp.196-7.
16 Conway (1904).
17 The journals of Hall (1605 and 1606) and those of Gatonbe and Baffin (1612) are printed by Gosch (1911) vol. I.
18 Baffin's journal of 1615 is printed by Markham (1881) pp.138-55.
19 Wright (1966) pp.89-118; Nutt (1969).
20 Rundall (1849) p.50.
21 Christy (1894) I, p.85.
22 The documents on Hudson's last voyage are printed by Asher (1860) pp.93-144.
23 Information on Button's voyage was collected by Luke Foxe: Christy (1894) vol. I, pp.162-200.
24 Baffin's journal is printed by Markham (1881) pp.103-37.
25 Munk's journal is printed in Gosch (1911) vol. II.
26 The two books are reprinted by Christy (1894).
27 'The Rime of the Ancient Mariner', in *Lyrical Ballads* (1798).

Chapter 6

1 Ross (1923) pp.251-81; Wright, I.A. (1920) pp.448-50.
2 Hakluyt (1903) VIII, 11-2; X, 95.
3 Lanctot (1963) I, 422 ff.
4 *Ibid*, I, 77.
5 *Ibid*, p.79.
6 Burrage (1906) p.329.
7 *Ibid*, p.330.
8 *Ibid*, p.331.
9 *Ibid*, p.332.
10 *Ibid*, p.333.
11 *Ibid*, p.334 n.1.
12 *Ibid*, p.342.
13 *Ibid*, p.346.
14 *Ibid*, p.346 n.4.
15 *Ibid*, p.349.
16 *Ibid*, pp.348-9.
17 *Ibid*, pp.347, 351.
18 Andrews (1964) vol. I, p.79 n.1 & 2.
19 Burrage (1906) pp.360-1.

20 *Ibid*, p.362.
21 *Ibid*, pp.364-7.
22 *Ibid*, p.377.
23 *Ibid*, pp.379, 394 n.1.
24 *Ibid*, pp.358-9.
25 Andrews (1964) I, 80.
26 *Ibid* p.83.
27 Burrage (1906) pp.398-417.
28 *Ibid*, pp. 418-9.
29 *Ibid*, p.404.
30 *Ibid*, p.405.
31 *Ibid*, p.407.
32 *Sagadahoc Colony*, ed. H. O. Thayer, in *Gorges Society*, IV (1892) p.186.
33 Burrage (1906) pp.414-5.
34 *Ibid*, p.419.
35 *Ibid*, p.418 n.5.
36 Arber-Bradley (1910) I, p.90.
37 *Ibid*, I, cxxix, pp.93-4.
38 *Ibid*, I, lxi.
39 Barbour (1969) I, p.141.
40 *Ibid*, I, p.52.
41 Arber-Bradley (1910) I, p.104.
42 Barbour (1969) I, p.43.
43 Arber-Bradley (1910) I, p.56.
44 Strachey (1953) p.130.
45 *Ibid*, pp.126, 124.
46 Arber-Bradley (1910) I, p.51.
47 *Ibid*, I, lxii.
48 *Ibid*, I, lxxxii.
49 *Ibid*, I, p.155.
50 *Ibid*, I, p.157.
51 *Ibid*, I, pp.141-2.
52 Barbour (1964) p.97.
53 Arber-Bradley (1910) II, p.498.
54 Strachey (1953) pp.38, 123 n.1.
55 Wright, I.A. (1920) p.449.
56 W. F. E. Morley (1966) I, pp.209-10.
57 Champlain, ed. Biggar (1922-36) III, p.309.
58 *Ibid*, III, p.308.
59 Trudel (1966) I, p.188.
60 *Ibid*, I, p.188.
61 Champlain, ed. Grant (1907) pp.34 n.4 & 42.
62 *Ibid*, p.45.
63 *Ibid*, p.46.
64 *Ibid*, p.68.
65 *Ibid*, p.165.
66 *Ibid*, p.185; cf. C. W. Butterfield, *History of Brulé's Discoveries and Explorations*, Cleveland, 1898.
67 *Jesuit Relations*, ed. Thwaites (1896-1901) LXV, doc. clxx.
68 Asher (1860) p.81.
69 *Ibid*, pp.xxv, 148.
70 Jameson (1909) p.67.
71 Bradford, ed. W. T. Davis (1964) p.301.
72 Purchas (1906) XIX, pp.272-3.
73 *Ibid*, XIX, p.274.
74 *Ibid*, XIX, p.283.
75 Arber (1897) pp.409-10.
76 Bradford (1964) pp.94-5.
77 Arber (1897) pp.407-17, including subsequent quotations in this paragraph.
78 *Ibid*, p.418.
79 *Ibid*, p.433.
80 *Ibid*, p.450.
81 Bradford (1964) pp.115-6.
82 Arber (1897) p.458.
83 *Ibid*, pp.470, 473.
84 *Ibid*, p.476.
85 *Ibid*, p.517.
86 Jernegan (1959) p.122.
87 Winsor (1884) III, p.10.
88 Jernegan (1959) p.126.
89 Morgan (1964) pp.231, 227.
90 *Ibid*, p.225.
91 *Ibid*, p.227.
92 *Ibid*, p.238.

ACKNOWLEDGEMENTS

The authors and publishers are indebted to the following individuals, libraries, museums, archives and organizations for permission to reproduce maps, engravings, paintings, drawings and photographs:

The National Maritime Museum, Greenwich: 1, 2, 6, 18, 95, 100, 161, 299, 301; courtesy of the Trustees of the British Museum: frontispiece, 3, 4, 5, 9, 12, 14, 15, 16, 19, 20, 21, 24, 26, 29, 33, 35, 37, 38, 40, 50, 51, 55, 56, 57, 58, 59, 60, 61, 63, 64, 65, 77, 80, 81, 83, 84, 85, 86, 88, 89, 90, 91, 92, 93, 94, 96, 97, 101, 103, 104, 106, 107, 108, 109, 110, 111, 112, 113, 114, 116, 118, 119, 121, 122, 123, 125, 126, 127, 128, 129, 130, 131, 132, 135, 136, 137, 138, 139, 140, 142, 144, 153, 154, 155, 156, 157, 158, 159, 162, 164, 165, 166, 167, 169, 170, 171, 172, 173, 174, 175, 176, 177, 187, 188, 189, 190, 191, 192, 195, 199, 201, 202, 204, 205, 206, 207, 208, 209, 212, 213, 215, 216, 217, 218, 219, 220, 221, 222, 223, 225, 226, 227, 228, 229, 230, 232, 233, 234, 235, 236, 237, 238, 240, 241, 242, 244, 245, 246, 247, 248, 249, 250-3, 255, 259, 260, 261, 265, 267, 268, 269, 270, 271, 273, 275, 276, 279, 282, 283, 284, 285-6, 287-8, 290, 291, 294, 296, 297, 304, 305, 306, 307, 309, 310, 311, 312, 313, 314, 315, 316, 317, 318, 319, 320, 321, 322, 323, 324, 326, 329, 330, 331, 333, 334, 335, 336, 337, 338, 339, 342, 343, 344, 345, 347, 348, 349, 350, 351, 352, 353, 354, 355, 356, 357, 358, 360, 361, 362; Magdalene College, Cambridge: 7; Bibliothèque Nationale, Paris: 8, 11, 76, 340; Crown Copyright, Public Record Office, London: 10, 194; Academia das Ciencias, Lisbon: 13, 62, 75; Biblioteca Apostolica Vaticana: 17, 73, 115; Universitetets Oldsakamling, Oslo: 22, 23, 25, 42; Yale University Press: 27 (reproduced by their permission from *The Vinland Map and Tartar Relation*, by R. A. Skelton, Thomas E. Marston, and George D. Painter. Copyright © 1965 by Yale University), 242; Biblioteca Nazionale Marciana, Venice: 28; Museo Naval, Madrid: 29, 168; Biblioteca Nazionale Centrale, Florence (photograph by G. Sansoni): 30; Royal Geographical Society, London: 31, 39, 277, 278, 280, 281, 289, 295, 302; Det Kongelige Bibliothek, Copenhagen: 32, 34, 272, 274, 298, 300; Biblioteca Nacional, Madrid: 36, 69, 117, 264; Fot. Bent Fredskild: 41; Historisk Museum, Bergen: 43; Copyright Rikantikvaren, Oslo: 44; Fot. Jörgen Meldgaard: 45, 47; Ministry of Defence, Hydrographic Department: 46, 303; National Museum of Denmark, Copenhagen: 48; Gyldendal Norsk Forlag, Oslo: 49 (from Helge Ingstad, *Land under the pole star*); Biblioteca Estense, Modena (photographs by Fot. Cav. Uff. U. Orlandini): 52, 53; Koninklijke Bibliotheek, The Hague (photographs by A. Fréquin): 54, 152, jacket; Biblioteca e Musei Oliveriani, Pesaro: 60; Herzog August Bibliothek, Wolfenbüttel: 66; Archivo General de Indias, Seville: 67, 68, 133; The Pierpont Morgan Library, New York: 70; John Carter Brown Library, Brown University, Providence: 71, 211; Biblioteca Mediceo-Laurenziana, Florence: 72; Archivo Marchesi Castiglioni, Mantua (photograph by Calzolari Studio Fotografico): 74; Houghton Library (Fogg Art Museum), Harvard: 78; London Library: 79, 102, 120, 266; Arents Collections, The New York Public Library, Astor, Lenox and Tilden Foundations: 82, 239, 328, 341; courtesy of The Hispanic Society of America, New York: 87; Maritiem Museum 'Prins Hendrick', Rotterdam: 98, 257, 263; Photographie Giraudon, Paris: 99, 141, 147, 163; The Newberry Library, Chicago: 105, 143, 160, 308; Rare Book Division, The New York Public Library, Astor, Lenox and Tilden Foundations: 124, 148, 149, 150, 151, 178, 179, 180, 181, 182, 183, 184, 185, 186, 196, 197, 198, 210, 231, 327; Los Angeles County Museum of Natural History, History Division: 134; Bayerische Staatsbibliothek, Munich: 145, 146, 243; Archivo Historico Nacional, Madrid: 193; The Free Library of Philadelphia: 200; National Portrait Gallery, London: 203; Paul Mellon Collection, Upperville: 214, 224; Charles Swithinbank, Scott Polar Research Institute, Cambridge: 254; Nürnberg Germanisches Museum: 256; Collection of Rudolf Schmidt on loan to the Österreichische Nationalbibliothek, Vienna: 258; Library of Congress, Washington: 262, 332; Property of Mrs. R. A. Skelton: 292, 293; Algemeen Rijksarchief, The Hague: 325 (photograph by A. Fréquin), 359; courtesy of the Pilgrim Hall Museum, Plymouth, Massachusetts: 346. Many of the photographs of originals at the British Museum were taken by Peter Parkinson and John R. Freeman.

Acknowledgement of author and title for all extracts quoted from published works is given in the text. However, the publishers would like to acknowledge permission in particular for the following: extracts from *The Vinland Sagas*, translated by Magnus Magnusson and Hermann Pálsson, from Penguin Books Ltd; the extract from *Landnámabók* in Gwyn Jones, *The Norse Atlantic Saga*, from Oxford University Press; extracts from the Hakluyt Society publications are used by permission of the Society and the publishers, Cambridge University Press; extracts from George P. Hammond and Agapito Rey, *Don Juan de Oñate, Colonizer of New Mexico, 1595–1628* (copyright 1953 The University of New Mexico Press); extracts from *The Journal of John Winthrop*, from Houghton Mifflin Company; the extract from Jean Ribaut's report to Admiral Coligny in the *English Historical Review* XXXII, from the Longman Group Ltd; extracts from *Bradford's History of the Plymouth Plantation*, edited by W. T. Davis, the *Voyages of Samuel de Champlain*, edited by W. L. Grant, and *Spanish Explorers in the Southern United States*, edited by Hodge and Lewis, from Barnes and Noble Inc.

BIBLIOGRAPHY

Books and articles referred to in the notes and selections

Andrews, Charles M. *The colonial period of American history. The settlements, vol. I.* New Haven and London, 1964.

Arber, Edward (ed.) *The first three English books on America.* Trans. by Richard Eden. Westminster (England), 1895.

Arber, Edward (ed.) *The story of the Pilgrim Fathers, 1606–1623.* Boston, 1897.

Arber, Edward (ed.) *Travels and works of Captain John Smith.* With bibliographical and critical introduction by A. G. Bradley. Edinburgh, 1910. 2 vols. (Referred to as Arber-Bradley in notes.)

Ascensión, Father Antonio de la. *Relacion de la jornada que hizo el General Sevastian Vizcayno al descubrimiento de las Californias el eno de 1602.* (Manuscript in Newberry Library, Chicago: Ayer Collection 1038.) Trans. in Wagner, H. R. *Spanish Voyages to the northwest coast of America in the 16th century.* San Francisco, 1929, pp.180-272.

Ashe, Geoffrey. *Land to the west.* London, 1962.

Asher, G. M. (ed.) *Henry Hudson the navigator.* London, 1860.

Bakeless, John. *The eyes of discovery: the pageant of North America as seen by the first explorers.* New York, 1950.

Bandelier, A. F. *Contributions to the history of the Southwestern portion of the United States.* Papers of the Archaeological Institute of America. American series V. Cambridge, 1890.

Barbour, Philip L. (ed.) *The Jamestown voyages under the first charter, 1606–1609.*

Barbour, Philip L. *The three worlds of Captain John Smith.* Boston, 1964.

Baudry, René. 'Marc Lescarbot'. *Dictionary of Canadian Biography,* I, 469-71. Toronto, 1966.

Benzoni, G. *See* Bry, Theodore de.

Biggar, H. P. (ed.) *A collection of documents relating to Jacques Cartier and the Sieur de Roberville.* Canadian Archives Publication no. 14. Ottawa, 1930.

Biggar, H. P. 'Jean Ribaut's Discoverye of Terra Florida.' *The English Historical Review,* XXXII (1917) 253-70.

Biggar, H. P. (ed.) *Précurseurs de Jacques Cartier, 1497–1534: collection de documents relatifs à l'histoire primitive du Canada.* Canadian Archives Publication, no. 5. Ottawa, 1911.

Biggar, H. P. (ed. and trans.) *The voyages of Jacques Cartier.* Canadian Archives Publication, no. 11. Ottawa, 1924.

Biggar, H. P. (ed.) *The Works of Samuel de Champlain.* Toronto, 1922–36. 8 vols.

Bolton, H. E. (ed.) *Drake's plate of brass.* California Historical Society (Special Publication, no. 13). San Francisco, 1937.

Bolton, H. E. *Spanish exploration in the Southwest, 1542–1706.* New York, 1916.

Bradford, William. *The history of Plymouth Plantation, 1606–1646.* William T. Davis (ed.) New York, 1964.

Brebner, John Bartlet. *The explorers of North America, 1492–1806.* London, 1933.

Brereton, John. *A brief and true relation of the discovery of the north part of Virginia.* London, 1602.

Brereton, John. *A brief relation of the discovery and plantation of New England . . .* Published by the President and Council of New England. London, 1622.

Bry, Theodore de. *America (Historia Americæ sive Novi Orbis).* Parts I-XIII. Frankfurt, 1590-1634. Part I. Harriot, Thomas. *A briefe and true report of the new found land of Virginia.* Frankfurt, 1590. Part I. Harriot, Thomas. *Admiranda narratio . . . Virginiæ.* Frankfurt, 1590. Part II. Le Moyne de Morgues, Jacques. *Brevis narratio eorum quæ in Florida Americæ provincia Gallis acciderunt.* Frankfurt, 1591. Part IV. Benzoni, Girolamo. *Americæ pars quarta . . . historia . . . Occidentali India.* Frankfurt, 1594. (cont.: Part V, 1595; Part VI, 1596; Part X, 1618.) Part XIII. Merian, M. (ed.) *Decima tertia pars historiæ Americanæ . . . Novæ Angliæ, Virginiæ . . .* Frankfurt, 1634.

Burrage, H. S. (ed.) *Early English and French voyages, 1534–1608.* New York, 1906.

Butterfield, C. W. *History of Brulé's discoveries and explorations.* Cleveland, 1898.

Cartier, Jacques. *See* Biggar (1924).

Castañeda, Pedro de, de Najera. Trans. by G. P. Winship. *See* F. W. Hodge and T. H. Lewis (1907) pp.273-387.

Champlain, Samuel de. *Works. See* H. P. Biggar (1922–36).

Champlain, Samuel de. *Voyages. See* W. L. Grant (1959).

Christy, Miller (ed.) *The voyages of Captain Luke Foxe . . . and Captain Thomas James . . . in search of a north-west passage, in 1631–32.* London, 1894.

Churchill, Awnsham and John. *A collection of voyages and travels.* London, 1732, vol. VI.

Clissold, Stephen. *The seven cities of Cibola.* New York, 1962.

Collinson, Richard (ed.) *The three voyages of Martin Frobisher.* London, 1867.

Connor, Jeannette Thurber (trans. and ed.) *Jean Ribaut, together with a transcript of an English version in the British Museum.* Florida State Historical Society, publication no. 7. DeLand, Florida, 1927.

Conway, Sir William Martin (ed.) *Early Dutch and English voyages to Spitzbergen.* London, 1904.

'Coppie d'une lettre venant de la Floride, envoyée à Rouen, et depuis au Seigneur d'Eueron; ensemble le plan et Portraict du fort que les François y ont faict.' A Paris, pour Vincent Norment et Ioanne Bruneau . . . 1565. In Ternaux-Compans, H. *Voyages, Relations . . .* Paris, 1841. Vol. XX, pp. 233-45.

Cortesão, Armando, and Avelino Teixeira da Mota. *Portugaliæ monumenta cartographica.* Lisbon, 1960–62. 6 vols.

Crone, G. R. *Maps and their makers.* London, 1953.

Cumming, William P. (ed.) *The Discoveries of John Lederer.* Charlottesville, Va, 1958.

Cumming, William P. 'The Parreus map (1562) of French Florida.' *Imago Mundi,* XVII (1963) 27-40.

Cumming, William P. *The Southeast in early maps.* Chapel Hill, North Carolina, 1962. 2nd edition.

Davies, James (?) *The relation of a voyage unto New England. See* Burrage (ed., 1906) pp.398-417. *See also* Thayer (ed., 1892) pp.35-86.

Day, John. Letter to the 'Lord Grand Admiral' of Spain. *Archivo General de Simancas, Estado, Leg.* 2, fo. 6. *See* Williamson (1962) for text used. *See* Vigneras (1956) for first publication.

Delanglez, Jean S. J. *El Rio del Espíritu Santo.* New York, 1945.

Dictionary of Canadian Biography. Vol. I, 1000-1700. Toronto, 1966.

Dicuil. *De mensura orbis terrae* (ed.) A. Letronne. Paris, 1814.

Dodge, Ernest. *North-west by sea.* New York, 1961.

Elvas, a Gentleman of. *Relaçam verdadeira . . . feita per hũ fidalgo Deluas.* Evora, 1557.

Elvas, a Gentleman of. *The discovery of Florida.* Trans. by Buckingham Smith. *See* F. W. Hodge (1907) pp.127-272.

Final report of the United States de Soto Expedition Commission, 76th Congress, 1st Session, House Document no. 71 (J. R. Swanton). Washington, D.C., 1939.

Fink, C. G. and E. P. Polushkin. *Drake's plate of brass vindicated.* California Historical Society, special publication no. 14. San Francisco, 1938.

Fite, E. D. and A. Freeman. *A book of old maps delineating American history from the earliest days down to the close of the Revolutionary War.* Cambridge, Massachusetts, 1926.

Foxe, Luke. *North-West Fox, or Fox from the North-West Passage.* London, 1635.

French, B. F. (ed. and trans.) *Historical collections of Louisiana . . .* New York, 1846–53. 5 vols.

Ganong, W. F. *Crucial maps in the early cartography and place-nomenclature of the Atlantic coast of Canada.* With introduction, commentary, and map notes by T. E. Layng. Toronto, 1964.

Gerritsz, Hessel. *Descriptio ac delineatio geographica detectionis freti.* Amsterdam, 1612.

Gosch, C. C. A. (ed.) *Danish Arctic expeditions, 1605 to 1620.* London, 1897.

Grajales, Francisco Lopez de Mendoza. *Memoir of . . . Menéndez de Avilés.* In: *Historical collections of Louisiana and Florida . . . 1527–1702.* Second series, trans. and ed. by Buckingham Smith. New York, 1875, pp.191-222.

Hakluyt, Richard. *Collection of the early voyages, travels, and discoveries of the English nation.* London, 1809–12. 5 vols.

Hakluyt, Richard. *Divers voyages touching the discoverie of America.* London, 1582.

Hakluyt, Richard (?) *The famous voyage of Sir Francis Drake.* In *Principall Navigations.* 6 folio leaves inserted between pp. 643 and 644. London, 1589.

Hakluyt, Richard. *The principall navigations, voiages and discoveries of the English nation.* London, 1589.

Hakluyt, Richard. *The principall navigations, voiages and discoveries of the English nation.* London, 1598–1600.

Hakluyt, Richard. *The principal navigations, voyages, traffiques and discoveries of the English nation.* Maclehose for Hakluyt Society, extra series I-XII. Glasgow, 1903–5.

Hall, E. H. (trans.) *Cèllere Codex. See* Verrazzano, G. da.

Hallenbeck, Cleve. *Álvar Nuñez Cabeza de Vaca . . .* Glendale, California, 1940.

Hammond, George P. *Coronado's Seven Cities.* United States Coronado Exposition Commission. Albuquerque, 1940.

Hammond, George P. (ed.) *The discovery of Florida, by a Gentleman of Elvas.* Buckingham Smith (trans.) Grabhorn Press, Book Club of California, 1946.

Hammond, George P. (ed.) *The discovery of Florida, by a Gentleman of Elvas,* trans. Buckingham Smith. Grabhorn Press, Book Club of California, 1946.

Hammond, George P. and Agapito Rey. *Don Juan de Oñate, colonizer of New Mexico, 1595–1628.* Albuquerque, 1953. 2 vols.

Hamy, E. T. (ed.) *Le livre et la description des pays de Gilles Le Bouvier.* Paris, 1908. (pp.157-217, the Bruges Itinerary.)

Harriot, Thomas. *A briefe and true report of the new found land of Virginia.* London, 1588. *See also* Quinn (1955) I, 341-74.

Harriot, T. *See* Bry, T. de.

Heizer, Robert Fleming. *Francis Drake and the California Indians, 1579.* University of California Publications in American Archaeology and Ethnology. Berkeley, 1947.

Hodge, F. W. and Lewis, T. H. (eds.) *Spanish explorers in the Southern United States,*

1528–1543. New York, 1907.

Hoffman, Bernard G. *Cabot to Cartier: sources for a historical ethnography of Northeastern North America, 1497–1550.* Toronto, 1961.

Hulton, Paul, and Quinn, D. B. *The American drawings of John White, 1577–1590.* London and Chapel Hill, North Carolina, 1964.

James, Thomas. *The strange and dangerous voyage of Captain Thomas James, in his intended discovery of the Northwest Passage into the South Sea.* London, 1633.

Jameson, J. F. (ed.) *Narratives of New Netherland, 1609–1664.* New York, 1909.

Jernegan, Marcus Wilson. *The American colonies, 1492–1750.* New York, 1959.

The Jesuit Relations and allied documents: travels and explorations of the Jesuit missionaries in North America, 1610–1791. Ed. by Reuben Gold Thwaites. Cleveland, 1896–1901. 73 vols.

Jode, G. and C. de. *Speculum orbis terrarum.* Antwerp, 1593.

Jones, Gwyn. *The Norse Atlantic saga.* London, 1964.

Krutch, Joseph Wood. 'The eye of the beholder.' *The American West,* IV, no. 2 (May, 1967) 18.

Lanctot, Gustave. *A history of Canada. Volume one: from its origins to the royal régime, 1663.* Cambridge, Mass., 1963.

La Roque de Roquebrune, Robert. 'Jean-Françoise de la Rocque de Roberval.' *Dictionary of Canadian Biography,* I, 422-24. Toronto, 1966.

Laudonnière, René de. *L'histoire notable de la Floride . . . mis en lumière par M[artin] Basanier.* Paris, 1586.

Laudonnière, René G. de. *Notable historie containing foure voyages made by certayne French captaynes unto Florida.* Trans. by R[ichard] H[akluyt]. London, 1587.

Le Jeune, Father Paul, S. J. *Brieve relation du voyage de la Nouvelle-France.* Paris, 1632.

Le Moyne de Morgues, Jacques. *Narrative of Le Moyne . . .* Trans. by Fred B. Perkins. Boston, 1875. *See also* Bry, T. de.

Lewis, Clifford M. and Loomie, S. J., Albert J. *The Spanish Jesuit mission in Virginia, 1570–1572.* Chapel Hill, North Carolina, 1953.

Lorant, Stefan (ed.) *The New World . . .* New York, 1946.

Lowery, W. *A descriptive list of maps of the Spanish possessions within the present limits of the United States, 1502–1820.* Ed. by P. L. Phillips. Washington, D.C., 1912.

Lowery, W. *The Spanish settlements within the present limits of the United States, 1513–1561.* New York, 1901.

Lowery, W. *The Spanish settlements within the present limits of the United States. Florida, 1562–1574.* New York, 1905.

MacBeath, George. 'Pierre du Gua de Monts.' *Dictionary of Canadian Biography,* I, 291-5. Toronto, 1966.

MacNutt, Francis Augustus (trans.) *De Orbe Novo:* modern English translation of the eight *Decades* of Pietro Martire d'Anghiera. New York and London, 1912. 2 vols.

Magnusson, Magnus and Pálsson, Hermann (trans.) *The Vinland sagas.* Harmondsworth, 1965.

Mapas españoles de América, siglos XV-XVII. Madrid, 1951.

Markham, A. H. (ed.) *The voyages and works of John Davis.* London, 1880.

Markham, C. R. (ed.) *The voyages of William Baffin.* London, 1881.

Matire d'Anghiera, Pietro. *P. Martyris ab Angleria Mediolanensi. Opera.* Seville, 1511. *See also* MacNutt, F. A.

Merás, Dr Gonzalo Solís de. *Pedro Menéndez de Avilés, Adelantado Governor and Captain General of Florida: memorial.* Trans. by Jeannette T. Connor. Florida State Historical Society, no. 3. Deland, Florida, 1923.

Morgan, Edmund S. (ed.) *The founding of Massachusetts: historians and the sources.* Indianapolis, 1964.

Morgan, Edmund S. *The Puritan dilemma: the story of John Winthrop.* Oscar Handlin (ed.) Boston, 1958.

Morison, Samuel Eliot. *Portuguese voyages to America in the fifteenth century.* Cambridge, Mass., 1940.

Mourt's Relation . . . London, 1622. *See* Edward Arber (ed., 1897) pp.397-508.

Munk, Jens. *Navigatio septentrionalis.* Copenhagen, 1624.

Nansen, Fridtjof. *In northern mists.* London, 1911.

Navarrete, M. Fernández de. *Collección de los viajes y descumbrimientos . . .* Madrid, 1858–80. 5 vols.

Nordenskiöld, N. A. E. *Facsimile–Atlas . . .* Stockholm, 1889.

Nunn, G. E. *The geographical conceptions of Columbus. A critical consideration of four problems.* New York, 1924.

Nutt, David C. 'The North Water of Baffin Bay.' *Polar Notes.* (Stefansson Collection, Dartmouth College Library), no. IX (May, 1969) 1-25.

O'Donoghue, Denis. *Brendaniana.* Dublin, 1893.

Oko, Captain Adolph S. 'Francis Drake and Nova Albion.' *California Historical Society Quarterly Magazine,* XLIII, no. 2 (June, 1964) 1-24.

Oré, Luis Jerónimo de. *Relacion de los martires . . . de la Florida.* (Madrid ?, 1617 ?)

Oviedo y Valdés, G. F. de. *Historia general y natural de las Indias . . .* Madrid, 1851–5. 4 vols.

Pacheco Pereira, Duarte. *Esmeraldo de situ orbis,* ed. G. H. T. Kimble. London, 1937.

Paez, Juan (?) (Voyage of Juan Rodriguez Cabrillo). *See* H. R. Wagner (1929) pp.29-30.

Pelham, Edward. *God's power and providence: shewed in the miraculous preservation of eight Englishmen left mischance in Green-land.* London, 1631.

Percy, George. *Observations gathered out of a discourse of the plantation of the southerne colonie in Virginia by the English, 1606. See* Purchas, *Pilgrimes* (1625) IV, 1685–90. *See also* Barbour (1969) I, 129-44.

Phillips, P. L. *A list of geographical atlases in the Library of Congress.* Washington, D.C., 1909–20. 4 vols.

Porten, Edward P. von der. 'Our first New England.' *U.S. Naval Institute Proceedings.* (Annapolis) December 1960, pp.62-6.

Power, Robert. 'Drake's Estero or Golden Gate?' *Marin Magazine: Independent-Journal* (San Rafael, Marin County, California), Aug. 8, 1959, pp.M7-M11.

Pring, Martin. *A voyage set out from the citie of Bristoll, 1603. See* Burrage (1906) 343-51.

Purchas, Samuel. *Hakluytus posthumus or Purchas his pilgrimes.* London, 1625. 4 vols. MacLehose: for the Hakluyt Society, extra series, XIV-XXXIII. Glasgow, 1905-7. 20 vols.

Purchas, Samuel. *Purchas his Pilgrimage,* 4th edition. London, 1626.

Quattlebaum, Paul. *The land called Chicora . . .* Gainesville, Florida, 1956.

Quinn, David B. and Dunbabin, Thomas. 'David Ingram.' *Dictionary of Canadian Biography,* I, 380-1. Toronto, 1966.

Quinn, David B. (ed.) *The voyages and colonizing enterprises of Sir Humphrey Gilbert.* London, 1940. 2 vols.

Quinn, David B. (ed.) *The Roanoke voyages, 1584–1590.* London, 1955. 2 vols.

Ribaut, Jean. *The whole and true discoverye of Terra Florida.* London, 1563. *See also* Biggar (1917) pp.253-70. *See also* J. T. Connor, ed. Florida State Historical Society, no. 7. Deland, Florida, 1927.

Rosier, James. *A true relation of the most prosperous voyage made this present yeere 1605 by Captaine George Waymouth . . .* London, 1605. *See also* Burrage (1906) pp.355-93.

Ross, Mary. 'French intrusions and Indian uprisings in Georgia and South Carolina (1567–70).' *Georgia Historical Quarterly,* VII (1923) 251-81.

Ross, Mary. 'The French on the Savannah.' *Georgia Historical Quarterly,* VIII (1924) 167-94.

Rundall, Thomas (ed.) *Narratives of voyages towards the north-west, in search of a passage to Cathay and India, 1496 to 1631.* London, 1849.

Sauer, Carl O. *Northern mists.* Berkeley and Los Angeles, 1968.

Scisco, L. D. 'Track of Ponce de Leon.' *American Geographical Society Bulletin,* XLV (1913) 721-7.

Settle, Dionyse. *A true reporte of the laste voyage by Captaine Frobisher.* London, 1577.

Shea, John Dawson Gilmary. 'Ancient Florida.' In Justin Winsor (1884–9) II, 231-98.

Sixteenth-century maps relating to Canada: a check-list and bibliography. Public Archives of Canada. Ottawa, 1956.

Skelton, R. A. *Explorers' Maps.* London, 1958.

Skelton, R. A. *The European image and mapping of America, A.D. 1000–1600.* Minneapolis, 1964.

Skelton, R. A. 'The Vinland Map.' In: Skelton, R. A., Marston, T. E., and Painter, G. D. *The Vinland Map and the Tartar Relation.* New Haven, 1965, pp.107-240.

Smith, John. *The generall historie of Virginia, New-England, and the Summer Isles.* London, 1624.

Speed, John. *A prospect of the most famous parts of the world.* London, 1627.

Starr, Walter A. 'Drake landed in San Francisco Bay in 1579: the testimony of the plate of brass.' *The California Historical Society Magazine,* XLI, no. 3 (1962) 1-29.

Stefansson, Vilhjalmar. *The three voyages of Martin Frobisher.* London, 1938.

Stokes, I. N. P. *The iconography of Manhattan Island, 1498–1909.* New York, 1915–28. 6 vols.

Strachey, William. *The historie of travaile into Virginia Britania.* (c. 1612.) Louis B. Wright and Virginia Freund (eds.) London, 1953. London, 1953.

Taylor, E. G. R. 'Master Hore's voyage of 1536.' *Geographical Journal,* LXXVII, no. 5 (1931) 469-70.

Ternaux-Compans, H. (ed.) *Voyages, relations et mémoires originaux pour servir à l'histoire de la decouverte de l'Amérique.* Paris, 1837–41. 20 vols.

Thayer, H. O. (ed.) *The Sagadehoc colony.* Gorges Society Publications, IV. Portland, Maine, 1892.

Thwaites, R. G. (ed.) *The Jesuit Relations and allied documents.* Cleveland, 1896–1901. 73 vols.

Tooley, R. V. 'Maps in Italian atlases of the sixteenth century.' *Imago Mundi,* III (1939) 12–47.

Trudel, Marcel. 'Jacques Cartier.' *Dictionary of Canadian Biography,* I, 165–72. Toronto, 1966.

Trudel, Marcel. 'Samuel de Champlain.' *Dictionary of Canadian Biography,* I, 186–99. Toronto, 1966.

Unamuno, Pedro de. (Voyage: untitled MS., Archives of the Indies, 1-1-3/25.) Trans. in Wagner, H. R. *Spanish voyages to the northwest coast of America in the sixteenth century.* San Francisco, 1929, pp.143-5.

Vaca, Álvar Núñez Cabeza de. *The journey of Álvar Núñez Cabeza de Vaca and his companions from Florida to the Pacific, 1528–1536.* Trans. by Fanny Bandelier; ed. by A. F. Bandelier. New York, 1905.

Vaca, Álvar Núñez Cabeza de. *La relación de la jornada que hizo a la Florida con el adelantado Portfilo de Narvaez.* Zamora, 1542.

Vaca, Álvar Núñez Cabeza de. 'The narrative of Álvar Núñez Cabeza de Vaca.' In F. W. Hodge and T. H. Lewis (eds, 1907), pp.1-126.

Verrazzano, Giovanni da. *Giovanni da Verrazzano and his discoveries in North America, 1524. According to the unpublished contemporaneous Cellère Codex.* Trans. and ed. by Edward Hagaman Hall. In: New York Scenic and Historic Preservation Society, *Fifteenth Annual Report.* Appendix A, pp.135-227. Albany, 1910.

Vigneras, L. A. 'The Cape Breton landfall: 1494 or 1497?' *Canadian Historical Review,* XXXVIII (1957) 219-28. (English translation of John Day's letter to the Admiral.)

Vigneras, L. A. 'New light on the 1498 Cabot voyage to America.' *Hispanic American Historical Review,* XXXVI (1956) 503-9. (Spanish text of John Day's letter to the Admiral.)

Vigneras, L. A. 'A Spanish discovery of North Carolina in 1566.' *North Carolina Historical Review,* XLVI (1969) 398-414.

Villagrá, Gaspar Pérez de. *Historia de la Nueva Mexico.* Alcalá de Henares, 1610.

Villagrá, Gaspar Pérez de. *History of New Mexico.* Gilberto Espinosa (trans.), F. W. Hodge (ed.) Quivira Society Publications, IV. Los Angeles, 1933.

Von Sant Brandon. Ulm, 1499.

Wagner, Henry R. (ed.) 'California voyages, 1539-1541', *California Historical Society Quarterly Magazine,* III, no. 4 (1924).

Wagner, H. R. *The cartography of the northwest coast of America to the year 1800.* Berkeley, California, 1937. 2 vols.

Wagner, H. R. 'A map of Sancho Gutiérrez of 1551.' *Imago Mundi,* VIII (1951) 47-9.

Wagner, H. R. *Sir Francis Drake's voyage around the world: its aims and achievements.* San Francisco, 1926.

Wagner, Henry R. 'Some imaginary California geography.' *American Antiquarian Society (Magazine)* April, 1926. Worcester, Mass.

Wagner, H. R. *The Spanish Southwest, 1542–1794. An annotated bibliography.* Berkeley, California, 1924.

Wagner, H. R. *Spanish voyages to the northwest coast of America in the sixteenth century.* San Francisco, 1929

Waters, D. W. *The art of navigation in Elizabethan and early Stuart times.* London, 1958.

Weeks, Stephen B. 'The Lost Colony of Roanoke; its fate and survival.' *Papers of the American Historical Association,* V (1891) 107-46.

Wheat, Carl I. *Mapping the Transmississippi West, 1540–1861.* San Francisco, 1957. 5 vols.

Williamson, James A. *The Cabot voyages and Bristol discovery under Henry VII.* (With R. A. Skelton. *The cartography of the voyages.*) Cambridge, 1962.

Winship, G. P. 'The Coronado expedition, 1540–1542.' *Fourteenth Annual Report* of the United States Bureau of American Ethnology, 1892–93. Part I, 329-613. Washington, 1896.

Winship, George P. *Sailors' narratives of voyages along the New England coast, 1524–1624.* Boston, 1905.

Winslow, Edward. *Good news from New England.* London, 1624. *See also* Arber, pp.511-600.

Winsor, J. *Cartier to Frontenac, Geographical discovery of the interior of North America and its historical relations, 1534–1700.* Boston and New York, 1894.

Winsor, J. (ed.) *Narrative and critical history of America.* Boston and New York, 1884–9. 8 vols.

Winthrop, John. 'The history of New England: the journal of John Winthrop, March 29, 1630–May 14, 1634.' In *The founding of Massachusetts: historians and the sources.* Edmund S. Morgan (ed.) New York, 1964, pp. 204-82.

Wright, Irene A. 'Spanish policy toward Virginia, 1606–1612.' *American Historical Review,* XXV (1920) 448-50.

Wright, John K. 'The open polar sea.' *Geographical Review* (New York) XLIII (1953) 338-65. Reprinted in *Human nature in geography,* Cambridge, Mass., 1966, 89-118.

Zeno, Nicolò. *De i commentarii del viaggio in Persia di M. Caterino Zeno . . . Et dello scropimento dell'isola Frislanda, Eslanda, Engroueland, Estotilanda ed Icaria, fatto da due fratelli Zeni, M. Nicolò il K. e M. Antonio.* Venice, 1555.

Pena, Pierre and M. de l'Obel. *Stirpium adversaria nova.* London, 1570-1.

Pohl, F. J. 'The Pesaro map, 1505.' *Imago Mundi,* VII (1950), pp.82-3.

Porcacchi, Thomaso. *L'isole più famose del mondo.* Venice, 1572.

Ptolemy, Claudius. *Geographia.* Strasbourg, 1513.

Ramusio, Giovanni B. *Navigationi et Viaggi.* Venice: I, 1554; II, 1559; III, 1556. 2nd ed., 1565.

Ramusio, Giovanni B. *Summario de la generale historia de l'Indie Occidentali.* Venice, 1534.

Rink, Henry. *Tales and traditions of the Eskimos.* London and Edinburgh, 1875.

Roukema, E. 'A discovery of Yucatan prior to 1503.' *Imago Mundi,* XIII (1956), pp.30-7.

Settle, Dionyse. *Beschreibung der Schiffart des Haubtmans Martini Forbissher . . . im Jar 1577.* Nürnberg, 1580.

Smith, John. *A description of New England: or the observations and discoveries of Captain Iohn Smith.* London, 1616.

Smith, John. *A map of Virginia.* Oxford, 1612.

Smith, John. *New England's trials.* London, 1620.

Stobnicza, Johannes de. *Introductio in Ptholomei Cosmographiam.* Cracow, 1512.

Thevet, A. *Les singularités de la France Antarctique,* Paris, 1558.

Tooley, R. V. 'California as an island.' *Map Collectors' Circle,* no. 8, p.4. London, 1964.

Vaughan, W. *Cambrensium Caroleia.* London, 1625.

Veer, Gerrit de. *Waerachtige beschryvinghe van drie seylagien.* Amsterdam, 1598.

Vigneras, L. A. 'El viaje de Esteban Gómez a Norte America.' *Revista de Indias,* XVII (1957), pp.13-14.

Williams, Edward. *Virginia in America.* London, 1651.

Wood, William. *New Englands prospect.* London, 1634.

The World Encompassed: an exhibition of the history of maps held at the Baltimore Museum of Art, Oct. 7–Nov. 23, 1952. Published by the Walters Art Gallery, Baltimore, Maryland, 1952.

Wytfliet, C. *Descriptionis Ptolemaicae Augmentum.* Louvain, 1597.

Books and articles referred to in the captions to the illustrations in addition to the above

Aa, Pieter van der. *De Aanmerkenswaardigste en alomberoemde zee-en landreizen.* Leyden, 1706–1727. 8 vols.

Alexander, Sir William. *The map and description of New England.* London, 1630.

Benzoni, Girolamo. *La historia del Mondo Nuovo.* Venice, 1565.

Best, George. *A true discourse of the late voyages of discoverie; for finding a passage to Cathaya.* London, 1578.

Bigges, Walter. *A summarie and true discourse of Sir Francis Drake's West Indian voyage.* London, 1589.

Brown, Alexander. *The genesis of the United States.* New York, 1890.

Bry, Johann Theodor de. *Florilegium renovatum et auctum.* Frankfurt, 1641.

Calvert, Cecil, Lord Baltimore. *A relation of Maryland.* London, 1635.

Cortés, Ferdinand. *Praeclara Ferdinãndi Cortesii de Nova maris Oceani Hyspanica Narratio.* Nuremberg, 1524.

Cortés, H. *Historia de Nueva Espagna.* Mexico, 1770.

Cortesão, A. 'Note on the Castiglioni planisphere.' *Imago Mundi,* V (1954), pp.53-5.

Davies, Arthur. 'The Egerton MS 2802 and the Padrón Real of Spain in 1510.' *Imago Mundi,* XI (1954), pp.47-52.

Destombes, Marcel. 'Nautical charts attributed to Verrazzano (1525–1528)'. *Imago Mundi,* XI (1954), pp.57-66.

Dodoens, Rembert. *Frumentorum, leguminum, palustrium et aquatilium herbarum.* Antwerp, 1566.

The English Pilot, Fourth Book. London, 1689.

Gerard, John. *The herball or generall historie of plantes.* Englished by T. Johnson. London, 1633.

Gilbert, Sir Humphrey. *A discourse of a discoverie for a new passage to Cataia.* London, 1576.

Gómara, Francisco L. de. *Historia de las Indias.* Saragossa, 1552.

Gómara, Francisco L. de. *Historia de México.* Antwerp, 1554.

Grynaeus, Simon and John Huttich. *Novus orbis regionum ac insularum veteribus incognitorum.* Basle, 1532.

Hakluyt, Richard. *Divers voyages.* London, 1582.

Hall, Charles F. *Arctic researches and life among the Esquimaux.* New York, 1865.

Harrisse, H. *The discovery of North America.* London, 1892.

Hennepin, Louis. *A new discovery of a large country in America.* London, 1698.

Jomard, E. F. *Les monuments de la géographie.* Paris, 1842-62.

Laet, Johan de. *L'histoire du Nouveau Monde ou description des Indes Occidentales contenant dix-huict liures.* Leyden, 1640.

Laet, Johan de. *Nieuwe Wereldt ofte beschrijvinghe van West-Indien.* Leyden, 1630.

Lescarbot, Marc. *Histoire de la Nouvelle France.* Paris, 1609 (later editions, 1611, 1612, 1617, 1618).

Lescarbot, Marc. *History of New France.* W. L. Grant and H. P. Biggar, (eds.) The Champlain Society. Toronto: I, 1907; II, 1911; III, 1914. 3 vols.

McCrary, Ben C. *John Smith's map of Virginia.* Williamsburg, Va., 1957.

Magnus, Olaus. *Historia de gentibus septentrionalibus.* Rome, 1555.

Manby, G. W. *Journal of a voyage to Greenland in the year 1821.* London, 1822.

'Mason, John.' *Dictionary of National Biography,* XXXVI, pp.428-9.

Mattheoli, P. A. *Compendium de plantis omnibus.* Venice, 1571.

Monardes, N. *Joyfull newes out of the newe founde world.* Englished by J. Frampton. London, 1577.

Mook, M. A. 'The ethnological significance of Tindall's map of Virginia.' *William and Mary Quarterly Historical Review,* 2nd series, XXIII (1943), pp. 371-408.

Münster, Sebastian. *Cosmographia.* Basle, 1550.

Parry, Sir W. E. *Journal of a second voyage for the discovery of a North-west Passage . . . in 1821–3.* London, 1824.

300

INDEX

All references are to page numbers. Roman numerals refer to the text, *italic* numerals to the captions for maps and illustrations.